LIFE, LAND AND WATER IN ANCIENT PERU

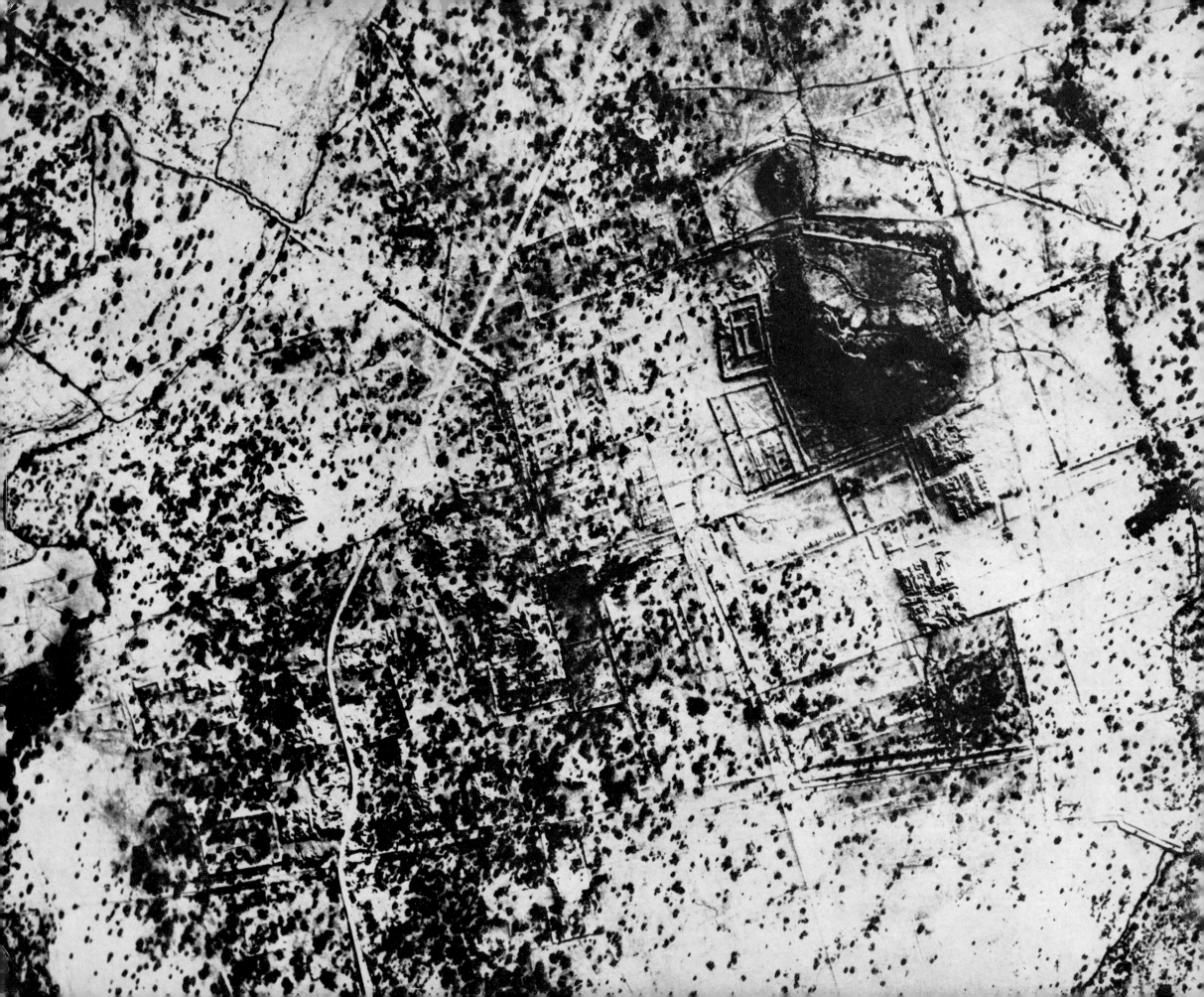

Large ceremonial center of over 25 pyramids, also walled compounds and canals at *Apurle*, located in the desert in northwestern Peru. *Servicio* (Details on pp. 172-173. Pan American Highway — large white line at left — runs through the site.)

LIFE, LAND AND WATER IN ANCIENT PERU

〜〜〜〜〜

An account of the discovery, exploration and mapping of ancient pyramids, canals, roads, towns, walls and fortresses of coastal Peru with observations of various aspects of Peruvian life, both ancient and modern.

By PAUL KOSOK, Ph. D.

Long Island University

NEW YORK: 1965

LONG ISLAND UNIVERSITY PRESS

General Editor, Nathan Resnick
Editor, Elliott S. M. Gatner
Scientific Editor, Richard Paul Schaedel

Designed and printed in
the United States of America by
The John B. Watkins Company,
New York City

Library of Congress
Catalog Card No.: 65-14627

Ancient ceremonial adobe pyramid (*huaca*) in
the Chicama Valley. *Kosok.*

PREFACE

Some books are planned, others just grow. The present volume belongs to the latter category. In 1948, I had been sent to Peru by Long Island University to complete a previously begun study of the ancient irrigation systems of the Northwest Coast of Peru and their possible relationship to important ruins of the past. On my return I was requested to present a limited report of my field work in Peru during the years of 1948 to 1949, to which was to be added aerial and ground photographs of some of the principal ancient ruins and canals. As the writing progressed, it soon became clear that a chapter would have to be devoted to each of the individual valleys and that additional, significant aerial photographs would have to be included for each chapter to make the presentation intelligible.

However, when I showed the preliminary draft and the collection of photographs to various persons, both professional and non-professional, they strongly urged that, since this volume would have more than professional interest, I should include information and photographs giving the general reader a better understanding of the life of the ancients who built the canals and the sites shown in the photographs. It was further suggested to me that the people of the past should be considered not merely as the dead, but also as the ancestors of the living, about whom some reference also should be made. Finally, it was suggested that I describe some of the professional and personal experiences encountered by myself and my oldest son, Michael — who accompanied me on the trip — while carrying on our field work and while occupied with the tens of thousands of aerial photographs that both the American and Peruvian governments had taken.

The present volume represents an attempt to carry out the aforementioned suggestions. While objections may be raised that too many aspects of Peruvian life have been included, I feel, nevertheless, that the *integration* of these aspects has provided a more vivid picture of Peruvian life of the past. The volume thus serves as a kind of descriptive-pictorial introduction to the general reader of the relatively unknown culture of the ancient Chimús and associated peoples inhabiting the irrigated river oases of the desert coast of Peru. At the same time the volume contains much new archaeological information and many hitherto unpublished photographs of ancient sites.

A great deal was contributed to the volume as a result of many long discussions with the archaeologist Dr. Richard P. Schaedel, formerly of the Institute at Trujillo and also of the U. S. State Department. He wrote many of the archaeological descriptions in the text as well as most of the captions of the photographs of archaeological sites and checked the others which I wrote. He read and corrected the various drafts of the book as well as the galley and page proofs. Without his help this book would not have been possible.

I wish to extend thanks to the large number of Peruvians, from the simple field workers to the highest government officials who have aided me in collecting the information for this book. They are too numerous to mention though some of their names appear in the text.

Likewise in the United States many people have aided me extensively in making this book possible. Of greatest aid were Professors Nathan Resnick, Elliott Gatner, William Korey and John Dunbar of Long Island University. Professor Gatner not only checked all the technical details but finally submitted to the tedious task of making the index and the bibliography.

Last but not least many thanks are due to Miss Frances M. Cornish who ingeniously planned all the beautiful layout work that gives this book its distinctive artistic form.

PAUL KOSOK

Ancient ceremonial water jug (*huaco*) — Mochica period.

CONTENTS

The material basis of the ancient coastal cultures. Remains of an ancient aqueduct at Ascope, Chicama Valley, Northwest Coast of Peru. *Kosok.*

FOREWORD

On these pages and in the pictures spread before him the reader will encounter a record of one of mankind's great stories of the past: the rise of one of the most important native American civilizations in ancient Peru. As the magnificent photographs of this book attest, it is a story engraved and molded upon the surface of one of the most unique regions of the world: the rainless desert coast of Pacific South America. In the valleys whose rivers rise in the Andes and fall to the ocean across this arid narrow coastal strip are found the remains of the first man who entered western South America. This early man was a hunter, fisher, and gatherer of wild foods; his numbers were few; and the material comforts of his life simple and crude.

Gradually, he came to assume mastery over his strange environment. He became a farmer, skilled in irrigation and in a knowledge of plants. His villages grew larger; craftsmanship in stone, pottery, and metals was discovered and improved; and he built great monuments to his gods, palaces for his leaders, and fortifications to defy his enemies. Villages became cities, and small tribal holdings expanded to the dimensions of statehood. From the pages of history we know that this development culminated in the fabulous Inca Empire, but little is generally known of the Chimú Empire which flourished on the desert Coast of Peru as a competitor of the Sierra Incas and whose achievements are described and illustrated in this volume.

The *how* and *why* of these ancient American civilizations — separated by oceanic expanses of thousands of miles from the Old World — are questions which still puzzle the archaeologist, anthropologist, and the philosopher of human history. In what manner did civilization — in many ways so similar to that of the Old World — come to the New? Many pre-historians (I would estimate a majority) hold that the rise of agricultural civilizations in the Americas was an independent growth with no significant direct Old World ties and that the presence of such similar phenomena in the New World is a demonstration of man's basic unity. Dr. Kosok shares this belief.

Among those who consider American civilizations to be independent developments there is no unanimity of opinion as to the causality of their growth. Dr. Kosok, as expressed in this book, feels that groups of mankind with similar cultural antecedents have responded to like natural and social environments in a comparable manner on all parts of the globe. He sees in the rise of irrigation and early agriculture in the coastal desert cases of Peru the same inner forces that shaped man's history in the important irrigation centers of the Near East, India and China during the late Neolithic and early Bronze Ages. Not all archaeologists or culture historians will agree with all aspects of Dr. Kosok's views, and I find myself in some disagreement. Nevertheless, Dr. Kosok has written a very significant and scholarly book.

It is, I believe, the most fascinating book ever written on the subject of Peruvian prehistory for the general reader. To the uninitiated, a marvelous realm of the past will be revealed that will astound him with its scope and grandeur. For many of the ancient settlements of Peru were not Indian camps; they were great *cities* with all the meaning that the word *city* has for the urban dweller. It took millions of adobe bricks carried upon the backs of thousands of workers to build a pyramid like the one at Moche, and all the king's engineers must have exercised their skill and wisdom to construct the mammoth aqueduct of Ascope.

For the professional archaeologist there is a wealth of new information assembled here for the first time. This is particularly true of the excellent aerial photographs of prehistoric sites. Because of the barrenness of the Peruvian coastal countryside the outlines of these ancient walls and buildings stand out in sharp relief in the air pictures. The number and size of these sites is surprising. How many professional archaeologists in the Peruvian field have ever heard of the site of Morro Solar? It is within a mile of Las Palmas, on the outskirts of Lima, and the photograph which Dr. Kosok presents reveals several acres of walls, courtyards, and buildings. Yet this great site is virtually unknown to the scientific world. Similarly, in the Chancay, Santa, Jequetepeque, and Lambayeque Valleys there are vast architectural clusters, photographs of which are presented here for the first time.

We cannot deny the past. Its enormous weight crowds upon us, the living. The sojourner in Peru, whether in person or vicariously by means of this book, will rapidly be made aware of this fact. We may stand uncomprehending before the symbols of antiquity, unable to decipher their meaning. But surely a message is there. For the form of the present is born of the action of the past, and the moment of today holds within itself the design of tomorrow.

GORDON R. WILLEY,
Bowditch Professor of Archaeology
Peabody Museum, Harvard University
Formerly with Bureau of Ethnology,
Smithsonian Institution,
Washington, D. C.

I

Why Study Ancient Peru?

WHY STUDY ANCIENT PERU? Why single out the Chimús and associated peoples who once inhabited the numerous river oases that lie scattered over the long, narrow, desert Coast of that wondrous country? What contribution can such a study make toward an understanding of the complex development of the whole of human society?

These basic questions excited our interest as we ventured into our study of the fascinating land of Peru. Many times were we confronted by these same questions from others. They demand an answer!

The answers, in many ways, are relatively simple. First of all, ancient Peru represented one of the highest cultures attained by the American Indians. But more important, the ancient Chimús and other peoples of the irrigated coastal plains developed, from early priest-dominated cultures, the most advanced forms of secular society in the western hemisphere. Finally, knowledge of Chimú society and culture sheds new light on the early stages of the ancient Afrasian irrigation societies of the eastern hemisphere that once formed the main stream of human evolution. These answers naturally require further elucidation.

However, before the answers are drawn in detail, we must pause to point out briefly the position of ancient Peru in the general stream of social evolution. In doing this we must keep in mind two basic principles: *mankind is diverse*, yet *mankind is one!* In fact, the interplay of these opposite yet complementary characteristics is an expression of the dual nature of all social groups. Each group is unique, but each is also part of the whole human family. Since its earliest appearance, mankind has developed into many distinct but related groups which gradually spread over our planet. Varying environmental and hereditary conditions — both natural and social — have produced, in each group and in each series of groups, a variety of social characteristics, so that today mankind is divided into a multiplicity of local, national, and international economies and cultures, each representing different levels of social evolution. But, despite their diversity of form, all groups have common characteristics because they are a part of mankind.

Most basic among the forces accelerating mankind's evolution to newer, more complex and more efficient levels of production have been *the rise and growth of agriculture* (and animal husbandry) in prehistoric times,

---

Fig. 1 (left). Huge pyramid (*huaca*) built of sun-baked brick (adobe), located in the small Virú Valley. Now called El Castillo de Tomaval, the structure probably dates back to Early Chimú (Mochica) times. *Kosok* • Fig. 2 (right). Ceremonial portrait water jug (*huaco*), with stirrup spout, typical of the highest form of plastic art of ancient Peru. This *huaco* is a product of the Early Chimú (Mochica) Period, a period which appears to have extended from the latter part of the first millenium B.C. to the first part of the first millenium A.D., if not later. The portrait is that of an important ruler as attested by the ear lobe plugs. *Guillen.* NOTE. Drawing next to initial, copied from a portrait *huaco*, is that of an important personage of the Mochica Period. *After Doering.*

with the resultant appearance of early civilizations and class societies, and *the industrial revolution* in modern times, with the resultant and still continuing struggles for democracy. Both of these major transformations represent man's *increasing control* over nature and society, not merely an "adjustment" to them. Clearly, neither agriculturalization nor industrialization took place simultaneously in all human societies. Each evolved at first in specific areas, then spread at different rates and in different forms, but neither has yet extended to all of mankind. This *uneven development* of both agriculture and the industrial revolution has increased the degree of diversity of present day economies, social structures, and cultural forms. At the same time, the industrial revolution and its social implications have been supplying *the very basis* for establishing *an increasingly unified human economy and culture, a level in social evolution which is now in the process of formation.*

The availability of a large amount of documentary material makes it relatively easy to reconstruct, historically, the rise and development of the industrial revolution and the resultant social transformations. Much more difficult is a reconstruction of the rise of agriculture and the resultant social changes, for they occurred during the prehistoric, pre-literate stage, possibly about eight to ten thousand years ago in the eastern hemisphere and half as long ago in the western hemisphere. Even when we do find archaeological material in Eurasia and Africa indicating the existence of early agricultural sites, it is

Fig. 3 (below). Schematic topographical cross-section of Peru. On pages 2 to 9 are photographs that show the natural and cultural characteristics of the country's three main regions, namely the Coast, the Sierra and the Montaña • Fig. 4 (left). A section of the desert Coast at the southern edge of the Moche Valley. In the foreground what appears to be white sand is mainly dry soil, which is not cultivated because it lies above the highest level of present day irrigation canals. In ancient times a canal passed between the two barren mountains in order to bring water to the fields adjoining the huge Huaca del Sol (extreme left of photograph). If rain should fall here, most of the desert landscape would be covered with grasses, flowers and trees, except in the limited areas that are saline or covered by sand dunes. The port of Salaverry is at the right. The vessels are landing barges, which are used in this modern port because steamers cannot enter the shallow waters. *Kosok* • Fig. 5 (p. 3). Another section of the coastal desert is shown in this view of a part of the lower Chao Valley. Note the different beach levels, the rows of sand dunes, and, as in Fig. 4, the foothills of the Andes extending into the Pacific Ocean. *Servicio, unnumbered series.*

COAST

1a. No Rain
Desert

1b. Irrigation Imperative
Canal Building Problems

2a. The Ancient Chimús and Other Coastal Peoples

2b. Highest Art Forms and Social Structures

SIERRA

1a. Moderate Rain
Complex hydrological pattern owing to great regional and seasonal fluctuations

1b. Some Irrigation
Not essential in many regions, but necessary for more regular, more efficient production

2a. The Ancient Incas and Other Sierra Peoples

2b. Wide Range of Cultural Forms and Social Structures

PREVAILING RAIN WINDS
from Atlantic Ocean,
3000 miles distant

MONTAÑA

1a. Too Much Rain
Jungle

PACIFIC OCEAN
Cold Humboldt Current

difficult to reconstruct the nature and dynamics of the social structures that prevailed among the people who built and inhabited these sites. It is still more difficult to relate these social structures to those much more advanced forms that we find at the beginning of early civilizations in Eurasia and Africa. Hence the nature and sequence of the various steps in the process of transformation from late tribal societies to early civilization are still none too clear. Here, as we shall see, knowledge gained from studying the New World can help us.

Tens of thousands of years ago — or even earlier? — when the "American" Indians — predominantly, but not necessarily solely, of Mongolian stock — began coming in numerous migrations from eastern Asia, they were still in the hunting, fishing, and food-gathering stage. They can therefore be considered a *branch* of the Eurasian and African *hunting, fishing and food-gathering societies* which, at that time, represented the *trunk* of the tree of man's social evolution. But, having established themselves in the western hemisphere, the Indians belatedly developed, *independent* of the *main trunk* of world agricultural production in Eurasia, a *secondary trunk* of agricultural production, together with such indigenous handicrafts, buildings, and social structures as are characteristic of evolving agricultural societies.

It thus becomes clear that, in a study of rising agricultural societies, we cannot limit ourselves merely to an analysis of the development of the *main trunk* of social evolution in the *eastern* hemisphere — which probably took place somewhere in the Near East — but we must also investigate the developments that took place in the *secondary trunk*, in the *New World*. For both developments show basically similar trends, though the forms in which they express themselves are different.

Naturally, such a study must be carried on — and is being carried on — by a multitude of archaeologists, anthropologists, and historians, each concentrating upon the people in a specific region. In our case, we decided to study ancient Peru and specifically those peoples who inhabited the desert Coast of that country. Thus we return to our first question: Why study ancient Peru?

Ancient Peru produced — as did ancient Mexico — one of the highest cultures in the western hemisphere. Like parallel peaks, these indigenous cultures grew out of the more primitive agricultural tribal societies which had, themselves, evolved from the earlier hunting and food-collecting tribal economies of America. The factors that produced such important evolutionary advances, while the other peoples of the two continents remained at relatively lower levels of economy, obviously merit inquiry. Indeed, this inquiry is an essential part of the study of man's social evolution in the Americas.

Another reason for studying the early Peruvians and Mexicans is the fact that their descendants still comprise the bulk of the population of Peru, Mexico, and some of the adjacent countries. But more than that, these people are now awakening from centuries of domination by a West European civilization, and in the future will undoubtedly play leading roles in the national revivals of the cultural, social, economic and political affairs of their

political matters they never progressed much beyond the establishment of local, priest-dominated, ceremonial centers with their associated population clusters. The theory, incidentally, that the ceremonial centers of the Maya had been city states — similar to those of ancient commercial Greece — quickly turns out to be fallacious when one compares the economic systems and population densities of the two societies. In the Americas, mercantile structures like those of ancient Greece never developed.

The Aztecs progressed considerably further towards a secular society than did the Maya. But, as the early Spanish Chroniclers clearly relate, even among the Aztecs the priesthood still played a very strong role. Moreover, recent investigations clearly indicate that the territorial extent and political control of the Aztec Empire was not as great as hitherto had been assumed.

In Peru, on the other hand, the Inca Empire attained a much larger territorial size and a far superior level of political maturity and administrative centralization than had the Aztecs in Mexico. More important to us, the coastal Chimú Empire and the smaller coastal confederations, all of which were eventually conquered by the Incas, had built up an economy unique in the Americas and had developed certain social, political and cultural forms that were the most advanced in the New World. The Peruvian area thus affords an unusual opportunity for studying special and important aspects of the transformation of primitive tribal societies into early civilizations with their emerging class structures and secular rulers.

But why stress the relatively unknown Chimús and other coastal peoples of Peru instead of the better known Incas who lived in the nearby Andean Sierras? We can now turn to this question and answer it in greater

---

Fig. 6 (margin). Children in a coastal port. *Kosok* • Figs. 7 to 10 illustrate what man has done to conquer the coastal desert by means of irrigation canals. The degree of his success has depended upon the amount of water in the rivers, the topography of the valleys, and the irrigation techniques at his disposal • Fig. 7 (left). The small valley of the large Ocoña River, on the South Coast of Peru, is a miniature of the larger valleys of the Central and Northwest Coast, which are characterized by their narrow "necks" and their wide, fan-shaped coastal plains. This photograph, taken at an altitude of 20,000 feet, is reproduced because the northern valleys we studied are too large to be encompassed by a single aerial photograph. At the extreme right side of the valley can be seen the bed of the Ocoña River as it runs into the Pacific Ocean. The coastal plain is cultivated by water brought from the river by means of canal systems. The white areas on both sides of the cultivated region are the desert coastal hills, which are above the level that can be reached at present by means of irrigation canals. *U. S. Army 123-R-53* • Figs. 8 and 9 (below). Unfortunately for man, most of the South Coast consists of a high *mesa* through which the rivers have cut narrow paths. Fig. 8 (lower left) shows a V-shaped southern valley where almost no land is available for cultivation. *Kosok* • Fig. 9 (lower right) shows a U-shaped valley where a slightly larger amount of cultivation is possible. *Kosok*.

countries. Furthermore, they will continue to interact — at an increasing rate — with their neighbors in the New World and with the *main trunk* of social evolution in Eurasia, until they become an integral part of an evolving unified humanity. It is, therefore, vital that we understand their historical roots!

In this study we concern ourselves only with ancient Peruvian civilizations since, in certain respects, they reached *higher political and social levels* than did ancient Mexican cultures. While the Maya produced impressive stone temples, accurate calendrical systems and unique recording devices superior to those of the Peruvians, in

4

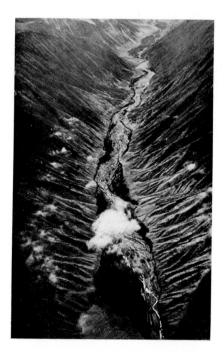

detail. After a long struggle against a priest-dominated society, the Chimús eventually produced a society dominated — to an extent unknown in other parts of the Americas — by *a secularized upper class.* In other words, the "Second Estate" had grown more powerful than the "First Estate." With the evolution of such an advanced secular society there developed new forms of property relationships, accompanied by the most advanced forms of social urbanization known in the western hemisphere.

The coastal societies produced the finest ceramics (Mochica and Nazca) and the finest textiles (Nazca and Paracas) of America. They also constructed hundreds of

Fig. 10. In contrast to the areas shown in Figs. 8 and 9, we see here the extensive, irrigated plains of part of the Chicama Valley, one of the large valleys of the Northwest Coast. In the Lambayeque Complex, farther north, the expanse of cultivated area is even greater. This situation helps to explain why the valleys of the Northwest Coast became the seats of important cultures and social developments, and comprised the main region of the Chimú Empire. The pyramid is Huaca Cucurripe, which probably was built in Early Chimú times. Note how the uniform patterns of canals and furrows of the modern sugar *hacienda* are interrupted by the different pattern of the walls surrounding the *huaca,* an illustration of how the past is still asserting itself in the present. Figs. 8 to 10 were taken in 1940-41 from a Faucett Line airplane. *Kosok.*

adobe pyramids that are scattered over the Coast. This cultural richness and social complexity developed in an area where agriculture depended *entirely on irrigation* — a unique form of production for advanced societies in this hemisphere! Such a complex of interrelated factors, obviously, requires investigation.

The beautiful ceramics and textiles of coastal Peru are well-known throughout the world and have been studied for some time. Scholars have sensed the advanced nature of the socio-political structure of at least some of the coastal peoples. But thus far no one has investigated the nature as well as the social and cultural implications of their irrigation economy. It seems vital, therefore, to ascertain in some detail the nature and extent of this form of agricultural production and its interrelationship with other factors. Only against such a background can the life processes of these societies be understood as a whole. Such an irrigation study also provides the basis for evaluating the nature of the interrelationship of the cultures of the Coast with those of the Andes.

True, in New Mexico, Arizona and adjacent arid sections of northern and western Mexico, an irrigation economy was also essential for existence. But as a result of specific, limiting geographic conditions, these early irrigation societies developed *on such a small scale* that they could never hope to reach an economic, social and political level in any way comparable to that of coastal Peruvian

Fig. 11 (left). In the mighty Andes we enter a different world. Here, man in his conquest of nature has had many more difficulties to overcome than on the Coast. In thousands of years he has painfully hacked out of the hills and built up, with earth and stone, the endless number of terraced farms (*andenes*) that cover many of the mountainsides of Peru. Dependent upon moderate but irregular rain, he has often had to build irrigation canals to supplement his water supply. Indeed, he probably practiced irrigation here before he permanently entered the desert Coast some three thousand years ago. The two white spots at the extreme right and left of the photograph, as well as the one in the center, are villages that are connected by long narrow paths, which wind tortuously up and down the mountainsides. Often one or two days are required for the journey — by foot or on mule back — between two neighboring villages, while on the Coast only a few hours are needed for a walk between neighboring villages. This photograph shows the upper limits of cultivation. In the background are the barren windswept *puna* and the snow-covered mountain tops. *U. S. Army 210-R-13* • Fig. 12 (left margin). Andean farmer. *Kosok* • Fig. 13 (right). The region of eternal ice and snow that towers above the cultivated fields of man. *Servicio 2692:R:34.*

societies. These societies may, therefore, be eliminated in a presentation of our main problem.

It is true that irrigation was carried on — and still is carried on — in the Andes, which rise precipitously from the narrow coastal desert. But the social significance of Sierra irrigation was different from that of the Coast owing to the complex topography and climatology of the Andes. The seasonal rainfall found throughout the Andes is sufficient to permit an *exclusively rainfall* agriculture in the higher altitudes. In contrast, the arid bottoms of some of the intra-Andean valleys receive so little

rain that they *require irrigation* in order to produce a crop. Along the vast slopes of the Andean mountains, where much of the Sierra population lives, there is a moderate but annually fluctuating amount of precipitation. In many parts of this region irrigation is *not essential for physical existence;* but it was introduced and developed as a *supplementary* form of water supply, because it helped to *stabilize* agricultural production and to *raise the level of subsistence*, until finally a *regular surplus* became possible. By producing a stable economy with such a surplus, irrigation probably played an *essen-*

In the Montaña, which stretches from the foothills of the Andes to the far Atlantic, man has to this day conquered only some of the banks of the thousands of tributaries of the Amazon. The evolution of his economy and culture was drastically retarded by too much water and too much rain. Man could conquer the deserts of the Coast and the heights of the Sierras but not the depths of the jungle (Fig. 19, p. 8, lower right, *Servicio 0:9173* and Fig. 22, p. 9, upper right, *Servicio, unnumbered series*). From Iquitos, Peru, to the Atlantic Ocean, a distance of some 3000 miles, the river drops only 300 feet. As a result, there is considerable flooding and meandering of the branches of the Amazon (Fig. 14, p. 8, left margin, *Servicio 109:2*, Fig. 22). Moreover, during the wet season when the Amazon sometimes rises more than 30 feet (the branches somewhat less), permanent habitation sites are often difficult to maintain. In the area where the floods occur, houses are built on stilts (Fig. 15, p. 8, upper left, *Kosok*, and Fig. 18, p. 8, upper center, *Kosok*), on rafts (Fig. 17, p. 8, lower left, *Kosok*) or on hillocks. Dugout boats are used everywhere in the area (Fig. 16, p. 8, center left, *Kosok*) • Fig. 20 (p. 9, upper left). Giant horsetails, one of the oldest types of plants, found near Tingo Maria. *Kosok* • Fig. 21 (p. 9, lower left). An interesting group of three palm trees near Iquitos. *Kosok* • Fig. 23 (right margin). A typical señorita of the Montaña carrying home drinking water. *Kosok*.

9

tial role in the rise of early class societies and political empires in the Andes — a role whose nature and importance, however, has not as yet been determined. Supplementary forms of irrigation were probably also significant in the advanced societies of the Mexican plateau.

But, in the coastal desert valleys of Peru, irrigation has always been *the sine qua non of agricultural production. Without it, life would be impossible.* It is true at present — it was true in the past!

What are some of the implications of an irrigation agriculture? In such an economy, as contrasted with one that depends entirely on rainfall, man exerts *considerable control over one of the basic natural productive forces, i.e., water.* While the rainfall community goes through a cycle of hoping, praying and sacrificing for the coming

of rain — at the right time and in the right amount — the irrigation community draws upon the river when necessary. True, the river levels fluctuate considerably, but never to the extent that rainfall does in specific local regions. Thus, water control *increases* and *stabilizes* agricultural production. Such *control* must also give man *a consciousness of his own power* in the struggle with nature, a feeling that undoubtedly also reflects itself in his attempts *to control his own social life.*

At the same time, the building, cleaning, repairing and defense of a network of irrigation canals imposes on the tribe or community a greater need for *collective work and thought* than is required in communities dependent merely on rainfall agriculture. Other irrigation communities often arise on adjacent terrain and thereby often partici-

pate in a joint use of common major canals. As a result, a *growing interdependence of thought and action among communities evolves,* which is far more intricate than that existing in the Sierras where neighboring communities are often separated from one another by high mountain ridges or deep valley gorges. Finally, as a coastal valley becomes more and more populated, a still greater complexity of closely-knit social relations develops out of the need for a still more extensive joint water control. Such kinds of social relationships do not evolve in exclusively rainfall societies.

There are other aspects of an irrigation economy that must be considered. When irrigation agriculture develops in desert valleys where the rivers, in their annual floods, have deposited rich alluvial soils, the accumulation

of the latter over centuries and millenia generally provides a basis for better yields per unit of land than do the relatively thinner mountain soils. As a result, many more people can live in a specified coastal area than in one of equal size in the nearby Andean Sierras. In other words, there is an *increased density of population* and with it, as has already been pointed out, there develop *closer and more complex social relationships* within and among coastal communities. Secondly, an *increased efficiency of* production develops, i.e., a greater amount of *food* can be produced by the same number of people expending *the same or even a lesser amount of labor,* than is the case in the Sierras. With this increased efficiency of production, a *regular surplus food supply* can be obtained much more rapidly. Finally, the fact that a crop can be raised

An outstanding achievement of ancient coastal Peru was the large scale production of adobe pyramids of various sizes and shapes (see Chapter VII). On the basis of our field work we estimated that there existed almost a thousand pyramids, the majority of which we visited. They appear singly or in clusters of up to twenty-five. Their greatest significance lies in the fact that they were built mainly for ceremonial purposes, as attested by the presence of ramps leading to the tops of most of them. Apparently, they were built mainly for the priests — also for secular rulers? — who lived on them or near them. When we compare the model (made by Storck and based on the ground plan of Rodríguez SuySuy) of the important Huaca Chotuna in the lower Lambayeque Valley of Peru (Fig. 25, p. 10, top. *Gotlob*) and the ceremonial Ziggurrat pyramid of the priests of ancient Babylonia (Fig. 28, right), we are struck by their basic similarity. Both structures are of adobe and have similar external forms with ramp approaches. Both are products of an intensely irrigated desert economy in a *proto-urban* stage. Chotuna in its present form was probably built in the latter part of the pre-Spanish period, while the Ziggurrat belongs to the early period of Babylonian civilization. By thus specifically linking these two cultures there becomes possible a comparative analysis that throws new light on both of them • Fig. 24 (p. 10, far left). A vertical aerial view of the Chotuna Complex, showing the main pyramid (Fig. 25) at the bottom. At the top is a two-step pyramid, with ramp, similar to Huaca Miguelito (Fig. 4, Chapter XV), while between the two are remains of a small but important third pyramid. To the right are walled semi-urban compounds attached to the main *huaca*. *Servicio 3330:843* • Fig. 26 (p. 10, lower center). Front view of Huaca Chotuna. The circumferential type of ramp of this *huaca* was also used in the Tigris and Euphrates Valleys in the post-Ziggurrat periods. *Kosok* • Fig. 27 (p. 10, lower right). Rear view of the same *huaca* taken from the walled compounds. The figures standing on top of the *huaca* give a concept of its height, almost sixty feet, approximating that of the Ziggurrat. *Kosok.*

The pyramids shown here, unlike those that appear on the previous pages, were apparently built primarily as stately burial places for secular rulers. Figs. 29 and 30 are Chinese pyramids that are located near Sianfu • Fig. 29 (above left) is a Han Dynasty burial "mound" with a base measuring 532 feet by 532 feet and a height of 80 feet. On the top is a structure 10 feet high. Surrounding the pyramid are the walls of a compound that is 1276 feet square • Fig. 30 (above right) is the tomb of Emperor Shi-huang-ti, who lived in the third century B.C. and is known as the founder of the Chinese Empire. The dimensions of the pyramid base are 1600 by 1700 feet, and the height is 250 feet. The walled compound around the structure is 2300 by 2750 feet. This is the largest pyramid in China; indeed, its base area is about five times that of the Great Pyramid of Egypt. However, all burial pyramids in China are constructed of earth and required relatively less labor than the stone pyramids of Egypt. The above information has been taken from Kiroku Adachi's *Chōan Shiseki no Kenkyū* (Study of Historical Remains at Ch'ang-an), Tokyo Oriental Library, 1933. This volume contains photographs of more than a dozen other Chinese pyramids, with ground plans, dimensions and descriptions • Fig. 31 (lower left) is a vertical aerial photograph of the well known Step Pyramid of Djeser in Egypt. Pointed pyramids, like the famous Pyramid of Gizeh, are unusual. *Grinsell* • Fig. 32 (lower right) is a cross section of the Djeser pyramid showing the different earlier forms as well as the underground burial vaults. *Edwards* • Figs. 33 (p. 13). Three basic styles of Chinese pyramids with compounds. *Adachi* • Fig. 34 (p. 13). Ground plan of a Chinese pyramid. Measurements are in units equivalent to the American foot. *Adachi*. It is still a moot question why the pyramids of Babylonia, Peru and Mexico apparently served primarily as ceremonial centers for the living while those of Egypt and China seemed to have been built primarily for the dead. Perhaps both forms were used everywhere in earlier times as, for example, in the Mississippi Valley cultures; later on, special conditions and developments favored the one form or the other. Moreover, it must be remembered that the ceremonial pyramids built for the living were also often used as burial sites for the dead, while the pyramids for the dead in turn were used as ceremonial shrines by the living. This interplay of the dead and the living as significant factors in the evolution of society — expressed here in architecture — is a fascinating but still unexplored subject.

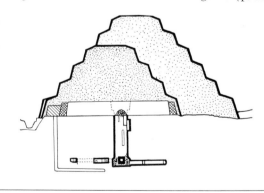

on the warm Coast in about four months, whereas a much longer period is required in the cold Sierras, means that the coastal peoples have *much more time to develop arts and handicrafts* and carry on other activities. Thus, a greater number of cultural activities can be developed on the Coast. These activities, moveover, take on forms that are different from those of the Sierras.

But these very factors contained *the material preconditions for the rapid evolution of a class society on the Coast of Peru!* The priests or chiefs, or both, could — and did — rapidly expand their existing prestige and power by demanding and exacting increasing amounts of surplus food products, an increasing number of handicraft objects and, most important, an *increasing amount of "leisure" time which people had at their disposal due to the increased efficiency of production.* This "leisure" time was put to use by the rulers, who forced the people to build the numerous pyramids, temples, roads, walls, fortresses and other constructions that still litter the whole Coast of Peru. As a result of the growth of the power of the rulers, the *free labor* of the inhabitants was turned into *forced labor.* This domination by the priests and chiefs was naturally facilitated by the density of population mentioned above. To further consolidate their power, the rulers set up a centralized water-control bureaucracy whose function was to develop, regulate and safeguard the large irrigation systems and to control the distribution of the life-giving waters to their subjects. While these activities increased the quantity of crops, they also increased the amount of tribute for the rulers.

Thus, coastal irrigation societies, by contrast to Sierra societies, tended to be precocious in their development of class societies, which were an integral part of all early civilizations. This precociousness expressed itself, not only in the tempo of growth and in the amount of material wealth, but also (in certain regions and during certain periods) in the higher artistic levels of ceramics, textiles and metal objects.

This precocious social development also expressed itself in changes in architectural forms. It is generally accepted that the first great outburst of coastal culture in Peru came with the priest-dominated societies when villages were apparently grouped around *a local ceremonial center consisting of a pyramid or a group of pyramids* — the churches of the ancients. However, as internal social differentiation and conflicts evolved and military-economic expansion set in, the secular chiefs as military specialists grew in power until they dominated the priest-

hood. This development was expressed architecturally by the gradual growth of *large, walled urban centers* — the palaces and ruling centers of the chiefs — while the pyramids of the priests were reduced to minor proportions or placed outside the walled compounds themselves. The rate and nature of these changes obviously were not uniform throughout the Coast.

With the rise of the secular authority, modifications in property relations and in the forms of political administration must also have taken place. But we are still somewhat in the dark as to what these changes were and how they were actually achieved.

ChanChan, the capital of the Chimú Empire — with a possible population of some fifty thousand — emerged as *the largest and richest of the many secular urban sites, not only of Peru, but of all the Americas.* Here, the Grand Chimú held court, and from here he ruled his many subjects living in more than a dozen irrigated valley oases along the Coast. When the Incas finally captured Chan-Chan, they were amazed by its luxury and accumulated wealth. Immediately they carried off the loot to Cuzco, their Sierra capital, only to be relieved of it soon after by the even more rapacious Spanish conquerors.

The rainfall and partial-irrigation mountain societies of Peru also developed class societies with corresponding early civilizations. Here, the process of development must have been somewhat different from that on the Coast. The economy was of a less specialized type, embracing both rainfall and irrigation forms of agriculture. The more generalized economy of the Sierras was also exemplified by the fact that the people there raised not only the coastal crops of maize and beans but also the mountain crops of quinoa and potatoes and made use of domesticated llamas and alpacas. Furthermore, the mountain peoples had to struggle harder with nature to extract a living — and the necessary surplus products for their rulers. This mode of existence must have been reflected in their somewhat different political and social institutions as well as in their artistic achievements. The specific forms of the development of class societies in the Sierras, compared and contrasted with evolving coastal forms, is a fascinating subject which some day must be studied!

It is true that the precociously developed coastal peoples were richer, more cultured, more urbane and more sophisticated than the mountain peoples. These characteristics, however, were based on an economy and a social structure that were more specialized, more "arti-

ficial" and more vulnerable than those of their Sierra neighbors. A thorough, detailed analysis of the above-mentioned characteristics of the coastal irrigation societies can only be accomplished in the future when more material is available than is the case at present, though we have already indicated some of the specialized, "artificial" and vulnerable aspects of their life.

We can, in addition, indicate some aspects of the military vulnerability of the coastal peoples. The *exposed position of their isolated valley oases* in the desert plains and the fact that they owed their very existence to a complex set of *artificial waterways, the canals, which could easily be destroyed,* made them very vulnerable to attacks from one another as well as from the mountain peoples that periodically poured down from the Sierras. The Sierra peoples were ultimately victorious in their conquest of the coastal peoples; we have only one tradition indicating a temporary conquest of Sierra territories by coastal peoples (the Chinchas). Nevertheless, it is these "hothouse" cultures of the Coast that must attract our attention, since they reached certain levels which their Sierra neighbors did not attain.

In answering the question as to why we have chosen to study the Chimús we have given the clue for answering our final query: What contribution can a study of the coastal cultures of Peru make toward a better understanding of the evolution of human society in the mainstream of its development in Afrasia? Although we find that the agriculture of coastal Peru, based *entirely* on irrigation, was unique among the higher cultures of the Americas, this type of economy had similar but much further developed counterparts in the eastern hemisphere, namely, in ancient Egypt, Babylonia, the Indus and Yellow River Valleys, and parts of Central Asia. We also find, in these counterparts, the transformation of primitive tribal societies into early class civilizations. These Afrasian societies, like those of coastal Peru, were also characterized, at a certain stage, by a precocious cultural development in contrast to that of their mountain neighbors, who subsisted on a rainfall economy.

However, in Afrasia there are *considerable gaps* in our knowledge of the long period of transformation from the more primitive tribal societies to the fairly well established class societies that confront us at the dawn of the so-called historical period. In Egypt and Babylonia, this period extended for several millenia before the first part of the third millenium B.C. At present, it is difficult to reconstruct much of this early transition period, for the

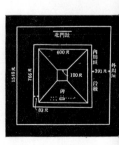

13

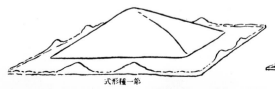

式形種一第

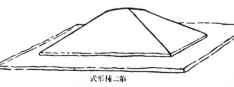

式形種二第

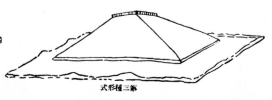

式形種三第

archaeological remains of this period have been greatly obliterated or lie buried under the accumulated structures built and rebuilt during the last five thousand years.

But in the case of coastal Peru, the various steps in the early phase of this period of transition can be traced archaeologically and can — by indirection — be given a social interpretation with an increasing degree of accuracy and detail. The reason for this is as follows: When the Spaniards arrived in the sixteenth century, the Indian population of coastal Peru had reached a stage of economic, social and political development that was somewhat on the same level as that found *at the beginning* of the historic periods in Afrasia. Despite the havoc that the Spaniards wrought among the conquered Indian peoples, the 400 years of colonial and republican rule destroyed *only a part of the archaeological remains of the past.* In addition, several Spaniards wrote some valuable, albeit meager, descriptions of some of the institutions and customs of the people they conquered.

Consequently, on the basis of the limited archaeological and archival research thus far accomplished, it has been possible to trace, to some extent, the various steps of the social, economic, political and cultural development on the Coast. We have been able to establish the fact that after the introduction (probably before 1000 B.C.) of small, priest-dominated communities, based on an irrigated, maize agriculture and associated with the *Very Early* Coastal Chavín (Cupisnique) Period, there developed the artistically outstanding *Early* Chimú (Mochica) Period. Then followed the somewhat confused and ill-defined *Middle* Period (Tiahuanacoid), and finally the secular, urban *Late* Chimú Period. During the latter period, a coastal empire, including probably more than

half a million people, was established. This empire, as indicated above, was finally absorbed by the conquering army of Inca mountaineers only a few generations before the arrival of the Spaniards.

The cultural and social sequence, presented above and discussed in more detail in Chapter VIII, has been quite definitely established for the Northwest Coast of Peru, economically the largest and most important part of the whole Coast. Similar parallel sequences have also been determined for the Central and the South Coast cultures, though in a less complete form. But such definite and detailed sequences of economic, social and cultural levels for the early periods of the higher Afrasian irrigation cultures *have not yet been established*.

The continued investigation of the evolving economies and cultures of ancient Peru will become increasingly important as more archaeological and archival materials are brought to light and studied. Utilizing the Peruvian data, we will one day be able to reconstruct more clearly certain basic aspects of the late prehistoric — and even the early historic — period of the Old World. And, as we have already pointed out, such a reconstruction is fundamental, since Afrasia, during the period of transition from tribal societies to early civilizations, represented the *main trunk* of human social evolution.

At the same time, as new material concerning the late prehistoric and early historic periods of Afrasia is discovered, further light will be thrown on the significance

of certain aspects of ancient Peruvian cultures. For in Afrasia there evolved social and cultural levels that ancient America began to approach but never attained. Knowledge of these more advanced levels is important, for, *from the vantage points of higher levels, we can understand more clearly the unsolved problems and undeveloped potentialities of emerging lower levels!*

A word of caution must be added. It would, of course, be unscientific to transfer specific Peruvian forms of development mechanically to Afrasia — and vice versa. But the general sequences in the developments of early class-stratified societies in Peru and Afrasia are so strikingly parallel, although separated in time and space, that they not only justify but make imperative the use of the comparative method. By applying this method with intelligence and with critical understanding of the concrete issues involved, we can draw ancient Peruvian cultures from their apparent exotic isolation in world development and place them in their true perspective as important landmarks in the evolution of the great human family. Thus, we can further substantiate the basic principle that under similar conditions mankind has developed similar institutions and similar ideas, while differences in the specific forms of these institutions and ideas are the result of the manifold combinations of specific local conditions, specific local traditions and specific local needs. *Peru furnishes striking evidence of this basic law!*

II

Preparations

THE ROLE that irrigation had played in the transformation of primitive tribal societies into the early stages of civilization in ancient Afrasia had always attracted my attention. In 1936, I received a grant from the Social Science Research Council that enabled me to make a survey study of important sections of China, India, Iraq, Egypt and other irrigated regions. After my return to the United States some of my findings were presented in a paper before the American Oriental Society.

At this point ancient Peru attracted my attention. As I began to read some of the available material, I decided it would be worth while to investigate in greater detail the early cultures of that fascinating country. This, I felt, would give me a deeper and more detailed insight into the problem of early social transformations.

Most important, I wanted to visit Peru to obtain a concrete picture of the country. Fortunately, in 1939, my former wife, Rose Wyler, and I were able to make a brief tour of South America. While there, we made a preliminary ground survey of some of the ancient canal systems of the Northwest Coast of Peru and came to the conclusion that a further study of the problem would yield important results. The results of our preliminary survey were presented in 1940 in Washington, D. C., before the Eighth American Scientific Congress, and published in the *Proceedings* of the Congress.

It became clear, even after this short survey, that it would be possible to do in coastal Peru what had not yet been done in any of the archaeologically explored areas of irrigated Afrasia, namely, to enter on the existing maps the remains of all the major ancient irrigation systems and to determine the *maximum cultivated area of each valley in ancient times*. The areas of all the valleys could then be added together to obtain the total cultivated area for the whole Coast. A clear picture of the actual geographic-economic framework, within which the economy, politics and culture of each valley developed, would then emerge — together with the geographic-economic relations of the valleys to one another at their maximum stages of development. Moreover, in this desert land, it would be possible to locate and map the most important ruins still remaining from ancient times without laboriously hacking down dense jungle vegetation. On the basis of this wealth of basic material, we could then *reconstruct graphically the main physical aspects of pre-Columbian coastal Peruvian societies during their maximum stage of development*. Truly a worthwhile project!

As stated in Chapter I, such a project would be extremely difficult to carry out in India, Egypt, Iraq and China, not merely because of the greater areas involved, but also because constant rebuilding activities during the past 5000 years have precluded determination of the extent of the areas once under cultivation. These activities have destroyed or covered over the main ruins of the period of transition from the late stages of primitive societies to the early stages of civilization.

Fig. 1. Part of an exterior wall of Huaca el Dragón in the Moche Valley. The whole *huaca* was recently excavated by Dr. Schaedel and his assistants (see Chapter IX). The unusual designs discovered on the adobe walls may be of calendrical significance. *Schaedel.*

During our cursory survey of Peru in 1939 we noticed that most of the ancient canals and fields no longer in use today were located mainly along the Northwest Coast. This puzzled us. We made inquiries and were truly astounded to learn that an unusual botanical phenomenon was the cause of this situation!

Before discussing this problem, let us first contrast certain hydrological aspects of ancient and modern crops. In ancient times the main coastal crop was maize — and a

subsidiary one, beans. Cotton was also grown, for it was the raw material from which practically all clothes on the Coast were manufactured. But both maize and cotton are crops that require *little water per acre*. Thus the limited amount of water in most rivers was used to irrigate rather *extensive land areas*.

When the Spaniards came, the population along the coast shrank tremendously and so did, though to a lesser extent, the size of the irrigated areas. But the nineteenth and twentieth centuries saw the rapid growth of exports of agricultural crops, of which cotton proved to be the most profitable. Since cotton requires little water per acre to cultivate, the amount of water available in each river could therefore irrigate much land. As a result, many of the ancient canals began to be put back into operation and the old fields again placed under cultivation.

But soon difficulties arose. In the extensive and economically most important region of the whole Coast, namely, from the Supe Valley on the Central Coast to the Motupe Valley on the Northwest Coast, the cotton plants were generally attacked by a destructive disease. Why these valleys suffered and not the others is still unexplained. As a result, the planters turned to the next most profitable crop, namely, sugar. Sugar cane had already been introduced by the Spaniards in some of the northern valleys soon after the conquest, but this was done to satisfy their own local needs.

But sugar requires two or three times more water per acre each year than does cotton! Rice, which is also grown here, but for Peruvian consumption only, requires even more water! Therefore, the limited amount of water in most rivers necessitated the cultivation of a *much smaller area than had been the case with a maize or maize-cotton economy of the ancients. This left considerable areas, once cultivated in ancient times, without the essential water.* Thus was the mystery explained!

For topographical reasons the land thus cultivated was generally in the part of the valley closest to the river itself. Consequently the ancient canals, fields and ruins in *the more distant peripheral areas* remained untouched by modern agricultural expansion.

Because these sugar-producing valleys contain most of the ancient canals and fields no longer in use, they would naturally attract the attention of the paleohydrologist. But by a peculiar coincidence these same valleys also constituted *the main region of the Chimú Empire*. By determining the form and size of the areas previously cultivated in these valleys, we could thus obtain a clear picture of the geographic-economic aspects of the Empire itself.

Most of the canals we were later to find were of course already known to engineers and to many local inhabitants. Some of the ruins of important sites which we were to map had already been studied by archaeologists who had, moreover, drawn valid conclusions concerning the general sequence of cultures along some parts of the Coast. But it became essential that an *integrative survey* be made

which would give the geographic-economic framework within which the social structures and cultural activities of the coastal irrigation societies of the past could be studied in a more concrete and systematic way.

After having better acquainted myself with the geographical, historical and archaeological literature dealing with ancient Peru, I took a year's leave of absence from Long Island University in 1940, in order to return with my wife to Peru. During that year we collected all available hydrological data on the various coastal rivers in the Dirección de Aguas y Irrigación. We also combed through the historical materials in the National Library and in the Geographic Society of Lima. Some of these materials were subsequently destroyed by fire.

Most important, we began a ground survey of the individual valleys on the Northwest Coast. But we were badly handicapped by the absence of aerial surveys of these valleys and by our financial inability to hire a truck or car for our field work. The Peruvian Ministerio de Fomento, which was then in the process of building the Pan American Highway, happily overcame in part our second obstacle by placing its trucks at our disposal whenever possible. Various *hacendados* along the Coast also kindly loaned us cars, trucks and horses for our work.

We were given additional assistance by Señor Pardo y Miguel of Hacienda Pátapo in the Lambayeque Valley. He took us on several flights in his private airplane over the many ancient sites in this and neighboring valleys. Mr. Faucett, the director of the Faucett Line, the local Peruvian aviation company, also generously came to our assistance by giving us a pass for planes of the company flying along the Coast. We made full use of this valuable privilege and were thus able to locate additional ancient canals and archaeological sites. Moreover, the Peruvian Government gave us permission to take photographs from these planes. Thus we were able to obtain numerous low-elevation photographs of important ancient canals and sites. Some of these are reproduced in this volume.

But the main work was discovering and localizing canals and ruins by ordinary ground work and then mapping them with a sufficient degree of accuracy so that the

Fig. 2 (left). Another portrait *huaco* of a Mochica ruler or official whose high rank is indicated by his ear lobe plugs. *Chiclin-Kosok* • Fig. 3 (below). Detail of a Paracas textile. *Courtesy of the Brooklyn Museum* • Fig. 4 (p. 17). A collection of late Chimú gold objects supposedly found in the Huarmey Valley. *Courtesy of the American Museum of Natural History (AMNH).*

final results would be satisfactory. Our method of work was simple. Before we arrived in a valley we usually had collected some advance information about the location of ancient canals and associated ruins by studying old maps and by interviewing irrigation engineers and other officials.

When we arrived in a valley we visited each settlement and *hacienda* located there, and, after the customary polite formalities, we would ask a series of pertinent questions. Have you any ancient canals or ruins on your property? Do you know of any others in the neighborhood? Where are they? What are their names? Is there anyone here to guide us to the sites? We were generally overwhelmed with answers!

With this additional information in our possession and usually accompanied by a local guide, we then set out with either car, truck or horses to locate the canals and ruins about which we had heard. We marked their position on our maps and made short descriptive notes of each of the sites. In the process of carrying on this field work we were often rewarded by finding more canals and archaeological sites than our informants and guides had known of. Gradually, we were able to piece our information together bit by bit until we obtained a unified picture of an entire valley. The work was fascinating — a kind of archaeological hunting expedition!

But because this procedure had to be repeated in each valley our work often tended to become rather monotonous. However, the repetition tended to have compensating, attractive aspects, for each new valley was a new adventure into an unknown region and among unknown people. We were brought into continuous contact with persons from all walks of life of present day Peru, rich and poor, educated and uneducated, many of them, at least in part, descendants of the ancient Indian peoples whose work we were now studying. It was heartening to find so much interest in our project and so much willingness to help us in completing it. Here along the Coast, where the Indian component of the Peruvian population is less than in the Sierras, we were surprised to find among many people a vague, though persistent awareness and pride in the achievements of their Indian ancestors, who had been an independent people free from foreign domination.

The mapping itself became a relatively simple problem. Fortunately, Peruvian Army maps were available with the convenient scale of 1:100,000 for the coastal area from Lima to the Ecuadorian frontier, a distance of more than

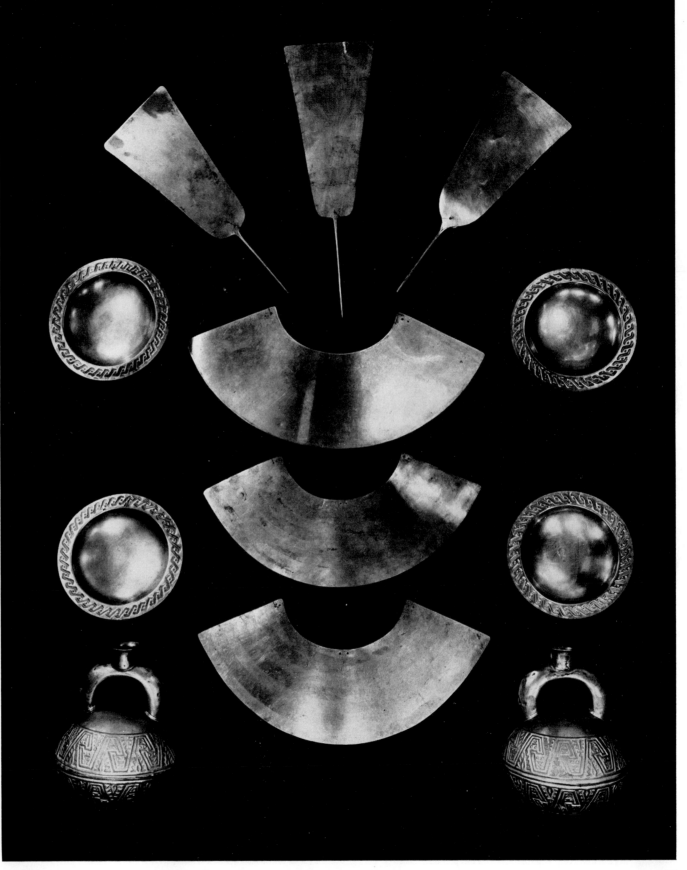

six hundred miles. These maps thus covered the area of the ancient Chimú Empire as well as part of the region to the south of it. On these maps we entered the results of our field work.

The scale of the maps was such that one centimeter on the maps represented one kilometer on the ground. The maps contained not only topographical features but also the location of towns, villages, *hacienda* buildings and roads.

Figs. 5 to 8. Mochica type *huacos*. Fig. 5 (left center). Bird with captured fish. *AMNH.* Fig. 6 (right center). Typical drawing of a Mochica warrior-priest on a wide-handled stirrup spout. In their drawings, the Mochicas never reached the high technical level of expression that they did in their plastic arts. *AMNH.* Fig. 7 (top). Only a few *huacos* of clenched fists have been found so far. The significance of the fist is unknown. *Chiclin-Kosok.* Fig. 8 (bottom). The white head, with painted eyes and eyebrows, as well as the black stirrup spout of this *huaco* are unique. *Chiclín-Kosok.* Fig. 9. A Paracas textile (Early Period) from the South Coast, the region where the finest textiles of ancient America were woven. A study of the design indicates that it probably had calendrical significance (see Chapter VI). *AMNH.*

Starting out from a fixed place on the map we would, by following the odometer (distance recorder) on the car or truck, easily determine how many kilometers we were from that particular place. Then we entered the distance in centimeters on our maps. Cross checking was, of course, necessary. When we worked in the open desert, far from a road, we often had to follow a triangulation method, utilizing those hills and structures that also appeared on the maps. The results usually were sufficiently accurate for our purposes.

World War II interrupted our work. During the war, however, the United States Army made a fairly complete trimetrogon aerial survey of much of Peru. In this type of aerial survey the plane carries three large cameras: one takes vertical photographs, while the other two cameras, which are fixed in the plane at an angle to the ground, simultaneously take oblique photographs, one to the left, the other to the right. Then the three overlapping photographs can be joined together to form a composite trimetrogon picture from which an extensive vista, from horizon to horizon, is obtained. At the same time, since the vertical photographs also overlap one another, it is possible to line them up in one continuous strip containing more than a hundred photographs. By this method a tremendous area can be surveyed in one flight.

Through the aid of Dr. John Wright, then Secretary of the American Geographical Society, who had shown keen interest in the Peruvian study and had given us much intellectual advice and moral support, these photographs were made available to us. There were about 20,000 of them! It took a good part of the summer of 1946 in Washington to wade through this mass of material. The photographs were unfortunately taken at a very high altitude and sometimes during midday when shadows of objects are almost non-existent. As a result, many important details were not visible. Early morning and late afternoon are the best times for taking aerial photographs, for then shadows are longer, and slight differences in contour of natural formations as well as *man-made* structures stand out in bold relief. But since these were the *first* comprehensive aerial photographs ever taken of a great part of Peru, they were highly welcome. They gave not only an over-all picture of each valley, together with some of its major ancient canals, roads and sites, but also a comprehensive, though often somewhat indistinct, view of the *inter-valley desert areas*. Almost none of these latter areas has ever been photographed again. Thus the American Army photographs became a valuable supplement to our

previous field survey. Some of the most dramatic of these photographs are reproduced in this volume.

Before World War II, Robert Shippee and Lt. George R. Johnson spent some time in Peru where they took a large number of excellent oblique aerial photographs of various important archaeological sites and geographical landmarks. A few of these are reproduced in this volume. A larger, more representative number, was published in

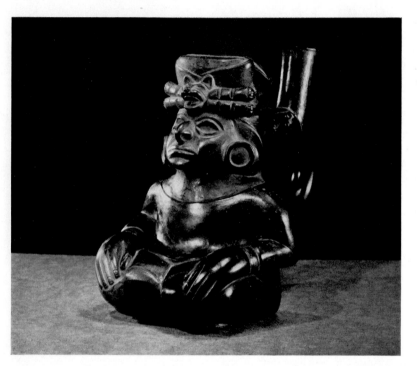

Fig. 10. The consummate arrogance of an important chief is well portrayed in this *huaco* made by a great anonymous artist of ancient times. The polished black surface and the squatting position of the ruler are not typical of Mochica type water jugs. A study of most of the portrait *huacos* indicates that the rulers were almost always portrayed as stern, domineering characters. *AMNH*.

literature dealing with the geography, economy, archaeology, history, and culture of ancient Peru. This included, of course, a detailed investigation of the Spanish Chroniclers and their commentators.

Because of the paucity of the material in the Chroniclers dealing with the Coast of Peru and the dispersion of this material in a variety of places it was necessary, first of all, to "dig out" all the isolated sections and passages relevant

1930 by the American Geographical Society under the title, *Peru from the Air*, with an excellent text furnished by Raye Platt, one of the leading geographers of the Society. The bulk of the photographs, however, remain unpublished and are at present in the possession of the Wenner-Gren (Viking Fund) Foundation for Anthropological Research, Inc., in New York.

In the latter part of 1946, I obtained another year's leave of absence from Long Island University. I spent this time writing up my field notes and making a systematic study, mainly at the Library of Congress, of the

to the subject. These extracts will eventually be published as a source book with an English translation and a commentary.

On the basis of some of this material, I prepared an article which attempted to analyze the limited and conflicting accounts of the conquest of the Coast of Peru by the Incas during the latter part of the fifteenth century. Ironically, the conquest of the Chimú Empire, the most important aspect of Inca coastal expansion, is barely mentioned by most Chroniclers. Moreover, there appear contradictions in their accounts, indicating that there may

have been several campaigns or conquests. It soon became clear that certain aspects of Garcilaso's much-criticized account of this conquest must be treated more seriously than has hitherto been the fashion in most scientific circles.

Another article, together with a chart, dealing with the absolute chronology of the leading peoples of North and South America was also prepared. The results of the study indicate that the official Inca list of rulers dates back only to the latter part of the thirteenth century and that the conquest of the Coast took place only in the latter part of the fifteenth century, a conclusion which Rowe (1946) also reached. Both articles will be published after the completion of our major study.

During the same period an article dealing with the peculiar astronomical markings of the ancient Nazca region in the southern part of Peru (Chapter VI) was completed and published by Maria Reiche and myself. This article was based in part on material collected in 1940-41 and appeared in the May 1947 issue of *Natural History*. Some of our findings are presented in Chapter VI.

In 1948, the Board of Trustees of Long Island University, through the good offices of the late President Tristram Walker Metcalfe, sent me and my son Michael to Peru for a year to complete the field work of our irrigation studies. The detailed results of this work, together with four large maps, we expect to publish in the coming year under the title of *Water and Life in Ancient Peru*. In the meantime, we present here a summary of some of our main findings about ancient canals, cities and pyramids, together with other significant and interesting information on Peru, both past and present.

20

III

Off to Peru!

WE LEFT NEW YORK during the middle of July, 1948, traveling by the *Silver Meteor* to Miami. There we decided not to take the direct "night express" plane to Lima, but rather to stay overnight and go on the "day local". Since it took two days instead of the customary one night, the "day local" would give us a chance to see, even though superficially, the nature of the country over which we were flying.

Early in the morning the plane rose above the sandy shores of Miami Beach, and soon the glistening blue-green of the Caribbean spread out below us. Before long, we were flying over Cuba, and then over Jamaica. In spite of the limited time we spent over these islands we obtained a vivid impression of the varying topography, the lush vegetation and the scattered population centers, which book-reading by itself could hardly produce.

The plane arrived at Barranquilla, Colombia, at about lunch time. There we fortunately had a three-hour stopover until the plane for Panama was ready, and we spent the time in making a short sight-seeing trip through this interesting town with its old Spanish buildings. Though not as picturesque as the rival port of Cartagena, it surpasses the latter in prosperity. We wandered through the colorful streets, carried on some intriguing window shopping and then relaxed in a small café where we sipped our first strong South American coffee.

The flight over the Caribbean to Panama turned out to be a dramatic climax to the exciting day's trip. As we approached land, we witnessed from our position high in the heavens the overwhelming majesty and power of an approaching thunder storm. The entire horizon before us was covered with towering layers of dark, awesome clouds, tinged with vibrant shades of red and orange from the rays of the setting sun! This inspiring scene came to a close as the plane suddenly plunged downward through this thick wall of clouds — to land safely at the airport.

Panama City, with its old, narrow, winding streets lined with many balconied colonial style houses, is one of the most fascinating centers of Latin America. Having left modern Miami only the same morning, we were now transplanted suddenly into the past. We stayed at the large Hotel Central, a typical old-fashioned structure in the old part of the city. That evening we enjoyed ourselves wandering leisurely through the maze of fascinating streets that were lighted by lamps attached to old-fashioned lampposts. Here we watched the ever moving procession of peoples from all over the world.

Early the following morning we flew southward over the shimmering Pacific. Before long, the plane again approached land and then began climbing up over the Andes of southwestern Colombia. After a brief stop at the important town of Cali, the plane mounted still higher

Fig. 1 (far left). Ecuadorian woman from Otavalo. *Kosok* • Fig. 2 (left). Snow-covered volcano in highland Ecuador. In the foreground are typical terraced farms (*andenes*) that have been laboriously built everywhere along the steep sides of the vast Andes. *Panagra* • Fig. 3 (right). View of a section of Quito. Notice the palms which are growing at an altitude of 9000 feet. *Kosok.*

over the ever-rising Sierras, until we crossed into Ecuador and landed at the capital city of Quito. This attractive city, with its wonderful, year-round temperate climate, lies more than 9000 feet high on an extensive rolling plateau from which rise the majestic peaks of extinct ice- and snow-covered volcanoes (Fig. 2).

During the descent from Quito to the coast, the plane soon became engulfed in a mass of white clouds which obscured the rugged mountains around us. But after a short time the clouds suddenly dissolved, and we were abruptly transported into an entirely different world! Below us stretched an extensive flat region covered with lush green tropical vegetation and segmented by numerous rivers meandering lazily into Guayaquil Bay. We

Both of these countries also abound in even more extensive and significant remains of the long pre-Incaic past, which are even less explored and understood than those of Peru. We were tempted to pry into some of their secrets, but the whole problem was far beyond the range of our own studies. We did, however, later return to the coast of Ecuador to ascertain the dividing line between the region of rainfall agriculture, and the small dry region of potential irrigation agriculture (see Chapter XXIV).

Following a brief stop at the city of Guayaquil, the plane crossed over the wide bay and within minutes we approached the coast of Peru. Again a sharp change in landscape attracted our attention! This time it was a change from the tropical jungles of coastal Ecuador to

bringing with it a heavy rainfall. The larger one, the cold Humboldt Current, comes from the Antarctic Ocean and flows northward along part of the coast of Chile and along the whole of the coast of Peru. The Humboldt Current has the effect of turning this entire coastal region into an almost complete desert and of reducing the temperature considerably below the level expected for these latitudes. The two currents meet near the border of Peru and Ecuador and thus help to account for the abrupt changes of climate and vegetation at this point.

The relative strengths of the two ocean currents vary from year to year. The result is an annual northward or southward shift of the zone where these two currents intermingle. This, in turn, creates a considerable vari-

Fig. 4. A section of Guayaquil, the largest port of Ecuador. *Panagra.*

Fig. 5. Sierra Ecuadorians, in their native costumes, going to market. *Kosok.*

soon landed at attractive, modern Guayaquil, the principal city and harbor of Ecuador (Fig. 4).

Before the coming of the Spaniards in the early sixteenth century much of Ecuador, and even a part of southern Colombia, had been under the domination of the Incas, who left us a number of archaeological remains.

the desert plains and mountains of Peru (Figs. 6 and 7).

This change in climate is due largely to the meeting in this region of two opposing ocean currents. The smaller one, the warm Niño, (the child), flows from the west across the Pacific and then continues in a southward direction down along the coast of Colombia and Ecuador,

ation in the annual rainfall of the Peruvian-Ecuadorian border region. Thus in the Peruvian valley of Tumbes, near the Ecuadorian border, the annual rainfall rate shifts between two inches and seventy-five inches! As a result, rainfall agriculture is possible during certain years, while during others, irrigation becomes indispensable.

came into existence. And it is in these small cultivated valleys that there evolved the coastal Indian cultures with their large pyramids, walled cities, roads and fortresses, beautiful pottery and textiles, elaborate gold and silver ornaments and utensils; cultures parallel to those of very early desert Egypt, Babylonia and India. It was to the remains of these early Peruvian cultures that we were returning, intent upon obtaining a better and more concrete understanding of their geographical extent and material basis.

Flying from north to south over this coastal area is a most fantastic experience. On the one side lies the vast blue Pacific stretching to the distant horizon; on the other rise the towering Andes, whose foothills at times extend into the ocean, and whose steep, barren slopes reflect, especially at sunset, many subtle shades of gray, brown, purple and red; while directly below stretch the brownish-yellow desert lands dramatically interrupted every ten to twenty-five miles by lush green valley oases! Such a flight presents in dramatic form the basic climatic-topographic problems which have confronted man ever since he entered this barren desert region.

During the voyage, our view, unfortunately, was ob-

Fig. 6. When approaching the northernmost part of the Peruvian Coast, between Tumbes and Talara, one is greeted by these desert hills. Farther south, the hills give way to desert plains that are cut at fairly regular intervals by river-irrigated oases. The small settlement, Galeta Grau, can be seen in the center of the photograph, while Talara is located in the upper right hand corner. Still farther south runs the Chira River. The white ribbon, following the irregular coast line of the Pacific Ocean, is the Pan American Highway. *Servicio 0:4349* • Fig. 7 (below). Flying over *loma* clouds along the desert Coast of Peru (see text). *Kosok* • Fig. 8 (right margin). Young Ecuadorian girl. *Kosok.*

The long narrow desert zone which stretches more than 1400 miles along the coast of Peru and Chile is but a few dozen miles wide, extending from the Pacific Ocean almost to the Continental Divide in the Andes. In the extreme northern part of Peru the average annual rate of rainfall barely reaches three inches, while in Iquique in northern Chile, the rate is estimated to be one hundredth of an inch a year, the lowest on record in the world!

This inhospitable region, one of the driest on earth, is dotted, nonetheless, with a series of wonderfully green oases produced by man. Each of these oases clusters around one of the dozens of small rivers that flow in a westerly direction from the nearby Continental Divide into the Pacific. From these "miniature Niles," man has been taking water during the past three thousand years and spreading it by means of complex irrigation systems over the parched soil. Thus, the present exceptionally productive, cultivated lands of these valley oases gradually

structed part of the time by banks of *loma* clouds which, for a period of from four to five months of the Peruvian winter, remain almost continually suspended, at an altitude of from one to two thousand feet, over much of the narrow coastal area. These peculiar clouds never produce rain; at best, a slight drizzle reaches the ground! The climate, as a result, is moist and cool during the winter. While this coolness and moisture are most welcome, the absence of sunlight for weeks at a time often makes one feel extremely depressed.

Along the narrow strips on the edge of the mountains where the *loma* clouds rest, there is generally a sufficient condensation of moisture to permit the growth of some grasses, flowers, and even shrubs. Flying along the desert Coast after the *loma* clouds have lifted, one can often see this green strip stretching along the mountain sides, sandwiched between an upper and lower layer of arid soil.

Our plane arrived above Lima after dark. We had an eerie feeling as it circled many times over the clouds, searching for a hole through which to drop. But none appeared! Finally the plane plunged through the thick, wide cloud blanket, and suddenly, as though produced by the wave of a magic wand, a fairyland of innumerable lights of the city of Lima lay spread out below, winking, as it were, a bright welcome to us!

At Limatambo airport customs and passport inspections were carried out with an unheard-of speed. "We did it in seven minutes flat," Michael's diary records. A taxi soon sped us to the old-fashioned, spacious Hotel Maury, which had been our main headquarters during our previous visits to Peru.

Fig. 9 (margin). Young Ecuadorian boy. *Kosok* • Fig. 10. Maguay plant found in certain parts of the Andes. *Kosok*.

24

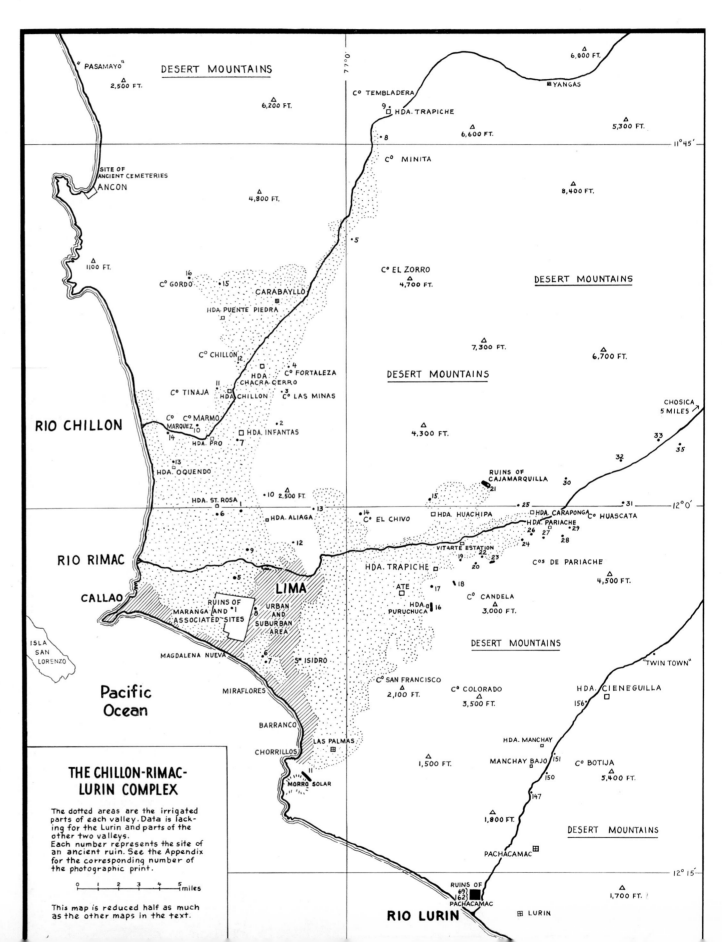

THE CHILLON-RIMAC-LURIN COMPLEX

The dotted areas are the irrigated parts of each valley. Data is lacking for the Lurin and parts of the other two valleys.
Each number represents the site of an ancient ruin. See the Appendix for the corresponding number of the photographic print.

0 1 2 3 4 5 miles

This map is reduced half as much as the other maps in the text.

IV

Lima and Peru: Past and Present

PERU IS STILL, in many ways, a country of the Indian, a fact which appears to be contradicted by the distinctly Latin flavor of Lima and some of the coastal cities. To understand the true nature of Peruvian affairs, the traveler must leave Lima, which is indeed atypical of Peru, and go up into the Sierras. There he will find a world in which the Indian and his way of life still predominate.

The 1940 Census — the first systematic one in the history of Peru — lists almost half of the population as being of Indian racial stock! This means that out of a total population exceeding six million about three million are Indians. The Census makes no distinction between Whites and White-Indian mixtures, which together constitute the rest of the population, but lumps them as one group. Various estimates, however, indicate that most of this group are probably White-Indian mixtures. This means that the total non-White stock probably makes up about 90 per cent and the White no more than 10 per cent of the population! Since it is common knowledge in Peru that people tend to list themselves in the "more desirable" social categories, the actual racial composition of the population is probably even more on the Indian side than the Census would indicate.

But there are great variations in the distribution of the

Fig. 1. View of Lima, capital of Peru. Contrast the living city and adjacent irrigated lands with the surrounding desert foothills of the Andes. *Servicio, unnumbered series.* NOTE: The line-cut above and those on pp. 32, 33 and 38 are of Early Lima *huacos. Handbook II.*

Indians throughout the country. When we turn to the Sierras, we find that the Indians predominate, especially in the central and southern parts. Here the actual Indian stock ranges from about 60 to 90 per cent. (For details see column 8 of the Table, p. 27). In the northern part of the Sierras, however, the proportion of Indians among the population is considerably less. Even so, the Indians together with the Indian-White mixtures probably comprise more than three-quarters of the population here. The White population is strongest on the Coast, especially in the Spanish colonial towns of Arequipa and Lima. Yet, even on the Coast the Whites definitely represent a minority of the population.

But more important than racial composition are the *linguistic* and cultural aspects of the population problem. We find that more than half the population of Peru over five years of age still speak one of the Indian languages!

Fig. 2. Viewed from a balcony of the City Hall is the famous Plaza de Armas, the oldest plaza of Lima. The Cathedral, just opposite, contains the body of Pizarro; in front of the Cathedral stands an equestrian statue of the conqueror of Peru. To the left is the Bishop's Palace with its finely carved wooden balconies. Further left is a section of the President's Palace. *Grace and Company* • Figure 4 (p. 27, margin). Guard before Presidential Palace. *Kosok*.

Of these, *Quechua*—the language of the ancient Incas—is by far the most widely used. The related *Aymara* also plays an important role in the extreme southern Sierra zone (see column 6). What is even more surprising is that *more than two-thirds of those who speak an Indian language — this means one-third of all the people of Peru — know no Spanish at all* (see column 5).

In the Sierras the situation becomes linguistically even more astonishing. In the five provinces of the Southern Sierras — the home of the ancient Incas — from 79 to 86 per cent of the population speak *only* Indian languages (see column 5, lines 1 through 5). If we add to that the percentage of persons who speak both Indian and Spanish (see column 4) we find that *more than 98 per cent of the population here speak Indian tongues* (see column 6)! Furthermore, less than 20 per cent speak Spanish (see columns 3 and 4)! Spanish alone is spoken only by a little more than one per cent of the people (see column 3). *And this after four centuries of Hispanization!*

We are here living, so to speak, among an Indian nation, or people, with a distinct language, distinct culture and in some ways distinct economy. Here the Spanish-speaking top level administrators need interpreters to relay their orders. This is not surprising for these administrators have not grown racially or culturally out of the people themselves. They form a ruling group superimposed from the outside as a result of a past conquest.

In the Central Sierras — Huánuco, Ancash and Junín — the situation is only somewhat less striking (see lines 6 through 8). However, in the northern part of the Sierras the Indian languages of the past are now spoken by only a small minority of the population. But one has merely to visit this region to realize how strongly the Indian way of life persists to this day.

Solely on the Coast do we find that Spanish has triumphed completely! The reason why the coastal departments, especially those in the south, are listed in the Census as containing peoples speaking Indian languages is that these departments include part of the neighboring Sierras.

In ancient times, a number of languages were spoken along the Coast. These languages were quite distinct from those in the Sierras. Along the Northwest Coast the most important was the so-called Mochica which continued to exist longer than all other coastal languages, dying out only in the course of the last hundred years. Today a few individuals in Lambayeque remember some words — a pathetic finale to a great living past!

The question immediately arises: Why this lack of resistance to the inroads of Spanish culture here? We are not yet in possession of all the data to answer this question satisfactorily. However, it is clear that, unlike the Sierras, almost every valley of the Coast was immediately and suddenly hit by the full force of the Spanish conquerors and settlers who easily and rapidly seized the relatively defenseless coastal plains. Moreover, the irrigation economy and social structure here were more highly specialized and more vulnerable to the Spanish forms of economic life and political control than the more generalized and more resistant Sierra pattern.

A radical change in the mode of water distribution and settlement pattern which the Spaniards introduced was in certain ways a lethal blow to coastal social organization. The abruptness with which the change was effected on the Coast was the result of the facility with which the coastal valley economy could be directed. In the course of a very few days whole settlements of Indians could be deprived of water, the *sine qua non* of their existence. Such changes, while effected in key areas in the Sierras, took much longer to bring about there; consequently, the Indians had time to accommodate their economic and social relations to the innovations.

Other factors obviously contributed to the rapid breakdown of indigenous coastal society. Certain of the Spanish Chroniclers frankly allude to the virtual depopulation of many valleys caused in part by the brutality of the conquerors and in part by the civil wars among the conquerors themselves. Some Indians were killed, others fled temporarily to the somewhat safer Sierras (Kubler:1946). In the case of uprisings, the coastal Indians were much more susceptible to violent reprisals than those of the Sierras. For guerrilla warfare cannot be maintained on open terrain — a fact confirmed by many incidents of World War II.

As some of the Coast later on became repopulated — partly by Sierra Indians — the cultural life came much more thoroughly under Spanish Church and governmental control than was the case in the Sierras. Although the so-called Mochica language survived along parts of the Northwest Coast and was even used by the Church for missionary purposes, the intensive domination of coastal life by the Spaniards, nevertheless, led to the gradual annihilation of the last linguistic vestiges of an ancient people.

Thus, today, as in the past, the Coast is linguistically divorced from the Sierras. But the Coast now has the

FIG. 3. PERCENTAGE OF POPULATION OVER 5 YEARS OF AGE SPEAKING DIFFERENT LANGUAGES

		1	2	3	4	5	6	7	8
	Name of Department	Spanish and Foreign	Spanish Only	Spanish and Indian	Indian Only	Total % Who Speak Indian Cols. 4 & 5	Total Population Over 5 Years of Age	% of Population Listed Racially as Indian
Southern Andes	1. Apurímac	0.04	0.37	13.37	86.22	**99.59**	216,243	70.02
	2. Ayacucho	0.05	0.86	16.70	82.39	**99.09**	299,769	75.94
	3. Huancavelica	0.05	1.17	19.94	78.84	**98.78**	203,128	78.68
	4. Puno	0.08	1.29	15.19	83.44	**98.63**	463,080	92.36
	5. Cusco	0.16	1.45	18.95	79.44	**98.39**	411,298	71.73
Central Andes	6. Huánuco	0.29	11.45	35.71	52.55	**88.26**	193,235	63.46
	7. Ancash	0.26	15.18	29.65	54.91	**84.56**	354,892	55.83
	8. Junín	0.74	20.43	47.12	31.71	**78.83**	361,878	60.85
South Coast with Parts of Southern Andes	9. Tacna	1.30	46.92	35.69	16.09	**51.78**	31,684	52.17
	10. Moquegua	0.36	51.12	24.19	24.33	**48.52**	29,034	46.17
	11. Arequipa	1.24	63.62	17.98	17.16	**35.14**	225,244	26.44
Montaña with Parts of Andes	12. Loreto	1.79	59.50	25.25	13.46	**38.71**	137,931	38.16
	13. San Martín	0.28	66.87	20.31	12.54	**32.85**	77,197	25.02
	14. Amazonas	0.14	76.10	18.48	5.28	**23.76**	53,982	20.37
	15. Madre de Dios	7.64	75.33	11.66	5.37	**17.03**	4,098	25.88
Central and North Coast with Parts of Andes	16. Ica	2.03	83.44	12.71	1.82	**14.53**	118,371	29.19
	17. Lima	8.23	77.68	11.66	2.43	**14.09**	721,818	15.30
	18. Callao	9.63	84.78	5.59	—	**5.59**	72,295	2.87
	19. Cajamarca (Northern Sierras)	0.08	93.32	5.49	1.11	**6.60**	405,975	12.13
	20. Lambayeque	0.64	92.35	4.21	2.80	**7.01**	162,967	30.09
	21. La Libertad	0.95	97.77	1.11	0.17	**1.28**	319,514	12.86
	22. Tumbes	0.22	99.30	0.48	—	**0.48**	21,362	1.46
	23. Piura	0.54	99.34	0.09	0.03	**0.12**	343,357	37.82
	Total for Country	1.67	46.73	16.61	34.99	**51.60**	5,228,352	45.86

language of the conquerors, while the greater portion of the Sierras has retained the language of the conquered.

Much of the story of the disruption and transformation of coastal society and culture since the time of the conquerors remains to be told. Many aspects of this story undoubtedly lie hidden in the numerous unexplored archives of the Coast.

Representatives of a few other nationalities are also scattered throughout Peru. There are Chinese merchants and landowners in various parts of the country. Most of them are descendants of former contract laborers who were imported into Peru during the nineteenth century because they could be forced to work for even lower wages than the few centavos paid to the Indians and liberated Negro slaves. The descendants of these liberated slaves live along the Coast, mainly in the Lima-Callao region and in the Ica Valley. Add to this mixture a sprinkling of North Americans and Europeans, as well as some non-Peruvian Latin Americans, and the population picture is more or less complete. There has always been a considerable amount of intermarriage among the various groups, with the result that Peru, especially in the coastal areas, has become a true melting pot of races and nationalities.

In the daily life of the people of Peru, as in other Latin American countries, there is no sharp color line of the kind found in many parts of the United States. Nevertheless, color is reflected in the social structure of the country. As a result of the Spanish conquest, the upper class consists largely of White business men and White *hacendados*. The middle classes are made up mainly from some of the Indian-White mixtures. The great mass of farmers, agricultural laborers, and industrial workers is composed of Indians or Indian-White mixtures. Thus the economic and social class distinctions of Peruvian society express themselves here in racial forms.

Let us now turn to Lima, situated in the lower part of the rich, irrigated Rimac Valley. It is not only the political capital; it is also the outstanding city of the country. With a population of more than three quarters of a million — and growing by leaps and bounds — it is far larger, according to the 1940 Census, than the leading provincial cities of Arequipa (110,000), Trujillo (45,000), Cuzco (45,000), or Iquítos (40,000). The possibilities of obtaining a good position in a powerful and rapidly expanding government or in private business and industry, the various modern conveniences, the fine hotels and restaurants, as well as the many cultural and social activities of Lima,

have made this city the magnet which yearly attracts thousands of the most ambitious and energetic middle and upper class Peruvians from the provinces.

At the same time, even larger numbers of poorer people from both Coast and Sierras have been coming to Lima and its port, Callao, to find work on the docks as well as in the newly developed textile and other light industries.

Lima's cultural life reflects this general growth. It pos-

sesses a good symphony orchestra — the only one in the country — which for years has been presenting a standard orchestral repertoire under the able direction of its conductor, Dr. Buchwald. One can also hear concerts in which outstanding Indian musicians and music groups from various parts of the Andes present some of their wonderful folk music and dances. Several Peruvian composers, especially the late Señor Daniel Alomía Robles and the late Teodoro Valcárcel, have used this folk music as the basis for their compositions and thus helped to initiate a renaissance of one of the forms of ancient Peruvian culture. Lima also possesses a number of legitimate theatres which have a regular drama repertoire. In addi-

28

Figs. 5 to 9. Scenes in Lima. Fig. 5 (far left). Religious procession moving through a narrow street of old Lima. *Kosok* • Fig. 6 (left). Church portal carved out of stone. *Kosok* • Fig. 7 (top). One of the modern, workers' hospitals. They are also found in other chief cities of Peru. *Panagra* • Fig. 8 (center). Trolley cars passing down the Colmena to Callao harbor. *Kosok* • Fig. 9 (bottom). Typical booth in the large municipal market. *Kosok*.

tion, there are motion picture theatres everywhere, of which the beautiful and modernistic Tacna Theatre is the outstanding example. Several dance schools teach both Spanish and modern ballet.

Two anthropological and archaeological museums, one under the direction of Dr. Luis Valcárcel, and the other at Magdalena Viejo under Dr. Rebeca Carrión, house many valuable collections. The latter museum was founded and developed by the late Dr. Julio Tello, one of Peru's leading archaeologists, who has left the impress of his work in many parts of the country. Various scientific societies such as the Geographic Society of Lima and the Engineering Society carry on important activities. Mention must also be made of the National Library and the National Archives as well as of a number of parochial and private archives, which contain extremely valuable books and manuscripts. These institutions proved most helpful to us in our work.

When we arrived in Lima we found that, in many ways, the city looked the same it did when we saw it in 1941. The same thoroughfares with many of the same business houses and stores greeted us as they had done previously. And the city was still divided between the fine mansions where the wealthy lived and the great mass of adobe houses in which the poor existed.

But one external change was apparent. As a result of the war and post-war prosperity, the small middle class had grown rapidly in size and wealth. This growth expressed itself not only in the greater number of expensive and imported items found in the stores, but also in the large number of architecturally attractive houses that had been built in newly-opened suburban areas. Many of these houses, even the smaller ones, represent a successful integration of some of the best characteristics of both modern and colonial architecture. Artistically, they are generally superior to most of those we find in the suburbs of North American cities. Workers' housing projects are also being built. We were pleasantly surprised to find in Lima and in other coastal towns, a number of modern and attractive workers' hospitals built with government controlled social security funds.

But the very site which Lima and its suburbs now occupy also contains many relics of past civilizations. In ancient times, the large Rimac Valley, together with the adjacent small Chillón (Carabayllo) Valley, had become economically and politically the most important unit along the whole Central Coast. In fact, a Rimac Federation, which included several other valleys to the north

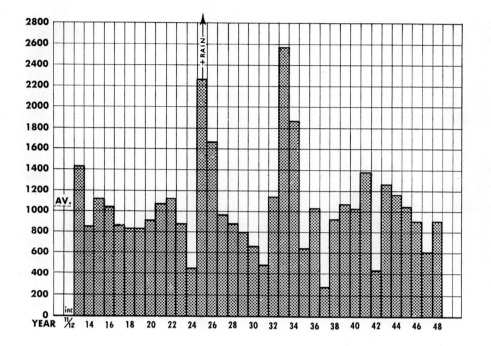

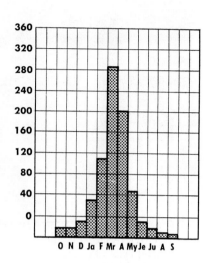

Fig. 10 (top left). Annual water discharges of the Chicama River, in millions of cubic meters. The measuring gauge is at Salinar in the upper part of the valley. The figures given are for each *agricultural* year starting from the beginning of October, when the annual rise of the river begins, to the end of September of the following year. Note the great annual fluctuations, which seriously affect agricultural production. The year 1925 was cursed by heavy rains — so rare on the Coast — that wrecked canals, roads, buildings and ancient ruins to an extent unknown since the Spanish Conquest. Some months later — as if in atonement for this destruction — the whole desert landscape was covered by a carpet of beautiful grass and flowers! *Kosok* • Fig. 11 (top center). Average monthly discharges of the Chicama River, in millions of cubic meters. Note the tremendous seasonal fluctuations which, moreover, establish an agricultural year beginning with October. This month corresponds to April in our northern hemisphere. *Kosok* • Fig. 12 (bottom). This chart shows the daily discharges, in cubic meters per second, of the Chicama River during the *agricultural* year, October 1937 to September 1938. The tremendous day by day fluctuations, especially during the most important months of February, March and April, create great excitement among the *hacendados* and the owners of the small *chacras* who daily plead with the government irrigation officials to divert as much as possible of the life-giving water onto their lands. Although each parcel of land has its own water rights passed down, with modifications, from time immemorial, pressure is often successfully exercised by the larger landowners to obtain extra water. Note the preliminary increase of water in November-December. This is useful for wetting the hard dry soil before planting. *Kosok* • Fig. 13 (right). Porch of Perricholi Palace, built by one of the Viceroys for his favorite lady. *Kosok*.

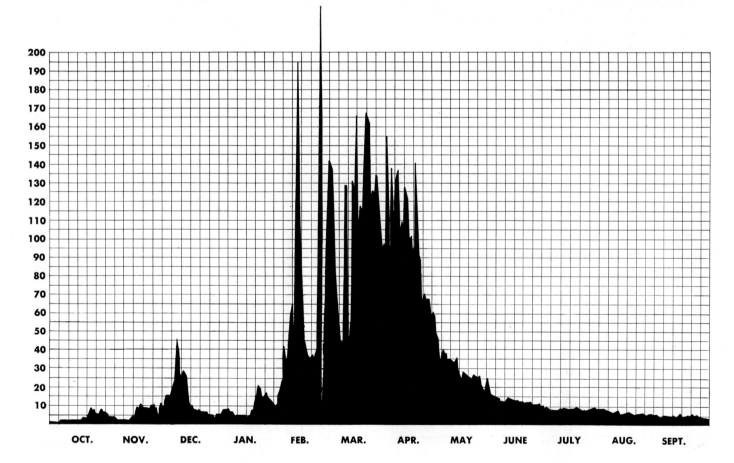

OCT. NOV. DEC. JAN. FEB. MAR. APR. MAY JUNE JULY AUG. SEPT.

and south, had apparently existed at the time of its so-called peaceful submission to the Incas who took over these valleys less than a century before the arrival of the Spaniards.

There are a large number of ancient ruins in these two valleys, most of which have been ignored by archaeologists. Of the ancient sites which have been studied, the extensive centers of Cajamarquilla and Maranga (Huadca) are by far the most important. The former, situated on a dry plateau 18 miles up the valley, is still fairly well preserved (Fig. 24). The latter has been largely destroyed by the rapid expansion of nearby Lima. Only the bulky structures remain, of which the main pyramid —

29

one of the largest in volume along the whole Coast — has been partly cut by the modern highway to the port of Callao! Both of these sites have been studied by archaeologists, primarily Middendorf (1893), Means (1931), Giesecke (1939) and Jijón y Caamaño (1949). Nevertheless, no thorough excavation and analysis has yet been made of them. During 1952, Mr. Louis Stumer and Dr. Schaedel made a survey of numerous sites in the Rimac Valley and came to interesting new conclusions on the basis of surface finds.

Since the ruins of this valley complex did not fall within the immediate limits of our study, we did no field work here in 1948-49. Later on, however, we found so many fine aerial photographs of this region that we could not restrain ourselves from having enlargements made. We

Fig. 14 (left). A modern national fair in Lima. The names on each of the large panels are those of the various Departamentos of Peru. In adjoining booths the characteristic products of each Departamento are for sale. Most of these products were brought by truck to Lima over the Pan American Highway and the large network of connecting roads in the Sierras and in the Montaña. *Kosok* • Figs. 15 to 17 (left to right, above). Sierra visitors at a national fair in Lima. • Fig. 15. A woman from Puno with an "Al Smith" brown derby, commonly worn by women in this region as well as in the neighboring Sierra regions of Bolivia. *Kosok* • Figs. 16 and 17. People of the Cuzco area. *Kosok* • Fig. 18 (below). This unusual advertisement in a Lima paper shows plans for a modern real estate development to be built adjacent to an ancient pyramid (*huaca*). Such a modern development destroys all the surrounding ancient walls and habitation structures, thereby isolating the pyramid and making reconstruction of the site impossible. With the expansion of modern cities such areas should be maintained as national monuments. When utilization of the land becomes absolutely necessary owing to population pressures, plans of the site, based on available aerial photographs and on ground surveys, together with stratographic excavations by archaeologists, should first be made.

reproduce some of them in this volume (Chapters IV and V). We also entered all the sites located on the aerial photographs on a map (Page 24). Villar Córdova (1935) has described a number of sites in this valley unit and published a map containing their locations. Carlos A. Romero (1934) has also published a map containing names and locations of various sites in the Rimac Valley. Since we were unable to devote any time in localizing the sites in the field, it was impossible for us to correlate clearly the maps of Villar Córdova and Romero with ours and with the actual ground locations of the sites. Perhaps some young Peruvianist can be induced to carry out this project.

Ironically, the ruins of this valley are among the most

accessible in Peru. Many of them can easily be reached by bus or car from the center of Lima. Indeed the slogan could be: "Archaeology by Taxi!" Already in 1940-41 we had discovered that all along the Coast many important and impressive ancient ruins were situated near modern towns and cities or along the Pan American Highway and its associated roads. It seems strange that there is not enough money and interest to investigate these outstanding and easily accessible vestiges of a great past!

Just south of the Rimac lies the small valley of Lurín. Its historical and archaeological significance lies in the fact that here was built the great temple "city" of Pachacamac, formerly the leading ceremonial and pilgrimage center of much of the Central Coast. In Chapter V, we present an aerial photograph of this famous place together with three important ground plans. Cieza de León (I, Chap. LXXII), who visited the site shortly after

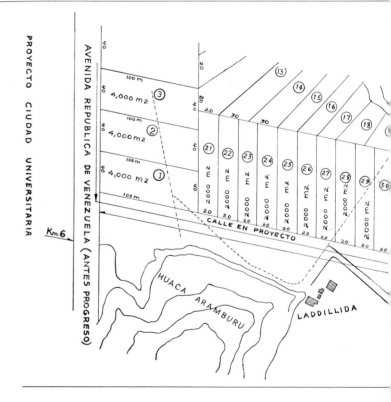

the Spanish conquest, commented on its former great wealth. He also shrewdly noted that the priests were much reverenced and that the chiefs obeyed them in many things. This power of the priests over the lay rulers indicates the undeveloped nature of the secular state in this region. It is reminiscent, in a way, of the status of Aztec society at the time of the Spanish conquest.

We visited only one site in the Lurín Valley and that shortly after our arrival in Lima. Our attention was drawn to it by the archaeologist, Dr. Hans Horkheimer, who had discovered it on an oblique aerial photograph. He did not know its name, but estimated it to be some fifteen miles up the valley.

The actual visit to this site was quite accidental. While discussing some aspects of Peruvian agriculture with the late Mr. Anderson, an American soil expert of SCIPA (see below), I mentioned the site to him. His immediate reaction was, "Fine, let's go and visit the place in my car next Sunday and see what it's like." When Sunday came, we drove up this pleasant valley to the approximate region in which we expected to find the ruin. After much questioning, we finally found it in a *quebrada* (dry valley) on the southern bank of the river, just above the present irrigated areas (Chapter V, Figs. 7 to 10).

As the large photograph indicates, the site has the form of a minature twin settlement. The two parts are separated by a small spur running from the nearby mountains. The ruins consist mainly of adobe houses, together with what appeared to be a large rectangular ceremonial center. Above the western part of the settlement another rectangular ceremonial area was located. Remains of the terraces used for habitation were clearly visible on the small hills surrounding the settlement, while a sizeable ancient canal could still be traced running partly above and partly through the settlement. The ruin appeared to belong to the Late Period.

The site was not an outstanding one, yet it gave us quite a thrill to feel that we were the first to have reported on it! We had had such experiences before; we were to have them often again. Indeed, that is what makes the archaeologists' work so fascinating in Peru. The country is littered with so many ancient sites, which so few people seem to know or care about, that it is easy to "discover" new ones almost every day.

But we have run ahead of our story. Let us now present an account of how we spent our time in Lima. After we had settled ourselves and mapped out our work, we set out at once to renew our acquaintance with old friends in various government agencies. We had numerous conversations with members of the Dirección de Aguas y Irrigación, and especially with Ingeniero Carlos Sutton, the dean of irrigation engineers in Peru. He was an American who had settled in Peru more than thirty years before and had become a citizen of that country. Because of his intimate knowledge of the irrigation systems and problems of almost every valley in Peru, and his interest in the irrigation systems and economy of ancient Peru, he was able to give us much invaluable information and advice which we could not obtain elsewhere. In addition to his great engineering knowledge, his understanding and sympathy for the great mass of Indians of both past and present made him altogether a most unusual man. As in 1940-41, we spent many pleasant and informative hours with him. We were greatly shocked when near the end of our stay in Peru news came of Señor Sutton's sudden death. Although in his seventies, he was still a man of great vigor and enthusiasm and had just embarked upon a new irrigation project.

Our first work at the Dirección de Aguas y Irrigación was to bring the material we had collected in 1941 covering the amount of daily, monthly and annual water discharge of each of the coastal rivers up to date, for this data is vital to the study of irrigation. Some of the records go back over twenty-five years; some of them cover a shorter period of time; for some of the minor rivers no

Figs. 19 and 20. Children enjoying themselves at the national fair. *Kosok* • Fig. 21. One of the many unexplored ruin sites in the Rimac Valley. The densely packed structures are crowded into the limited amount of land of a *quebrada*. The general amphitheatre-like effect (found also in other sites) of the plan of the settlement was produced by the terracing of the shoulders of the two projecting hills which enclose the settlement. The dark region at the bottom of this vertical aerial photograph shows the present irrigated and cultivated area. *Servicio 340: E 142 N 177.*

Fig. 22. Ruins of Armatambo located near Molo Solar, about a mile from the Servicio headquarters at Las Palmas, a suburb of Lima. This is another of the many ancient sites in and around Lima which can be reached by bus or taxi, but so far it has failed to attract the serious attention of archaeologists. Especially interesting is the well-preserved compound, lower center. Here can be seen, to the left, a large, high building and a series of courts and terraces and, to the right, a number of less well-defined courtyards. This place may well have been the palace of one of the Late Period Chiefs of the Rimac Valley. In the background of the main part of the site can be seen habitation terraces for the populace, together with contour canals that meander through the ruins. Some of the white lines are modern paths. The ruin is now used as a garbage dump! *Servicio 340: E 126 N 156, E 126 N 157½, E 124 N 157½.*

data on water discharge has so far been collected. Luckily for our study, the most complete records existed for the rivers along the Northwest Coast. This is not accidental, for this area is at present, as it was in the past, the largest and most important agricultural zone on the entire Coast.

On the basis of the material collected, we made two comprehensive sets of graphs, both of which will be reproduced in *Water and Life*. One set shows the consider-

able year-by-year changes of the water content of each of the coastal rivers which largely determines the amount of land that can be irrigated (Fig. 10).

The other set of graphs shows the average monthly discharges of each of these rivers. These graphs provide a clear picture of the tremendous seasonal fluctuations, with a high point generally in March and a low point about six months later (Fig. 11). This water pattern defines the agricultural season in each valley. The monthly varia-

tions reflect the general rainfall pattern in the Sierras but show a lag of a month or two. Thus, while the peak of the rainfall season in the Sierras comes generally in January and February, the highest water discharges on the Coast usually come in March. During our summer and early fall months, when there is no rain in the Sierras, the water content of the coastal rivers reaches its minimum. Indeed, some of the smaller rivers run completely dry. For the newcomer, a trip along the coastal valleys during this time

32

is often disappointing, for he keeps asking: "Where is the river?"

We also copied numerous graphs showing the tremendous day-by-day variations of the water content of each river throughout the year. These variations vitally affect the development of the agricultural process throughout the growing season (Fig. 12).

The reason for studying and graphing this data is obvious. The amount of land in each coastal valley that *can* be irrigated depends upon the average annual water content of each river. This does not mean that all the

water in a river was necessarily utilized in the past — or is so at present. Indeed, in the case of the Santa, the Chira and the Tumbes, the three largest coastal rivers, the absence of large coastal plains has made it possible to utilize only a small fraction of the water in these rivers. But even in valleys like the Lambayeque and the Chicama where there is more land than can be irrigated with the water generally available in the rivers, the unequal seasonal distribution of the water results in having much of it discharged into the Pacific during the period of abundance. These problems were always present among the ancients; they still exist today. But now they can be solved technically. What delays their solution is a host of financial problems and conflicting private property interests.

Mr. Sutton pointed out to us that annual fluctuations in crop yields are not as sharp as the annual fluctuations in the available water. Thus, if during a certain year a particular piece of land has only 75 per cent of the normal water supply, it still can produce 90 per cent of the normal crop, while a 50 per cent supply can still produce 75 per cent of the normal crop. This phenomenon later proved significant when we tried to correlate water supply, cultivable land, and population density in the different valleys.

At this point, several basic facts which emerged during the progress of our work must be stated. In the first place, in most of the coastal valleys *the amount of land cultivated in ancient times was equal to or greater than that at present*. In the second place, *practically all the land areas actually cultivated now were also cultivated in ancient times* during the period of maximum irrigation. As we stated in Chapter II, this land is near the river. Consequently, *the land formerly under cultivation, but now in disuse, is found in the peripheral areas of the valleys*.

In order to determine the *maximum* amount of land cultivated in *each* valley in ancient times, we had to determine first the amount of land cultivated today and then the additional amount of land cultivated formerly.

It seemed a simple project to determine the present size of the cultivated area in each valley. The available Peruvian Army maps indicate approximately the zone which is usually cultivated now. By means of an engineering instrument, called the intograph, which is moved around an enclosed zone on the map, the area of the zone can easily be calculated. Mr. Sutton did this work for us. Unfortunately, this zone represents *gross* area since it includes roads, villages, smaller elevations and swamps.

But, even though we allowed for these factors, difficulties arose when we compared the net areas for each valley with those found in government reports. Not only are the areas given in the latter generally lower, but those of different agencies contradict one another, especially in the case of the most important valleys. Thus the Department of Irrigation has one set of figures based on the amount of water furnished, while the Department of Agriculture has another set based on crop returns. What complicates matters further is that some returns are based on estimates of local government representatives and others on those of local *hacendados* who, for tax purposes, tend to send in returns that are definitely on the low side.

One of our problems was the ironing out of these differences, valley by valley. This we did in part by repeated conferences with various leading officials of each department. In addition, we enlisted the aid of the local representatives of both departments in each valley or group of valleys.

Two other government agencies entered the picture and complicated matters still further. One was the Direc-

---

Fig. 23. This hitherto unpublished ground plan of a site near Lima was made by Bandelier. In addition to Bandelier's ground plans of Pachacamac and ChanChan, reproduced in Chapters V and VIII respectively, there also exist his still unpublished ground plan of the ruins near Magdelena del Mar (Rimac Valley) and those of Tambo Colorado (Pisco Valley), both preserved in the vaults of the American Museum of Natural History. *AMNH.*

ción de Catastro, a kind of land record office, listing the amount of land owned by each individual. In some cases, the figures of this office were similar to those of the Agricultural Department, but in others there were divergencies due to the fact that all arable land is not necessarily cultivated each year. The other office, a new one, was connected with the tax bureau. Here the cultivated areas, as seen on the aerial photographs, are measured by intographs and compared with estimates from other bureaus. This project had, however, just been started, and in the few valleys studied considerable dis-

crepancies appeared. Thus we spent part of our time in Peru trying to establish some figure for the present amount of cultivated land of each valley that would approximate the truth as closely as possible.

Of course, the areas of cultivation fluctuate somewhat each year, especially in those valleys where there is an overabundance of land in relationship to the water content of the rivers. In such valleys more land is cultivated during years in which there is a great deal of water than in "dry" years when some land is allowed to remain fallow. In valleys where there is little land, in relation to the water supply, the variation is not so great, since here all the land is usually cultivated every year. But such variations exist in the agricultural economy of every country. Maximum areas of cultivation were usually the ones finally accepted.

The problem of calculating the *additional* amount of land cultivated in ancient times depended, of course, upon the results of our field work. Once this work had been completed and the results mapped, the amount of additional land was roughly calculated by means of the intograph. The two sets of figures were added together and the total maximum area cultivated in ancient times was ascertained.

Although the results will be presented in detail in *Water and Life in Ancient Peru*, it may be stated here that on the South Coast approximately the same amount of land is cultivated today as in pre-Columbian times. Along the Central Coast the amount is *slightly* less, but along the Northwest Coast — always the main agricultural center — present day cultivated areas are *considerably* less than in the past. In all, probably 15 to 20 per cent more

land was cultivated along the whole Coast in the past.

Since Peruvian government officials have calculated the present day cultivated area along the whole Coast to run between 1,250,000 and 1,500,000 acres, it follows that in ancient times about a quarter of a million acres more land had been under cultivation. However, since most of this additional amount of land is found on the Northwest Coast the problem of ancient versus present day cultivated areas centers mainly around this region.

On the basis of the maximum amount of cultivated land in each valley in ancient times, we of course could estimate the *relative* sizes of the populations of the various valleys. As a result, we were able to show that more than half the coastal population lived in the valleys along the Northwest Coast, the region of the Chimú Empire.

We entered on tempting though dangerous ground when we tried to establish some kind of an *absolute* population size for each valley in the past. This we did by preparing an operational population coefficient based on a series of factors which will be discussed in our main study. By adding up the data for each of the valleys, we arrived at a total coastal population figure definitely in excess of a million at the period of maximum development. Obviously, the validity of our calculation depends entirely upon the correct magnitude of the coefficient.

Then, by additional but even more tenuous calculations, which will be treated in our main study, we arrived at a tentative figure for the size of the population of the *entire Inca Empire* at the time of the Spanish conquest. The population may have been possibly about seven or eight million, a figure which is somewhat of the same order as that given by Spanish estimates made in the sixteenth

Fig. 24 (upper left). A part of the large pyramid at Maranga in the process of being demolished. This photograph strikingly illustrates the tremendous number of adobe bricks that went into the building of huge structures such as this. *Means* • Fig. 25 (lower left). Middendorf, in his *Peru* (1893:80), gives a plan of the ancient town of Maranga (called Huadca in Middendorf's time), situated in the lower Rimac Valley just west of Lima (see map, p. 24). Compare this plan with the present day aerial photograph on the opposite page • Fig. 26 (right). At first glance, this photograph appears to be an unorganized mass of black and white blotches. Actually, the white areas are ancient mounds, some with structures on top of them, while the dark or striped areas are modern irrigated fields. Most of the connecting walls and other small structures that were once located in these fields have been ploughed back into the soil. Structure No. 17 in Middendorf's plan is at the extreme right of the photograph. At the left of it is No. 16, the unusually large rectangular pyramid with walled structures on top of it. To build the modern road from Lima to Callao (wide oblique line in the photograph), a corner of each of Nos. 16 and 18 had to be demolished (see Fig. 24). No. 19, in which many ancient burials were found, was almost completely destroyed. No. 15, with its peculiar form, can be easily located, as well as Nos. 20 and 23. The remains of the long wall can be seen in the photograph (parallel to the top edge). The slightly bent wall with entrances at 2 and 3, as well as part of the wall running perpendicular to it, can also be clearly seen. The aerial photograph covers only the upper and middle part of Middendorf's plan and thus does not show the lower part of the wall that surrounded the city (A) or the structures below and to the right of this wall. The volume by Middendorf contains a detailed key to his plan. Significant is his observation that the large pyramids were built *outside* the town walls, a phenomenon of urbanization similar to that found in ChanChan (see Chapter VIII). *Servicio, 340 series.*

century. These calculations are naturally subject to revision before final publication of our data.

While working in Lima, we also decided to investigate the possibilities of making some kind of a rainfall map of all Peru. The desert Coast obviously presented no problems, for here practically no rain falls. We were interested mainly in the Sierras, for they are the source of the waters that flow through the desert valleys. Besides, the topographical and climatological complexity of this mountain region must have been the geographical basis for the uneven growth of the various Sierra economies and cultures, which in turn interacted with the more homogeneous coastal economies and cultures.

Considerable variations in annual rainfall occur along the sides of each valley. The bottom of one of the deep intra-Andean valleys may be semi-arid and require irrigation for agricultural purposes; the regions near the top may have sufficient precipitation to permit regular

rainfall agriculture; while the sides of a valley may have moderate but fluctuating precipitation requiring irrigation mainly as a stabilizing factor. Considerable variations in rainfall, moreover, occur throughout the length of each of these valleys, as well as between valleys of the Northern and those of the Southern Sierras. A good rainfall map is therefore essential for the understanding of the complex climatic foundations of Sierra economy and society and their relations to coastal economy and society, both past and present.

We therefore visited the Meteorological Institute to find out what data existed. To our dismay, we learned that most of the weather stations were on the desert Coast where there is practically no rain, while those in the mountains were few and far between! Such a distribution of stations may make work easier and more pleasant for the meteorological agents, but the resulting lack of data for the Sierras is extremely deplorable.

We then visited the meteorological office of Panagra Airways Company at Limatambo airport. Here we also searched in vain! We did, however, find some good material concerning the neighboring countries of Ecuador, Bolivia and Chile. The data published by the Ecuadorian government is especially comprehensive. Consequently, we were soon able to make a preliminary meteorological map of Ecuador, which demonstrated very graphically the great extremes of rainfall in closely related regions. It is the kind of a map which we hope some day to have of the Peruvian highlands.

But in addition to the difficulties in obtaining and calculating all the above data, we had two other immediate problems before us in Lima. One was to obtain a jeep for our rather extensive and widespread field work; the other was to examine the aerial photographs which the Peruvian Government had taken of the various valleys of

Fig. 27 (right). Cajamarquilla, whose extensive ruins attest to its former greatness, is situated at the end of a *quebrada* about ten miles from Lima. It was one of the main Late Period centers of the Rimac Valley. Occupied by the Incas, it is mentioned by the sixteenth century Spanish Chroniclers. The dense concentration of contiguous house walls, shown in the center of the photograph, indicates that Cajamarquilla had a population numbered in the thousands. The many-walled structures of the city appear to be separated by streets, but such is not the case; the people probably moved about by walking on top of the walls! At the right is a large, spacious compound, possibly the quarters of the rulers. At the left, the large pyramid, probably the religious center, stands out sharply. The irregular white lines cutting across the ruins are modern paths, while the area at the bottom of the photograph represents modern fields and orchards. Visited and described in part by a number of archaeologists, Cajarmarquilla, by its very size and complexity, has prevented a systematic exploration. As a result of its position above the irrigated level, this site has escaped the fate of the equally large and important site of Maranga (Huadca). *Servicio 340: E 138 N 178½* • Fig. 28 (above). This is not a jack-o'-lantern or a Halloween pumpkin; it is an ancient ceremonial water jug (*huaco*) supposedly found in the Rimac Valley. *AMNH.*

36

Fig. 29. The middle part of the Lurín Valley south of Lima, shown in this oblique aerial photograph, presents the sharp contrast, typical of all Peruvian coastal valleys, between the green irrigated fields and the desert foothills of the Andes. Further down the valley are the famous ruins of Pachacamac, photographs and ground plans of which are presented in the following chapter. *Servicio, unnumbered series.*

our irrigation study. He gave us all available data on cultivated areas and crops which his organization had collected. In addition, he generously offered to put a jeep at our disposal whenever one was not in use — possibly in October.

Unfortunately, in October the promised jeep had to be sent, for some time, on an emergency mission to Piura, where a slight smallpox epidemic had broken out. In fact, it was the end of the following spring before a SCIPA jeep did become available. When it arrived, we were happily surprised to discover that Mr. Neale had arranged to send along on our trip not only a chauffeur-mechanic, Señor Portugal, but also a brilliant young engineer, Señor José Vivas. They not only were excellent companions, but gave us much help in collecting our data. In the meantime, Mr. Neale made it possible for us to use the jeeps at the local offices of the SCIPA, located in the various valleys. The SCIPA engineers here proved most cooperative and gave us considerable assistance.

Transportation facilities, however, came also from another direction. While in Lima, we met the American archaeologist, Dr. Richard P. Schaedel, who was the Director of the newly-founded Anthropological Institute of the University of Trujillo. He came to our house late one afternoon for a discussion of mutual problems. Michael spread the maps and graphs on the floor in order to show what we had done and what we still needed to do in order to complete the study. Soon we too were spread out on the floor tracing canals and studying the extension of irrigated areas, as well as locating and discussing the significance of the main population and ceremonial sites of ancient times. Reinforced by sandwiches and wine, we continued our discussions until, by the early hours of the morning, we were in a complete state of exhaustion.

We had established many common approaches to the problem of ancient Indian societies. Dr. Schaedel put all the facilities of his Institute at our disposal; these included a somewhat aged but still usable jeep, together with an excellent chauffeur. We made extensive use of this jeep at different times during our entire stay in Peru. Together with the SCIPA jeeps, and the trucks and cars of various *haciendas* and local Peruvian Government offices, we were able to carry out our field work fairly satisfactorily even though it often meant a loss of time resulting from the necessity of continually rearranging our schedule of activities. But, as we had learned previously, time was not of great importance in a basically preindustrial society.

the Coast during and since World War II. The problems we encountered working with the aerial photographs are discussed in the following chapter.

We had expected to be able to rent a jeep for our field work, but contrary to the information we had obtained previously in the United States, jeeps were very scarce in Peru. It is true they had been plentiful right after World War II. But many had worn out rapidly because of excessive use and poor maintenance, and, as a result of the stringent monetary exchange regulations in force during our stay, it was almost impossible to im-

port new jeeps and replacement parts for the rundown vehicles. We were thus faced with a real problem.

After vainly soliciting many organizations and government institutions, we finally met Mr. John Neale, the American director of SCIPA. This organization, which has the impossibly long name of Sociedad Cooperatíva Interamericana para la Producción Alimentícia (SCIPA), is a joint Peruvian-United States governmental organization formed for the purpose of improving agriculture. Mr. Neale, a cultured, well-trained and experienced American agronomist and rancher, showed immediate interest in

V

Aerial Photography in the Reconstruction of the Past

 AERIAL PHOTOGRAPHY! This new technique has become a wonderful tool in reconstructing the past. Indeed, it has raised archaeology to a new level. By a kind of preliminary "armchair exploration," many unknown ancient sites, whose discovery by conventional field methods would often take considerable time and tremendous physical effort, can now be located easily and rapidly. But more important, aerial photography makes it possible to obtain, almost at a glance, a comprehensive and dramatic picture of the archaeological remains of a valley as a whole! Indeed, one can easily establish the relationship of the various ruins not only to one another, but also to present day sites and structures, as well as to the whole topographical setting of the countryside. Accurate ground plans of the larger complexes — a factor of great importance in field work — can also be obtained with little difficulty.

Therefore, we decided to visit the modern offices and laboratories of the Servicio Aerofotográfico Nacional which is the mapping unit of the Ministry of Aeronautics of Peru. The Servicio is situated near Barranco, one of the attractive suburbs of Lima. We had heard that during and since World War II the Servicio had made aerial surveys of many of the coastal valleys of the country. We were received in a most kindly way at the laboratories and all the facilities of the Servicio were put at our disposal. But when we began to make a survey of the photographs available, we were overwhelmed. And no wonder. There must have been about 20,000 photographs covering the areas of our interest! This was more than we had bargained for. But after we had recovered from the shock of hearing too much good news, we settled down to our task of making a thorough study of the material.

True, the photographs had not been taken specifically for archaeological studies, but rather for various governmental and private purposes of which the most important was the determination of the size of each land holding. It thus became possible for government officials to "go after" the numerous large landowners who in the past had evaded paying their just share of taxes by purposely underestimating the sizes of their estates —

apparently a universal failing. But for us, the photographers had unwittingly uncovered the existence and location of a vast multitude of ancient canals and archaeological sites, many of them unknown to professional archaeologists! Furthermore, they had brought into sharper focus the geographic pattern within which mankind on the Coast had evolved, a pattern which, at the same time, mankind itself had partly helped to create. By transforming deserts by means of irrigation into rich agricultural lands, man had changed the very face of the earth!

First of all we wanted to check the results of our extensive 1940-41 field trips. Then we were anxious to see whether we could locate canals and ruins which we might have missed in our previous field work. Five of the valley "mosaics," or composite maps made from photographs in series, we had studied in Dr. Junius Bird's office at the American Museum of Natural History in New York. But here, at the Servicio, mosaics of many other valleys were available, together with the original individual prints from which the mosaics had been made.

We spent about a month at the studios of the Servicio poring over the material concerning the Northwest Coast before we embarked on the field work in this region. But it proved necessary to return to the Servicio a number of times during our year's stay in Peru, not only in order to study other valleys, but also to check the findings of each of our field trips. Since the work was of a painstaking nature and required a great deal of time, the officials of the Servicio assisted greatly by permitting us to work long hours in their elaborate offices and laboratories. We generally stayed until ten each night —

Fig. 1. On a hill overlooking the Pacific Ocean stands the Inca Pyramid of the Sun. This partly excavated and rebuilt structure dominates the extensive ruins of Pachacamac in the Lurín Valley. Compare this oblique aerial photograph with the views shown in the lower left of Figs. 3 to 6 (pp. 40 to 43). *Servicio 0:1621* • Fig. 2 (right margin). Carved wooden idol found in Pachacamac. *Guillen* • NOTE: Cuts in margins are designs found at Pachacamac.

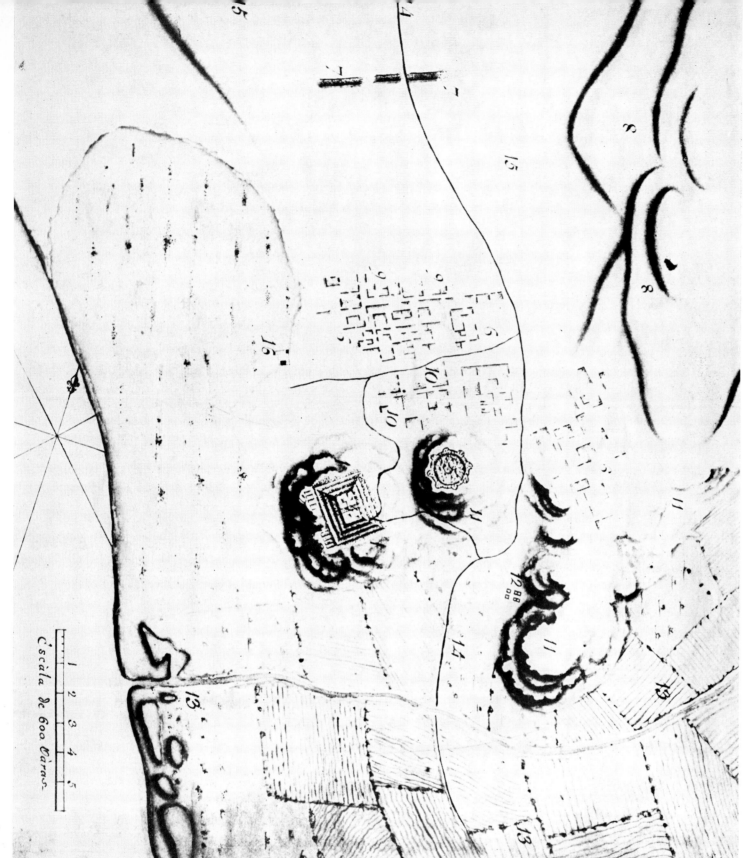

Escala de 600 Caras

including Saturdays and Sundays. Despite such hours and the use of a "belt system" for handling photographs, this laborious, but exciting and productive work consumed more than three months of our stay in Peru!

The Director of Aerophotography, the Fairchild Photographic Mission to Peru which served as technical advisor to the Director, and the officer staff of the Servicio Aerofotográfico Nacional and its personnel assisted us in every way possible in our studies. They gave freely of their time and their knowledge of the new technique of aerial photography; we spent many a pleasant hour with them being inducted into the secrets of their profession.

In order to simplify the account of our activities at the Servicio, we have found it advisable to describe them as a unit rather than to present them in the piecemeal fashion in which they were actually carried on.

And the work was exciting! A real treasure hunt! As

Figs. 3 to 6. Pachacamac, situated in the Lurín Valley, was one of the most famous of the religious shrines and pilgrimage centers in all of ancient Peru. Its extensive area and the many nearby graves have since made it a favorite place for treasure seekers. During the last century and a half, a number of ground plans were made of part or all of this site. Three of these plans are presented on pages 40 to 42 (Figs. 3 to 5). Recently the Servicio made an aerial photograph of these ruins, page 43 (Fig. 6), which shows not merely their present state of preservation, but also furnishes a check on the validity of the different ground plans. The three plans, as well as the photograph, here reproduced, clearly show the main Pyramid of the Sun — so named by the Incas — situated on a hill on the left (see also Fig. 1). To the right of the pyramid can be noted a smaller structure, the older shrine of Pachacamac. The rest of the site consists largely of remains of ancient living quarters. A modern road, which was apparently built over a previous path, winds its way through the site (see Figs. 4 to 6). The Lurín River, which runs south of the ruins, can be seen in Figs. 3 and 4. The Pacific Ocean is on the left. Fig. 3 shows the main part of the oldest ground plan that we could locate. It was made in 1793 by Joséf Juan and is now in the British Museum (Additional Ms. 17671). Photostatic copies are in Lima and in the Library of Congress. Accompanying the original plan is a detailed description of the various numbered places in the site. Considerations of space requirements have forced us to place this description in the Appendix. Our reproduction of the plan is turned sidewise in order that it can be better compared with the other drawings and the photograph. During the nineteenth century, more accurate and detailed drawings were made of parts of Pachacamac and are found in the works of Squier, Middendorf and others. The most comprehensive of these plans was made in 1892 by Bandelier (Fig. 4) and has until now remained unpublished. *Courtesy of the American Museum of Natural History.*

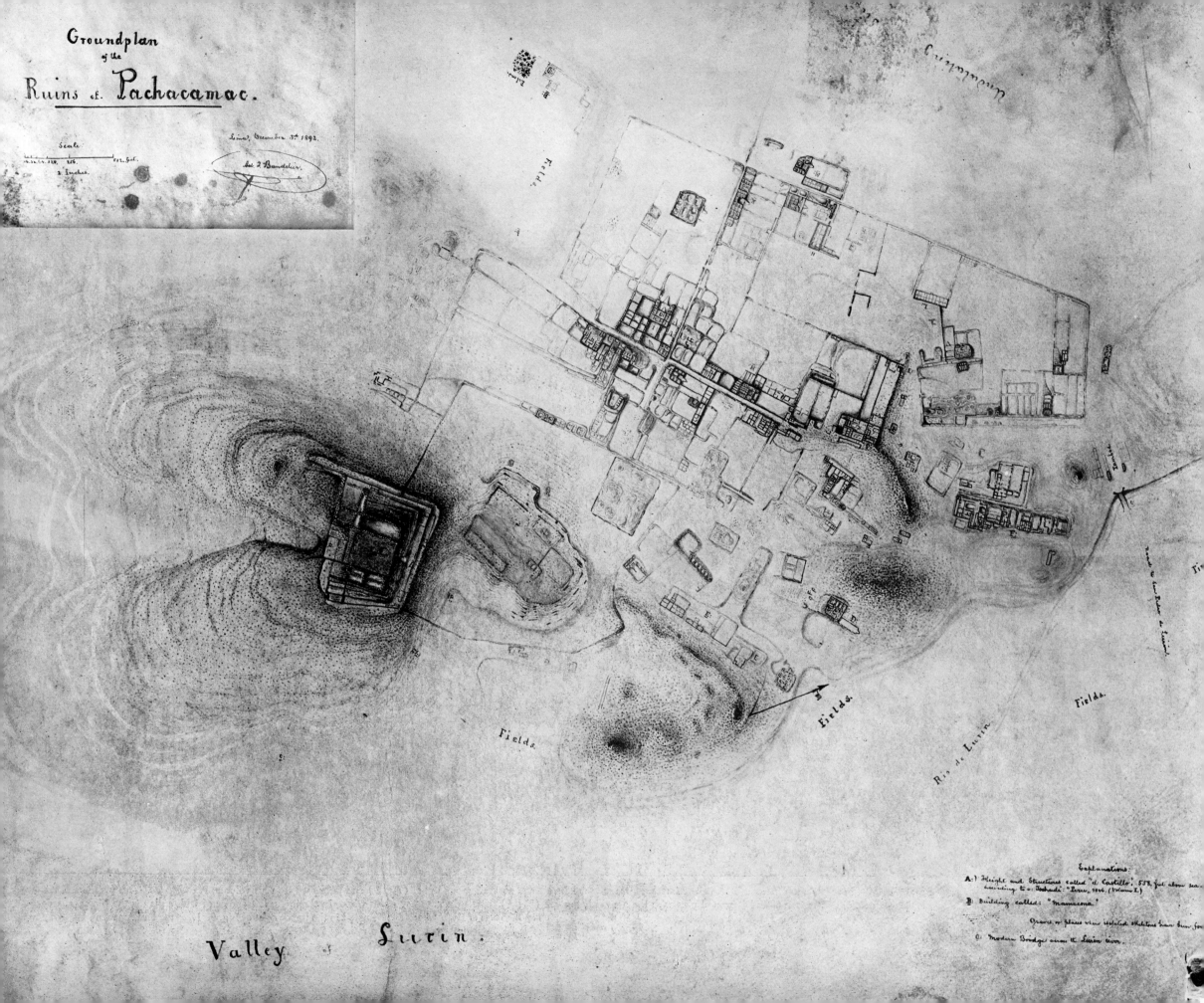

Groundplan
of the
Ruins of Pachacamac.

Scale:

2 Inches.

Lima, December 3rd 1892.

Ad. F. Bandelier

Fields

Fields

Fields

Fields

Fields

Rio de Lurin

Valley of Lurin.

Explanations:

A: Height and Structures called "el Castillo"; 558 feet above sea according to v. Tschudi: "Peru", 1846. (Volum I.)

B: Building called: "mamacona."

Graves, or places where isolated skeletons have been found.

C: Modern Bridge over the Lurin river.

Fig. 5 (above) and Fig. 6 (right). In 1902, Max Uhle, the father of Peruvian archaeology, made the elaborate and accurate ground plan (Fig. 5) and published it in his volume, *Pachacamac*. This plan is still the standard one used by archaeologists. A careful comparison of Uhle's ground plan with the aerial photograph (Fig. 6) reveals the accuracy of his work. In the upper left corner of Uhle's plan is the Mamacona or Temple of the Sun Virgins, since reconstructed by Tello (see Fig. 6). The encroachment of modern civilization on the ruins of Pachacamac can be noted in the upper right of Fig. 6. Here the Pan American Highway (black line) cuts through a corner of the site where a small settlement has been built on some of the unexcavated structures. Most of the extensive ruins of Pachacamac have yet to be cleared. *Servicio 1003: 69.*

43

we studied photograph after photograph we were actually carrying on an intellectual quest for the dead but unburied treasures of the past. There was always tremendous satisfaction in discovering new pyramids, settlements, fortifications, walls, roads and canals on a photograph. Indeed, it was even exciting to find such ruins on photographs after we had seen them in the field. For here they looked quite different! We would often exclaim: Why didn't we see that there was another ruin right nearby when we were in the field? Why didn't we see that this wall extended all the way up the hill? Why didn't we follow the "end" of this canal for another half mile and find its continuation?

Sometimes it was difficult to decide whether a certain mark on a photograph was a section of a road or of a canal — or perhaps just a scratch on the negative! But even if a set of pictures yielded no "pay dirt," the beauty of some of the photographs was often a reward in itself!

After a preliminary survey of the files of the Servicio, we found that there were aerial photographs (individual contact prints) of the following valleys (from north to south): Tumbes, Jequetepeque, Chicama, Moche, Virú, Chao, Santa, Nepeña, Fortaleza, Pativilca, Supe, Huaura, Chancay, part of Chillón, Rimac, part of Lurín, Mala, Chilca, Chincha, the branches of the Río Grande, and finally, Ocoña and Sihuas. The Ica Valley has been photographed since then, the project having been financed by a private association of agriculturists.

Unfortunately, the Casma, part of the Chillón, part of the Lurín, the Cañete, the Pisco, as well as practically all the valleys to the south of the Río Grande, had not yet been photographed. Most disappointing was the fact that when we first arrived in Peru no aerial survey had been made by the Servicio of the northern valleys of Chira, Piura, Motupe, Leche, Lambayeque and Zaña. And these were precisely the valleys which were among

the most important for our study. But the story had a happy ending!

Shortly before we left Peru the Servicio made a low-altitude aerial survey of the Zaña and the upper middle Lambayeque and Leche valleys. Since the photographs turned out to be excellent and brought to light new aspects of the territory we had studied in our field work, we extended our proposed stay in Peru by another month. We utilized this time to study these photographs and to make a short field trip to investigate some of the new archaeological sites which the photographs had revealed.

Even from the beginning, we were not without some aerial photographs of this northern region. We discovered that the Servicio also possessed photographs which it had made under contract for the International Petroleum Company and which the company graciously permitted us to use. These had been taken as part of an oil prospecting survey and covered the lower and middle Lam-

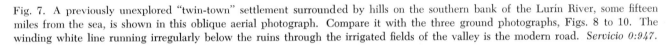

Fig. 7. A previously unexplored "twin-town" settlement surrounded by hills on the southern bank of the Lurín River, some fifteen miles from the sea, is shown in this oblique aerial photograph. Compare it with the three ground photographs, Figs. 8 to 10. The winding white line running irregularly below the ruins through the irrigated fields of the valley is the modern road. *Servicio 0:947.*

Fig. 8. Part of the "twin-town" ruin seen from the ground. The buildings constructed of mud-brick (adobe) and stone. The dark areas to the right irrigated fields. *Kosok* • Fig. 9 (top, p. 45). Another part of the ruin. *Ko*

Fig. 10. This wall in "twin-town," where the plaster has fallen off, reveals significant details of its construction: layers of stone held together by mud "cement." *Kosok* • Fig. 11. Design based on carved wooden figures from Pachacamac. *Bedia - Cornish.*

bayeque and Leche, the Motupe, Piura, Chira and Tumbes Valleys, as well as the whole Sechura Desert. But because these photographs were taken from a much greater height than that normally flown by the Servicio, the ruins and canals naturally appeared much smaller and were therefore much harder to detect. Nevertheless, these photographs turned out to have some use. Since the negatives were very sharp and on fine-grain film, enlargements up to eight times the original size turned out to be surprisingly clear. Once we had learned from our field trips the approximate location of certain significant ruins, we were able to obtain excellent photographic enlargements of the sites. On them the general ground plan and many structural details, which frequently were difficult to ascertain from ground exploration, could then often be seen at a glance.

We also had enlargements made of photographs of various uninvestigated areas, which were difficult to survey by field work alone, in order to see if we could locate ancient sites there. We were especially successful with the enlargements of the extensive Morrope-Lambayeque desert area which showed a wealth of archaeological remains that had not been previously known to exist.

In addition to these individual contact photographs, the Servicio possesses mosaic maps of many of the coastal valleys of Peru. Its technicians construct them by taking the individual overlapping contact prints and then fitting them together in such a way that their corresponding images match. All of these fitted prints of an area are then pasted together on a huge board and a complete picture of the valley is obtained.

This is, however, a complex process. For here the problem of displacement and distortion arises. As the photographing airplane follows its course in "flying a strip," obviously it cannot always maintain the same altitude nor prevent a certain amount of tilting. As a result, some scale differences in both the negatives and the corresponding contact prints become unavoidable. By elaborate calculations in the laboratories these scale differences are eliminated and more uniform prints are made before the mosaic map is put together.

As a result of the inherent nature of the photographic process, there is also a slight displacement and distortion at the edge of each negative and in its corresponding contact print. In the making of mosaic maps this is counteracted by having the original aerial photographs made in such a manner that each photograph automatically overlaps about 60 per cent of the area of the next one.

45

The technicians then discard the slightly distorted and displaced edges of each photograph and use only the more accurate center sections. In our type of exploratory work these imperfections played no important role. But they might have to be taken into account in making very accurate ground plans directly from the photographs.

When the mosaic of a valley has been completed, longitude and latitude lines are carefully drawn on it. The mosaic is then divided into rectangular sections of 40 by 50 centimeters (about 16 by 20 inches). Then a full-sized negative and a corresponding print are made of each section. All the large-sized prints of each valley can then be aligned correctly next to one another on a huge table and a truly sweeping and comprehensive picture of the whole valley can thus be obtained. Indeed, this is what we often did. For practical reasons, these mosaic sections are filed in large looseleaf books where they can be consulted with ease.

The problem of correctly mapping a ruin or canal had often troubled us in our previous field work. But now our problem was solved! For by studying these mosaics we could at once determine the exact location of such ruins and canals and map them correctly. We soon succeeded in correcting the position of some of the ruins whose sites we had entered in 1940-41 on the Peruvian Army's topographical maps scaled 1:100,000. We even discovered a number of topographical errors in the Army maps themselves which resulted from the process by which they were made. Consequently, we had to "move" certain hills, *quebradas,* and even coast lines on the maps in order to have their position conform with the more accurate aerial surveys.

We also made extensive use of individual contact prints in our work. Since a mosaic map is a photograph of photographs, it naturally is not as clear as the original contact prints. Therefore, it is usually a good idea to have enlargements made from the contact prints. The increased clarity of detail in the enlargement, thus achieved, more than compensates for the slight displacements and distortions in the prints.

There is another important advantage in studying the contact prints directly. As we have mentioned, when the airplane "flies a strip" of territory, the photographs run in a sequence with an overlapping of 60 per cent. This permits two adjoining photographs to be used in a stereoscopic apparatus. When they are correctly aligned — not always an easy task — a three-dimensional effect of part of the overlapping area is produced. This apparatus

46

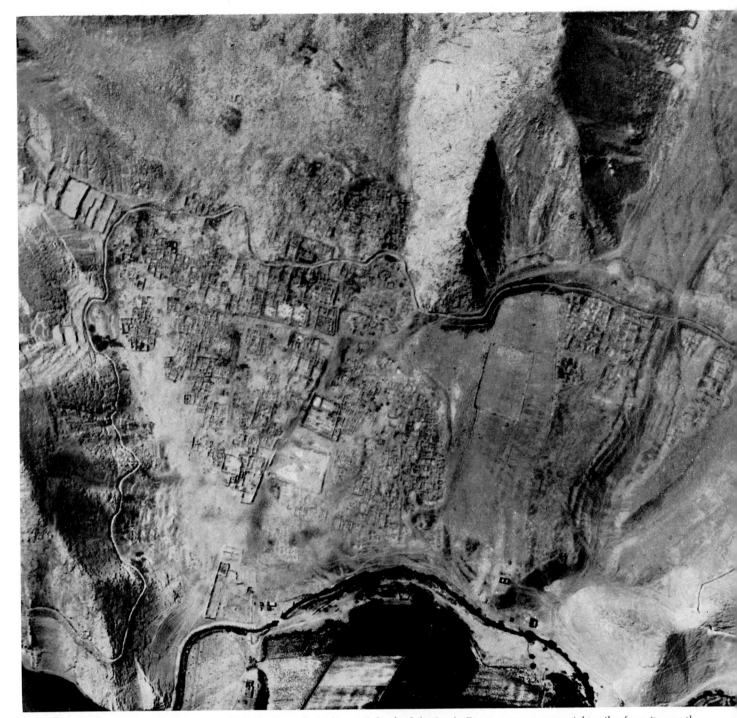

Fig. 12. Here is another unknown ruin which we located on the south bank of the Lurín River, some seven to eight miles from its mouth. Additional structures continue along the sides of the hills farther up the river. The heavy line running in an irregular fashion around and through the ruins is a modern irrigation canal not yet in use when the photograph was taken. With the functioning of the canal, parts of the ruin will be plowed under and the land cultivated. *Servicio 1003:150.*

is, moreover, so constructed that vertical elevations appear greatly exaggerated in relation to horizontal distances. Thus slight elevations of mounds and ruined walled structures stand out prominently while large pyramids dramatically jump up to meet the eye. Depressions, characteristic of canals, likewise stand out in bold relief. It was, therefore, possible at times to trace clearly the almost ruined courses of canals as they wound around steep hills. In this way we could find and map certain canals much more rapidly and accurately than was possible by field work. It was sheer joy to thus find and "follow" a canal in a few minutes in the laboratory, a process which in the field had previously taken us many painful hours or even days on horseback and on foot.

Working with the stereoscopic apparatus, however, requires much time and patience. The stereoscope consequently was used only when doubts arose about the nature of a ruin after photographs of it had been viewed with the naked eye or with a simple magnifying glass.

Contact prints had to be used exclusively for some valleys for which mosaic maps had not yet been constructed. In other valleys, of which mosaic maps existed, photographs of desert areas located at some distance from the cultivated lands, and thus of little interest to the Agriculture and Tax Departments of the Peruvian Government, had not been incorporated into these mosaics. Yet these areas were often of prime interest to us. We were thus forced to depend entirely upon the contact prints for our work in such areas. One of the areas which we studied in this way was the large desert plain to the north of ChanChan, the ancient capital of the Chimús.

By carefully studying each mosaic map and by examining individual prints with a magnifying glass and sometimes with a stereoscope, we were able to locate and map probably all of the major canals and ruins, as well as most of the secondary ones that could be seen on the aerial photographs.

Since the photographs of the various valleys were taken for different purposes, with several types of aerial cameras, and were sometimes made under unfavorable weather conditions, the negatives were not always of the same standard. Consequently, the degree of enlargement of the negatives which the Servicio could produce for us varied in different valleys and areas. Nonetheless, whatever the size of the enlargement, it always turned out to be of help to us.

We had enlargements made of photographs of over five hundred sites. Copies of most of these are at Long Island University. Others are at the Anthropological Institute of the University of Trujillo, Peru, or with Dr. Schaedel. A list of these vertical aerial photographs can be found in the Appendix. Some of the most important ones are reproduced in this volume. Dr. Schaedel published an article entitled "The Lost Cities of Peru" in the *Scientific American* for August 1951, in which he describes how he used some of these aerial photographs in furthering his own specific archaeological studies.

The use of aerial photographs nevertheless had definite limitations for our work. As has been said, the photographs in the files of the Servicio generally covered only the irrigated areas of the valleys together with small strips of the adjacent desert areas. The ruins and canals in the unphotographed desert areas between the various valleys therefore *had to be located by ground reconnaissance alone*, a slow and tedious operation which we carried on by means of a jeep, car, horse, or on foot.

The field work, however, consisted of more than merely covering the areas not recorded on the aerial photographs. We visited canals and ruins located on the aerial photographs mainly to obtain a concrete and more detailed knowledge of them. Moreover, badly destroyed ruins and canals photographed under unsuitable conditions, often could not be recognized as such on the photographs. Field trips were necessary to determine whether certain ill-defined spots on the photographs were natural mounds or ruins of man-made edifices. Such trips were important, especially in the large and complex Lambayeque area, where the cumulative power of occasional rains during the past centuries has transformed many adobe pyramids into apparently shapeless mounds. Thus, by intensive field reconnaissance, we sometimes established the existence of secondary sites that we could not discern in the photographs. When we returned to the Servicio, we could, since we now knew the location of these ruins, "rediscover" them on the photographs.

On the other hand, a re-examination of the photographs after field trips would at times show complexities and extensions of sites and their interconnection with others which were not apparent during the field work itself or which we had not noticed in our preliminary study of the photographs. This meant that we had to revisit most valleys at least once, some several times, to check the information obtained from the aerial photographs.

But the great aid of aerial photography in making an archaeological survey of an extensive region is obvious. It provides an *over-all* picture of the region, makes possible the *rapid location* of major and even minor sites, helps determine the *structure of major sites,* and can be used to accelerate the drawing of preliminary ground plans. Thus it tremendously reduces the time needed for general survey work in the field.

But field work still remains basic. Only by such work can the actual canals and structures of the past be studied and analyzed thoroughly, and the innumerable details be discovered that escape aerial photography, but that are essential for a real archaeological survey. As in the military field, aviation, while important, is, after all, chiefly an accessory to ground action!

Fig. 13 (below, left). Part of the reconstructed Pyramid of the Sun at Pachacamac. *Kosok* • Fig. 14 (below, right). A typical scene in an excavated, ancient graveyard at Pachacamac. Note the many human bones scattered about the site. *Kosok.*

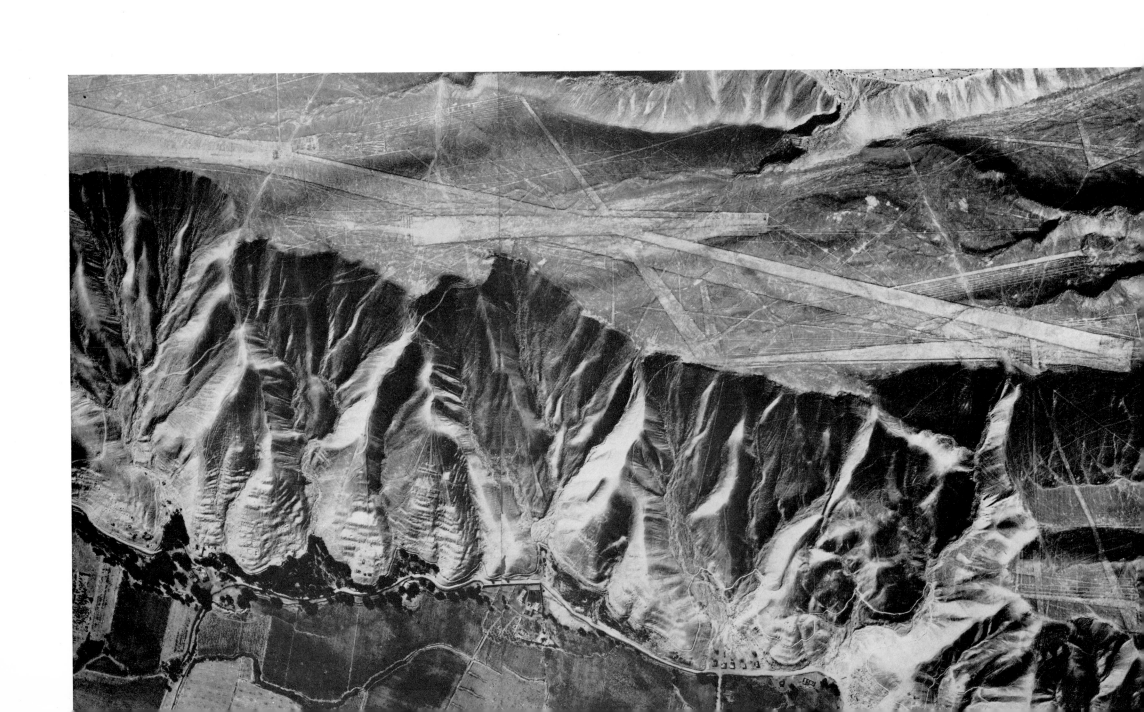

VI

The Largest Astronomy Book in the World: New Aspects of Ancient Nazca

ACROSS THE SOUTHERN COAST of Peru, about 250 miles from Lima, there runs a river called the Río Grande. Like most southern rivers, it has cut a narrow gorge through the coastal *mesa* and produced a valley where there is barely enough room for cultivation. But in a large plateau region beginning about thirty miles from the sea, this large river "dissolves itself," so to speak, into eight small branches, which furnish the water necessary for irrigating the adjoining fields. These fields are not extensive, for the rivers are small and contain water only four to five months a year. Each valley supports today, as it undoubtedly did in the past, a population of

Fig. 1 (left). This fantastic and mysterious complex of overlapping lines, "roads," triangles and trapezoids was probably built and used by the ancients for astronomical observations and related ceremonial cults. These markings cover the top of a plateau, situated just above the Palpa Valley, which is part of the Río Grande system; even the eroded slopes of the plateau were used for making these sacred markings. On the lower parts of the slopes are habitation terraces, while in the foreground are the fields of the Palpa Valley. *Servicio, 543 series* • Fig. 2 (right). South of the Ingenio Valley stretches an even greater maze of markings. It continues for some fifteen to twenty miles farther south into the Nazca Valley and even beyond it! The small size of the cultivated area of the Ingenio Valley (right) illustrates graphically why this valley, like the others of the Río Grande system, could support only a small population (see also Fig. 12). In contrast are the huge plateaus, on which the ancients were engaged in searching for the secrets of the Universe. It seems incredible, in view of their small populations, that these little valleys should have produced such an amazingly large number and variety of desert "records." *Kosok.*

a few thousand, and contains only one or two villages.

Because of location and elevation—about 1500 feet above sea level—this region is not strictly coastal. It is even less Sierra. Indeed, its character includes elements of both. Thus, it forms the beginning of an increasingly elevated series of intensively cultivated branch valleys of the western semi-Sierra region, which extends southeast

towards Arequipa, and which includes such an important and historically interesting small valley as the Colca (Johnson, 1930). Furthermore, the Río Grande region has always been the natural southern coastal entrance into the southern Sierras proper—connecting this section of the Coast with Ayacucho, Abancay, Cuzco and even Lake Titicaca (Tiahuanaco), once the seats of ancient cultures,

and still the chief centers of Indian life. Finally, the Río Grande branch valleys, together with the neighboring Ica Valley, comprise, in a way, the southern geographical and cultural terminus of the South Central Coast.

In this *peculiar transition zone*, the famous ancient Nazca culture evolved. Named for the Nazca Valley, the most important branch of the Río Grande, it has in many

50

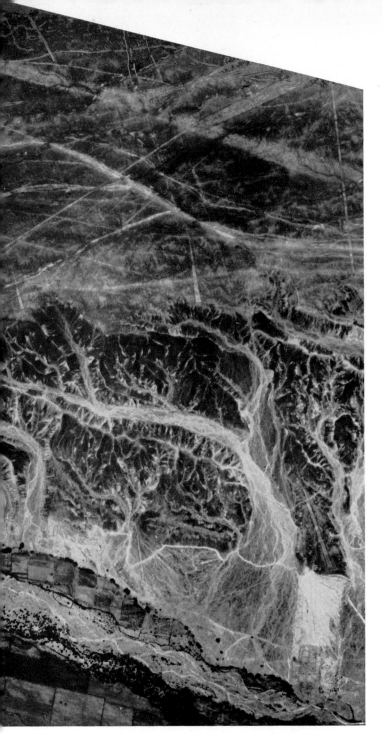

Paracas textiles have been found. In the Nazca area, the ancients developed a distinct type of ceramics characterized by their fine shapes, complex designs and beautiful color combinations. Of peasant, "ceremonial" character, the cultural products of Nazca contrast sharply with the rather secular nature of the best Mochica material of the Northwest Coast and the mass-produced Late Chimú goods. Intriguing and important as it is to unravel the socio-historical roots of the Nazca culture, we cannot attempt it here.

On the contrary, we have another mystery to add — namely, the so-called Nazca markings! Flying over the dramatic desert plains and hills that stretch between the lower branches of the Río Grande in southern Peru, one sees strange and unique networks of lines and geometric figures. They are visible in many places; sometimes lacing back and forth in extremely complex and apparently chaotic ways across an area possibly *more than forty miles long and five to ten miles wide!*

On more careful inspection, these fantastic networks are found to consist of long stone and dirt lines, roads, triangles, and trapezoids, as well as drawings of animals, plants, spirals and other figures, some of which are still meaningless to us. The raised edges of the various figures were made by the simple process of removing some soil and small stones from the enclosed areas and piling them up in a uniform way along the sides. Many of the sides are now only a few inches high and barely perceptible from the ground, even at dawn or dusk when the shadows are longest.

Some of the straight lines and roads are from four to five miles long! The triangles and trapezoids are usually immense, often measuring thousands of feet in length. The modern inhabitants of the valley of Ingenio,

Fig. 3 (left). In this vertical aerial mosaic which covers much of the region shown in Fig. 2, the multiplicity and complexity of the markings become even more apparent. Note, near the middle of the photograph, a typical "center" from which many lines, roads, triangles and trapezoids radiate. Numerous centers of this kind are found throughout the Nazca area. At the lower left hand side of the picture can be seen faint traces of an ancient settlement whose inhabitants probably helped make the manifold markings in the desert (see also Fig. 2). The size of the markings is indicated by the fact that the oblong white spot within one of the trapezoids near the lower left hand corner of the photograph is a modern football field! The black line running across the photograph is the Pan American Highway, while the white line with white blotches on each side of it is a dirt road leading to nearby Cahuachi. The irregular white lines are modern foot paths. *Servicio 524: 96, 99, 101* • Fig. 4 (below). Maria Reiche made this plane-table drawing after completing extensive field measurements of a small section of Fig. 3. The area covered is just above the bend of the Pan American Highway where the "white" road branches off. The drawing brings out the many details that are not visible on the photograph, thus indicating even more clearly the overwhelming mass of markings that the ancients constructed. Indeed, the very richness of the available material often overwhelms the individual field worker and suggests the need of a collective survey of at least the main areas. The dotted line indicates the Pan American Highway.

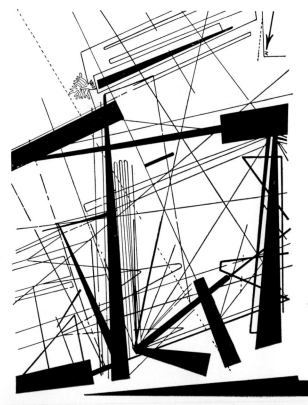

Fig. 5 (below, right). This photograph shows what the lines and "roads" actually look like on the ground. Notice how straight they are and how they radiate in different directions. The irregular white tracks in the foreground were made by a modern truck. *Reiche* • NOTE: In the margins of this chapter are pictured Nazca type *huacos*. *Kosok-Rein*. The two with wooden bases are from the *AMNH*. The line cuts of Nazca figures found in the margins are from *Mead* and from *Guillen*.

ways been a socio-archaeological puzzle. For here in these minute, isolated valleys that lie scattered over one of the world's driest deserts, the inhabitants produced technically the most advanced, and artistically the most beautiful, textiles of the Americas. In its broader sense, this area should include the neighboring Ica Valley as well as the Pisco, near whose mouth the wonderful ancient

Fig. 6. An oblique aerial view of another desert region covered by sets of markings. *Servicio, unnumbered series.*

one of the branches of the Río Grande system, built a football field in one of the trapezoids, where it occupies only a small fraction of the enclosed space! The dirt drawings of some of the plants and animals are likewise done on a large scale, extending sometimes hundreds of feet in length.

So far, no traditions that might indicate the purpose of these drawings have been discovered. The early Span-

ish Chronicler, Cieza de León (I: Chap. LXXV), mentions that all the Indians in the Nazca Valley were killed in the civil wars in which rival groups of Spaniards fought for possession of both the soil and the Indians. And with the Indians, their traditions apparently also perished. None of the known records of the early Spanish Chroniclers explains the nature of the lines; however, unexplored local archives may in the future yield some information about them. The physical existence of these drawings is well known to many people in Peru today, for they can be seen clearly from the Faucett planes that fly regularly over this region. Sections of these markings can be noticed even from the well-traveled Pan American Highway, which cuts right across some of the most important of these sites!

In an article published in the *Proceedings* of the 27th Congress of Americanists (1939), Mejía Xesspe proposed that the roads were of a ceremonial nature, and he is probably quite correct. But he goes no further in his analysis. Later on, in 1947, Dr. Hans Horkheimer published a monograph in which he suggested that connecting lines represented kinship lines connecting the graves of the various members of the local clans. This explanation sounds rather labored, especially since no graves have ever been found at these centers, some of which are situated on small natural hillocks.

While investigating this region in 1941, I was suddenly struck with the thought that these remains could have had some connection with early calendrical and astronomical observations. For many years, I had been interested in the development of primitive science and realized the great importance of astronomical observations and calendrical calculations in helping to regulate the life of evolving agricultural societies throughout the world.

The ancient astronomer-priests supervised the construction of sight lines of dirt, or of individual large stones, toward points on the horizon where the sun rose and set at different times of the year, especially the summer and winter solstices and the two equinoxes. Sight lines were also made indicating where the annual appearance and disappearance of important stars took place on the horizon. Such markings defined the beginning and ending of important periods in agricultural life. Later on, the study of the stars and the calendar was undoubtedly also used to "predict" the coming of important events.

To us the Nazca lines seemed to be similar to the astronomical-calendrical marking techniques of other peoples. What, however, makes them unique in the whole

Fig. 7 (left). This figure, attached to a long trapezoid of which only a part can be seen here, was the first one we discovered in 1941. It is on a plateau south of Palpa and just east of the Pan American Highway. What the drawing portrays we do not know. *Reiche* • Fig. 8. A ground view of a "bulb" at the end of one of the "fingers" of the drawings in Fig. 7. Such "bulbs" can be seen on one of the murals at Pañamarca, Nepeña Valley (see Fig. 10b, Chapter XX), as well as in some Maya drawings. *Reiche* • NOTE: When an elongated triangle is cut across, both a triangle and a trapezoid are produced. These two forms and their relationships to each other may have had a special meaning for the ancients since none of the large enclosures have any other geometrical forms.

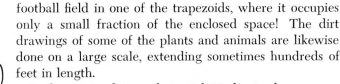

Fig. 9. Ceremonial lines "etched" into a hillside. *Reiche.*

Fig. 10. Maria Reiche standing in front of a part of a trapezoid to which two triangles and some "roads" are attached. *Kosok* • Fig. 11. Set of markings just north of Nazca. The Pan American Highway is the black line that runs across the picture. *Kosok.*

world is *the vast number and the complex networks they form* as they spread over the large desert plateaus. As we contemplated this vast achievement of early man, it occurred to us that we might well call it *The Largest Astronomy Book in the World.* Once we can read this "book," we may have a better understanding of a statement by Cieza de León: "These Indians watched the heavens and the signs very constantly, which made them such great soothsayers."

After spending several weeks in 1941 in the field taking astronomical alignments of some of the important markings, I found that a number of them pointed to the solstices. Others might have pointed to the Pleiades — a very important constellation for the ancients. I also found certain lines in *different* regions that had the *same* direction, which indicated observations in *different* places of the *same* celestial phenomena! When I returned to northern Peru, I found the same situation. Pyramids in different valleys had similar sets of azimuths! I had no time to continue the work; but it was clear to me that a new aspect of ancient Peruvian astronomy had come to light.

Before leaving Peru, I was fortunate in being able to interest Miss Maria Reiche of Lima, who was well-trained in mathematics and astronomy, in this problem. She continued the field work and further developed the theoretical aspects of the problem. A preliminary report of some of our findings was published in the May 1947 issue of *Natural History.*

Later Miss Reiche received a grant from San Marcos University in Lima to continue her investigations. Her main interest lay in trying to identify the direction of the important sight lines with the points on the horizon where the present heliacal risings or settings of associated stars can be seen. This is important, for every year each of the stars rises and sets at a slightly different point on the horizon. Tables have been computed giving the amount of annual change for all the important stars. By calculating the difference between the present position of a star and its former position, as indicated by an associated or nearby sight line, *the approximate date of the construction of a sight line can be determined!*

This method of dating has been used successfully in European astro-archaeology. It was developed during the latter part of the nineteenth century mainly by the famous British astronomer, Sir Norman Lockyer. In his well known volume, *Stonehenge* (1906), he calculated the date of the construction of this great prehistoric monument to be about 1630 B.C. This conclusion was proved to have

been of the correct order by recent Carbon 14 measurements which give the date as 1848 B.C. with a probable error of ± 275 years. Miss Reiche based much of her work on the method of *astronomical* dating. It is a form of dating which with few exceptions has been unjustifiably neglected in the archaeological work of the Americas. In Nazca, moreover, the enormous number of sight lines makes possible the use of a quantitative, semi-statistical method of study, the general results of which *should be far removed from the category of the accidental.*

The question at once arises: Why should people entering the early stages of civilization have taken such an

Fig. 12. Two solitary triangles pointing to the narrow Nazca Valley. The change in direction of the "road" part of the triangle is characteristic of several other "roads" found on the *pampa.* The two parallel lines that cross the markings are irregular modern paths. *Servicio, unnumbered series.*

Figs. 13 to 17. Enlarged photographic details of the Palpa Valley region • Fig. 13 (above). A detail showing a "cat-demon" figure closely associated with a complex of roads and trapezoids. This "cat-demon" figure is also found on textiles and water jugs of this region and is probably based on the numerous mountain "tigers" of Peru. *Servicio 543:24* • Fig. 14 (right). Two rather crudely-made spirals are here associated with parts of a large triangle. The black spots within the triangle are small heaps of stones and are possibly recording devices. They have been found in many other enclosures. *Servicio 543:24* • Fig. 15 (opposite page, upper right). Part of an "exposed" dirt drawing. *Reiche* • Fig. 16 (opposite page, lower right). The two stylized angular spirals and the two sets of "pan pipes" appear to be interconnected so that the lines of their design form a continuous path. At the top of the photograph are remains of what appear to be crudely-constructed human figures. The irregular light lines running horizontally across the photograph are modern paths. The irregular lines running vertically across the photograph are natural run-offs. *Servicio 543:24* • Fig. 17 (p. 56, lower left). Another detail showing small heaps of stones.

intense interest in astronomical observations? An analysis of social developments during this period will answer the question. With the rise of a more advanced type of agriculture and the transformation of tribal society into the early period of civilization, there developed a more complex and organized social life. This must have resulted in an increasing realization that there likewise existed a complex organization among the heavenly bodies. When it became clear that the annual movements of the heavenly bodies could be correlated with the annual progress of the seasons, *around which the whole productive and social process revolved,* a fuller understanding of astronomy became imperative.

But there was more than correlation! Indeed, the *precise, unrelenting regularity* of the movements of heavenly bodies appeared to have *created and directed the more fluctuating regularity* of the annual seasons and the even more fluctuating social life of mankind. The very heavens seemed to *control* the events on the earth beneath! *Thus astronomy as an organized science had to be born.* From the outset it was a *practical* science, for its main function was to produce a complex *calendar* which became *the regulative mechanism of the newly developing agricultural productive process.*

In a *rainfall* economy, astronomically determined prediction and "making" of rain become the essential parts of practical astronomy. However, in an *irrigation* economy, prediction of the appearance, the rise, the fall and the disappearance of the life-giving waters in the rivers plays the main role. With the emergence of a practical calendar, special astronomical-calendrical rituals and ceremonies begin to evolve around the whole water-determined productive process. And with these ceremonies a series of heaven-determined "auspicious" as well as "evil" days and periods is established that eventually influences every aspect of man's life from the cradle to the grave.

But such organized astronomical investigations of the movements of the sun, the moon, the planets and the stars, together with the building up of a complex calendar, an involved ceremonial cycle and an organized method of prediction could not be done by the average person. A group of specialists was required — *the astronomer-priests.* These specialists built up an extensive system of observations and calculations and established involved rituals of supplication addressed to the heavenly bodies, which seemed to dominate the very life on earth. This combination of truth and ignorance, of scientific honesty and social deceit, gave the priests a *tremendous control*

over the people — for only the priests could know and apparently influence the forces that controlled human destiny. A whole new system of interacting forces thus emerged, which, once established, grew through its own internal momentum until a complex system of astronomical-calendrical knowledge gradually came into existence. Like the highly accurate Maya calendar, Nazcan astronomical activities probably expressed a kind of precocious achievement that went *far beyond the practical needs of the people themselves.*

These astronomer-priests undoubtedly found that the more complex and artificial their astronomical-calendrical knowledge and ceremonial forms became, and the more they kept that knowledge secret, the more they could impress the populace with their own mysterious supernatural powers. These powers then became a valuable asset in strengthening their growing privileged position. Indeed, some of this socially unnecessary "knowledge" was probably used quite consciously to mislead the people and thereby to rule them. The German scientist, Alexander von Humboldt (1814:131), in discussing the artificial nature of the priestly ceremonial calendar of the Chibchas of Colombia, succinctly summarized this aspect of the problem as follows: ". . . the power of a class of society is often founded in the ignorance of the other classes. . . ."

When Michael and I arrived in Peru, Miss Reiche had

already returned to Nazca to carry on additional field work. We were anxious to see how far she had progressed in her new work and to find out how we could aid her. When Mr. Neale of the SCIPA offered us a trip to Nazca in one of his jeeps, we gladly accepted.

At Nazca we settled down at the government-owned Hotel de Turistas. Such government-owned tourist hotels are now operated in most of the important cities of Peru, and are of a high quality. Coming, as we did, out of the hot, dusty desert, the Nazca hotel appeared to us at first like a wonderful mirage. Built only a few years ago, in a partly Spanish style, around a large patio, it had beautiful flowers growing alongside its walks. In the center of the patio a fine swimming pool gleamed. Swimming in the desert! This seemed fantastic! Around the patio was a covered terrace with tables and chairs set for afternoon coffee or evening dinner. It was an inspiring experience to sit evenings in an easy chair and gaze through the open patio at the black desert sky illuminated by thousands of bright stars — the same stars that the ancient astronomer-priests of Nazca had once studied in their attempts to control nature and society!

While in Nazca, we called on Señor Bocanegra, whom I had met in 1941 at the time he was Mayor of Nazca and the editor and owner of the local newspaper. He was still the owner of the newspaper and, in this capacity, lost no time in introducing us to the local Director of Agriculture, the Director of Irrigation, and other officials who supplied us with information on present day agricultural conditions. They also provided some of our transportation into the desert areas.

Nazca was suffering from a shortage of meat and other foods, a situation typical of other valleys on the Coast. Every day one could see people waiting in line at the market. This shortage was due to the fact that large parts of the valleys, from the Huaura on the North Central Coast to the Nazca region, are devoted to the cultivation of cotton, amounting in some cases to as much as 80 to 90 per cent of the total area of each valley! Cotton is grown mainly on large and medium-sized estates and exported to obtain the highly desirable American dollar. This foreign currency, unfortunately, is not used primarily for importing food and manufactured products for the people. It is, instead, invested abroad or used for the purchase of more land, more foreign machinery and more imported luxury items that have become very popular among the middle and upper classes. The inadequate food production of the coastal valleys has to be supplemented by imports from the Sierras and from foreign countries.

One official whom I questioned stated the problem simply. "No one can eat cotton. What we need is food production. Even though our soil is very rich, we are gradually starving because the land is not being used in the interests of the people." The same problem holds true for those valleys in the north which grow sugar for export purposes, while food has to be imported.

These conditions dramatically illustrate the difference in production among the ancients and the moderns. Then, security and self-sufficiency of each region was basic to the people — even to their own rulers. With our modern complex economy and its alienation of property much of this security and self-sufficiency has disappeared for most of the people.

While awaiting Maria Reiche's return from an extended field trip to Palpa, we used the SCIPA jeep which had brought us down from Lima and made some trips over the desert, revisiting some of the old sites known from our 1941 visit. In addition, an intelligent local guide took us to a nearby place called La Estaquería, a peculiar ancient site, which contained the remains of twelve rows of nineteen wooden posts each. Kroeber had visited this site (1926) and published photographs of it (1944). However, we found the place had been partly destroyed since then. As a result of the growth of the nearby grape industry, many of the poles have been dug up and used as vine supports (Fig. 27). Other sets of posts were found implanted near the main structure, but no regular design could be established there. Some miles further down the river, we found a smaller but even more dilapidated set of posts. These two sites date back to pre-Spanish times. The posts may have supported the roofs of houses, but they are placed too close together to furnish space for a living quarter. Were the sites perhaps ceremonial centers related to an astronomical-calendrical cult?

That evening we met Maria Reiche, who had returned from her three-day field trip in the nearby Palpa Valley. She had many things to tell about her discoveries of new desert drawings and of new centers from which lines and trapezoids radiated. Most important, she had again found, in a number of valleys, lines with the same orientation, indicating that the ancient Indians had made observations in *different* places of the *same* celestial phenomena!

The next few days we spent jointly visiting some of the important sites in the desert that Miss Reiche had located in her extensive field reconnaissance, which was aided by the few aerial photographs available. Then we decided to

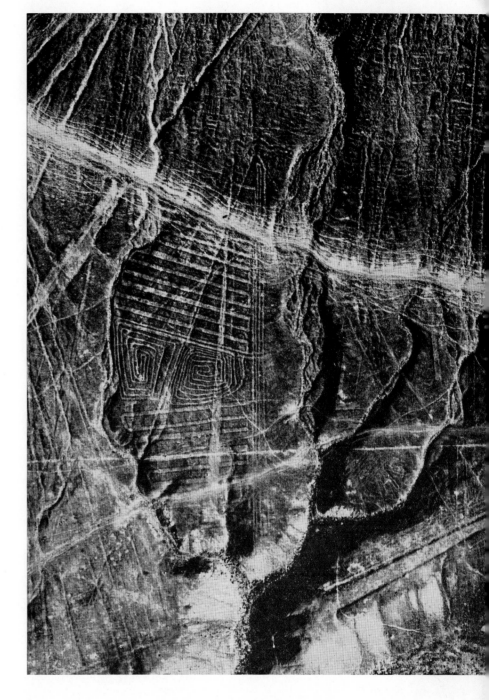

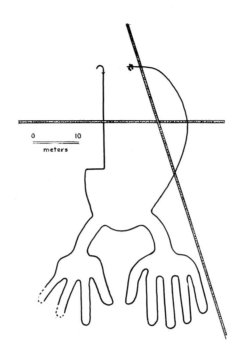

split up our field work. Miss Reiche continued to roam over the desert in search of new finds, accompanied by her field assistant, who carried her theodolite — the principal surveying instrument necessary for determining the azimuths of the various lines. Michael and I, on the other hand, decided to visit some of the desert drawings whose general position Miss Reiche had located. We had found only one in 1941 and we were anxious to uncover more of them.

Most of those we studied were within an hour's walking distance from the Pan American Highway. Since we had no jeep at our disposal during this time, we generally boarded an early morning bus going towards Ica and had the chauffeur drop us off at the desired locations. We wandered around in the desolate desert until we struck "pay dirt"; then we began to work. Since we were out all day we had to take along our lunch. This usually consisted of rolls, bananas, oranges and a peculiar carbonated beverage called Cola Inglés, which, after having been exposed to the hot sun for half a day, tasted like some horrible witches' brew of ancient Nazca!

We had to do all our field work on foot. The region was too rocky for trucks or even jeeps, but, more important, the lines were so faint that the wheels of a vehicle would have ruined the drawings. Towards evening we would return to the Highway and hail the first truck that was returning to Nazca. The time it took to return varied, depending upon the *espíritu* of both truck and driver.

As a result of centuries of strong desert winds, the drawings are sometimes rather difficult to uncover and piece together. The line of the drawing is generally a path from one half to three yards wide with raised edges of dirt and small stones, which in some cases are now barely visible. The only way we could find out what a drawing was like was to shuffle with our boots along a discovered path, thereby disturbing the darker oxidized surface of

the soil and exposing the lighter soil below. Since these drawings were made like certain kinds of childrens' drawings, where the pencil never leaves the paper and no line crosses the other, it was often possible to shuffle along the whole path from the beginning to the end. The result was generally a huge, light-colored drawing. It was very important not to walk absent-mindedly off the path of the drawings, since this would ruin the original design.

Despite the heat, the work was exciting, for after we had begun to uncover a drawing it was always a guess as to what kind of design we would uncover! But our labors did not always yield positive results. Sometimes a large part of the drawing had been obliterated by the winds of the centuries, or by other drawings later superimposed by the ancient builders.

Most of the drawings we uncovered represented birds or fishes, though other animals, many spirals and some plant figures were found (Figs. 18 to 26). A unique drawing was one of two hands with only nine fingers (Figs. 18 and 19). Most of the figures seemed to be similar to those found on Nazca pottery. Some of them may have been representations of sacred animals or clan totems. They may have been "walked on" by the priests or the clan during ceremonial processions, for each figure is always associated with a ceremonial trapezoid or triangle. In fact, the path generally starts from one side of a trapezoid or triangle and then returns to it.

Fig. 18 (above, left). A pair of hands with only nine fingers! This unique drawing is found near a trapezoid close by the Pan American Highway. Although such hands are known on ancient Nazca pottery, this is the only dirt drawing of its kind so far discovered. The number *nine* is found in other parts of Peru; it is considered by many peoples of the world as important and sacred. Note the *nine* gods of the underworld of the Maya. *Kosok-Reiche* • Fig. 19 (above). Partial view of the pair of hands of Fig. 16 as seen from a specially constructed ladder. The four fingers and thumb of one hand and the thumb of the other hand can be easily recognized. The truck in back is passing along the Pan American Highway. *Kosok* • Fig. 20 (below). One of the many animal-like figures constructed in Wisconsin by North American Indians. Though made in the form of elevated dirt mounds, these figures and their Nazca counterparts were apparently built for ceremonial — totemic? — purposes. The actual size of the figure below is about the same as that of the one shown in Fig. 21. *Davis and Squier (1848, pl. XLIV).*

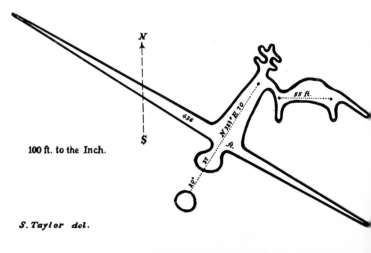

100 ft. to the Inch.

S. Taylor del.

We almost always found a small pile of stones near one or both ends of the trapezoids. These stone piles may have been altars used for ceremonial purposes. The extreme length and the narrowness of some of the enclosures suggest that they may also have been used for ceremonial races, a custom prevalent among many peoples of a corresponding stage of development in other parts of the world.

We carefully copied the drawings that we found. Some of them appeared with explanatory text and descriptions in the December 1949 issue of the magazine *Archaeology.* A number of them are reproduced here. The drawings can be dated once their associated enclosures and sight lines are dated. In the meantime they could be stylistically dated by comparing them with similar designs on textiles and pottery which have been classified into various periods. Much work remains to be done!

In 1949, Miss Reiche published, both in Spanish and in English, a monograph describing her work at Nazca. The monograph contains many photographs and drawings of sight lines, enclosures, and dirt drawings not included in the article in *Archaeology.* Since then she has continued her work in the field with unrelenting ardor and it is to be hoped that she will soon publish the results of her extensive work.

Lines, roads and enclosures have been found in other valleys of the Coast, though only as rare specimens. They have been reported in some valleys south of the Nazca region. Miss Reiche also found centers with radiating lines and roads in several places in the vicinity of Lima. Mr. P. L. Thommen took us on a trip to another group of roads in a *quebrada* between the Rímac and Chillón Rivers. The roads at Queneto in the Virú Valley and the wide road in the Zaña Valley may also belong to this category.

However, in most of these larger valleys to the north such astronomical-calendrical lines, if they existed, have been destroyed in the course of time. And that is not surprising. As the population there *grew in size and wealth* and the government *increased its power,* such simple astronomical-calendrical lines, roads, enclosures and drawings as may have existed were gradually replaced by *the much more elaborate and expensive roads, walls, pyramids, temples and friezes, whose remains still litter these valleys.*

Besides, as already pointed out, with this growth of wealth, a secular military power gradually emerged and established a secular state that finally brought the priest-

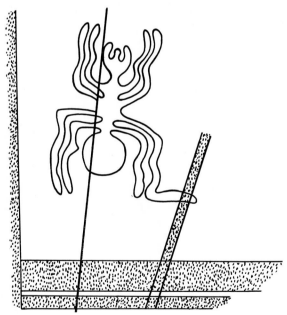

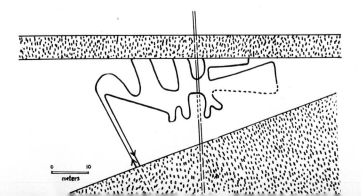

hood under control — at least in part. While the secular rulers needed the priesthood in order to obtain the aid of the heavenly bodies in ruling their own people and conquering new ones, they were, at the same time, interested in restricting the activities of the priesthood to those forms which were useful in expanding the interests of the

Figs. 21 to 25. These huge drawings are found closely associated with trapezoids and triangles. Are they clan totems? Symbols of heavenly bodies? Or both? Such huge animal drawings have been found also in other parts of the world • Fig. 21 (top). A well-defined, stylized drawing of a bird about 400 feet long. The "road" paralleling the wings is a solstice line. *Reiche* • Fig. 22 (next to top). This peculiar and undeciphered "fishing pole" drawing is almost half a mile long! Spirals like the one here shown are found on other drawings. *Reiche* • Fig. 23 (next to bottom). The two body divisions and eight legs of this figure indicate that it is a spider. *Reiche* • Fig. 24 (photograph). Ground view of spider drawing. The outlines of the drawings are so low that generally they can be seen only at sunrise and sunset when the shadows are long. They can be made more distinct, as in this case, by carefully dragging a stone attached to a rope along the slight ridge, so as to expose the lighter colored soil beneath the surface of darker pebbles. The straight line running across the drawing is an astronomical observation line. *Reiche* • Fig. 25 (bottom). This drawing appears to be a crude representation of a flying pelican, a bird which is common along the coast of Peru. Here both lines that form the beak become long sight lines continuing in a parallel direction. *Kosok.*

state. It was no longer astronomy for the priesthood's sake! It was now *astronomy for the sake of the state!* The dominance of a secular power must have affected the quantity, the nature and the social role of astronomical observations, calendrical calculations and public ceremonies.

57

The question remains: Why should such a poor region as Nazca have produced such elaborate and peculiar forms of culture? This question is not easy to answer since we do not yet have all the elements to fit the puzzle. But as the result of an extended association with this material, we can venture a general hypothesis which may in a way encompass the problem.

Specific hydrological problems of the Nazca area may have furnished a reason for such elaborate astronomical observations. While the larger rivers in the north have water for a good part of the year, the branches of the Río Grande have water for only about five months. During "bad" years there is even less water; during "very bad" years there is none! True, in the Nazca Valley itself, this condition led to the building of tunnels that tapped the underground waters of the nearby mountains, but the amount of water collected had only supplementary value. It is therefore not surprising that the priesthood would press their astronomical observations as well as their astrological predictions and exhortations to the limit in the hope of increasing the supply of the life-giving waters.

Another factor is significant. In the small valleys of the Río Grande no great wealth could accumulate; thus no large constructions could be undertaken. At best, a few small adobe mounds could be erected. Consequently, conditions never arose whereby a secular state could appear — except at rare intervals and then probably only as an outside intrusion. And the Nazca area was too poor to attract any but the temporary interest of passing conquerors. Consequently, these valleys, with very limited potentialities, in all likelihood *sustained mainly priest-ruled peasant societies throughout their two thousand or more years of history.* Since no great structures could be erected, the priests and the people had to content themselves with easily built ceremonial lines and centers in the adjoining deserts. As they continued to build, generation after generation, century after century, and as the dry desert carefully preserved these markings, there slowly emerged those vast networks of figures that today strain our credulity and challenge our understanding!

Such heavy emphasis on astronomical-calendrical ceremonialism in Nazca society brings to mind the cultural forms of the Maya in Central America. The early priest-dominated Maya had evolved an astronomy and a social-astrological cult that in certain aspects were probably similar to those of ancient Nazca. But here a curious fact emerges. As the Maya began to get richer and more powerful, they did not — like the North Peruvians — evolve a centralized secular state! They produced no walled urban compounds, no fortresses, no palaces. *On the con-*

Fig. 26. This peculiar bird figure with the snake-like neck is the only one of its kind so far found. Moreover, it is one of the largest drawings encountered. Each line represents a path about two feet wide and the figure can be "walked" from one end to the other without crossing the path. The entrance to the figure and the exit run parallel for almost 100 meters and then disappear in a "washout." The shaded area at the bottom is part of a trapezoid which is more than half a mile long. The darker band just above it represents the edge of the trapezoid and is about two feet high. The small round circles represent small piles of stones. The broken lines represent parts of the paths that have been destroyed by the elements. Note that the bird has *eleven* feathers. *Eleven* is a significant number in other areas of Peru, as it is, indeed, in other parts of the world. It was used to signify the difference between the number of days in twelve *lunar* months of 29½ days each (i.e., 354 days), and the number of days in a solar year (i.e., 365 days). These extra days were generally devoted to festivities. One of the Spanish Chroniclers informs us that these eleven days were celebrated by the Incas, but that the great ruler, Pachacutec, abolished calendrical *lunar* months by introducing 30-day administrative months, thereby reducing the number of feast days at the end of the year to five. *Kosok-Reiche.*

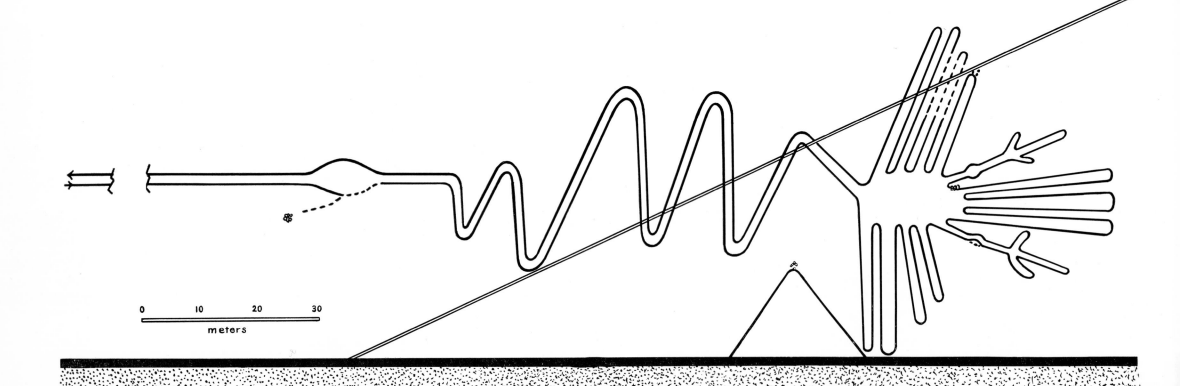

0   10   20   30

meters

trary, they merely built bigger and better ceremonial centers controlled by a priesthood that maintained its astronomical-calendrical cult. A kind of glorified Nazca!

The problem, therefore, is not one of explaining the retention of the religious ceremonial emphasis among the poorer Nazcans, but of explaining its retention among the richer Maya. Although this is not basically our field, we may venture some possible explanations. May not the answer have something to do with the jungle geography and economy of the Maya in contrast to the irrigated agriculture of the milpa system with its many periodically discarded fields — and the existence of dense jungle areas desert life of the Peruvians of the Northwest Coast? Apparently the low density of population around the ceremonial centers of the Maya — as a result of the extensive separating the individual ceremonial centers from one another, helped to prevent a successful integration of

Fig. 27 (above). A view of the few remaining posts of La Estaquería (see p. 55). Kosok • Fig. 28 (below). Part of the patio of the Hotel Turista in Nazca. Kosok • NOTE: The rare puma figure (right margin) is taken from a Paracas textile. John Wise.

these local centers into a secular state. By contrast, the intensive, irrigated agriculture of the coastal Peruvians in the larger northern valleys, their greater efficiency of production, their greater density of population clusters, and the closer proximity of these to one another, were undoubtedly factors favorable to an early development of a centralized, secular state in Northern Peru. The answer to the problem undoubtedly lies somewhere within this complex of factors.

But let us now turn to another problem: How highly developed was the astronomical and calendrical knowledge of the Peruvians, and how did it compare with that of the Maya? Although the Spanish Chroniclers give us some information about the calendrical system of the Incas, they are virtually silent about the astronomical-calendrical knowledge of the coastal peoples. This is most deplorable, since the latter probably reached a higher level in their astronomy and their calendars than did the Incas. We are, therefore, dependent upon the "records" left by the ancient Peruvians themselves. But here our efforts are blocked by the undeveloped nature of the Peruvian recording devices and by our own limited ability to decipher those which we know exist. As a result, our present knowledge of much of ancient Peruvian astronomy is extremely limited or even non-existent!

But this low level of Peruvian recording devices does not necessarily indicate a low level of astronomical development. We often forget that only because the Maya priesthood developed a glyph recording system, some elements of which accidentally have been preserved and are now partly deciphered, do we have knowledge of the high level of Maya astronomical knowledge and calendrical systems. Without this recording system and its survival, we would know as little today about Maya as we do about Peruvian astronomy and calendars!

We must, of course, admit that a definite relationship exists between the degree of development of a priestly recording system and that of a priestly-controlled astronomical-calendrical system. But the correlation is not necessarily so close that a less developed recording system necessarily means a similarly low level of astronomical observations and calendrical calculations. In other words, the correlation is not one to one. We, therefore, cannot discount the possibility that Peruvian astronomy and calendar construction reached higher levels than the undeveloped nature of the recording system would indicate. In fact, the nature of the deciphered parts of some recording systems and the amount of the undeciphered

recording systems suggest that both astronomy and calendars reached fairly well developed levels — at least in some parts of Peru.

The main problem in Peru, therefore, is the deciphering of recording systems. Once this is done, we may be able to lift the veil, at least in part, from the still shrouded mysteries of the past.

The best known Peruvian system was that of knotted cords or quipus (Fig. 32). From the Spanish Chroniclers we know (Locke:1923) that the Incas had trained a special group of administrative officials called quipucamayocs (quipu keepers) whose function was to keep (by means of the quipu) detailed local, district, regional and federal administrative records of the size of the population, the amount of agricultural and manufactured products, the size of llama and alpaca herds, the number of soldiers, and most important, the amount of the annual tribute! This information remained "top secret" among the ruling Inca. But the very efficiency and secrecy of the quipu system made it unnecessary for the Incas to develop any form of "writing" in order to carry on the complex administrative system of their far-flung Empire. Indeed, Montesinos (ms. 1648) mentions a tradition according to which one of the Inca rulers prohibited, on pain of death, the continuation of a kind of writing on palm leaves that existed among one of the conquered tribes. A politically logical decision made in the interest of the ruling Inca group! For why should subject peoples possess the means of recording and transmitting information, especially if they were under the control of a priesthood, antagonistic to the rising power of secular rulers?

There is an indication that some of the quipus or parts of them were also used as a mnemotechnic device for remembering certain historical events and traditions. It was mainly from the quipucamayocs that the Spanish obtained various historical data including the official lists of the Inca rulers and some of their achievements.

Finally, the limited study of the quipus by Nordenskiöld (1925) indicates that some of the knotted cords may have been used by priests for recording astronomical-calendrical data. This should not be surprising, for a recording system once established can be used to record anything within the range of its own potentialities.

Deciphering quipus which were used as mnemotechnic devices is out of the question. It is barely possible that some of the specific knowledge locked up in the administrative quipus may one day be recovered. Most likely of reconstruction are the astronomical-calendrical quipus,

59

since they must contain a limited variety of key calendrical numbers, most of which, moreover, are universal. At present, Mr. August De Clemente, a research associate of mine, is making a systematic study of several hundred *quipus*, loaned to Long Island University by Mr. John Wise, to see what information can be extracted from them in regard to the calendrical systems of the past. Such a broad systematic study of a large number of *quipus* should also bring out more details and more variants of this system of recording than have so far been presented by Locke and Nordenskiöld.

Only a relatively small number of *quipus* are still in existence, because the Church burned most of them in its seventeenth century campaign to liquidate the still powerful "heathenism" among the Peruvians. This destruction parallels the burning of hundreds of Maya codices, of which only three have been saved for posterity!

Knotted cords are not unique to Peru; they have been found in many parts of the world. It is known that the Chinese used them in earliest times before they developed their own picture-writing. Even the Mayas are supposed to have used them before they had glyphs! It is interesting to note that *quipus* have been reported to be still in use by shepherds in the remote parts of the Peruvian-Bolivian highlands in order to keep records of their flocks.

But even in ancient times *quipus* were not the only recording devices that were employed. By a careful study of ancient bags containing beans and by examination of paintings on ancient *huacos*, Señor Rafael Larco Hoyle, the Director of the Chiclín Museum on the Northwest Coast, has come to the conclusion that the Early Chimús scratched markings on beans in order to record messages and possibly other information. (Handbook, Vol. II).

Fritz Buck of Bolivia has made a study of several thousand Peruvian *huacos* and has come to the conclusion that many of the symbols moulded or painted on them refer to calendrical-astronomical or numerological data of that time. Unfortunately, most of his material has not yet

Fig. 29 (margin). Beans with different markings painted on *huacos*. According to Rafael Larco Hoyle, they are ideographic signs (Los Mochicas, Vol. II) • Fig. 30 (top, center). Drawing from a *huaco* showing a messenger carrying what appears to be a bag. Such bags, containing beans with various markings, have been found in ancient graves • Fig. 31 (right). Rafael Larco Hoyle suggests that this *huaco* painting represents officials deciphering symbols on the beans.

been made available. However, in several published articles dealing with the well-known Lamabayeque gold plaque and with some unusual Mochica ceramics, Buck has tried to prove that ancient Peru once had a *tzolkin* calendrical system of 13 months of 20 days each, similar to that of the Maya. His theory has been met with skepticism; but the fact that Alexander von Humboldt (1814) found a 20-month ceremonial cycle among the Chibchas indicates that the unit of twenties had developed in South America.

Arthur Posnansky (1945) attempted a rather logical calendrical interpretation of the ancient sun portal at Tiahuanaco, though his datings of the site are impossibly early. Stansbury Hagar and Zelia Nuttall also deciphered some Peruvian calendrical material.

Irrespective of the validity of the specific interpretations of the data by these various authors, it must be realized that sufficient material has already been accumulated to indicate *the existence of early recording techniques.* This is not surprising, for even more primitive people try to keep a record of important events.

As a result of our work in Peru, we were able to discover several more ancient recording devices! While tramping over the deserts of Nazca, and while studying some of the aerial photographs, we discovered that some of the triangular and trapezoidal enclosures contained many small heaps of gravel (Figs. 13, 14 and 17). It appeared that these heaps of stones could have been numerical-calendrical-astronomical recording devices. The heaps we visited had unfortunately been partly demolished by modern paths or by the winds of centuries, so that we could not be certain of the exact number of heaps in each enclosure. Perhaps a systematic survey of all such enclosures would yield some positive results.

But the most important recording devices on the desert plains of Nazca are, of course, some of the lines and roads themselves. Once they are deciphered, we will know *when they were built and to which heavenly bodies they were oriented.* This information should give us a key to the astronomy of the past for at least the Nazca area.

We were also to discover still another form of recording device of ancient Peru! While looking through Dr. Wagner's collection of Peruvian antiquities in Lima, our attention was attracted by a large Nazca textile whose

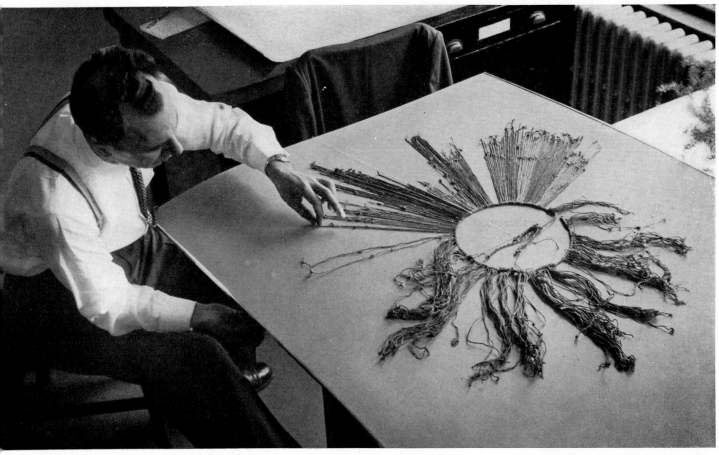

of theocracy which, in other places, was later brought under the control of a rising secular state.

However, we must indicate some other achievements of these astronomer-priests. As they attempted to correlate the accumulating mass of astronomical data — much of it of a numerical nature — they began to speculate about the *numerical* aspects of the motion of the heavenly bodies, hoping thereby to obtain an insight into some aspects of the unity of the celestial Cosmos. One method of speculation consisted of taking astronomical-calendrical numbers and giving them cosmic significance. Another method was to look for a *least common multiple* embracing, for instance, the number of days in lunar months, lunar "years," solar years, Venus years, and so forth. Indeed, the ultimate goal was probably an all-embracing number for all the phenomena of the Universe!

Such a numerology tended to become a study in itself, a study in which certain numbers lost their original astronomical-calendrical significance and appeared abstractly as "sacred" or "evil" numbers that explained and governed the Heavens and the Earth. (Even today, in our modern industrial society, many people still balk at the "evil" number *thirteen* — without knowing why!) The growth of an astronomical-calendrical-cosmological-numerical complex was characteristic of such peoples as the Egyptians, the Babylonians, the Indians, the Chinese, and the Maya, and apparently also the Peruvians. Moreover, many of the "sacred" and "evil" numbers were identical throughout the whole world. And no wonder! For they had grown out of man's observation of the *same motions* of the *same heavenly bodies* of the *same Universe!*

Fig. 32. Mr. De Clemente, in the History Workshop of Long Island University, mounting a *quipu* in preparation for an analysis of its knot system. This *quipu*, one of the larger ones, consists of more than two hundred strings. *Abbott* • Fig. 33. The ancient Maya priests possessed a number of natural and "artificial calendars." A small section of the Dresden Codex (see below) seems to contain numerical vestiges of a former three-thirteen calendar (see Chapter XXI). In the Maya recording system a dot represents the number 1, a line the number 5.

design consisted of rows of rectangular figures. Our preliminary analysis, summarized in the caption to Fig. 34, indicates that this design incorporated basic calendrical data! Since then, Mr. De Clemente and I have begun to study photographs of many additional textiles. Although the study is still in progress, results so far obtained tend to confirm the hypothesis that *some* of these ancient textiles did record calendrical-numerological data. It is not at all surprising that the ancient astronomer-priests should have had woven for themselves valuable textiles *incorporating important secret and sacred knowledge of their profession.* And it is not surprising that they were buried with these sacred keys to the heavens and the hereafter! Thompson

(1950) found, in several graves of Maya priests, what appeared to be traces of ancient codices, indicating the existence of a similar burial custom among the Maya.

Finally, we must mention the extensive friezes on Huaca el Dragón, situated in the Moche Valley. On close inspection the markings and designs of the frieze seem to suggest a calendrical record of some sort.

In this chapter we have pointed out how organized astronomical observations and calendrical constructions arose out of the practical needs of an evolving agricultural society. We have also indicated that the astronomer-priests used their knowledge to achieve a position of power over the rest of the people, thus establishing a kind

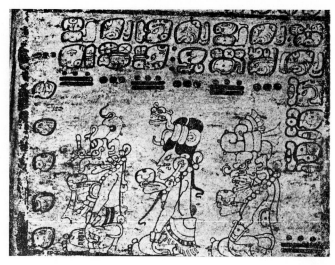

We were to discover still another form of recording device of ancient Peru! While looking through the late Dr. Wagner's valuable collection of Peruvian antiquities in Lima, our attention was attracted by a large Nazca textile whose design consisted of rows of rectangular figures. Our immediate analysis seemed to indicate that this design incorporated basic calendrical data! Due to lack of time it was then impossible to make a systematic study of this textile. Several years later, however, we received a good photograph of it. Mr. De Clemente and I at once began to work on an enlargement of the photograph. The

textile consisted of 14 rows of rectangles. In the sixth row there were 37 rectangles. They were narrower than those of the other rows and each rectangle was surrounded by dark edges.

We were delighted to find the number 37, for it is a number that characterizes certain ancient calendrical systems throughout the world. The number is made up of the sequence 12+12+13. Each of these numbers represents the number of moon-months in a solar year. In this type of month i.e., the solar-lunar month, it takes 29½ days for the moon to make a complete "cycle" in relation to a given position of it to the sun. Twelve of such "months" give a "lunar year" consisting of 354 days. Thus this lunar year is about 11 days short of the *basic* solar year. There are several ways of solving this quandary. The method here used is to start the second "lunar year" right after the first one ends. Then at the end of the second "lunar year", the count is about 22 days behind the second solar year, and at the end of three years the count

is about 33 days behind. To get rid of this great discrepancy a thirteenth moon-month is intercalated. Thus the sequence 12+12+13 is created and the well known ceremonial cycle of 37 is obtained. (Of course after so many cycles a 12+13+13 cycle is intercalated since there are always extra days left over). We had now found a definite record of a calendar that had once existed on the Coast of Peru, the only record of which we then knew! Later on we were to find other references to the 3-13 system in Peru and other parts of ancient Latin America.

But more was in store! When we analyzed the other 13 rows of rectangles, we discovered that basically each one had 28 rectangles, except that the top line had one extra and the bottom line two extra rectangles. After some calculation it became clear that this was another calendar but that it was a siderial-moon calendar, i.e., one in which the number of days are counted between the appearance and reappearance of the moon in a *given stellar* constellation. The number of days is 27⅓. Since people in early stages of society did not use fractions, they created moon-months of either 27 or 28 days. Calendars of both types have been found in India. The significance of our find was that it represented a 28-day month, and a 13-month year thus producing a 364-day year. The extra rectangle of the first row thus produces a 365-day average solar year and the extra two rectangles of the bottom give the 366 days of the leap year.

Not only were we thrilled at having found a second type of calendar on the Coast of Peru, the first one of its kind so far discovered, but that both calendars were on the *same* textile and presented in a way that seemed to indicate *interrelationships* between the two calendrical systems. Thus we are confronted with additional problems, especially since each rectangle has within it one of five distinct designs. Attempts to study the rectangle-design has so far yielded no satisfactory positive results. There are tentative indications that such a calendar *might* have existed among the very early Maya (Willson) and among some of the peoples conquered by the Aztecs (Kosok).

Results so far obtained tend to confirm another hypothesis that other textiles in the museums of New York, Philadelphia and Washington which were examined, contained calendrical-numerical information.

Fig. 34 (left). Calendrical textile. *Kosok.* Fig. 35 (top). Detail of textile. *Kosok.*

VII

The Trip to Trujillo

AFTER having spent several months with Nazcan astronomy, aerial photographs and irrigation statistics, we decided it was time to get out into the field. Just about then Dr. Schaedel informed us that his jeep had been repaired and was ready for us. So we decided to leave Lima for Trujillo at once.

Lima is strategically situated for travel in Peru. Several airplane lines, a network of highways, and even a few railroads, connect Lima with the most important points on the Coast, in the Sierras and also in the Montaña (the jungle region). Outstanding among the roads is the Pan American Highway, which runs along the desert Coast from Ecuador in the north to Chile in the south, a distance of more than 1400 miles. Two other important highways have been built. One runs over the Sierras to Pucalpa, a town on one of the branches of the Amazon; the other, the so-called Central Highway, winds its way in a southeasterly direction through the most populated section of the southern Sierras until it reaches the Bolivian frontier at Lake Titicaca. In addition, there are several shorter

Fig. 1. Bus transportation in the Sierras. *Kosok.*

Fig. 2. Llama trains moving along the Central Highway. *Kosok.*

Fig. 3 (right). Passengers boarding a Central Railway train at La Oroya, mining and smelter city high in the Peruvian Andes. The Central Railway climbs from Lima at sea level to nearly 16,000 feet in less than 100 miles. It is the world's highest standard gauge railway and is a marvel of railway engineering. *Panagra.*
Fig. 4 (far right). These three bridges at different levels indicate how, in order to gain elevation, the trains of the Central Railway wind their way through 65 tunnels and across 67 bridges in the narrow Rimac gorge. The photograph was taken from the Central Highway which, for the most part, parallels the railroad. *Kosok.*

in another four hours, be in the steaming hot jungles of the Montaña which contain the headwaters of the mighty Amazon! These sharp contrasts within a small area are characteristic of most of Peru. They have affected its history enormously. They also make an overwhelming and inspiring appeal to the traveler.

Possibilities of travel by car and bus extend to other countries of South America. As early as 1939 we made a trip from Venezuela through Colombia, Ecuador and Peru to Bolivia, largely by bus! This trip carried us through a wonderland of dramatic, ever-changing landscapes and

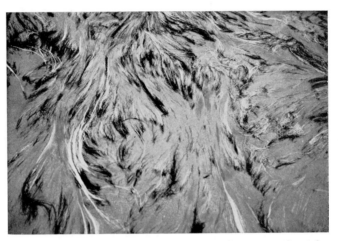

tain people; while on the Coast, where the Spaniards killed or drove out a large portion of the indigenous population, the mixed Indian and white laborers, shopkeepers and professionals predominate. Since the people are all very friendly and open, opportunities for conversation are boundless. In this way, in the course of time, one obtains innumerable snapshots, figuratively speaking, of various aspects of the life of the people.

At times we also used the local Faucett planes, which connect the important towns along the Coast with one another and with some of the main mountain centers. These planes were inestimable time-savers, but they also had an additional value for us. They flew at fairly low altitudes, enabling us to spot many significant ruins.

Our 300-mile bus trip to Trujillo took us about ten hours. Traveling along the Coast is not as exciting as riding through mountainous regions. But it has its own charm. Here are only two kinds of landscape: the endless, ever-present desert — flat, hilly or undulating, but always the same desert — and the beautiful, green, irrigated valleys. Entrance from the bleak, arid regions into these valleys is like the transition from death to life — man-made life. As the bus — this capsule of human cargo — whips across the desert from valley to valley, one feels as though projected in a spaceship through a vacuum — from one center of life to another.

Trujillo, which lies in the valley of Moche (called Chimor by the ancients and Santa Catalina by the Spaniards), is an old colonial town established by Pizarro in 1535, immediately after the conquest of Peru. It was built adjacent to the ruins of the much larger ChanChan, the former capital of the Chimú Empire, and like Chan-Chan in ancient times, was the leading city on the Northwest Coast in colonial times. For a long time, Trujillo remained a small fortified city; only during the last century did it, like other cities in the country, break down its walls and spread out rapidly. Today it numbers about fifty thousand inhabitants and is the third largest city in Peru. Its nearest rival in size on the Northwest Coast is Chiclayo, further north in the Lambayeque Valley. After the Wars of Independence, Trujillo became the capital of the Departamento de La Libertad, and it was here that Simon Bolivar — the George Washington of South America — founded the present University of Trujillo. The latter has grown steadily and has made Trujillo the leading cultural center of Northwest Peru, both Coast and Sierra.

In Trujillo we were warmly greeted by Dr. Schaedel and his sweet and hospitable wife who invited us to stay

Fig. 5. The fishing village and summer resort of Ancón with its ancient graveyards nearby. The Pan American Highway is at the right. *Kosok* • Fig. 6. Seaweed pattern on the beach at Ancón. *Kosok* • Fig. 7 (margins). Ancón mummies and designs. *Reiss and Stübel.*

roads that leave the coastal Pan American Highway and lead up into the high Sierras and, in some cases, down into the Montaña. Add to this the numerous spurs that lead out from these roads and we see that Peru has an extensive network of roads that connects deserts, mountains and jungles.

How closely these three zones have been brought together by the modern road system is dramatically indicated by the following example. One can leave Lima, on the desert Coast of Peru, and travel by car over the Central Highway, which steadily winds up the steep sides of the towering Andes, until one reaches the glaciers and snowbanks of the Continental Divide at an altitude of 16,000 feet — all in less than four hours! Then, descending the precipitous valleys to the east of the Divide, one can,

climatic zones ranging from the arctic to the tropic. Since then there has been an extension of roads and a corresponding increase of travel facilities.

Peru today has a large number of bus lines with low fares and steadily improving service. The buses do not compare in size or luxury with those in the United States, for they are built and equipped to fit the low incomes of the Peruvian people. Our main objection to them, however, was that they were too small and the seats too close together. As a result, Michael and I were anxious to get the front seats where we could stretch our long legs.

Bus travel is always interesting. One continually encounters people of different classes — with the exception of the upper class. In the Sierras, the passengers are mainly Indians, direct descendants of the ancient moun-

at their home. There we met many of their interesting friends. As soon as we were settled, we began our work. Dr. Schaedel took us over to the headquarters of his Institute of Anthropology, at the University of Trujillo, where he was training students in anthropology and archaeology. Dr. Schaedel's project was very commendable, for its purpose was to enable many of Peru's young people to better understand and reconstruct their own heritage. The Institute was the only one of its kind in Peru and had been organized by Dr. Schaedel the previous year.

At the Institute, we met the staff members and some students actively engaged in archaeological field work. Among these were Señor Luis Guttiérrez, the secretary of the Institute, formerly curator of the Rafael Larco Herrera Museum at Chiclín in the neighboring Chicama Valley; José Manuel Cacho, the draftsman of the Institute; and Emilio González, a student who spoke and wrote English fluently. Each aided our work in various ways.

Antonio Rodríguez SuySuy, Dr. Schaedel's leading student, was of greatest aid to us on a number of field trips. He is a native of the old Indian village of Moche, in the valley of the same name, and, as his maternal family name, SuySuy, indicates, is partly of old Mochica-Chimú stock. Indeed, Soriano Infante discovered that SuySuy

was the name of the *caciques* (local rulers) of Huambacho in the Nepeña Valley. Antonio developed so rapidly in his studies that at present he is carrying on independent investigation of ruins as well as making ground plans of sites. On the basis of these plans, plaster models of pyramids have been made at Long Island University by Mr. John Storck (see Chapters I, IX and XV).

We met Dr. Schaedel's friend, Don José Eulogio Garrido, another resident of Moche who, with Señor Rodríguez SuySuy, accompanied us on several of our trips. A highly cultured gentleman, Señor Garrido knows many parts of Peru extremely well, has written on many facets of Peruvian life, and possesses a penetrating understanding and an intimate and sincere feeling for the life and customs of his people. We enjoyed his excellent sense of humor and his sharp, lively wit. Although over sixty, he is vigorous, and on expeditions tears up and down hills like a young man.

Having established ourselves in Trujillo, we brought our maps, photographs and other material to the Institute. We had many fruitful discussions with Dr. Schaedel which ranged from basic geographic factors to details of cultural sequences. Our general approach to these problems was so similar that we found that we were able to

complement each other's thoughts and activities to a great degree. This combination of efforts yielded an improved manuscript and an improved set of maps. As already stated, Dr. Schaedel also contributed generously in the preparation of the present volume.

Our first practical move was to devise a method of numbering the ruins which we already had entered on our three large Army maps in such a way that we could record additionally discovered ruin sites on the maps later on without disturbing the established numbering

Fig. 8 (left). The famous "Pasamayo" — a spectacular stretch of the Pan American Highway between Ancón and Chancay. In this typical scene, southbound vehicles are lined up waiting for the road crews to clear the highway, which is constantly being covered by sand that slides down from the steep hills above. *Kosok.* • Fig. 9 (center). Aerial photograph showing the Pan American Highway passing through a section of the coastal desert. The short parallel grooves leading up to the highway are the markings left when bulldozers pushed soil to the highway in order to provide material for the roadbed. *Kosok.* • Fig. 10 (lower right). The Pan American Highway winding along the coastal hills just to the north of the Ocoña Valley, southern Peru. *Kosok.* • Fig. 11 (upper right). The Pan American Highway here cuts into the side of the coastal plateau in southern Peru. Note the waves breaking against the bottom of the plateau. *Kosok.* On the relatively level Coast, the Pan American Highway follows in general the route of the ancient north-south trunk highway. In the Sierras, however, where modern roads cannot exceed a certain gradient, a factor of no significance in building ancient "roads," the routes of the former rarely follow the latter.

Fig. 12 (above). This unusually large sand dune, called Cerro PurPur, lies north of the vegetation zone (black area at top of photograph) of the Virú Valley. This kind of large sand dune, unique for most of the Coast of Peru, is found mainly in the extensive Sechura Desert, much further north. The black line at the bottom left of the photograph is the Pan American Highway. *Servicio, unnumbered series.*
Fig. 13 (below). View of Salaverry, the main port for the Moche and Chicama Valleys. Note the ocean breakers at the bottom of the photograph, and at the top and right, the surrounding desert plateau. *Kosok.*

system. Our next step was to work out a uniform system of symbols for the different classes of ruins. Finally, we decided to add a comprehensive "key" to each map, with the name, pertinent archaeological data, and bibliographical references for each site. This meant a great deal of tedious work, but when completed these maps would be a kind of guide to prehistoric Peru.

While we were engaged in these various activities, Michael was given a special job. We decided that it was necessary that the maps be traced in preparation for future publication. When the tracings were completed, we left two copies, reproduced by the Ozalid process, in Trujillo with Dr. Schaedel and the Institute. Later, as

we located new canals and new sites from aerial photographs or from our field trips, they too were entered on the maps. These will be published in our main study.

In order to assist in dating by cultural periods those sites that we were planning to visit, it was decided that Michael and I should make surface potsherd collections wherever possible. As it turned out later, some mounds and pyramids (*huacas*) yielded few if any potsherds. The latter were generally found in previously excavated cemeteries often situated at a short distance from the pyramids. In all, we made between sixty and seventy such collections and deposited them at the Institute at Trujillo, where they are at present.

Our project, which in 1940-41 had begun merely as one of locating and mapping ancient irrigation systems, had by now grown into one that included locating all major archaeological sites, associating them where possible with the irrigation systems, "dating" additional archaeological sites by means of surface collections, and compiling a list of bibliographical references to the known sites. At first we did not realize how much work this involved. But we soon became aware of the fact that we had to work at top speed to complete our survey project within the allotted time.

A word about making surface collections of pottery. Excavation of ancient graves for stratigraphic purposes as well as to see what articles the ancients cherished is always intriguing and highly informative. But that was not our field of activity; it was that of professional archaeologists. However, the latter have made only a very small number of such excavations. Most of them have been made by amateur or professional grave robbers, the so-called *huaqueros*. Excavating graves without permission is illegal in Peru. But since there are no law enforcement officers to prevent grave robbing, it is a widespread profession — sometimes even organized in syndicates. Indeed, a special instrument has been invented — a long, pointed metal rod four or more feet long with a handle at one end — which the *huaqueros* push gently into the ground wherever there is a suspicious depression. Some of the *huaqueros* have developed such skill that they can often tell, by the way the rod feels when it strikes an object as well as by examining the point, whether they have hit metal, cloth, ceramics or only dirt and stones.

These *huaqueros* have operated along the whole Coast for centuries and have dug up many of the tens of millions of graves that must have accumulated during the last several thousands of years. They are such an integral part of the social scene of the Coast that a popular song has even been written about them.

It has been said that the only difference between archaeologists and *huaqueros* lies in the fact that the former dig in the daytime and the latter at night! Yet the difference is much more vital. The archaeologists keep a careful, written account of the contents of the graves, as well as of their stratigraphy, to provide a permanent scientific record of the work accomplished. But the *huaqueros* destroy much scientifically valuable material as a result of their methods of excavation. Moreover, since the *hua-*

queros sell their goods surreptitiously, they fear to disclose the nature and place of origin of the articles. Summing up the situation, Dr. Julio Tello once remarked that more than 95 per cent of the materials in museums and private collections have no "birth certificates." These undocumented objects are useful for demonstrating the different culture *periods* and art *styles*. But until sufficient scientific excavations are carried out that can relate the new material to the old, most of the latter will possess more aesthetic than scientific value.

Since we were not planning excavations — though we

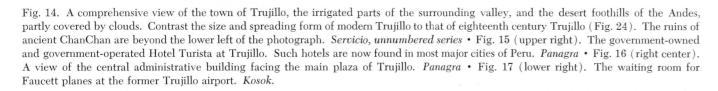

Fig. 14. A comprehensive view of the town of Trujillo, the irrigated parts of the surrounding valley, and the desert foothills of the Andes, partly covered by clouds. Contrast the size and spreading form of modern Trujillo to that of eighteenth century Trujillo (Fig. 24). The ruins of ancient ChanChan are beyond the lower left of the photograph. *Servicio, unnumbered series* • Fig. 15 (upper right). The government-owned and government-operated Hotel Turista at Trujillo. Such hotels are now found in most major cities of Peru. *Panagra* • Fig. 16 (right center). A view of the central administrative building facing the main plaza of Trujillo. *Panagra* • Fig. 17 (lower right). The waiting room for Faucett planes at the former Trujillo airport. *Kosok.*

67

Fig. 18. Dr. Richard Schaedel in his office at the Institute of Anthropology at the University of Trujillo. *Alvarez.*

The task of looking for surface potsherds is often thrilling. The collector does not pick up everything; for then trucks would often be needed to carry off the materials from one site alone. One has to be selective and pick out only those fragments of pots that seem most significant. This work, of course, requires knowledge of the various styles of ceramics and their developmental sequence (see Chapter VIII).

To make pottery more attractive, various devices were used by the ancients — devices which help us to classify the period and general region of origin. One very effective, yet relatively simple, method of applying adornment consisted of lightly "spanking" the pot, while still wet, with a paddle, on the surface of which a design had been carved. It may be pointed out that the potter's wheel (or for that matter any other type of wheel) had never been developed by the prehistoric inhabitants of the Americas. Therefore all pots were "hand made."

Pressed ware was a modification of paddled ware. In this type of pottery the design was pressed on the still wet clay. Sharpened reeds were often used as styli to incise patterns, while cut ends of reeds were pressed on the wet clay to produce small circles. Sometimes even an ornament in the form of an animal head or a human figure was made at the edge of the pot. Most of these decorative devices seem to have been applied to ordinary everyday utensils, usually referred to as utility ware. It appears that most of the common people of the past were buried with such pots — sometimes still covered with the soot from the fire — for they have been found plentifully in the cemeteries along the entire Coast. Similarly, the common people appear to have been interred in their everyday clothes — the only ones they possessed.

In contrast, the priests, rulers, and officials were buried with more elaborately prepared water jugs (*huacos*) apparently made only for ceremonial and burial purposes. Here the professional artisan — and in many cases artist — had full rein in expressing his abilities. While he utilized the techniques already described, he also employed *painting* and *relief modeling.* The painting was of two types, positive or negative. Negative painting is essentially what a child does when he draws a design on an Easter egg with a wax pencil before dyeing it, so that the design retains the original white of the egg against a colored background. In positive or "normal" painting the design is of course applied directly.

In Nazca and related areas, the pot decorators used a

Fig. 19. A student of the Institute of Anthropology. Note the aerial mosaic of several valleys hanging on the wall. *Alvarez.*

whole palette of beautiful colors — and the designs were either abstractions (later period) or intricate compositions of highly stylized cat-demons and other animals, in a way reminiscent of similar priest-dominated and demon-infested cultures of Tiahuanaco, Chavín and the Maya.

In northern Peru, the emphasis was placed upon developing novel forms rather than new colors in ceremonial water jugs. Here the unique *stirrup spout* became very popular among the Early Chimús (Mochicas). Here we also found the development of excellent realistic forms comprising plants, animals, houses, boats, humans (including some pornographica). This trend culminated in the admirable *portrait huacos, the finest ceramic product of the Americas.*

In baking the clay in open hearth ovens, the Mochicas usually produced reddish pots on which they painted various designs, generally in brownish-yellow hues. This is the method used in the finest Mochica ware. But among the Late Chimús, pots were generally baked in closed ovens where lack of oxygen produced the typical Chimú blackware. Molds are known from very early Cupisnique times, but they were apparently used to the greatest extent by the Late Chimús on the Northwest Coast when a kind of "mass production" of various goods began.

watched some — we picked up broken pots where we found them. This we did either in excavated graveyards or in ancient garbage dumps (*basurales*). Such work may appear to be rather gruesome, but the scientific value of the results obtained overrides one's sensitivities about the dead of the distant past.

The importance of ancient pots lies in the fact that archaeologists have discovered that changes in cultural forms are reflected in changes in pottery styles. Therefore, pottery has not only been a convenient but also a basic index for a relative dating of the period that produced it. Potsherds, if large enough, are almost as useful archaeologically as whole pots since they likewise give material, shape and design.

Since the chronological sequence of pottery types found on the Coast of Peru has been fairly well established, it is frequently possible to identify the cultural phases represented at a given prehistoric site by a careful examination of the *potsherds found on the surface.* This is always true for the last occupation or occupations of the site. Excavations are, however, sometimes necessary to establish the earlier occupations. But by means of simple surface collections one obtains, with a minimum of time and expense, certain key information about a site.

In almost every valley, as well as for each period, characteristic shapes, colors and techniques evolved. When one realizes the multiplicity of possible combinations that this situation produced, one may more readily understand the complex problem of potsherd analysis. One may also perceive why the systematic study of pottery has become such an essential technique for establishing relative chronology and regional distribution of cultures. In addition, modern methods of analysis and forms of statistical treatment of potsherds have become so sophisticated that many subtle changes and outside influences in a culture, which would otherwise escape attention, can be detected.

Picking up potsherds turned out to be a time-consuming, albeit exciting, job. But once we caught the "fever" it was difficult to resist stopping at every graveyard to

hunt for potsherds. The fever sometimes became so bad that while driving in a jeep we often had to make a resolution: "No matter what we see we won't stop!" Sometimes it worked; but sometimes it didn't! For after all we were human! To ride in a jeep, past a nice, ancient, partly-excavated graveyard, or a garbage dump well-stocked with much interesting material, and not to stop, was just too much to expect of us. So we would jump out and say: "Five minutes and no more!" But sometimes we ran into interesting prospects — then the five minutes stretched on and on until we lost all sense of time.

Whenever we came upon a ruin, we would naturally enter its position on our maps and walk around it so

as to be able to write a short description. If we encountered potsherds, it became almost impossible to refrain from looking for significant types. After a time our eyes became trained and we could detect minute variations at a glance. Our SCIPA mechanic, Señor Portugal, had such sharp eyes that he could often detect unusual kinds of ceramics from our moving jeep!

An outsider must have found it strange indeed to watch three or four people wandering around apparently aimlessly, with eyes intently cast upon the ground, occasionally picking up an object and then throwing it away or putting it into a paper bag. On one occasion, at one of the ancient graveyards, we saw a gentle young lady in search of treasures excitedly throwing around thigh bones, skulls, potsherds, and other rubbish. Her actions were not surprising, for grave robbing is merely a specialized, ghoulish form of treasure hunting. And everyone has a bit of the treasure hunter hidden away somewhere!

Before we left Trujillo for our field work, we were intrigued by an interesting problem, which, while not germane to our main study, nevertheless could not be ignored. One day a member of the Institute informed us that he had heard of an eighty-year old woman from the town of Eten in the lower Lambayeque Valley who still

knew some of the ancient Mochica language! We were astounded by this information, for we had been assured repeatedly that this ancient language of the Northwest Coast had by now become extinct. We immediately made arrangements to visit Señora Manuela Millones de Carrillo.

Mochica was the most important coastal language of Northwest Peru at the time of the Spanish conquest and was used as a missionary language by some of the Catholic priests. In fact, a grammar of the Mochica language was printed in 1644 by the Peruvian priest, Fernando de la Carrera, although a promised dictionary by the same author never appeared in print. There are fairly definite indications that it was written, though the manuscript has not been located so far — if it still exists! Middendorf (1892) published a revised version of the grammar in German and added a large number of words which he was able to collect in the Eten-Monsefú region of the Department of Lambayeque. By then the language apparently had disappeared everywhere but in this small area! Short vocabularies were also published later by Villareal (1921) and by Rafael Larco Hoyle (1939). In 1948 Jorge Zevallos Quiñones published a short, interesting account of the grammars and dictionaries that were reported to have been written during the sixteenth and

Fig. 20. A Mochica grave, containing water jugs (*huacos*) and remains of a body, excavated in the Chicama Valley by the Larco brothers. Water jugs, found in all graves, symbolize the life-giving properties of water in a desert economy. *Kosok* • Fig. 21. Examining a water jug that has just been excavated. *Kosok* • Fig. 22. Two charming laboratory workers in the Chiclín Museum, directed by the Larco brothers, trying to fit together the parts of broken water jugs. *Kosok* • Fig. 23 (upper right margin). Michael with a collection of bones. *Kosok*.

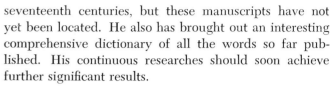

seventeenth centuries, but these manuscripts have not yet been located. He also has brought out an interesting comprehensive dictionary of all the words so far published. His continuous researches should soon achieve further significant results.

Accompanied by Antonio Rodríguez SuySuy, we visited the old Mochica lady who was temporarily staying with her married daughter, the owner of a small hat shop in Trujillo. The daughter told us that, while a child, she herself had always spoken Mochica with her parents, but by now had completely forgotten it. The mother, a lively and intelligent woman, was at first hesitant. She seemed to be unable to remember any of the language. But after the conversation got under way she began to recall some words. We tried to obtain at least the words dealing with family relationships, for we thought we might thus clear up the moot problem of the kinship system among the ancient Mochicas. But she could not remember enough significant terms to enable us to reconstruct the system.

In the course of several hours of questioning, she finally managed to recall about fifty words with their Spanish equivalents. Señor Rodríguez did much of the interrogation and took down the words. These are reproduced in the Appendix as List No. 1, with Spanish and English equivalents. Unfortunately, few new words were added to the known vocabulary of the language. But it is interesting to note that the forms of the words we obtained corresponded very closely to those given by Carrera some three hundred years ago!

Fig. 24. This unique eighteenth century map of the lower Moche Valley – *Valle del Chimo* as it was then called – was made by Michael Feyjóo, who also published a small informative volume on this and neighboring valleys (see Bibliography). Note the fortified nature and the small size – though given on an exaggerated scale – of Trujillo. Note also that only one main irrigation canal is shown, the Mochica – still so named and still in use today – which splits into three branches, thereby furnishing water for the lands surrounding Trujillo. The Mochica Canal once brought water to parts of the ancient capital of ChanChan. The map gives the site (incorrectly placed) of the latter, which Feyjóo calls "ruined houses of the Chino [Chimú] ruler," as well as the nearby Huaca Toledo. The two ancient canals, Vinchançao and Moro, which ran above the Mochica, had already been abandoned when the map was made. The two little ponds received their water from the drainage of the irrigated fields further up the valley and distributed it by means of the tail-like canals to the fields below. The lower pond we found to be still functioning today.

VIII

What Do We Know of Peruvian Pre-History?

THE SPANIARDS knew that many different peoples with ancient and extensive cultures had existed along the Coast long before the Incas came down from the mountains as conquerors. However, any sequence of development of the cultures of even the major valleys was unknown. Moreover, most of the Spaniards who studied the Indians strove to extirpate forms of religion and culture that still survived from the past. The problem of reconstructing the ancient cultures and their sequences was beyond the interest and abilities of the colonizers.

Max Uhle (1856-1944), the father of Peruvian archaeology, was the first to distinguish, in the Moche-Chicama area, between an *Early* Chimú (Mochica) Period and a *Late* Chimú Period, a distinction which became the key to establishing the culture sequences of the past. Uhle also showed that a rather ill-defined *Middle* Period existed between the two Chimú periods, in which, among other things, strong highland Tiahuanaco influence was present. Uhle made this classification largely on the basis of his excavations at the Huaca del Sol and the Huaca de la Luna in the Moche Valley and the resultant study of the excavated ceramics (1913).

Additions and modifications have since been made in

Fig. 1. An oblique aerial photograph of the remains of the main walled compounds that once comprised the ancient city of Chan-Chan, near the present city of Trujillo in the Moche Valley. *Shippee-Johnson* • NOTE: The above line-cut is that of a detail from ChanChan. The decorative designs used throughout this chapter are from adobe reliefs found on structures in or near ChanChan.

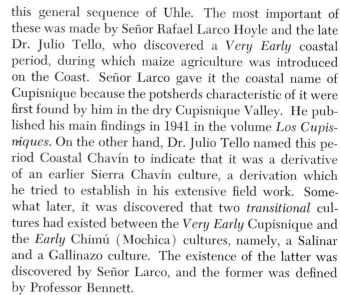

CHART I

Dates	Economic-Political Periods	Inferred Social Structures	Buildings	Cultural-Technological Designation	Cultural Sequence
Pre-3000 BC	**I. Pre Agricultural Stage** A. HUNTING—beginnings unknown. Chipped stones found, date unknown. Parallel to fishing and early agricultural stages.	Clans-? Hunting Bands	Temporary cave shelters	Pre-ceramic	Pre-agricultural
	B. FISHING—parallel to hunting but not related.	Settled village structures	Semi-subterrainean structures in coves along coast	Pre-agricultural Ceramic	Pre-agricultural
1000 BC	**II. Intra-Valley Agricultural Development** (Maize; Bean) A. FORMATIVE PERIOD—probably maize-raising settlers came from Sierras where they had already practiced elements of irrigation and spread into the coastal valleys.	Priest-dominated. Small communities. Village federation and proto-class structure	Mounds (burial?) and small ceremonial pyramids began (raised platforms?)	Cupisnique (Coastal Chavín) Salinar Gallinazo	Very Early Very early—transitional
	B. CULMINATION PERIOD— possibly the valleys have a maximum or near maximum in irrigated areas and in population size.	Culmination of Priest-dominated societies and beginning of growth of secular power. Class societies forming into a valley Federation?	Large Pyramids— by enlarging earlier smaller pyramids or by building new ones. Pyramid clusters evolve and/or previous clusters increase in size	Mochica or Early Chimú Highest quality of realistic ceramics	Early
750 AD	**III. Inter-Valley Economic-Political Forms** A. FORMATIVE PERIOD. During this period various valleys that are internally well populated and politically well organized make raids or more regular conquests on neighboring valleys. Invasions and intrusions from the Sierras also appear.	Secular power dominates? —or secular directed theocracy. Mochica Empire includes Chicama, Moche; extends to Virú, Chao, Santa and Nepeña Valley in south and probably parts of Jequetepeque in north	Walled compounds alone or in conjunction with pyramids	Coastal Tiahuanaco, coming from Sierra, gradually moves up the whole coast from the south and eventually succeeds the Mochica Empire and culture	Middle
1250 AD	B. CULMINATION PERIOD. The culmination along the northwest coast consists of the multi-valley (1) Chimú Empire (c.1250-1470) attempts at extension along central coast are only temporarily successful. (2) Inca Empire from Sierras, conquers whole coast, but with limited hold on coastal valleys (1470-1532).	A developed secular state. A central ruler, the Great Chimú with a standing army and administrative officials in various valleys. A developed class society. Priesthood plays secondary role— or has been absorbed by secular ruling powers.	Large walled compounds predominate as centers of power. Pyramids within walls are small. Large pyramids (from past?) are outside walls.	Late Chimú Mass produced ceramics, and gold and silver goods. Best coastal artisans are brought to Chan Chan	Late
1532 AD	**IV. Intercontinental Spanish**			Colonial	Colonial

this general sequence of Uhle. The most important of these was made by Señor Rafael Larco Hoyle and the late Dr. Julio Tello, who discovered a *Very Early* coastal period, during which maize agriculture was introduced on the Coast. Señor Larco gave it the coastal name of Cupisnique because the potsherds characteristic of it were first found by him in the dry Cupisnique Valley. He published his main findings in 1941 in the volume *Los Cupisniques.* On the other hand, Dr. Julio Tello named this period Coastal Chavín to indicate that it was a derivative of an earlier Sierra Chavín culture, a derivation which he tried to establish in his extensive field work. Somewhat later, it was discovered that two *transitional* cultures had existed between the *Very Early* Cupisnique and the *Early* Chimú (Mochica) cultures, namely, a Salinar and a Gallinazo culture. The existence of the latter was discovered by Señor Larco, and the former was defined by Professor Bennett.

A summary of the most recent refinements dealing with culture sequences was presented in several charts, together with much descriptive material, in a collective study made by leading Peruvianists. It was published in 1948 in a volume entitled *Reappraisal of Peruvian Archaeology.* Some of the main aspects of these cultural sequences are embodied in part of Chart I of this chapter. Without questioning the archaeological validity of these cultural sequences, it will be noted that their general chronological classification consists of a mixture of economic, technological, social, political and cultural categories, which has definite shortcomings *from the point of view of our study.*

It thus became necessary to establish some sort of chronological classification based on the nature and expansion of the productive process of the irrigated areas. Such a classification would have to take into account the fact that on the desert Coast each valley oasis became a kind of *geographic framework* within which the economy, government and culture of that oasis at first evolved. Later, some of these oases were united into larger economic and political complexes by federation and conquest. As a result of such an approach, it soon became obvious that the whole coastal sequence could be divided into several main periods:

I. Pre-Agricultural Hunting and Fishing Settlements. (These were partly parallel developments and often continued through the ensuing periods).

II. Organized *Intra*-valley Agricultural Development.

   A. *Formative Period.* The gradual settling of each

valley by *agricultural* tribes mainly from the Sierras, leading eventually to —

B. *Period of Culmination.* Extensive economic and political growth within each valley. This, when it reached a certain maximum, became the basis for —

III. Organized *Inter*-valley Economic and Political Expansion. (This represents a *qualitatively* different kind of expansion than *intra*-valley expansion).

A. *Formative Period.* The relatively long period of conflicting expansions of various coastal and mountain peoples and kingdoms, which eventually led to—

B. *Period of Culmination.* Establishment of the coastal intervalley Chimú Empire and finally the creation of an all-embracing Inca Empire. This was then superseded by —

IV. The Spanish Intercontinental Sea Empire.

This general classification has been worked out in considerably greater detail, and will be published as a chapter in *Water and Life.* Its main elements are presented here merely to clarify some of the material in the present volume.

To avoid misunderstandings, it must be noted that there are no sharp dividing lines between the various periods and sub-periods. In applying the various categories of our classification, it is important to distinguish *incidentals* from *essentials* in the politico-economic structure of each valley. Therefore, while a valley was in stage II B, (culmination of *intra*-valley expansion), *incidental sporadic* raids into neighboring valleys undoubtedly took place. But only when *systematic* attempts at organized conquest of neighboring valleys developed and became an *essential* aspect of the economy and politics of the conquering valley, can we put this valley in stage III A, (organized *inter*-valley expansion).

In conclusion, it must be borne in mind that similar stages of economic-political development, as outlined above, evolved *at different times and at different rates in different valleys.* Thus, some valleys entered their *initial agricultural stage* II A earlier than others. Likewise, some reached their *culmination stage* II B more rapidly than others. In fact, some may have reached certain aspects of this II B stage only when they were conquered by other valleys already in the more advanced III A or even III B stage. Moreover, some of the valleys, having achieved stage II B, never really reached stage III A. Finally, on the Coast it was only the Chimús who reached stage III B. The Rimac Confederacy and the Huarco Confederacy (see Chapter IV) were probably in stage

CHART II

Year	Lambayeque	Jequetepeque	Moche-Chicama	Inca	Europe
900					
925					
950				End of Classical Tiahuanaco in the Sierras—ca. 1000?	ROMANESQUE
975					
1000			Coastal Tiahuanaco		
1025	1. Naymlap and Ceterni came by boat from Equador region				
1050	2. Cium and Zolsdoni sons				1066 Norman Conquest
1075	3. Llapchillulli (Jayanca) Cala (Tucume) Escuñain (Lambayeque) Nor (Cinto) Cuntipullec (Collique) others (to other parts)				1096 First Crusade
1100	4. Mascuy				
1125	5. Cuntipallec		COASTAL TIAHUANACO PERIOD ca. 1000-1250?	Tiahuanaco influence in Sierra	
1150	6. Allascunto				
1175	7. Nofan-Nech				
1200	8. Mulumuslan				
1225	9. Llamecoll		1. Taycanamu—from north (Chimorcopac)		GOTHIC
1250	10. Lanipatcum		2. Gaucricaur—conquers the entire Moche Valley	1. Manco Capac	
1275	11. Acunta		3. Nançenpinco—conquers Pacasmayo to Santa (Empire of 6 valleys)	2. Sinchi Roca	
1300	12. Fempellec (Killed) (30 days Flood)	Pacatnamu? Set up by Chimús?	4. ? seven descendents	3. Lloque Yupanqui	
1325	Interregnum (how long?) "for many days" (Cabello)	Chimú attacks here or after?	5. ?	4. Mayta Capac	
1350			6. ?	5. Capac Yupanqui	Hundred Years War
1375	Was this due to Chimú Interference?		7. ?	6. Inca Roca — 7. Yahuar Roca	
1400	1. Pongmassa set up by Chimús		8. ?	Conquest to Pativilca and forays to central and south coasts — 8. Viracocha	
1425	2. Palesmassa		9. ?		
1450	3. Oxa (hears of Incas in Cajamarca)		10. Minchançamon— controls 600 miles of coast. Conquered by Incas	9. Pachacutec (1438-71) begins extensive conquests (Tupac takes command 1463)	War of Roses
1475	4. Llempisan (Independent ruler or set up by Incas?) 5. Chullumpisan 6. Cipromarca 7. Fallenpisan (Efquempisan) brothers		11. Chumun Caur set up by Incas	10. Tupac Yupanqui conquers Chimús (1471-93)	RENAISSANCE / Spain Unified
1500			12. Guaman Chumu Incas break up Chimú lands — 13. Ancocoyuch	11. Huayna Capac culmination (1493-1525) of Inca Empire	
1525	8. Fefuinpisan—murdered 3 brothers (Xecfuinpisan) —became Christian		14. Chimo Cajacimcim baptized as Don Martin	12. Huascar/Atahualpa civil war (1525-32)	
1550	9. Efuichumbi		15. ? 16. ? 17. ? 18. ? 19. ?		Spaniards Conquer Peru
1575					
1600			20. Don Antonio Chayhuac		

Sources
Lambayeque — Cabello; Rubiños

Sources
Chimú — Anonymous Trujillano (1614); Feyjóo; Pacheco

Sources
Inca — Cabello; Sarmiento (Dates in parentheses are those of Cabello)

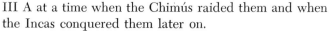

The Anonymous Trujillano (ca. 1614)

The following is a translation of pp. 2 and 3 of Chapter I of a history of Trujillo by an unknown author. The manuscript was found and published by Rubens Vargas Ugarte in the Revista Historica, 1936. *Page 1 could not be located; the missing words at the beginning of page 2 were eaten by mice! The manuscript itself appears to have since been destroyed by the fire that swept the National Library in Lima some years ago. The translation, as well as the other ones in this chapter, have been made as literal as possible, and retain practically all of the original punctuation. As a result, the original flavor of the manuscript has been maintained together with the ambiguity of certain passages, which in the usual "free" translations often take on a definiteness and clearness not inherent in the original manuscript. The only change that has been made was to capitalize uniformly the names of all the rulers.*

. . . . . . in this house remained for the period of a year, performing . . . . the said ceremonies and of the communication that he had with . . . . . Indians whom he was conquering he learned the language, who obeyed him and gave him their daughters. From then on he came to take the name of Chimor Capac [Chimor = Moche (Valley); capac = powerful, ruler].

It is not known whence came this . . . . except that he gave them to understand that a great lord . . . . *hera* [?] had sent him to govern this land *. . . . . .* from the other part of the sea. The yellow powders which he used in his ceremonies and the cotton cloths which he wore to cover his shameful parts are well known in these lands and the balsa of logs is used on the coast of Payta and Tumbez from which it is presumed that this Indian did not come from a very distant region.

This Taycanamo had a son who was called Guacricaur, who acquiring more power than his father, conquered the Indians and leaders of this valley, and he had a son who was called Ñançenpinco who was engaged in conquering the valley up to the *cabezadas* [the beginnings] of the Sierra and at the same time overran the Coast [to the south] as far as the *pueblo* named Mayao, where the village of Santa now stands, eighteen leagues [48 miles; actually the distance is about 64 miles measured in a straight line] from this city [Trujillo], and for the lower part [to the north] the valley of Chicama *as far as* [editor's italics] Pacasmayo [a former name for Jequetepeque] close to [!] the village of Saña, twenty-four leagues [72 miles] from this city. [From the above it is clear that Ñançenpinco never conquered Zaña. Actually Zaña is about 83 miles from Trujillo. It is on the northern edge of the cultivated lands of the Jequetepeque which are about 72 miles from Trujillo.]

After this Guacricaur [,] seven *caciques* [rulers] consecutively succeeded him, his sons and descendants, up to (*hasta*) Minchançaman [It is not too clear whether the seventh *was* Minchançaman or whether Minchançaman followed *after* the seventh] which was conqueror of the *pueblos* [*pueblo* can mean nation, land, people, town, or village] of this Coast up to Carbaillo [Chillon, near Lima] and Tumbez [near the Ecuadorian border] which is more than two hundred leagues [600 miles] of land, in whose time came down from Cuzco the Ynca called Topa Yupangui with a great force of arms and men; who subjected all the *llanos* [coastal plains] and made himself *señor* [lord, or ruler] of all his [Minchançaman's] land, killing a great number of Indians and taking away their gold, silver and other things that they had and he caused great destruc-

tion especially in this valley of Chimor [Moche] because of the resistance which he encountered and he took with him to Cuzco the said Minchançaman, where he married him to one of his daughters and as he had heard that said Minchançaman had a son called Chumuncaur who was in the valley of Gaura [Huaura; see Chapter XXIII] with his mother who was a *señora* [ruler] of this valley [and] called Chanquirguanguan [;] he [the Inca] had him [Chumuncaur] summoned and ordered him to go to govern this land in place of his father Minchançaman (who died in Cuzco) [this phrase crossed out in the ms.] with the order that he pay him [the Inca] tribute which they [he and his descendants] did until the coming of the Spaniards and they sent him each year to Cuzco silver, clothing and other things and women, daughters of the *caciques* [local rulers].

This Chumuncaur had a son called Guamanchumo who governed the whole land and at his death Ancocuyuch, his son, succeeded him in whose time the *pueblos* of the above-mentioned Coast were already divided into *cacicazgos* [apparently local administrative and economic (?) units headed by *caciques*] because as the sons [of the Chimú?] were multiplying they made *particiones* [divisions of land?] among themselves and they gave to each *pueblo* its head with the approval and consent of the Ynga of whom they were subjects. [The meaning of the above sentence is somewhat obscure. The translation appears historically the most logical one. It is obvious that such a breaking up of political and economic power of the Grand Chimú would be to the interest of both the Incas and the younger brothers of the Chimú "ruler."]

As a result of the death of Ancocoyuch [,] his brother, Cajaçimçim, took over the power and the lordship (*señorío*) of this valley of Chimor, in whose time the Spaniards entered this land and subjected all of its *caciques* [local rulers] and *señores* [lords], from Tumbez which was the first port where they disembarked in the year one thousand five hundred and thirteen [actually 1528]. The said Cajaçimçim became a Christian and took the name of Don Martin and when he died they interred him in the church of Santa Ana of this city from which the very next night the Indians took the body from the sepulchre and carried it to its interment according to the rites of their ancestors, and it has not been possible to discover where it is.

After this Cajaçimçim, six Christian *caciques*, descendants of the previous ones have succeeded up to Don Antonio Chayguar who is living today and is *cacique* of this valley of Chimor.

III A at a time when the Chimús raided them and when the Incas conquered them later on.

The length of each period in the economic-political sequence indicated in Chart I applies only to the Mochica-Chicama area, and must necessarily be different in other valleys. This results in thrusting into the foreground the whole complexity of the problem, for it means interrelating the *indigenous development of each valley* with the *external forces thrust upon it by conquest.* The concrete solution of the problem depends on much more archaeological knowledge than we have at our disposal.

Since cultural growth and expansion are interrelated with economic and political growth and expansion, an attempt has been made in Chart I to link these two developments in the Moche-Chicama area. This was not only the political and cultural center of Northwest Coast developments, but it was also *the only place where all the stages of political-economic evolution were consummated.*

In other valleys of the Northwest Coast, the cultural developments, though influenced and dominated at times

Fig. 2. A narrow passage between two high walls that surround one of the large compounds of ChanChan. The compound is known as the Rivero group and can be located in Fig. 4 and on the map p. 85, site 7. *Kosok.*

by the general Moche-Chicama sequence, nevertheless *had their own local history*. This is particularly true in the extensive Lambayeque region, whose cultural sequence has not yet been completely established. Thus, interrelationships of culture sequences and economic-political sequences have to be studied separately for each valley or group of valleys — a study barely in the initial stage of development.

In the Central and South Coast valleys, which were barely touched by the development on the Northwest Coast, different, though parallel, culture sequences have been roughly established. Details of all of these cultures can be found in *Reappraisal* (1948) as well as in Bennett and Bird (1949), Means (1931) and *Handbook of South American Indians* (II, 1946).

At present it is difficult to give a fairly reliable *absolute* dating of the main cultural periods, since archaeologists are now in the process of drastically revising their previous estimates. Until the last decade, it had been customary to make the cultural periods, especially the early ones, fairly long (see Means, 1931). In recent years, however, there has been a strong tendency to shorten considerably the duration of each stage. This is apparent in the charts in *Reappraisal.*

Some limited Carbon 14 datings done recently seem to have definitely upset this trend towards contraction. Dr. Bird's findings indicate a date of about 800 B.C. ± 100 for the Cupisnique remains that he excavated at Huaca Prieta in the Chicama Valley. This would push back the date of the *coming* of the maize-growing Cupisnique cultures into the coastal valleys to 1000 B.C., if not earlier. Dr. Bird *estimates* that the beginnings of the fishing culture at the same Huaca Prieta might go back well beyond 3000 B.C., while *the appearance of an incipient pre-maize agriculture,* supplementing the basic fishing economy, might be set tentatively at about 2500 B.C.

For the method used in making Carbon 14 datings and the particular difficulties encountered in making these datings along the Coast of Peru, see the article "Radiocarbon Dating" by Edward S. Deevey, Jr., in the *Scientific American,* February 1952. See also Dr. Bird's article, "South American Radiocarbon Dates" (1951).

Very tentative datings of Mochica grave material seem to indicate a Mochica period extending from the latter part of the first millenium B.C. through the first part of the first millenium A.D.

Such tentative early dating for the important Mochica period would definitely indicate that the *Sturm und*

Fig. 3. Ruins of a part of ChanChan, with the foothills of the Andes in the background. *Kosok.*

Drang Middle Period — when various valley and mountain peoples were marching up and down the Coast attempting to conquer one another — started earlier and was considerably longer than had been previously assumed. According to Dr. Schaedel, this is partly confirmed by the large amount of Middle Period ceramics and architectural remains which he found at various sites. Only the approximate dating of the Late Chimú Period in the Moche-Chicama area does not seem to require any important change.

It might be pointed out here that the Middle Period lasted longest in the North Central and South Central coastal areas. But, as we proceed north, we find that in each successive valley, the period appears to have been shorter. Indeed, in the Lambayeque Complex, Middle

Period potsherds are practically non-existent. However, it is best to wait until more concrete information is accumulated before drawing definite conclusions.

A word about the Incas. The records of various Spanish Chroniclers indicate that the Inca conquest of the Coast took place only sixty or seventy years before the Spaniards arrived in 1532. Scarcity of Inca potsherds on the coast supports the traditions of such a limited period of occupation.

Although more extensive Carbon 14 datings are essential in order to supply *absolute* dates more closely related to the actual cultural stages in the past, it is safe to assume that *the chronological sequence of cultures will not change;* only certain modifications and refinements will appear as our archaeological knowledge increases.

The short general survey of the cultural evolution of the coastal peoples just presented is based almost entirely on archaeological material. The question arises: Are there no legends and traditions *that were written down during early Spanish times* that tell us about the Indian coastal cultures and their history? There are, but they are few! And they tell us little!

The few who wrote about the Indians concentrated mainly on the history and institutions of the Incas — the great ruling power when the Spaniards arrived. Besides, the Incas had already destroyed the specific forms of political organization and part of the social structure of the Chimús. To the Spaniards, the Chimús were just one of the many constituent peoples of the conquered Inca Empire.

Systematic historical and archaeological research methods would have been necessary in order to collect and collate in early colonial times the enormous amount of information then extant concerning ancient Peru. But history and archaeology as sciences did not exist in colonial times; they were not established till the nineteenth century. Therefore, we have to content ourselves at present with the morsels at our disposal in the hope that future archival research will furnish more information, which would enable us gradually to push back certain aspects of the historic period into the now extensive but unknown prehistoric period.

The most important material on the Chimús and their Empire is found in Calancha (1638), the Quipucamayocs

Fig. 4. Vertical aerial photograph of the greater part of the remains of ancient ChanChan. The city, with a population of possibly fifty thousand, was undoubtedly the largest urban site in the Americas. Each one of the walled compounds, probably built at different times, appears to have been a distinct "ward" or section of the city, and was inhabited by distinct clans, tribes or other more developed administrative units of the Chimús. Within the compounds, each cubicle represents a storage bin or the living quarters of a family. Some of the larger units were undoubtedly reserved for the Chimú aristocracy. Note the virtual absence of pyramids within the city. It is only *outside* the city that a number of large pyramids are located. This probably indicates the superior position of the secular power and the inferior position of the priesthood. The dark sections of the photograph surrounding much of the city are mainly cultivated areas that have gradually encroached upon the ruins. The irregular dark areas at the right of the photograph are at a lower level than the city and are covered at present by reeds and brush which are fed by subsoil drainage. *Servicio 104: mosaic set ·* Fig. 5 (margin). Polished Chimú blackware. *Kosok-Rein.*

77

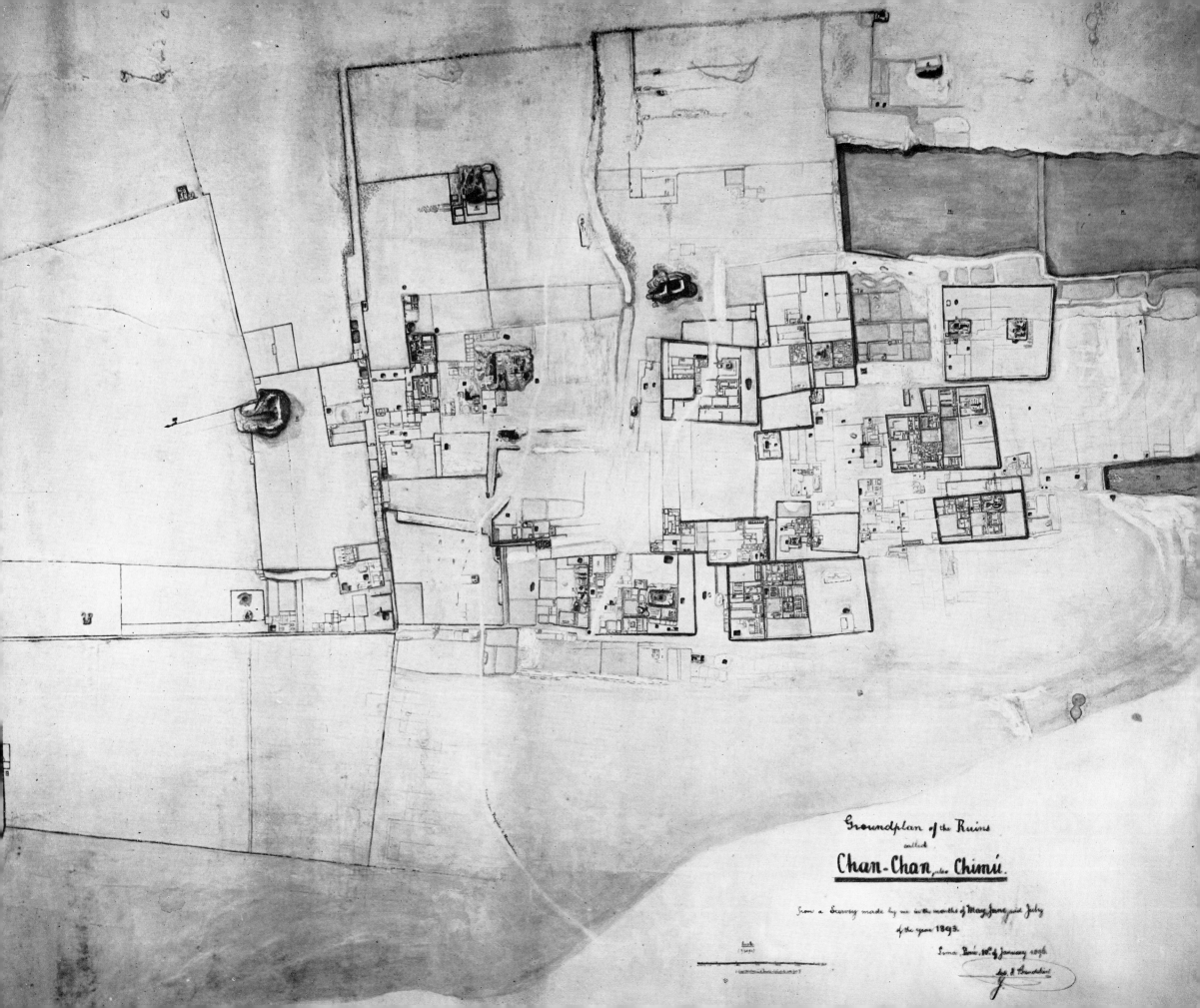

Groundplan of the Ruins

called

Chan-Chan, also Chimú.

From a Survey made by me in the months of May, June and July
of the year 1893.

Lima, Perú, 10th of January 1896.

(ms. 1544 [1924]) and Cabello (ms. 1586 [1951]). Calancha was a Jesuit priest who lived for some time in the Jequetepeque Valley. The Quipucamayocs represent a short account collected from the descendants of the *quipu* keepers (see Chapter VI). Cabello de Valboa was a priest who lived for a long time in Ecuador and then traveled in Peru, where he collected some of the folk legends. Cabello also gives an account of the northern Lambayeque area with a list of rulers of that region.

Recently, Rubén Vargas Ugarte (1936) unearthed two very crucial pages of a manuscript — part of a history of Trujillo — written in 1614 in Trujillo by an unknown author who will be referred to here as the Anonymous Trujillano. This document for the first time gives a traditional list of some of the rulers of the Chimú Empire and mentions some of their conquests.

Several partial accounts, often contradictory, of the Inca conquest of the Chimú Empire are extant. They shed some light on the latter period of the Chimú Empire as well as on parallel coastal cultures and political structures. This conquest is dealt with by Cieza (1553), Cabello (ms. 1586), Sarmiento (ms. 1571), Lizárraga (ms. before 1602), Montesinos (ms. 1642) and Garcilaso (1601), who gives by far the most detailed, though still incomplete, account of this significant military venture.

In modern times, Squier (1877) was the first to give a well-illustrated summary of the main coastal cultures, together with quotations from original sources of the material then available. Middendorf (1894), Holstein (1927), Means (1931) and Horkheimer (1944) followed with summaries incorporating more recent historical and archaeological material.

Professor Rowe, in his short and well-written monograph, *The Kingdom of Chimor* (1948), attempted the first organized account of Chimú society and the history of the Chimú Empire. However, he does not exhaust his subject. Therefore, we hope that in the near future he will be able to publish a more extensive and detailed

study, including a systematic presentation and critical evaluation of all the source material available.

In order to make the development of the Chimú Empire and its relationship to the Incas clearer, a schematic chronological chart (Chart II) has been made of the list of Chimú rulers as given by the Anonymous Trujillano, together with the generally accepted "official" list of Inca rulers. Limited Chimú material from Feyjóo (1763) has also been used. Cabello's list of Lambayeque rulers has been given, to which has been added some of the data

presented by Rubiños (1781) in his document on the colonial descendants of the Lambayeque rulers. The chart here presented is part of a larger one drawn up in 1946 in connection with our study on "Absolute Chronology in the New World."

We have, at present, no way of testing the validity of the list of kings. They may have been altered in transmission from generation to generation. Indeed, the early parts may have even been forged in order to give ancient roots and traditions to the ruling houses. However, the

Fig. 6 (left). A ground plan drawn by Bandelier in 1896, and hitherto unpublished, of the main parts of ChanChan. Compare the plan with the oblique aerial photograph above, right, and the vertical aerial photograph on pp. 76 and 77. Many of the compounds can be easily identified • Fig. 7 (above, right). Another oblique aerial view of ChanChan, affording a comparison with Bandelier's plan on the opposite page. *Shippee-Johnson* • Fig. 7a (margin). Ancient *huaco* of a step pyramid. *Baessler*.

more recent parts of the lists are probably closer to the truth. Whatever the validity of these lists may be, until further information is uncovered to prove or disprove them, they will remain useful in probing into the prehistory of ancient Peru.

We ignore Montesinos' list of more than one hundred Inca rulers, since no one so far has satisfactorily related the list to the accepted Inca chronology.

Since no absolute dates exist for the rulers of the Chimús and Lambayeque, each ruler has been assigned a reign of 25 years (i.e., a generation), a principle which is useful in obtaining a *relatively absolute chronology*

from traditional prehistoric lists of rulers. For the Incas, *two traditional lists* of dates have been handed down to us, one by Sarmiento (ms. 1571), the other by Cabello (ms. 1586). But these lists assign to many of the rulers impossibly long reigns of up to one hundred years each and are therefore useless. Modern writers have tried unsuccessfully to revise these lists. We therefore assume, as we did above, an average reign of twenty-five years for each Inca. Rowe (1945), however, accepts the traditional dates given by Cabello for the last four Inca rulers. Since the traditions about recent rulers are more likely to be nearer the truth and since the given dates are not un-

reasonable, we tentatively accept Rowe's proposal and include these dates in our chart.

A comparative genealogical study of rulers in Mexico and other parts of the world indicates that the *average* length of the reign of a ruler *tends to be closer to twenty years*. This is likely when we consider the fact that the generation principle, in which son succeeds father, rarely holds true for more than several generations. Succession is often through brothers and cousins — which shortens the length of each reign and thus shortens the duration of the dynasty. But until this problem has been analyzed in greater detail it might be well to be generous and allow a traditional 25 years for each reign. In any case, the *relative* lengths of the three dynasties which we present, i.e., the Inca, the Chimú, and the Lambayeque, will not be seriously affected by this act of generosity.

From Chart II, it becomes clear that both the Chimú and Inca dynasties began at about the same time, i.e., the middle (more probably the end) of the thirteenth century. From the analysis by Rowe (1945) of the conflicting accounts of Inca development as well as from the material presented by the Anonymous Trujillano, it may be provisionally concluded that both Empires became really extensive in size only during the reigns of their last four or five rulers. The earlier period was apparently utilized to consolidate local power and to conquer neighboring peoples.

If we study the list of Lambayeque rulers, several things stand out clearly. In the first place, no matter how short we make the so-called *Interregnum*, the beginning of the Lambayeque line, with Naymlap as the founder, appears almost two hundred years *earlier* than the beginning of the Inca and Chimú lines. Secondly, there is no indication that the Naymlap line ever developed an "Empire"; indeed, it is improbable that Lambayeque

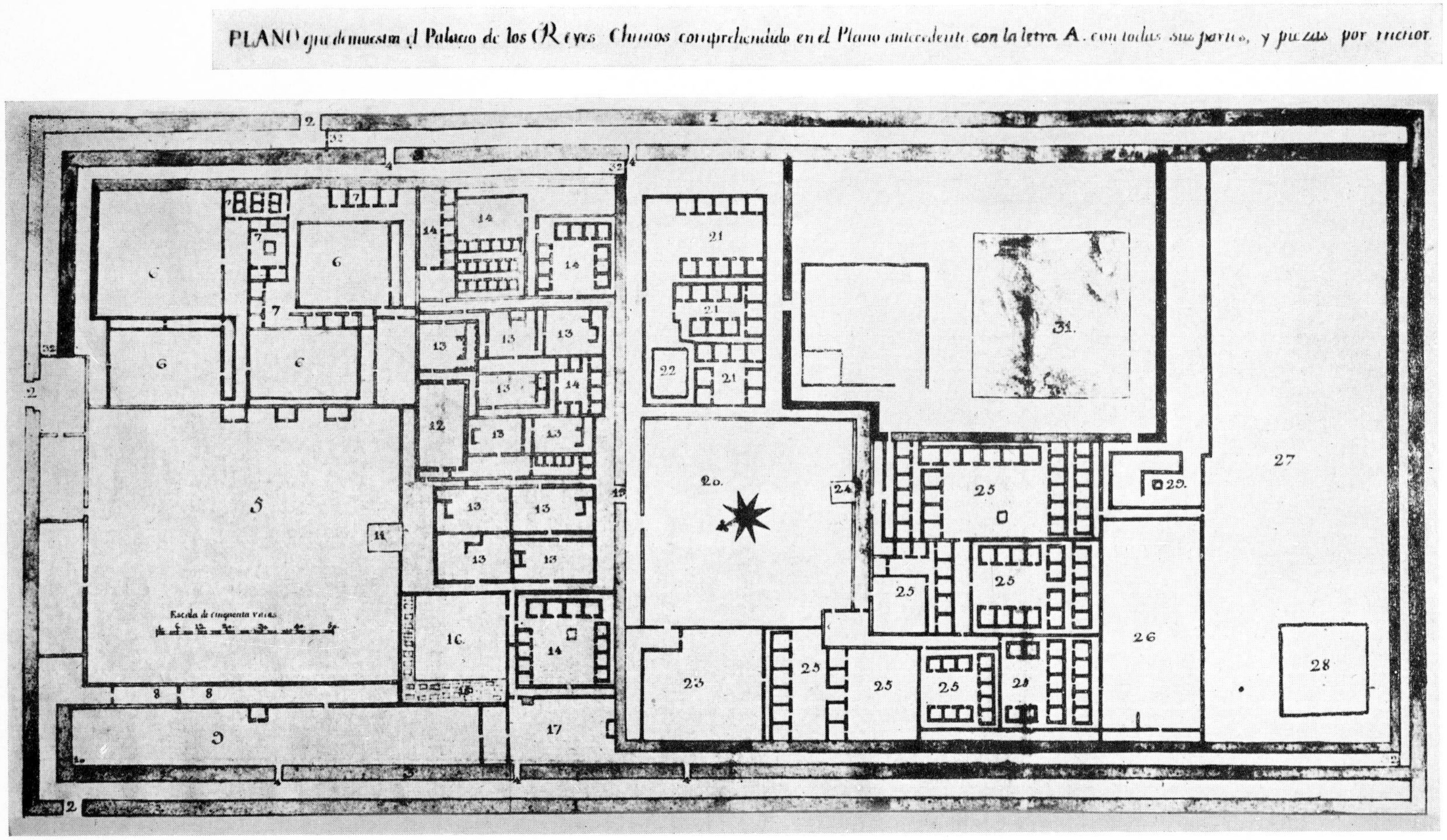

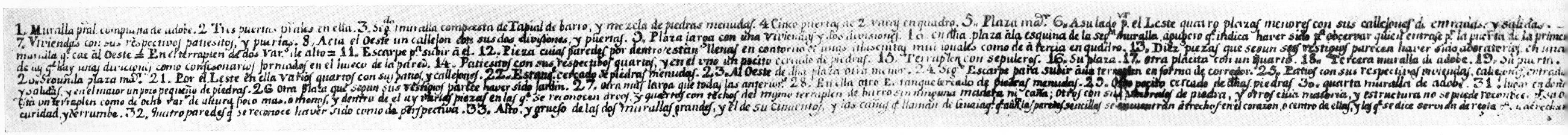

Fig. 8. Reprint of the drawing made by Bishop Martínez de Compañón of the "Palace of the Chimú Kings," one of the large walled compounds of ancient ChanChan.

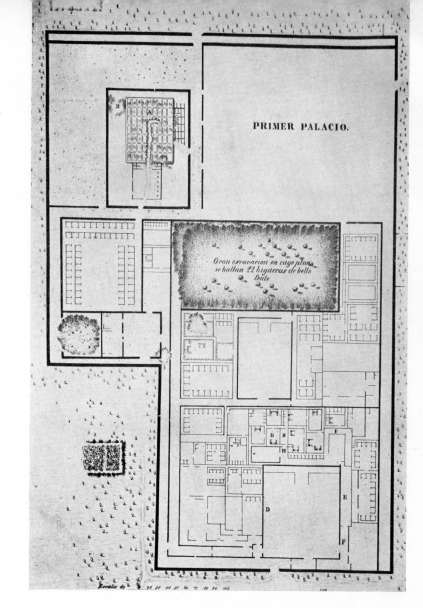

PRIMER PALACIO.

Gran escavacion en cuyo plan se hallan 22 higueras de bella brute

rulers ever organized a state comprising the whole Lambayeque Complex (see Chapter XVI). Thirdly, it is clear that after the *Interregnum* — caused by Chimú conquests? — the next three rulers were Chimú officials, while their successors were apparently local rulers appointed by the Incas. Their descendants appear to have continued their position during Spanish rule — with, however, only nominal powers. Owing to conflicting statements in Cabello — the main source of the Lambayeque list —, the identities and sequence of some Inca-appointed rulers are not quite clear and the list may have to be slightly revised if more accurate archival material is found.

Since the Inca conquest of the Coast probably took place about 1465-1475, some sixty or seventy years in advance of the Spanish conquest of Peru, we should expect to possess considerable Spanish data dealing with the Inca conquest of the Chimús, which might also throw some light on the institutions of the latter. But, as stated, only a few Chroniclers wrote of traditions they had heard concerning the Inca conquest. However, their accounts are incomplete and contain numerous contradictions which have not yet been successfully resolved.

Several distinct, but apparently unrelated, campaigns stand out. Two came down from the Sierras towards ChanChan (Cabello, Sarmiento). One campaign was none too successful, as the following quotation from Cabello (1586:497) indicates:

> . . . but it is known with great certainty that the army of the Yngas attacked suddenly those of the wide and spacious valley of the Chimo, and held its inhabitants in fear, and shut in for many days behind their high walls, from here without having achieved results for the time being (*sin hacer por entonces efecto*) they proceeded to the lands irrigated by the river called Pacaz mayo, and they upset (*turbaron*) all these valleys and by the upper part of the Nepos they returned to Cajamarca. . . .

Sarmiento (ms. 1571: Chap. XLIV) briefly mentions how Tupac Yupanqui conquered — apparently also from the Sierras — ". . . the valleys of Pacazmayo and Chimo which is now Trujillo, which he destroyed being that Chimo Capac [was] his subject. . . ."

These two short quotations furnish the only evidence, so far available, of an Inca invasion of the Chimú Empire by way of the Sierras. The two accounts — if correct — do not seem to refer to one and the same campaign, contrary to the general assumption. Cabello's account de-

Fig. 9 (above). Vertical aerial photograph of the Tschudi group (see Fig. 10). The small enclosures were probably living quarters while the open spaces were probably public squares used for various purposes. The dark rectangular area is a "tank" about twenty feet deep. At the time Tschudi visited it, fig trees were growing there. Now, there are only wild reeds that are fed by subsoil moisture. The "tank" may have been used in ancient times as a sunken garden or as a water reservoir. *Servicio 104:30* • Fig. 10 (right, top). Ground plan of the Tschudi group of ChanChan. The plan was made by Rivero and Tschudi in the first half of the nineteenth century. Compare this plan with Fig. 9 • Fig. 11 (margin). Chimú blackware representing a house with decorated pillars. Note the monkey, characteristic of Chimú ware, at the base of the spout. *Museo Nacional-Guillen.*

scribes what appears to have been a preliminary skirmish or an unsuccessful attack, whereas Sarmiento's brief and somewhat vague remark seems to refer to a punitive expedition following a previous conquest — or perhaps to the conquest itself.

Most of the information we have of the conquest of the Chimú Empire by the Incas is found in Book VI of Garcilaso, who devotes several chapters to this matter. According to him, the conquest *came along the Coast from the South.* Garcilaso not only takes up the conquest of the whole Central Coast, but also shows how, later on, the Incas and their coastal allies captured Paramonga, the southern outpost of the Chimús, and then drove them back to the Santa Valley. Here the story of the campaign ends without mention of the conquest of the main part

The Yungas, the Prehistory and Origin of the First Inhabitants of the Coasts of Peru

This is a translation of the most important sections of an article by Julio Víctor Pacheco entitled "Los Yungas, Prehistoria y Origen de los Primeros Pobladores de las Costas del Peru" and published in Trujillo in the now defunct magazine, Ciudad y Campo, *January 1926. The first part of the article is summarized in the first three paragraphs. The remainder is a literal translation of the article.*

Pacheco states that conditions of prehistoric life in Peru are revealed by archaeological remains. The highest civilizations were those that developed in desert lands which had to be irrigated. The Yungas, the ancient inhabitants of coastal Peru, dwelt in such a region and they achieved their splendor relatively early. The Quechua-Aymaras of the Sierras progressed more slowly, but because of their strength and youth were in a position to conquer and dominate the Yungas.

Pacheco then quotes directly from the lost manuscript of the priest Pedro de la Cruz: "The destruction and loss of this *pueblo* [can mean nation, land, people, town or village] was due to the Incas — and the Mochicas were the former inhabitants honored by their reputation as workers. We see that they had spent much gold in the construction of their great and populous city just like the cities of the Pentapolis; that all the products which they had in their kingdom were the results of labor and the fertility of the hot soil, indeed fertile for many reasons; the *omes* [keepers of history and legends] of their race say that the city was destroyed by evil and impious people and that their grandfathers fled to other regions; that *kon* [a deity] out of resentment had gone to the sea, leaving his people abandoned".

Pacheco then meditates on how ChanChan reflected all the hidden mystery of a lost civilization, and continues in his own words:

"Facts founded only on tradition, when they are turned into history, generally lose the criterion of truth in leaving [?] their source; and separating themselves deceivingly from reality they acquire in the imagination of the historian exaggerated tints of extravagance.

"These prostituted stories which are passed from father to son and which do not derive from orderly scientific principles, arrive in the course of time to succeeding generations profoundly altered and resist the analysis of investigation as well as the dissections of criticism severe and impartial.

"Because of the nature of the magazine and the narrowness of its columns, this small article which we now present cannot be amplified with citations of historic proof, which would occupy many pages. We have made this condensed article, which is taken in parts from fragments of a work which I have written, and which has been inspired by the testimony of stones and ceramics, which the obscure past hides with blind avarice, within the sarcophagi of its dead or in the piles of ruins of its monuments [;] serving as principal guides [were] the manuscripts (autografos) of the Dominican padre, Pedro de la Cruz, confessor of Vaca de Castro [an early viceroy of Peru] and those of the same order [:] Pedro Domingo de la Asuncíon de Santo Tomás and the historical notes of Father Meneses; these documents being found in the semi-destroyed archives of an ancient convent, written, partly on paper, partly on parchment, in the year 1545, and where the badly drawn Latin characters are mingled with the chainlike script of the author.

"The prosperous state of the Chimú, the extent of their dominions and the prestige of their arms, placed the coastal people (*pueblo yunga*) among the foremost in America, and of the Continent of Hot Lands, as they called it.

"As industrial people, they were the first to employ bronze for their ploughs, weapons, and other implements; they were great agriculturalists for, aided by the fertility of the soil, they sowed vast expanses of land and carried on a trade with the peoples (*pueblos*) of the Coast; it seems that some Phoenecian colonies left traces of their sojourn on these regions. [!]

"The prosperity of this kingdom aroused the covetousness of the Incas, and especially the fear caused by the fame of their conquests; thus it was that, beginning with the reign of Pachacutec, the troops of this Empire of the Sun were prepared for the military conquest of those settled north of the Tahuantisuyo.

"The campaign undertaken against this kingdom is one of the most important found among the military traditions and legends of the Inca Empire, not only for its political adroitness but also for the success of its imperial arms.

"The Incas initiated their conquest with expeditions of observations, [scouting expeditions] and various battles were fought intermittently for many years, in which fortune was generally adverse to the Imperial arms. So, after these defeats, it was decided in Cuzco to proceed with an all-out effort to conquer the Yungas.

"When the Inca Tupac Yupanqui ascended the throne, a great expedition was organized in command of his son Yupanqui, a young and brave general who had previously revealed exceptional qualities, distinguishing himself in the campaign against and the subjugation of the Cajamarcas and Huamachucas. Yupanqui launched his campaign against the Yungas with twenty-two thousand men. First he made an alliance with various powerful *caciques* [local rulers] who, having been conquered and subjugated by Fell-kum-Pisan, king of the Yungas, had been forced to acknowledge his suzerainty, and pay a corresponding tribute, being almost incorporated into the nationality (*nacionalidad*) of the Chimús.

"But the governing rulers (*regulos*) of those peoples (*pueblos*) who extended from Supe to Ica, and who [the rulers] were called Chuquimancu and Cuyusmancu, had kept a deep hatred of the Chimús, and proved to be a powerful help to the Imperial troops, who now found a safe base of operations, which permitted them to operate along the frontier against the armies of Fell-kum-Pisan.

"Battles were fought almost daily and sieges of fortresses lasted a long time, this is evidenced by the *huacos* found in the excavations carried out in the fortresses and in many places and *pueblos* of Yunga origin now destroyed, on which [huacos] can be seen the horribly mutilated remains of prisoners of war still dressed in their Quechua garb. [These mutilated figures are from the Early or Mochica Period (see Chapter XI, Fig. 43) and thus do not prove Pacheco's contention. However, this does not mean that the Late Chimús and Incas did not indulge in the practice of mutilation, common throughout the world until very recent times.]

"The stubborn resistance and the valor with which the Chimús defended themselves forced Yupanqui to abandon his military venture. He returned to Cuzco and after a long period of preparations, came back with three large armies, commanded by the finest generals of the Empire. The struggle was bloody and devastating. This is proven [!] by the multitudes of destroyed cities and abandoned villages which the Spaniards found when they came to Peru. The greater part of the inhabitants had been either removed to other regions, in accordance with Inca customs, or, as refugees in tiny hamlets, they lived a life of degradation and misery, which prevented them from offering the slightest resistance to the conquerors. [Recent studies tend to indicate that there was a partial depopulation of the Coast as a result of the Inca Conquest.]

"Finally, fortune turned against the Chimú, and defeated in Paramonga, he retreated to the North. The Quichuas advanced in a series of battles, capturing and destroying the greater part of the coastal fortresses. Among the most important was Chiquita Yap, an enormous bastion with many parapets which exists today. [Pacheco undoubtedly means Chiquitoy Viejo, on the southern edge of the Chicama Valley. He somewhat exaggerates the size of the site.]

"Fell-kum-Pisan, retreating precipitously, took refuge in the fortresses of his capital the city of ChanChan. Yupanqui laid siege but, since the area of the city was very extensive, they [the defenders] could fight to advantage, aided as they also were by immense supplies of maize, so they could not be starved out. And since on the other hand the Imperial troops were not sufficiently numerous to press the siege, it was very feasible to renew the supplies [of ChanChan.]

"As we know, the ancient Peruvians were very skillful in matters of hydraulics and irrigation. They [the Incas] therefore cut off the water which supplied ChanChan. Even today one may see the dry river bed whose water abundantly supplied the capital. [Pacheco apparently refers to the ancient canals now in disuse]. Yupanqui ordered the alteration of the course giving it another course which has not been discovered to this day; but ChanChan received water from hydraulic works located in a place called Challuacocha about seventy kilometers from ChanChan by means of hidden canals; for a long time they did not lack water, until the canals, revealed by a traitor, were destroyed and then the city deprived of its water surrendered [such hidden canals, if they existed, have not yet been located.]

"Fell-kum-Pisan withdrew with his troops, abandoning the city. Father Meneses relates that, when Yupanqui entered ChanChan as victor he was amazed when he saw the wealth and beauty of the great coastal city, built according to an immense plan with straight and aligned streets, full of light and sun and much superior to the coarse and semi-barbarian constructions of Cuzco.

"Possibly the Inca prince dreamed of making this city the capital of the Empire on ascending the throne of his ancestors as he later did, after conquering Quito."

Fragments of the Unpublished Work — History of the Valleys of Chicama, Virú and Santa

This article was published by Víctor Julio Pacheco in the Trujillo newspaper "La Industria," March 18, 1922.

As we have indicated previously, on conquering the kingdom of the Chimú, the Incas made no violent transformations in the religion or in the institutions [of the Chimús]; their [the Chimús'] king, Fell-Kum-Pisan, continued ruling with a certain independence after the peace celebrated in the temple of Kong, and imposed by Yupanqui [the Inca ruler] [;] and notwithstanding [after?] the fire and the destruction of their beautiful capital of ChanChan, the urban population took on a rural aspect, resettling in the Chicama, Chimú [Moche] and Virú Valleys, transferring the court to a place [*pueblo*], of which the ruins still exist, near the fortress of Chiquitayap, situated within the area of Hacienda Chiquitoy.

Through the intervention of Yupanqui the [old] animosities of the *caciques* Chuquimancu and Cuyus Mancu ruling to the south, against the Yunga king, Fell-Kum-Pisan, were weakened [;] but at his [Fell-Kum-Pisan's] death, his son and successor, Abhar-Occo, had very little influence in the administration [of the Chimús], as the policy of the [Inca] Empire daily reduced his power.

Following the Incas' doctrine of peaceful absorption, they began to mix the Yunga population with settlers from other regions, principally Quichuas, and they also brought many Cusqueños of illustrious ancestry, in order to make propaganda for the language and for the cult of the Sun; mixing the civilization and the gods of the Chimú with the civilization and gods of the Tahuantisuyo, absorbing them insofar as possible; and at the same time they were initiated into the farming practices of the coastal lands, trying to acclimatize the crops of the Sierra, principally the potato and the olluco, taking in exchange seeds and shoots of fruit [trees] and other products.

They tried to divide the fields [*terrenos*] into *topos* [Inca units of land measurement, varying in size in different regions] according to the practices of the Inca Empire, but those [the lands] of the Coast having a distinct topography from those of the Sierra and above all the methods of irrigation being different, the same [Chimú] distribution [of land] was maintained subject to the same custom and policy of concentrating vast extensions of land in [the hands of] a few proprietors, subdividing only production [produce] by the methods that we have studied, while covering [in the part of Pacheco's unpublished and lost work] the prehistory and the special section [dealing with] the Chimú Kingdom.

According to the Dominican Pedro de la Cruz, a tradition sustained by the natives and that was contained in the manuscripts of this *religioso* [monk], the lands [of Ascope] belonged to a noble Yunga who died in the year of the struggles that took place before the surrender of ChanChan; the same tradition says, that, at the time of the Spanish invasion, the vast extension of lands called As-cocp [Ascope], which in the Mochica language means mouth or entrance, belonged to the *Curaca* [ruler] Huasataca of the Imperial family [of the Incas].

When Pizarro, or better said Almagro, founded Trujillo in the year 1535, the family of the *curaca* that possessed them fled to the Sierra, and when the Spaniards distributed the land of the ancient Chimú the share of Capitan Don Bartolomé Tinoco y Cabero, was 132 fanegades (almost 1000 acres) within whose area is located today the city of Ascope. This assignment was made by the first Corregidor Don Diego de Mora, as were also those of the Chicama Valley and the other holdings of the Corregimiento of Trujillo; a century later when the land was already in the possession of his grandson Don Pedro Tinoco, he [Pedro] obtained legal title.

Fig. 12 (p. 82 margin). Chimú textile. *Metropolitan Museum of Art* • Fig. 13 (above). A detail of a partially destroyed frieze from ChanChan. *Kosok* • Fig. 14 (below). Two Chimú *huacos* excavated at ChanChan by members of the Trujillo Institute. Highly burnished surfaces are characteristic of Chimú ceramics. *Schaedel.*

of the Chimú Empire. We learn merely that the Chimú ruler submitted to the Incas.

The accounts of the three campaigns here presented are not necessarily contradictory; indeed, they may even complement one another. It is not impossible that the southern campaign took place during the interval between the campaigns mentioned only briefly by Cabello and Sarmiento.

A later, final conquest (or reconquest?) under Huayna Capac, the next to last Inca ruler, is mentioned by Garcilaso, Cieza and Cabello. But the three accounts of this campaign are in many ways conflicting. The existence of this last campaign is also confirmed by seventeenth century local traditions in Jequetepeque, as attested to by Calancha, and by existing local traditions in Lambayeque, noted and collated by Augusto D. León Barandiarán (1938). Other complete or partial campaigns, of which we know nothing or which are included in the contradictory accounts of what appears to be one campaign, may of course have taken place.

But even greater nebulousness surrounds the actual conquest of the Mochica-Chicama unit and the capture of the Chimú capital of ChanChan itself. Garcilaso omits this crucial part of the campaign entirely. Cabello and Cieza do likewise and defend their omission by referring to the vague and contradictory nature of local reports. This almost complete lack of information concerning these key events is surprising. Possibly, following the conquest of this region, or the suppression of an unsuccessful revolt, many inhabitants of this region were slaughtered and the remainder sent as colonists to other parts of Peru. In turn, colonists from other regions might have been settled in these crucial valleys. The vague and contradictory information about which the early Spanish Chroniclers complained could be accounted for in this way. But until new archival material is found, the prob-

Fig. 15. A partial view of the walls of ChanChan. *Kosok.*

Fig. 16 (above). The main outer wall of ChanChan. *Kosok* • Fig. 17 (below). A view of the so-called "dungeons" inside Chan-Chan. *Kosok.*

lem of the Inca conquest of the heart of the Chimú Empire, and especially the capture of ChanChan, must remain unsolved!

One day, as we were sipping *cinzano* at the Hotel Tourista in Trujillo, Dr. Schaedel, to our great delight, told us of an article that Señor Ortiz Silva of Trujillo had loaned him. This short article, written by Julio Víctor Pacheco, had appeared in 1931 in an obscure and now defunct local journal, *Ciudad y Campo* (City and Country). It dealt with the Inca conquest of the Chimús and was represented as being an extract from an unpublished work by the same author, entitled *History of the Valleys of Chicama, Chimú and Virú.* Pacheco claims that this work is based on unknown manuscripts of three sixteenth century priests, namely Padre Meneses, Padre de la Cruz, and Pedro Domingo de la Asunción de Santo Tomás. These manuscripts were supposedly written about 1545, i.e., only ten years after the Spaniards founded Trujillo!

This was electrifying news! The recovery of these early manuscripts of the three *padres* might become a landmark in our historical reconstruction of the Inca conquest of the Chimús and of the society and government of the latter.

However, our attempts to locate these manuscripts were unsuccessful, and our efforts to obtain information about their authors yielded only limited results. In the standard eight-volume biographical dictionary of Mendiburo, neither Padre Meneses, who is supposed to have left historical notes, nor Padre de la Cruz, father confessor to the Viceroy Vaca de Castro, are mentioned. Neither is the third author, Pedro Domingo de la Asunción de Santo Tomás, listed. But probably Pacheco meant Frey Domingo de Santo Tomás, who is known for his Quechua grammar. Not so well known is the fact that when Frey Domingo arrived in Peru around 1535, he helped to found the Dominican Order in Trujillo! He studied the native language spoken in the Moche-Chicama area and used it to preach the Gospel to the Indians, who admired and supported him because he always defended their interests. Apparently, he left this region about 1545. Such a man very likely would have written something about Indian life and traditions in this region.

It was found that the other two clerics had also belonged to the Dominican Order at Trujillo. To our dismay, we learned that the contents of the local Dominican archives in Trujillo had been removed to the main Dominican archives in Lima about ten years ago. Recent inquiries seem to indicate that non-members of the Order cannot use the archives, which, moreover, are uncatalogued!

Perhaps the manuscripts are not even in the Lima archives. Could they be among Pacheco's papers, together with the large volume which he claims to have written? Pacheco died more than twenty-five years ago without direct heirs, and attempts by Dr. Schaedel and Señor Garrido to locate his papers have so far proved unsuccessful.

Since these important manuscripts may not be unearthed for some years — if at all — and since the Pacheco article contains some new information, we decided to print a translation of the more important parts of the article (page 82). It is difficult to determine at present whether the flowery language of the article should be attributed to Pacheco or whether it is a mere rehash of some of the florid passages he found in the writings of his three Chroniclers.

In addition to this article, Señor Garrido found another, but shorter, article by the same author, printed in the issues of March 18 and 25, 1922, of the local Trujillo paper, *La Industria.* This article we present on p. 83.

As we read these articles, we are struck by the fact that Pacheco's account of the Inca conquest of the Chimús is in many ways similar to that of Garcilaso, though Pacheco's contains *more details of the campaigns* and gives information about *the surrender of ChanChan.* This indicates that Pacheco did not copy from Garcilaso. The question then suggests itself: Could the manuscripts of the three priests from whom Pacheco took his material have been also the source of at least part of Garcilaso's account? For Garcilaso had visited Trujillo during the period when these three clerics were supposed to have resided there. An answer to this question would then also resolve, in part, the question of the validity of Garcilaso's account, which was not actually written till the end of the sixteenth century.

What is also striking in these articles is the name given the ruler of the Chimús who was defeated by the Incas. Here he is called Fell-kum-Pisan, a name quite different from any of those given by the Anonymous Trujillano! In fact, the name resembles that of Fallenpisan, the Inca-controlled ruler of Lambayeque as listed by Cabello (see Chart II). Fallenpisan is the ruler Cabello mentions as having been taken as a hostage from Lambayeque to Cuzco by the Incas. What connection could there have been between the Lambayeque and the Chimú line? Could the two rulers mentioned above have been the same ruler — or related rulers? Could the Lambayeque line have been linked with the Chimú dynasty following the conquest of Lambayeque by the latter? Could the last names on the Chimú king list be another form of the Lambayeque names? Or could there have been a mistake made by Pacheco, the three Chroniclers, or the Anonymous Trujillano? These and a host of other enticing questions suddenly confront us — questions about which we can merely speculate as we grope in this twilight zone between history and pre-history.

To confuse things further, Fell-kum-Pisan is said to have had a son with the unusual name of Abhar Rocco. Here, likewise, there is no counterpart in the Chimú list of kings. But neither does such a name appear in the Lambayeque list!

We also hear for the first time of a coastal God *Kon* who fled to the sea — so reminiscent of the Sierra tradition which Heyerdahl and his famous Kontiki expedition used as one of the bases for their venturesome trip!

Fig. 18 (below). Antonio Rodríguez SuySuy standing before a part of ChanChan. *Schaedel* • Fig. 19 (right). Plan of ChanChan drawn on the basis of the aerial photographs. *González.*

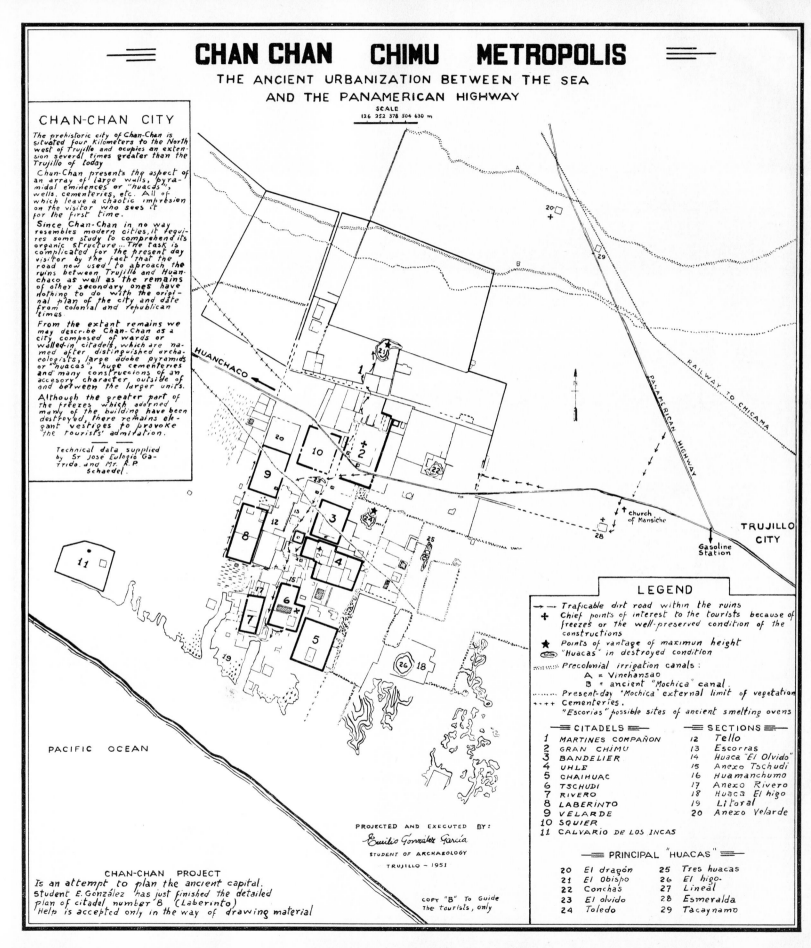

CHAN CHAN CHIMU METROPOLIS
THE ANCIENT URBANIZATION BETWEEN THE SEA AND THE PANAMERICAN HIGHWAY

SCALE
126 252 378 504 630 m

CHAN-CHAN CITY

The prehistoric city of Chan-Chan is situated four kilometers to the North west of Trujillo and ocupies an extension several times greater than the Trujillo of today

Chan-Chan presents the aspect of an array of large walls, pyramidal eminences or "huacas", wells, cementeries, etc. All of which leave a chaotic impresion on the visitor who sees it for the first time.

Since Chan-Chan in no way resembles modern cities, it requires some study to comprehend its organic structure... The task is complicated by the fact that the road now used to aproach the ruins between Trujillo and Huanchaco as well as the remains of other secondary ones have nothing to do with the original plan of the city and date from colonial and republican times.

From the extant remains we may describe Chan-Chan as a city composed of wards or walled-in citadels, which are named after distinguished archaeologists, large adobe pyramids or "huacas", huge cementeries and many constructions of an accesory character outside of and between the larger units.

Although the greater part of the freezes which adorned many of the building have been destroyed, there remains elegant vestiges to provoke the tourists' admiration.

Technical data supplied by Sr Jose Eulogio Garrido and Mr. R.P. Schaedel.

HUANCHACO

RAILWAY TO CHICAMA

PANAMERICAN HIGHWAY

RAILWAY TO CHICAMA

† church of Mansiche

TRUJILLO CITY

Gasoline Station

PACIFIC OCEAN

LEGEND

→-- Traficable dirt road within the ruins
+ Chief points of interest to the tourists because of freezes or the well-preserved condition of the constructions
★ Points of vantage of maximun height
⬭ "Huacas" in destroyed condition
Precolonial irrigation canals:
A = Vinchansao
B = ancient "Mochica" canal
..... Present-day "Mochica" external limit of vegetation
+++ Cementeries.
"Escorias" possible sites of ancient smelting ovens

CITADELS		SECTIONS	
1	MARTINES COMPAÑON	12	Tello
2	GRAN CHIMU	13	Escorras
3	BANDELIER	14	Huaca "El Olvido"
4	UHLE	15	Anexo Tschudi
5	CHAIHUAC	16	Huamanchumo
6	TSCHUDI	17	Anexo Rivero
7	RIVERO	18	Huaca El higo
8	LABERINTO	19	Litoral
9	VELARDE	20	Anexo Velarde
10	SQUIER		
11	CALVARIO DE LOS INCAS		

PRINCIPAL "HUACAS"			
20	El dragón	25	Tres huacas
21	El Obispo	26	El higo
22	Conchas	27	Lineal
23	El olvido	28	Esmeralda
24	Toledo	29	Tacaynamo

PROJECTED AND EXECUTED BY:
Emilio González García
STUDENT OF ARCHAEOLOGY
TRUJILLO - 1951

CHAN-CHAN PROJECT
Is an attempt to plan the ancient capital. Student E. González has just finished the detailed plan of citadel number 8 (Laberinto) Help is accepted only in the way of drawing material

COPY "B" To Guide the tourists, only

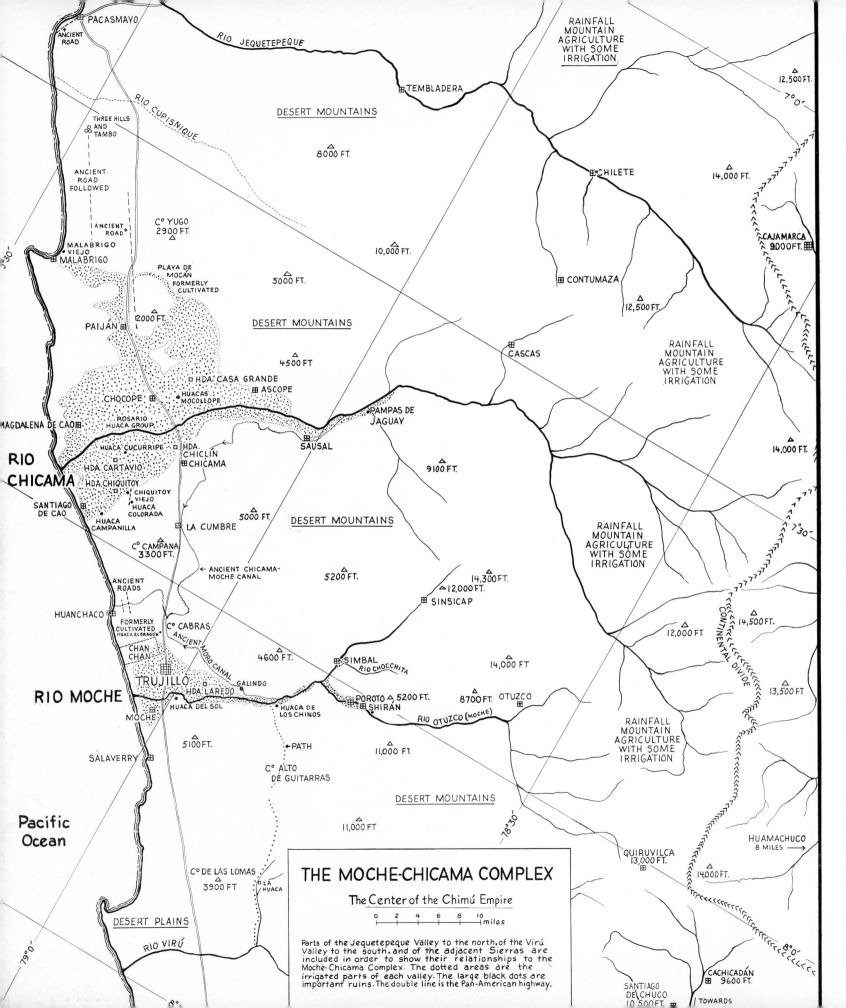

There is also mention of a temple, *Kong* (the seat of the god, *Kon*?) where the treaty between the Chimús and Incas was drawn up. It might be appropriate to mention that about 25 miles up the Moche River we came across the ruins of an ancient site which had the significant sounding name of *Kon-Kon*. The similarity of the name *Kon* in both coastal and Sierra legends seems hardly accidental.

According to Pacheco, the surrender of ChanChan was said to have been effected by the cutting of the water supply by the enemy rather than by force of arms. This account is similar to that of Montesinos (ms. 1642).

In addition, Pacheco's two articles contain the first known references to a fortress of Chiquita Yap from which the Chimú ruler carried on his last struggles against the Incas. The ruins of a walled, fortress-like compound called Chiquitoy Viejo can be seen today along the southern boundary of the nearby Chicama Valley (see Chapter XI) and is probably the compound Pacheco mentions. Incidentally, identification of ruined sites mentioned in early documents has so far been rare in Peruvian archaeology.

Perhaps of greatest significance is the one sentence in the second article citing the existence of a form of land tenure and tribute-collecting among the Chimús different from that of the Incas and apparently indicating a more highly developed form of land concentration among the former. Unfortunately, Señor Pacheco does not give us a direct quotation, nor does he develop his own statement.

What new insights into the lives, government and history of the Chimús will the lost manuscripts of the three Dominican priests yield us — if and when they are found? Undoubtedly, there is also additional, valuable material on the Chimús and other coastal peoples hidden in the archives of Lima, as well as in the local archives of the communities, churches, *haciendas* and certain notaries in the various valleys. No one has yet made a thorough survey of these archives. The results would of course have to be interrelated with additional archaeological investigations, thus bringing together the two basic sources for the reconstruction of ancient Peruvian society.

A systematic investigation of these archives may also yield rich material dealing with the virtually unknown sixteenth and seventeenth centuries in coastal Peru. It might throw *direct* light upon the transition from Indian forms of life and administration to Spanish forms, and, for the first time, *give a correct picture of a vital economic and cultural region of colonial Peru.*

IX

The Moche Valley: Region of Capitals

Visiting the Coast of Peru for the first time or studying the map of this region, one is often bewildered by the large number of valleys, most of them appearing to be very much alike and quite often possessing exotic, unpronounceable names. Only after one becomes acquainted in detail with this fascinating region does one realize that each valley has a distinct "personality," with its own geographical-hydrological, archaeological and cultural characteristics standing out in clear relief. To help the reader grasp the interrelationship of these apparently isolated valley oases, we shall present them in groups.

Since the main purpose of our study was to help reconstruct the ancient societies of the Northwest Coast of Peru, and since the most extensive political unit that evolved there was the Late Chimú Empire, these various valleys have been grouped according to what appear to have been the major zones of the Empire. In addition, each valley or valley complex has been given a "subtitle" in order to stress some important characteristic. These valley groupings are listed as sections C, D, E and F of this volume and are organized as follows:

Section C: *The Center of the Chimú Empire.*

This center consisted of the relatively small Moche Valley, containing the Chimú Capital of ChanChan, and the large neighboring valley of Chicama to the north. During the period of the Empire, if not earlier, these valleys were connected by means of a large canal which brought water from the Chicama Valley to the fields of ChanChan.

Section D: *The Northern Zone of the Chimú Empire.*

This zone included the large Jequetepeque Valley, which is separated from the Chicama by fifteen miles of desert. Farther to the north are the small Zaña, the large Lambayeque, the small Leche, and the very small Motupe Valleys. At present, the latter three form one irrigation unit. Our studies show that in ancient times this irrigation unit was connected by complicated irrigation systems with the Zaña and the Jequetepeque to the south. This five-valley unit was the largest contiguous economic area on the entire Coast of Peru and embraced probably about one-third of its cultivated area. Thus, it represented the most important economic section of the Chimú Empire. Considerable tension must have developed between the political center of gravity of the Empire situated in the Moche-Chicama region and the economic strength encompassed by this five-valley unit.

During its final expansion period the Chimú Empire extended still further north and included the Piura, Chira and Tumbes Valleys and possibly part of coastal Ecuador. This region, which may be characterized as *The Far Northern Extensions of the Chimú Empire*, is touched upon in Chapter XXIV.

Section E: *The Southern Zone of the Chimú Empire.*

South of the Moche Valley lay the Southern Zone of the Chimú Empire, composed of a number of small valley oases. Running from north to south they are as follows: the Virú, the miniature Chao, the Santa, the Nepeña, the Casma, the tiny Culebra and the Huarmey. These valleys are considerably isolated from one another, and we were able to determine that in the past they were never connected to one another by canal systems. Only when we come to the Pativilca area farther south do we find a multi-

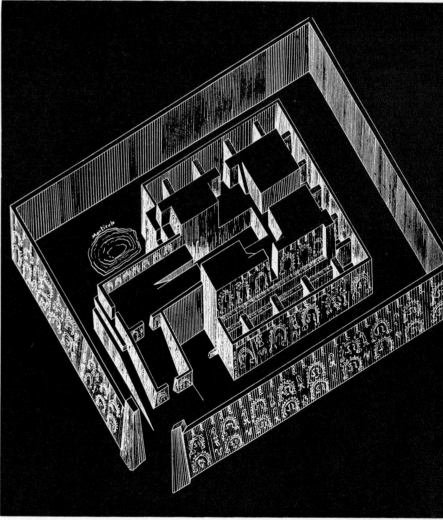

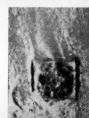

Fig. 1. Isometric projection of a reconstruction of Huaca el Dragón, drawn by Antonio Rodríguez SuySuy. See pp. 14 and 15 for a photograph of a wall of this pyramid · Fig. 2 (right). Aerial view of Huaca el Dragón before excavation. *Servicio 104 series.*

valley unit. It might not be amiss to consider this Fortaleza-Pativilca-Supe Complex, which in its Early and Middle Period was culturally part of the Central Coast, as the
southern anchor of the Chimú Empire during the latter
stage of its existence.

Section F: *The Southern Extensions of the Chimú Empire*.

The reports of several of the Spanish Chroniclers indicate that the Chimús had extended their power by
means of temporary conquests even further south along
the Central Coast. These extensions include the Huaura,
the Chancay, the Chillón-Rimac Complex (in which the
present city of Lima is situated), and the neighboring
small but important Lurín Valley. There is even some
evidence indicating that the Chimús had made excursions
into the South Central Coast as far as the Cañete Valley
and possibly as far as the Nazca (see Chapter XVII).

Having presented this general classification of valleys
in relationship to the Chimú Empire, we can now turn to
a description of some of our activities in the Moche
Valley. Since Dr. Schaedel is preparing a detailed
archaeological monograph about this valley, in which he
lived and worked for almost three years, we will restrict
ourselves to a bare outline of our activities there.

The Moche Valley, considered relatively small, at present has a cultivated area of some twenty-five thousand
acres. On the basis of our survey of the ruins of ancient
canal systems, we have tentatively concluded that this
area may have had almost twice as many acres under
cultivation in ancient times. As a result, the ancient
Moche Valley might be classified as having been almost
medium-sized. In contrast, the neighboring Chicama Valley to the north had, formerly, a maximum cultivated
area possibly triple that of the Moche.

Why did this small to medium-sized Moche Valley, and
not the larger and richer Chicama Valley, become the
political-military center of the Chimú Empire? This
question cannot be adequately answered on the basis of
our present knowledge. However, some suggestions may
be thrown out that may help to "fence in" the problem.

Perhaps it was *the level of development of the productive forces* reached by the coastal societies of ancient
Peru that made a small to medium-sized valley, with a
small to medium amount of water resources, the *most advantageous in size* for developing the greatest amount of
intravalley economic, social and political centralization.
And such a centralization of the greater part of the valley
would have been necessary before relatively permanent

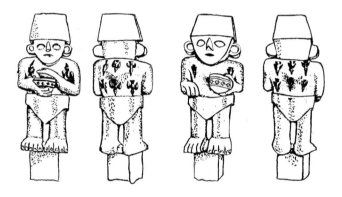

conquests of other valleys could have taken place. *Smaller*
valleys like the Virú, for instance, may have been able to
achieve an earlier political unity, but would *not have had
the strength* to conquer the larger neighboring valleys.
On the other hand, *larger* valleys, like the Chicama and,
even more so, the Lambayeque, *may have been too large*
to have become more than loose political federations.
Perhaps!

Environmental factors also undoubtedly help to explain the political predominance of the ancient Moche
Valley. To the south stretched the long protective desert,
beyond which lay the small, politically weak Virú and
the insignificant Chao Valley. On the other hand, to the
north, beyond the narrow desert, lay the large Chicama
Valley. But as a result of its very size, the latter may
have consisted of a number of political units that were
at best only loosely federated. Each of these units could

have been absorbed by the Moche through a combination of strong external military pressure and shrewd diplo-
matic maneuvers. This would have made the Chicama Valley a kind of "host" that economically fed the smaller
but better organized Moche Valley. The combining of
the two then produced the basis for a powerful economic-
political unit. Calancha refers to the marriage of Chacma,
the "ruler" of Chicama, with the Grand Chimú at Chan-
Chan, thus apparently symbolizing such a union. Once
such a relationship had been established, the Moche-
Chicama unit would become a key economic, political,
and military area, ready for further expansion.

Other environmental factors that may have aided the
early political growth of the Moche Valley were undoubtedly the specific geographic nature and social forms of
the nearby Sierra region and their interrelationships with
those of the Coast. But our information about this prob-

Fig. 3 (left and right). Wooden idols found by Dr. Schaedel when
he was excavating Huaca el Dragón. For details see the Spring
1951 issue of *Archaeology* • Fig. 4 (above). Bertha Rojas, student
of archaeology at the University of Trujillo, points to the relief
decorations on one of the outside walls of Huaca el Dragón.
Schaedel • Fig. 5 (below). Students and workmen of the Trujillo
Institute clearing the walls of Huaca el Dragón. The jeep frequently
used by the author can be seen here in its best condition. *Schaedel.*

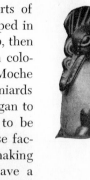

lem is now too meager to permit us to do more than mention it here.

Did the Moche contain capitals during previous periods? According to the archaeological studies of Rafael Larco Hoyle, there may have been a Mochica "Empire" consisting of six valleys: the Chicama, Moche, Virú, Chao, Santa and Nepeña. Mochica ceramics have also been found in the Jequetepeque and as apparent intrusions in the Lambayeque. But the discovery in a widespread area of the *same* ceramic and possibly architectural styles does not necessarily imply a correspondingly unified *political* organization. It is possible, however, that a mature theocracy interrelated in various ways with a strong group of rising secular chiefs, one or the other in control, *could have established such a rather unique "Empire".* Since the Huaca del Sol, the largest Mochica pyramid, lies in the Moche Valley, could not this *huaca* and its surrounding structures have been the capital?

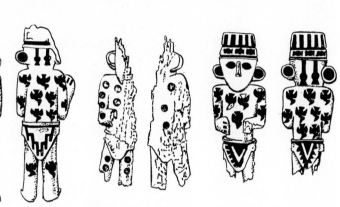

So little is known of the hectic sequence of highland and coastal influences that characterized the subsequent Middle Period that it is frankly impossible to state whether the Moche Valley continued for some part of this period as a capital. Was perhaps ancient Galindo (Fig. 11), in the middle part of the valley, the capital during this period?

Later on, according to the Anonymous Trujillano, Taycanamo, the legendary founder of the Chimú dynasty, began his reign by conquering a small portion of the valley. His descendants succeeded in uniting all of the valley and then commenced a series of conquests of neighboring valleys. These were governed by the Chimú rulers from the rapidly growing city of ChanChan.

After the defeat of the Chimús by the Incas, the latter, as was customary, left the ruling Chimús "in power," probably under the direction of an Inca "*Gauleiter*" and

a reliable Inca garrison. The Moche thus still remained the "capital" of the Chimús. But the "empire" had lost most of its territory and its rulers most of their power. When the Spaniards arrived they found a Chimú chief still living with some of his people in ChanChan, undoubtedly dreaming of the great power once wielded by his ancestors.

Why did the Spaniards, shortly after arriving in Peru, establish Trujillo, situated as it was next to the ancient capital of ChanChan, as their "capital" of the North? Were any of the factors that led to the building of Chan-Chan by the Chimús in the Moche Valley still present? Furthermore, did the Spaniards feel that it would be advisable to establish their northern "capital" next to that of the *largest coastal pre-Inca capital,* and thus through puppet Chimú rulers maintain better *control* over the people? The Spaniards, when they first arrived, after all knew little of the relative strength and resistance power of the coastal peoples. Besides, the Spaniards soon found out that the ancient "capital" of the Chimús and its surroundings still contained many buried treasures that had escaped the ravages of the Incas.

Trujillo's central location near the potential ports of Huanchaco, Guañape and Malabrigo may have helped in the decision. Salaverry, the modern port of Trujillo, then known as La Garita, was used only sporadically in colonial times. In addition, in the upper parts of the Moche Valley cutting directly into the Sierras, the Spaniards found important deposits of metals. These they began to mine and send via Trujillo and its nearby ports to be loaded on their ships bound for Spain. All of these factors collectively must have played some role in making Trujillo the northern "capital." Could we but have a record of the session at which the colonial authorities decided on the site of Trujillo!

Let us now turn to some of the archaeological aspects of the Moche Valley. The ancient city of ChanChan gives this valley its unique distinction (see photographs in Chapter VIII). This city, the largest of Indian America — with a former population of possibly about fifty thousand —, consisted of eleven huge living compounds, each one surrounded by adobe walls about twenty to twenty-five feet high. Most of the walls are still standing

Fig. 7 (below, right). A walled road that leads from the northern outside wall of ChanChan to one of the main canals in the Moche Valley is shown in this oblique aerial photograph. The canal can be seen in the background. The two parallel lines cutting across the road are the railroad and the Pan American Highway. *Kosok.*

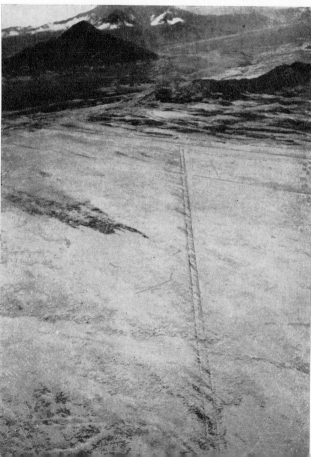

Fig. 6 (above). Ancient walled road, on the *pampa* north of ChanChan, leading from the Moche Valley to the Chicama. Its width of over seventy feet is unusual for an ancient road. *Kosok.*

Fig. 8. A section of the large canal that once connected the Chicama and Moche Valleys and transformed the desolate, barren landscape into one covered with green vegetation. *Kosok* • Fig. 9 (left margin). Water jugs showing (top) a "lean-to" type of house on a *circular* step pyramid (a very rare form), (center) a steep-roofed house with frogs on the gable, and (bottom) a similar type of house on a rectangular step pyramid. *Baessler.*

and make a dramatic impression upon both traveler and scientist. Each compound contains the remains of many rooms usually grouped around a court, long and labyrinthine corridors, elevated structures with rooms and passageways that appear to be palaces, and usually one small flat pyramid with adjoining plaza. It appears possible that each of these compounds was inhabited by one of the clans or tribes that made up the ruling groups of the Chimú Empire. A number of large pyramids are located *outside* the walled compounds, indicating the secular, urban nature of the compounds and the weakened power

90

of the priesthood. However, the Empire was destroyed by the Incas some sixty to seventy years before the Spaniards came, and the Spanish records, thus far discovered, tell us little about these people and their capital!

But even if new records should be discovered (see Chapter VIII), large scale archaeological excavations would nevertheless unearth a wealth of materials, expressive of the social and cultural life of this nerve center of the Chimú Empire, that documents by themselves could never yield. Moreover, it must be remembered that while documents are not always reliable, and traditions of the past are even less dependable, the existence of many physical structures and implements found by archaeological techniques can never be denied. It is only our *interpretation* of the social meaning of archaeological discoveries that may be incorrect.

We revisited ChanChan several times. Our main interest lay in seeing how the tremendous water demand of this large city related to the irrigation system of the whole valley. This system we had largely worked out and mapped in 1940-41, partly with the aid of Mr. Verne Grant. In 1948-49 we made, on the basis of the aerial photographs and additional field surveys, some modifications on our map. We wandered through the forlorn remains of this once great metropolis to see if we could connect the canals that had once brought water *into* the city with the remains of the canals *within* the city. But our attempts ended in complete failure. For we could find no canals within the city, with the exception of a few small modern ones! As we wandered around, we pondered the reason. The only explanation we could venture lay in the fact that centuries of destruction had completely filled the canals inside the city with debris. Archaeological excavations should show the presence of such internal canals. In this respect, ChanChan contrasts sharply with the large, archaeologically unexplored, urban center of Apurlé in the northern Motupe Valley, where the canal system in most of its details is clearly visible both from the air and the ground (see frontispiece).

Just to the east of the Pan American Highway and north of ChanChan is the medium-sized Huaca el Dragón, which Dr. Schaedel and his assistants were in the process of excavating. The last time we were there, a continuous adobe frieze more than 500 feet long had been cleared. The design gave us the impression that it was associated with calendrical records, and seemed to us another example of the many calendrical remains that so far have been overlooked by historians and archaeologists.

Fig. 10. An interesting region, northeast of Cerro Cabras (Goats Hill), where a major road, a major wall and a major canal cut across one another. *Servicio 104:595.*

Since our last visit, the interior of the *huaca* has been excavated by Dr. Schaedel and Señor Rodríguez SuySuy. As a result, it became clear that this *huaca* had not actually been constructed as a solid adobe pyramid but as a temple containing a series of rooms. But during the centuries the adobe walls had crumbled and filled the rooms, creating a ruin which appeared to be an adobe mound (Figs. 1 to 5). Some fifteen wooden idols, together with associated materials, were found in the course of excavation. These finds, along with other evidence, particularly the type and style of friezes, led Dr. Schaedel to date this site as belonging to the Middle Period, i.e., the period shortly before the building of ChanChan.

It should be pointed out here that on the walls of a small mound in the Chotuna group in the Lambayeque Valley further north, we found a small portion of a frieze similar, in many ways, to that of Huaca el Dragón (see also Horkheimer, 1944:42). This may well indicate cultural interrelationships that must have been strong during the Middle Period. But more excavation in this mound, as well as in some similar mounds, must be carried out before any relationships can be definitely established.

Outside of ChanChan we located some twenty-five archaeological sites in the Moche Valley, most of them pyramids and population centers. Many sites listed on our maps refer to more than one pyramid at each site. In some valleys there are clusters with as many as twenty-five pyramids in them! All of the pyramids are flat-topped, for they were probably used by the priests for carrying on religious ceremonies. A few of them contain vestiges of rooms on the top platform, indicating that they were probably inhabited by the priests — or by secular or semi-secular rulers during the long periods of transition towards a secular state.

Flat-topped pyramids with ramps or steps have been found in many parts of the world. As far as we know, such pyramids were built primarily for ceremonial purposes and played a role similar to that of churches in Christian communities. Situated, like these, on one side of a central square with secular structures opposite, pyramids, like churches, were *the centers of the living*. However, when priests and chiefs died they obviously desired to be buried in or beside the holy pyramid — just as in Europe rulers and bishops desired to be buried in or next to the holy church or cathedral. Likewise, the rest of the people wanted to be buried in the hallowed ground around or near the pyramid, just as in our own civilization many persons desired to be buried in the graveyard

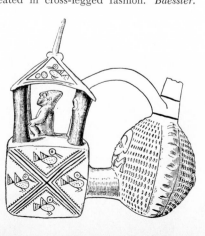

Fig. 11 (above). A part of the large Middle Period ruin of Galindo nestled in a *quebrada* at the foot of the hills. Note the large rectangular structure with a pyramid or palace at one end, apparently the former habitation of a ruler. Much of the rest of the ruin consists of hundreds of small stone-walled rooms (see text). *Shippee-Johnson* • Fig. 12 (left). Antonio Rodríguez Suy-Suy sitting on a stone on which has been carved the outlines of a face. The stone is located east of Simbal near Chachic on the northern bank of Río Chacchita. *Kosok* • Fig. 13 (below). An elaborate type of water jug showing a coastal house with pitched roof (indicating Sierra origin?) and high gable. The figure portrays an arrogant ruler seated in cross-legged fashion. *Baessler.*

adjoining the village church. Thus, near the centers of the living are often the centers of the dead! But such ceremonial pyramids must not be confused with tribal or royal *burial* mounds or pyramids whose *primary purpose* was the *honoring of the dead* (see p. 12).

But why were pyramids built by the priesthood at all? We cannot, so far, reconstruct much of the social psychology of the past. But one thing stands out. Pyramids are located on flat coastal plains; rarely are they found in mountainous regions. It seems quite likely that among mountain people the priest carried on services from a small hillock. When these people moved to the plains, artificial mounds were built for carrying on these services.

In addition, when conducting his services from an accustomed mound, the priest, by means of his elevated position above the worshippers, emphasized his *social, cultural and, later on, political superiority over the common people*. For, architecturally, a mound or pyramid is the easiest and most primitive way to achieve height.

While it is true that in Peru the growth of pyramid building appears to come with the growth of priestly power, at a later time pyramids may also have served

Fig. 16. Vertical aerial photograph of Huaca de los Chinos. The pyramid, which is made of stone and earth, apparently received its name in the nineteenth century from a nearby settlement or burial site of Chinese contract laborers. See Figs. 14 and 15. *Servicio 104:507* • Fig. 17 (below). Señor José Eulogio Garrido, former editor of *Industria*, the leading North Coast daily, now the director of the Archaeological Museum of the University of Trujillo. Beside him is an old *huaquero* from Moche who worked for Uhle in 1899 when the first excavations of Mochica ruins were made at the Huaca de la Luna. This pyramid can be seen in the background at the foot of the hill. *Schaedel.*

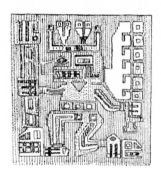 

Fig. 14 (above). Plaster of Paris model of Huaca de los Chinos and surrounding structures, made by John Storck on the basis of a ground plan drawn by Schaedel and Rodríguez. The steep ramps leading from level to level were probably composed of stone steps; the present condition of the ruin makes its reconstruction difficult. See Figs. 15 and 16. *Kosok.* • Fig. 15 (below). Ground view from an adjacent hill of the stone and earth Huaca de los Chinos, showing its present dilapidated condition. *Schaedel.* See also Figs. 14 and 16.

secular rulers. *For once an architectural form has been created it may then be used for other than its original purposes.*

In Peru most pyramids as well as other structures were built of sunbaked mud bricks (*adobe*). On the Central Coast very large rectangular blocks of sunbaked mud,

several feet wide and long (*adobónes*) were often used instead of adobes. In many of the constructions rough stones were set in mud. As a result of occasional rains some of the mud has washed off the adobe pyramids. Thus, most pyramids have lost the sharp contours they must have possessed originally.

On the huge plain north of the city of ChanChan there are no pyramids except the small Huaca el Dragón and the companion Huaca Tacaynamo just across the Pan American Highway. In this plain, where we spent time tracing canals and roads, we found three ancient roads that led toward the Chicama Valley. The most interesting of these roads paralleled the sea several miles inland and seemed to have come from ChanChan. It was about twenty-four yards wide and had walls of stone which had originally been about six feet high. These dimensions are unusually large and indicate that it must have been especially important. The walls suddenly ended in the desert in two well-built pillar-like constructions of stone that may have formed, at one time, the portals that controlled the entry from the north into the Moche Valley and ChanChan. Beyond these posts, faint traces of the continuation of the road, but with much lower walls, could be detected in the windswept desert to the north. Later, Dr. Schaedel made a trip in his jeep confirming these traces. But even the traces disappeared as he approached the Chicama Valley (Fig. 6).

One of the other roads, which paralleled the one mentioned above, was considerably smaller and was perhaps of another construction period. The third road (Fig. 10), much further inland, was probably part of the north-south trunk highway that passed the Huaca del Sol.

A fourth "road" remained a mystery to us. Flanked by

Fig. 18 (above). Huaca del Sol, presumably the largest pyramid in Peru. *Kosok* • Fig. 19 (lower left). Vertical aerial photograph of all that is left of Huaca del Sol. A large part of the original *huaca* was washed away by the action of the Moche River. The course of the river was slightly altered in Spanish times by a local landowner, who hoped eventually to wash away the whole pyramid in order to find the treasures that were rumored to be buried within it. Compare with Fig. 20. For a clearer view turn the photograph upside down. *Servicio 104:208* • Fig. 20 (lower right). Ground plan and side elevations of Huaca del Sol drawn by Bishop Martínez de Compañón • Fig. 21 (previous page, center column). A piece of cloth and a clay cup, both in Tiahuanacoid style, found in the Huaca del Sol. *Uhle.*

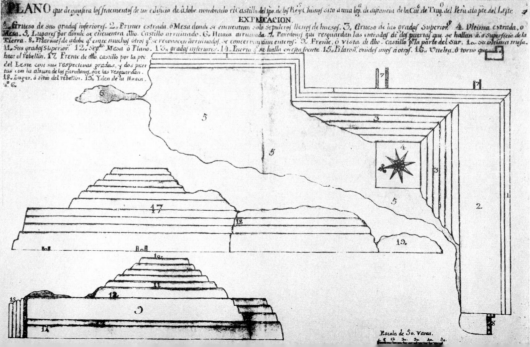

high walls, it led from ChanChan for a distance of only a few miles in a straight line to the nearby major Moro Canal. Was this a ceremonial road to the sacred waters of the main canal? Was its astronomical alignment a sacred one? Did it also carry water to the city? Perhaps it fulfilled all three of these functions (Fig. 7).

In checking the ancient canals that had run through the huge plain north of ChanChan, we concentrated on a canal that must once have had not only economic but also political significance. It was a large canal which had its intake quite a distance up the neighboring Chicama Valley and which brought water to the fields near ChanChan. If our field observations are correct, it also connected with the Moro Canal, the largest and highest *acequia madre* (mother canal) on the northern side of the Moche Valley. Did this canal indicate a control of the Chicama Valley by the Moche, or vice versa? If it already existed in Early Chimú times, its control *may* have been in the hands of the Chicama rulers. During the Middle Period, either of the two valleys could have controlled the canal. During the Late Chimú era, when, as we know, ChanChan dominated both the valleys, this long canal *must* have been under the control of the Chimú rulers in the Moche Valley. Such *intervalley* canals, of which we were to find a number, always indicate close *economic* relationships. *But they cannot by themselves give us a definite answer to the political relationships existing in the past.*

Since no aerial photographs of the area through which the Moche-Chicama canal ran were available, we had to follow it on the ground in order to map it. The terrain was too rough for the jeep and no horses were procurable at the time we were there, so we traced the canal on foot. It took two days to traverse this barren, lonesome and forbidding region which contained not the slightest sign of life. And here, less than five hundred years ago, a lush vegetation had flourished! During our walk alongside or inside the canal — which at times completely disappeared — we searched for potsherds that might help date the canal. We found very few, and they were generally crude ware from which no satisfactory cultural period affiliations could be established (Fig. 8).

While studying our aerial photographs at the Servicio, we were surprised to find the remains of a very extensive settlement that straddled several important canals near the "neck" of the Moche. These ruins were later studied in great detail by Dr. Schaedel and his assistants. Galindo, as the settlement is called, is an exceedingly fasci-

Fig. 22 (left margin). Late Chimú metal vase. *Muelle* • Fig. 23 (top). Señor Garrido and friends at a Moche village fiesta. *Schaedel* • Fig. 24 (above, left). A local music group in Moche preparing for a radio broadcast. *Schaedel* • Fig. 25 (above, right). Señor Garrido dancing at the Moche village fiesta. *Schaedel.*

We also investigated the ancient canal system on the narrower southern side of the valley. By means of our aerial photographs we were able to trace on the ground the large old main canal, which had once led the waters through a gap in the hills to the whole region south of the Huaca del Sol. We also found many parts of a smaller canal "intertwined" with the main canal and apparently dating from a different — earlier? — period. The misnamed Huaca del Sol, the largest pyramid of ancient Peru, together with the nearby Huaca de la Luna, was possibly the center of the ancient Mochica ceremonial

nating ruin. Extending for several miles, it is intersected by many roads and canals and is bounded by high perimeter walls and hundreds of rooms and house-foundations packed now in staggered form against the steep hillside, now filling the plain of a sloping *quebrada*. Not much evidence of desecration is to be found. Thus, it would seem to be a site which, if completely excavated, would reveal much data about the social organization and daily life of a typical North Coast town of the Middle Period of perhaps 1000 A.D. or earlier (Fig. 11).

cult in this and neighboring valleys (Figs. 18 to 21).

On this small southern side, and almost at the foot of the Huaca del Sol, lies the old Indian village of Moche. In 1945, the American anthropologist, John Phillip Gillin, published an interesting study of this village and successfully recorded some of its ancient traditions.

We also visited the small Huaca Pelada, situated between Trujillo and the sea, which was just in the process of being excavated by Señor Julian Castro, one of Dr. Schaedel's students. He had found, among other things, a carved box of balsa wood and some llama burials. *Huaqueros* have often found such burials along the Coast, indicating the wide use of the llama in this region, either for ceremonial purposes, food for the upper class, transportation of goods between Coast and Sierras, or for all three purposes.

One of the most important of our field trips was to the Poroto area approximately twenty miles up the Moche Valley. There we located an involved system of ancient canals running at different levels along the sides of the hills. On another trip, we discovered the main canal which we traced as far as Shirán, several miles farther up the valley. As a result of a trip on the other side of the Moche River, we located other ancient canals. These trips enabled us to determine that formerly a kind of irrigated "pocket" had existed here which was separated by a narrowing of the valley from the lower coastal part of the Moche Valley. At the same time it was separated by a long narrow chasm from the Sierra type of cultivated regions further up the valley.

In 1941 we had discovered the existence of similar pockets in the Nepeña Valley at Moro, in the Zaña at Oyotún and in the Lambayeque at Chongoyape. At present there are still cultivated areas in these pockets but, as at Poroto, they are much smaller than they had been in ancient times.

The Poroto pocket in the Moche is the smallest of the four mentioned. Each of the other three is still large enough to maintain an economic and social existence somewhat distinct from that of the main part of the valley. In fact, each has its own administrative unit and irrigation official and contains a town of at least several thousand inhabitants in which the life of the pocket is centered. In ancient times, when the area of each pocket was larger, and when transportation to the main part of the valley was not by bus or car, the economic, political and cultural independence of each pocket must have been considerably greater than it is today.

Archaeologically, these pockets should be interesting to explore. They were undoubtedly occupied when in the early past the first settlers moved down from the mountains. But it is possible that their full development may have taken place in those periods of the Peruvian Indian cultures when strong population pressures on the Coast reacted upon these pockets and forced the fullest utilization of all possible lands here. But no one has yet tackled this problem.

We were also concerned with some settlements and ruins along the sea. On several occasions we visited the old Indian fishing town of Huanchaco, situated in a cove to the northwest of ChanChan. Such fishing villages were established some five thousand years ago in the coves which line the desert Coast of Peru and Chile. Some of them exist till this day. Thus they represent the longest consecutively settled sites in coastal Peru and Chile!

As the original agricultural settlements expanded in size and number, the role of fishing and fishing communities must also have grown steadily. And no wonder!

Fish was the major source of animal proteins for the coastal population in ancient times. True, some llamas may have been slaughtered now and then, and some hunting done in the middle and upper reaches of the coastal valleys, but the amount of meat thus procured was so small that at best it sufficed only for the chiefs, priests and high officials. The great mass of people had a basic diet of corn (starch and minerals) and beans (*simple vegetable* proteins). Thus, for the more *complex animal* proteins they had to depend upon fish.

The cold Humboldt current as it passes along the Peruvian shore has always been teeming with enormous quantities of fish, more than enough to feed the whole coastal agricultural population. The sea has thus been the great food larder. It is therefore not surprising to learn from Calancha that the sea had been one of the important gods of the ancients. For the same reason, the fish motif was used extensively in pottery and textile designs.

How was the fishing done? Undoubtedly, as it still is done in Huanchaco and other coastal communities — by means of *caballitos* (little horses). These are flimsy vessels made by tying together bundles of reeds which grow in nearby marshes (Figs. 26 and 27). They are similar to those seen today on distant Lake Titicaca on the Peruvian-Bolivian highland border. They are manned by one or two persons and venture at most only a few miles off the coast. But this is sufficient, for the fish-laden Humboldt current hugs the coastline on its northward drive. Drawings on *huacos* from early Mochica times show

Fig. 26 (left). These boats for off-shore fishing, generally called *caballitos* (little horses), are made of several bundles of *totora* reeds tied together. They date from Mochica times, some two thousand years ago, if not earlier. The scene is at Huanchaco, an ancient fishing settlement north of ChanChan. When not in use, the *caballitos* are placed on end to dry. *Kosok* • Fig. 27 (center). Boy riding a *caballito* near Huanchaco. *Kosok* • Fig. 28 (right). Fishermen from Huanchaco. *Schaedel* • Fig. 29 (right margin). Priest sacrificing victim. *Baessler.*

similar boats, indicating their ancient origin. In fact some of them are shown with elaborate "royal" trappings, indicating that they were probably the boats of both the rulers and the people (see Chapter XVIII, Fig. 10).

But did not the ancients have larger boats? As far as we know, they did not. The principal tree that grows along the Coast is the small, gnarled algarroba, which is unsuited for boat building. Could they have used the large balsa rafts so common in the Guayaquil Bay region of Ecuador, copied and popularized by the modern Kon-Tiki expedition? True, the various Chimú rulers may have acquired some as curios or as booty, but there is no indication so far that they played any economic role in the life of the people.

This may seem odd. But, on investigation, it becomes clear that the ancients did not need such rafts for fishing purposes; their *caballitos* sufficed. For political and military purposes, the larger balsa rafts would, likewise, probably have proved of little help. The Pacific, unlike the Guayaquil Basin, is not an inland sea and therefore did not provide "short cuts" where balsas could be used to advantage by traders or conquerors. Since in Peru the sea merely follows the coastal plain, there was no advantage in sending troops, supplies, or booty by sea. Indeed, roads paralleling the sea and often alongside it made possible more rapid transportation of materials and men and thus were a more efficient means of keeping control over the component valleys of coastal "empires."

With the coming of the Spaniards, the sea began to play an entirely new political-military role. For by control of the sea from *without*, the invaders easily brought each coastal valley under control by landing troops and provisions from Spain at the numerous harbors which dot the coast of Peru. Some of these troops in turn were marched up into the Sierras to help maintain the initial conquest of the Incas by the Spaniards. As a result, the "dry Nile," i.e., the long north-south Sierra road that had been the political-military backbone of the Inca Empire, began to fall into disuse. In turn, the sea became the "wet Inca road," by means of which Spanish power could be maintained and the highly-prized loot of Peru sent to the "mother" country. Thus, for the first time, the sea became the prime factor in the political and military control of Peru!

Fig. 30 (left margin). Late Chimú metal vase. *Muelle.* • Fig. 31. Road leading into the Sierras. *U. S. Army.*

X

A Trip to Cachicadán in the Sierras

ONE DAY IN TRUJILLO, we learned that the Institute jeep was taking Captain Arboleda, a geographer and a former Peruvian Army officer, up into the Sierras for some work. Señor Garrido, Michael and I were invited to join him. We gladly accepted the invitation, for we had been working on the desert Coast for several months and were worn out with the steady grind. The Captain, who was in his seventies, was a jovial and lively fellow who kept us entertained during the trip with many stories of his various experiences, both professional and amorous.

I had been through part of this region in 1941 on my visit to Huamachuco, whose ancient hilltop fortress had once been the capital of a powerful mountain state. But it was a worthwhile experience to go up the Moche Valley again through the various vegetation and habitation zones ranging from the hot, dry coastal desert to the wet, cold Sierra. We welcomed every such trip up a coastal valley because it gave us a chance to study another connecting link between Coast and Sierra.

Of special interest here is the relatively uninhabited region that separates these two main population zones. Theoretically, this region can, of course, be cultivated by means of irrigation — but there is no land to cultivate! Here the Moche River, like most of the other rivers on the Coast, runs through a relatively deep, narrow chasm where the valley bottom contains practically no usable soil and where the sides are too steep and rocky to permit any cultivation. Only in a few favored spots, on some dizzy mountain heights, does one occasionally see rainfall crops. This comparatively uninhabited middle zone, which is a characteristic feature of all Peruvian coastal valleys, has separated the Coast and Sierra populations into two distinct economic, political and cultural units throughout their history.

The narrow paths and roads up the valleys have been the only links that have connected the peoples of the two zones. Paths and roads have always been the veins and arteries uniting geographically disparate peoples. At times these roads were used for peaceful, democratic trade purposes; at other times they carried brutal, conquering armies and their returning trains of loot and tribute. But in every case, *roads represent some form of union. They connect people and property.* This thought struck us on our trip, since we had, until then, spent much of our time studying walls and walled compounds whose function was to *separate peoples and property.* It then suddenly became clear to us — *walls divide, roads unite!* But both evolve simultaneously and interact upon each other's development, as mankind, in its struggle for property rights and control, rises from the primitive agricultural stage into modern industrial society.

The trip to Cachicadán in the Sierras took some eight hours. We zigzagged along dizzy roads up the steep and ever-changing mountain slopes for six hours. Finally, we reached the bleak, cold, wet and windy *puna* (high mountain pasture) that stretches throughout most of Peru along both sides of the Continental Divide. This desolate region, impressive in its vastness and loneliness, is beyond the limits of trees and cultivated crops. It is covered in part with *ichu,* a kind of tough grass generally not eaten by the small herds of sheep that occasionally graze here on the few softer grasses and herbs. Here we passed the large and dangerous copper mines of Quiru-

Fig. 1. Bell tower in the historic Sierra town of Huamachuco. *Kosok.*

97

Fig. 2. Modern highway crossing the cold, treeless and uninhabited *puna,* the lonesomest and most desolate part of the Andes. The black spots in front are small lakes. The white spots are islands of snow and ice or rock outcroppings. *U. S. Army 43-L-79* • Fig. 3 (margin). Child of the Andes. *Kosok* • Fig. 4 (right). Fiesta scene at Santiago de Chuco. *Schaedel.*

vilca, where the workers dwell in miserable houses near the ominous mineshafts.

We crossed the Divide at an altitude of some 14,000 feet, and shortly thereafter were happy to arrive at Santiago de Chuco, the largest mountain town of the entire region. After a hot drink, which cheered us up considerably, we descended the winding mountain road to the bottom of the warm and pleasant valley of Huay-

98

chaca, which connects with the Chuquicara Valley (see Chapter XIX). There the road ascended the other side of the valley until our jeep finally reached the attractive settlement of Cachicadán.

Cachicadán has a considerable number of thermal springs that have been known since ancient times. Situated on the charming mountainside with its many poplar and eucalyptus trees bordering the roads and walls, it has all the makings of an important watering place in the future. At present, however, it is merely a small, attractive Indian village, which is visited by a limited number of vacationists and moderately ill people who have heard of the curative value of its baths.

The important valley of Chuquicara, just mentioned, is a northern branch of the Santa. This valley, with its surrounding cultivated mountain slopes, is an area of fairly dense population that connects directly with the upper Santa area to the south (Callejón de Huaylas) and with the Cajamarca area to the north (see map, p. 180).

In ancient times, these areas also boasted a fairly dense population, as indicated by the many Indian villages dating back to the past, as well as by the numerous ancient ruined sites, most of them still unexplored. The Peruvian Army maps indicate extensive remains of an old north-south Inca road in this region, probably the main trunk line of the Inca Empire, connecting Cuzco with Quito. On the maps are also indicated a series of ruins dotting the mountain crest that separates the Chuquicara and the Chao Valleys. On the hills bordering the southern side of the Tablachaca, in the area constituting the present day province of Pallasca, Dr. Schaedel explored interesting remains of a number of important sites. Antonio Rodríguez SuySuy carried on some preliminary archaeological reconnaissance in the Santiago de Chuco region.

A broad archaeological survey of the whole Sierra region from Cajamarca south to the upper Santa should throw tremendous light not merely on the nature and interrelationship of the ancient cultures of these complex areas with one another, but also on the interrelationship of the Sierra cultures with those of the Coast. Such interrelations are indicated by some archaeological finds, and even by a few documentary references, but their extent and character are still only vaguely known.

In thinking about the nature of the interrelationship between Coast and Sierra, one is led immediately to the problem of trade. But unfortunately, with the exception of a few short remarks made by several of the Chroniclers, there is no indication of the nature and the amount of

trade that existed in ancient Peru. Nor is there mention of a *trading class,* so important among the less developed Aztecs of Mexico. True, the existence of local markets is occasionally mentioned, but these probably were bartering centers for various craft objects, specialties of one or another nearby village, and for certain fruits, vegetables and herbs whose cultivation may, for some reason, have been localized.

It may well be supposed that during several thousand years of occupation and growth a considerable amount of inter-valley specialization in many products took place. These products may then have been carried regularly by traders from valley to valley. Indeed, some objects may either have passed through many valleys and through many hands or have been carried all the way by "long distance" traders before they finally reached their ultimate

Figs. 5 and 6. Street scenes in mountain villages. The walls are made of mud brick, the roofs of orange tile. *Kosok*

buyers. Such trade was carried on by various peoples of a much lower cultural level and economy in both North and South America.

But we would expect an even greater amount of trade to have prevailed between the Sierra on the one hand and the Coast on the other. For Sierra and Coast each produced distinct raw materials and craftsmen's goods, a condition that undoubtedly led to an extensive exchange system between the two regions. The Sierra also yielded copper, silver, and gold, which were highly prized and worked in great quantities on the Coast but which were not mined there. Cieza de León (I, Chap. LXVII) mentions the fact that while in Motupe he was informed that the people there traded with those of the Sierra at certain seasons. But why did most of the Chroniclers fail to describe some of this trade or mention the traders?

With the growth of the Inca and Chimú Empires, several things probably happened to this trade. In the first place, as the result of conquest, *articles of trade became articles of tribute!* They still kept moving from valley to valley, but now mainly in one direction — to the capital of the conqueror! Many articles were still *transported*, but few were *exchanged*. It may well be said that in the Inca Empire — and probably in the Chimú — *transportation increased, but trade declined.*

Another aspect of the problem must be mentioned. When the Chimús — and later the Incas — conquered a wealthy region, they not only established a regular tribute but also sent back to their capitals the best craftsmen they could capture, thus making these cities the leading art and craft centers in Peru. This obviously reduced still further the amount of trade that had existed in previous times.

Finally, we must consider what may also be an important factor in our problem. In Calancha (Bk. III, Chap. II) there is an interesting passage:

The Chimo imposed upon all his vassals the duty of paying tribute, and among other things he employed six thousand Indians to bring to him from the highlands gold, silver, copper and other products.

Even if the number 6000 may be an exaggeration, the statement is still important. But some difficulty arises in interpreting it. No Chronicler mentions the Chimús as having permanently dominated territory in the Sierras. In the light of this, how could they obtain *tribute* from the Sierras? While absence of any reference in the Chroniclers to Chimú conquests of certain parts of the Sierras may not necessarily be proof that conquests did not occur,

Fig. 7. An unusually intensified form of terraced farming (*andenes*) found in the province of Huamachuco. *Shippee-Johnson* • Fig. 8 (margin and p. 97). Ceremonial wooden sceptres with Recuay motifs found in Mollepata near Cachicadán. *Garrido-Cacho.*

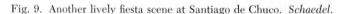

Fig. 9. Another lively fiesta scene at Santiago de Chuco. *Schaedel.*

the statement of Calancha may point to something else. Might it not be interpreted to mean that the Chimú ruler had a *trade treaty* with his Sierra allies, under the terms of which the latter shipped metals in exchange for fine cotton textiles and other coastal products much in demand in the Sierras? If this were true, would it have meant that the Chimú ruler, in addition to exacting the one way tribute within his empire, may also have taken over the formerly unregulated trade with his allies and converted it into a *state monopoly*? And if the Chimús had done this, why could not the Inca state also have controlled and taken over such trade?

Summing up, we can state that just before the arrival of the Spaniards apparently most large-scale *trade* had come under the control of the Inca state and had been largely transformed into *tribute*. In other words, there was much *transportation* of goods but little *trade*.

When the Spaniards arrived, they were so amazed at the wealth and organization of the Inca Empire that their main interest was to loot the wealth, establish an organized tribute system and develop their own inter-continental trading system. In other words, the conquerors did not care to — nor were they able to — understand important facets of the economy of the conquered. Only today can we begin to piece together our scant knowledge of the nature and development of ancient trade.

Fig. 10 (left). An unusual aerial view of a relatively level section of the Andes, showing an apparently endless number of *chacras* (small cultivated plots of land). *U. S. Army 82-R-49* • Fig. 11 (below). Typical mountain road with typical truck. *Kosok.*

XI

Heart of Mochicaland: The Chicama Valley

ALTHOUGH LITTLE IS KNOWN ABOUT TRADE and traders in ancient Peru, more information fortunately is available concerning priests and their activities. It has already been pointed out in Chapter VI that the priesthood played a leading role in the development and direction of early agricultural societies. Along the North-west Coast, this priesthood stage took place during the Very Early or Cupisnique Period and the two transitional Salinar and Gallinazo Periods. But it was during the outstanding Mochica (Early Chimú) Period that the priest-dominated society apparently reached the climax of its development in both creative abilities and power.

It is the ancient Mochica peoples who are famed for having constructed numerous large, steep adobe pyramids. But, even more important, the Mochicas produced, as a result of their highly developed artistic workmanship, the numerous beautiful ceremonial water jugs that are the pride of the Americas.

Of all the coastal valleys, it was the Chicama that developed this Mochica culture most widely and intensively. Moreover, it was probably maintained here after the other valleys farther south had entered the so-called Middle Period. Even today, when visiting various ruins in the Chicama Valley and examining excavated ceramics

Fig. 1. A side of Huaca Fachén, a typical solid adobe construction of the Mochica Period. The vertical streaks on the pyramid are the result of the occasional rains on the Coast of Peru. *Schaedel.* NOTE: The line-cut above is that of a Mochica *huaco. Guillen.* The decorative rules in this chapter are from Larco Hoyle's *Los Mochicas.*

three times that of the Moche River just to the south. The area under cultivation in this valley at present is likewise almost three times as large as that of the Moche Valley.

Like the Moche and many other rivers on the Coast of Peru, the Chicama flows southwesterly, thereby cutting the coastal plain in such a manner as to make the north bank the larger one. However, unlike many valleys on the Coast of Peru, the Chicama has more land in its coastal plain that can be cultivated by the amount of river water available. This is not only true today when the main crop of the valley is the water-consuming sugar cane, but it was also true in ancient times when maize, which requires

W. R. Grace & Company. At both of these *haciendas*, large mills are operated for the manufacture of white sugar, most of which is exported (Figs. 2 to 12).

Third in size and situated geographically between the above-mentioned plantations is Hacienda Chiclín, property of Señor Rafael Larco Herrera, a former Vice President of Peru. It contains the famous "Museo Arqueológico Rafael Larco Herrera," which is under the direction of Señor Larco's eldest son, Rafael Larco Hoyle, assisted by his brother Constante Larco Hoyle. Señor Rafael Larco Hoyle created and developed this excellent museum, which contains some of the finest Mochica and pre-Mochica ceramics and other artifacts. He has also

The Chicama Valley is one of the leading sugar producing centers in Peru. This series of photographs taken by the author on various sugar plantations on the Coast indicates some of the main steps in the growing and preparing of sugar • Fig. 2 (top, left). An aerial view of Hacienda Chiclín surrounded by fields of sugar cane • Fig. 3 (above, left). The planting process, in which short sections of cane are dropped into prepared furrows. Hacienda Paramonga • Fig. 4 (above, center). A field of growing sugar cane with the fortress of Paramonga in the background (see Chapter XXII) • Fig. 5 (above, right). The burning of a field after the cane has ripened. This is done to get rid of the dead "leaves" that would interfere with the sugar extraction process. At the same time the burning of the fields leaves the ashes as a fertilizer for the next crop. Since it is filled with sap, the sugar cane stalk does not burn. Hacienda Pátapo.

Fig. 6 (top, right). Workers with machetes cutting the soot-covered sugar cane after the fields have been burned over. Hacienda Cartavio • Fig. 7 (directly above). Empty railroad cars are drawn by oxen to the fields where they are loaded with the cut sugar cane. Hacienda Cartavio.

in the museum at Chiclín, one is struck by the predominance of Mochica cultural remains over those of other periods — a condition less marked in other valleys. Thus, the Chicama Valley can truly be called the heart of Mochicaland.

Before discussing further the problems of the culture and history of the Chicama Valley, let us glance at its geographical-sociological features. Through it courses the large Chicama River, which has an average annual water discharge in excess of one billion cubic meters, about

much less water than sugar cane, was the chief crop.

Today, the valley is dominated by four large sugar *haciendas*, Casa Grande, Cartavio, Chiclín and Chiquitoy, each of which represents an integration of a number of smaller ones. Casa Grande, the largest *hacienda* on the Peruvian Coast, extends mainly along the upper and middle portions of the valley, where, as in other valleys, the best soil is found and where the most irrigation water is available throughout the year. Farther down the valley, and next in size, stretches Hacienda Cartavio, owned by directed much of the field work necessary for making his collection.

Chiquitoy is the smallest of the four *haciendas*. It is situated in the lowest part of the valley's south side, and contains, among significant sites, the ruins of Chiquitoy Viejo, discussed in Chapter VIII.

The old Indian *communidades* have been largely forced out of the upper and middle part of the valley by the expansion of th*e haciendas*. Those which still remain intact, to a certain degree, are Ascope, Chocope and Paiján, on the north side, and Pueblo Chicama, on the south side. In the lower part of the valley, near the sea, are found Santiago de Cao and Magdelena de Cao. In early colonial times, these *communidades* still played a relatively important role, and despite the incessant pressure from the *haciendas*, the descendants of the ancient Indians here have to this day maintained some of their land and water rights and a limited amount of local self-government.

It is significant that today the large and wealthy Chicama Valley has no important towns, no administrative or cultural centers, no important ports. While Puerto Chicama, near the old port of Malabrigo, has been developed as a port for Casa Grande, the main port for this valley is Salaverry in the neighboring Moche Valley. Much of the political, economic, social and cultural life of the Chicama Valley centers around Trujillo, situated in the Moche Valley near ancient ChanChan. The relationship between the two valleys appears to be a continuation of the one that existed in Chimú times — if not earlier (see Chapter IX).

As in 1940-41, we made our headquarters at both Casa Grande and Cartavio, where we were lodged in fine guest houses and served excellent meals. In addition, we were given the use of cars, trucks, horses and guides. Hacienda Chiclín likewise generously furnished us with all the aid we requested.

At Casa Grande, the German engineer, Señor Kuks, gave us considerable help, as he had in 1941. By means of the detailed field maps of the *hacienda* and through knowledge gained in his own work during the past decades, he was able to direct us to a number of archaeologically unknown mounds on the lands of the *hacienda*. In fact, on his free days, he gladly joined us in our explo-

Fig. 13. Workers' houses on a coastal sugar *hacienda*. Although this is a model settlement, each family has only one room with a door but no windows. The "sentry boxes" in the middle of the street are outhouses; behind each one is a tap from which water is drawn for drinking and cooking purposes.

Fig. 10 (below, left). The cane is dumped into a trough from which it is drawn into chopping and grinding machines in the refinery to be prepared for sugar extraction in huge vats. Hacienda Pátapo • Fig. 11 (below, right). After the cane has been boiled in water and all the sugar has been extracted, the dry pulp of the cane is sent to the furnace and used as fuel for boiling other sugar cane solutions in the vats. Hacienda Pátapo.

Fig. 8 (below, left). Loading the railroad cars. The cane is brought on muleback from areas some distance from the tracks. Hacienda Cartavio • Fig. 9 (below). Loaded railroad cars at the sugar refinery. In the foreground are field workers. Hacienda Pátapo.

Fig. 12 (right). A scene in the sugar refinery at Hacienda Cartavio. The boilers are not visible since they are in another part of the building. After being extracted, the product has to be refined to become white granulated sugar. Most of this is exported; the rest is used by the middle and upper classes of the country. The great mass of the people, who cannot afford to buy white sugar, use the unrefined dark brown sugar which is produced in the many small extracting plants found throughout Peru. This product, called *chancaca*, is pressed into large cakes and sold in all the local markets.

rations. His interest in archaeological remains had led him to excavate partially a *huaca*, already in the process of destruction, in which he found several adobe columns, one with remains of polychrome painting (Figs. 31 and 32).

Our main tasks in the Chicama Valley were those of checking our previous work of locating and mapping the main canals and calculating the total area formerly under cultivation. We had previously discovered two large canal systems now no longer in use. The one on the north side consisted of a number of long, parallel canals that once had irrigated the whole of the large Pampa de Mocán (Fig. 19). We tried to follow some of the major canals of this system in order to see whether any of them continued around Cerro Yugo into the windswept desert area known as La Vaquita, in the direction of the Jequetepeque Valley. But neither by field work nor by aerial photographs were we able to find any traces of such an extension. Nor did questioning of local inhabitants unearth any tradition of former cultivation. All we could locate were some minor canals, west of the Pan American Highway, which at one time had extended the cultivated area of this lower part of the valley a mile or so northward into the desert.

On the south side of the valley, there are also a number of long, parallel, ancient canals, parts of which are

Fig. 14 (above). A section of the contour canal that once carried water for a distance of more than forty miles from the Chicama Valley to ChanChan, in the Moche Valley. *Kosok* • Fig. 15 (below, second from left). An unusually fine *huaco* from the Very Early or Cupisnique Period. *Guillen* • Fig. 16 (below and margins). Other *huacos* from the priest-dominated Cupisnique Period. *Handbook, II* • Fig. 17 (right). Another view of the huge canal described in Fig. 14. Inside the canal is the SCIPA jeep; alongside it are Señor Portugal, Ingeniero Vivas and the author. *Schaedel.*

still used (Fig. 27). The canals run southwesterly, pass Chiquitoy Viejo (Figs. 37 and 38) and the lone Middle Period Huaca Colorada with its walled compound (Fig. 36), and continue southward to a point where they completely disappear in a small desert *quebrada*. In tracing the canals, we encountered an ancient walled road that passed both Huaca Colorada and Chiquitoy Viejo and disappeared to the south in the desert in the general area of ChanChan (see Chapter IX) and to the north in the cultivated fields of the Chicama Valley.

One of the largest and most important ancient canals on the Coast is the Chicama-Moche Canal mentioned in Chapter IX. Originating in the upper part of the Chicama Valley above Sausal, it follows the contour of the hills and passes above the system just described until it reaches La Cumbre, the low dividing ridge between the

Fig. 18 (below). View of a garden at the home of one of the administrators of Hacienda Cartavio, Chicama Valley. *Kosok* • Fig. 19 (right). One of the old canals that run through the Pampa de Mocán. This photograph caught the typical atmosphere of the coastal desert shortly before sunset. *Kosok* • Fig. 20 (right, below). Part of the large contour canal that once connected the Chicama and Moche Valleys (see Figs. 14 and 17). *Servicio 171:348.*

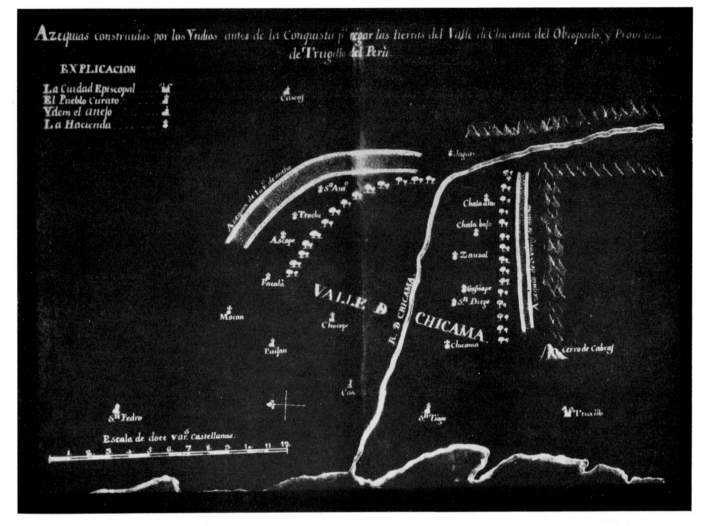

Chicama and Moche Valleys (Figs. 14, 17 and 20). From there it continues, as described in Chapter IX, until it reaches the fields of ancient ChanChan, having coursed a distance of some forty miles. While the canal obviously had been used principally to carry water into the Moche Valley, at least during one period, it had also been used to cultivate land within the Chicama Valley, a fact that became clear to us when we found a number of large branches of the canal that remained within the Chicama Valley itself. Indeed, it is possible that the latter branches had been built before it was decided to extend the canal into the Moche Valley.

Fig. 21 (left). A unique but rather crude map drawn by the eighteenth century bishop, Martínez de Compañón, showing the two main canals of the Chicama Valley.

Fig. 22 (above, left). An extension of the large Ascope aqueduct (opposite Preface). The massive left wall may be the remains of an earlier, lower canal that was filled in when the later, higher canal was built. *Kosok* • Fig. 23 (above, center). View of a partly destroyed canal at Sausal. *Kosok* • Fig. 24 (above, right). A section, at La Cumbre, of the large intervalley canal showing stone embankments. *Kosok*.

We also attempted to trace the course of the main ancient trunk road, as well as that of a secondary one, across the cultivated sections of the valley. Only near Pueblo Chicama, Paiján and the above-mentioned Chiquitoy Viejo are the entrances of the roads into these areas clearly visible. We tried to trace the roads farther across the irrigated region by studying aerial mosaics — the best way of discovering vestiges of ancient roads — but we were unsuccessful. Modern tractors and bulldozers of the *haciendas* have destroyed practically all traces of the roads.

Large and medium size adobe pyramids, most of which probably were built in the Mochica Period, characterize the Chicama Valley. But it is not unlikely that if tunnels were dug through some of these Mochica pyramids, the core would be found to consist of smaller pyramids of the earlier Gallinazo, Salinar, or even Cupisnique Periods! For mound building seems to have been typical of these older priest-dominated societies.

The pyramids of the Chicama Valley are generally quite steep, and some of them have remains of room structures on top of them. Many of them stand alone in the midst of green fields. Most of the associated structures such as plazas, houses, walls and connecting roads that once may have existed, have been destroyed by mod-

ern *hacendados,* who have ploughed back into the ancient soil all "obstructions" that were not too large to destroy.

Other Chicama pyramids, however, appear in clusters, in which there is usually one large pyramid surrounded by a number of smaller ones. These *huaca* clusters were probably large-scale ceremonial centers, just as the individual *huacas* were probably the seats of local religio-political units.

Examples of these clusters are Las Tres Huacas on the grounds of Hacienda Chiquitoy and the larger more important La Campanilla *huaca* group just to the east of the old town of Santiago de Cao at the southern tip of the cultivated area of the valley (Fig. 40). Near the buildings of Hacienda Cartavio is Huaca de Monjas, surrounded by a number of smaller mounds. The archaeologically unknown ruin of Malabrigo Viejo at the northwestern desert edge of the valley may also be considered a *huaca* complex. This site was seen by us from the air and later visited by a member of the Institute who reported finding many *huacas* and other structures. But the ceramics from the site had so deteriorated in the salty soil that a definite period dating was not possible.

The Mocollope hill, surrounded by various pyramids, walled compounds, and terraced earth and adobe mounds (Figs. 28 to 30), also represents a type of *huaca* cluster,

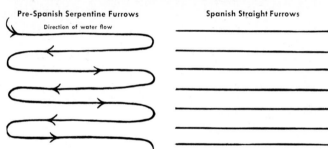

Pre-Spanish Serpentine Furrows
Direction of water flow
Spanish Straight Furrows

Fig. 25 (left and above). Typical *huacos* of the Salinar Period, which represents a transition from the Very Early or Cupisnique Period to the Early or Mochica Period. *Handbook, II* • Fig. 26 (top, right). Pre-colonial type, S-shaped furrows. See also drawing at center, right. *Kosok* • Fig. 27 (bottom, right). A series of parallel canals, dating from ancient times, extending from the southwestern edge of the present cultivated area of the Chicama Valley into the region around Huaca Colorada. The central canal is now used as a run-off for surplus water from irrigated fields. As a result, a narrow band of vegetation lines the edges of the canal. *Kosok.*

but it is different from the usual Chicama type. It is analogous, rather, to the much larger and more impressive Purgatorio group in the Leche Valley (see Chapter XVI).

Finally, we must call attention to what *may* have been the most extensive pyramid grouping in the Chicama Valley. The grouping consists of the large *huacas* of Ongollape, Salitral, Leche, Sonolipe and Rosario, all situated on the north side of the valley within a mile or two of one another. If these pyramids were once politically unified, they must have constituted the dominating *huaca* complex of the valley.

The aerial photographs of most of the individual *huacas* are, with a few exceptions, not reproduced, because they are not very impressive. This is due in part to their having been taken at too great an altitude to show details

Fig. 28 (top, left). Ruins of the large hillside site of Mocollope, one of the principal Mochica sites of the Chicama Valley. The numerous holes were made by *huaqueros*, who have unearthed a tremendous number of fine red and white *huacos* from the ancient graves that cover the whole ruin. Note the rectangular platforms on different levels of the hill. The rectangular enclosure in the lower center is probably a Late Chimú compound. *Servicio 171:336* • Fig. 29 (bottom, left). Mocollope Ceramics. *Schaedel-Cacho.* (a) Modeled animal, probably pre-Mochica orange ware. (b) Part of the inner surface of a grater bowl that was used to grate yuca roots. (c) Mochica red ware. (d) Mochica red ware. (e) Non-Mochica modeled blackware. (f) Mochica red ware. (g) Part of a mold. (h) Non-Mochica blackware. (i) Probably pre-Mochica ware. (j) Mochica red ware • Fig. 30 (below). Señor González with storage jars of the Mochica Period left by *huaqueros* at Mocollope. Below the jars is a stone-lined grave. *Schaedel.*

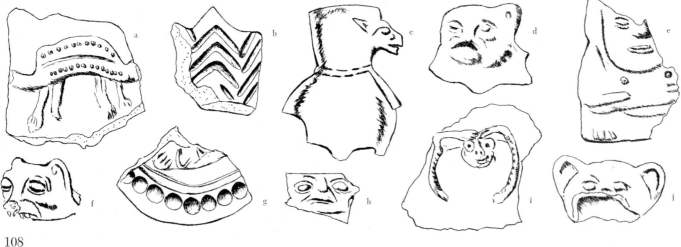

108

clearly. To some extent it is also the result of the *huacas* having been partly destroyed by occasional rains and by the depredations of treasure hunters. Consequently, ground plans of most of the structures are difficult to draw. Señor Rafael Larco Hoyle has had ground plans made but so far has not published them. Some archaeological surveys have been made by Dr. Schaedel, and a surface ceramic survey has been made by Dr. Ford, but reports of these surveys have not yet been published.

Señor Rafael Larco Hoyle and his staff at the Chiclín museum have done the major archaeological work in this

Fig. 31 (above). Ingeniero Kuks of Casa Grande Hacienda with his field crew excavating a small *huaca*. The excavation brought to light two adobe columns, rare structures in coastal architecture. To the left can be seen the ends of conical adobes, characteristic of the Very Early or Cupisnique Period • Fig. 32 (below). Ingeniero Kuks standing beside a column on which, barely visible, are the rare remains of a polychrome frieze. The column was found during the excavation of one of the mounds on Casa Grande Hacienda.

Fig. 33 (above). The large Huaca Rosario, situated on the north side of the Chicama Valley, a few miles from the Pan American Highway. This *huaca* and Huacas Ongollape, Salitral (see Fig. 34), Leche and Sonolipe may have once formed a huge *huaca* cluster (see text). *Kosok* • Fig. 34 (below). Vertical aerial photograph showing two large pyramids, probably from Mochica times (Ongollape at the left, Salitral near the center). The rectangular structures in the field may date from ancient times and may have connected the *huacas*. Dr. Ford examined the rectangular structure on the top of Ongollape and reported that it was probably built in the Late Chimú Period for secular, defensive purposes. During both the Coastal Tiahuanaco and Late Chimú Periods, various pyramids dating back to Mochica and even pre-Mochica times may similarly have been re-occupied and used as fortified sites. *Servicio 171:277.*

valley. Some of their results have been published in two monographs of a planned eight-volume series on the Mochica culture. Señor Rafael Larco Hoyle also has published reports on the Salinar and Cupisnique cultures, as well as various articles on related subjects. These reports are of extreme importance to our understanding of the prehistoric cultures of the Northwest Coast, but they are only the first part of a complete study.

The fact that Señor Rafael Larco Hoyle's main findings have not been published is regrettable, since the information he has gathered could possibly give us a better understanding of the social structure of the Mochica Period, the length of its duration, and the nature of its political-military expansion. At the beginning of this chapter, it was stated that the priest-dominated societies existed dur-

ing the Very Early (Cupisnique) and the two transitional Salinar and Gallinazo Periods and reached their *culmination* during the *Mochica Period* (II B in Chart I, p. 72). At its *culmination,* a development must, however, contain embryonic or formative elements of *new* social forms that break out as independent characteristics or forces in the succeeding period. The new forms may represent either degeneration or a development to a higher level.

We do know that after the Mochica came the Middle Period (Coastal Tiahuanaco). This period — to judge from our knowledge of other valleys — marked the growth of walled compounds, which eventually became the dominant form of architecture in the Late Chimú Period. But most important, this new architectural form was an expression of the rise of a secular military power in which the secular rulers eventually dominated the priesthood. In the process of doing this, the secular rulers not only conquered a single valley, but started a struggle for control over other valleys. In the case of the Chimús, this

110

intervalley conflict (III A and B in Chart I, p. 72) led to the establishment of the multi-valley Chimú Empire. Theoretically, therefore, we should expect to find the elements of secular power developing in some form during the Mochica Period, the period of *culmination* of priestly power and rule. The problem is this: How can we detect, or by indirection determine, that such secular forces existed? Moreover, how did these secular forces express themselves?

The available evidence is meager, though illuminating. Some of it is artistic; some of it is archaeological. If we study the many portrait *huacos* that have been unearthed from Mochica graves, we find that while some still have distinctly priestly decorative characteristics reminiscent of previous priest-dominated cultures, the

Fig. 35 (left). A group of Mochica style bird *huacos. Chiclín-Kosok* • Fig. 36 (above). Huaca Colorada, in the now barren region south of Chiquitoy Viejo. Significant is the large walled compound, adjoining the pyramid, which is characteristic of the Middle Period when the transition from priestly control to secular rule was taking place. Note the long ramp leading to the top of the pyramid. The black spots are areas of excavation. Note also the large canal at the top of the photograph; at the bottom is the same road as that shown in Fig. 38. *Kosok.* Fig. 37 (below, left). Vertical aerial photograph of a walled compound known as Chiquitoy Viejo, bordering the vegetation of the modern Hacienda Chiquitoy, on the south bank of the Chicama River. This may be the ancient Chiquita Yap, the citadel which, according to legend, was taken by the Incas before the Chimú capital of ChanChan surrendered. Note within the larger compound a smaller walled compound within which, in turn, is an elevated structure containing several rooms. Chiquitoy Viejo is one of the few walled compounds in the Chicama Valley. *Servicio 171:224* • Fig. 38 (below, right) An oblique aerial view of Chiquitoy Viejo, also shown in Fig. 37. In the upper right corner are remains of an ancient road that once connected the Moche Valley with the Chicama Valley. *Kosok.*

finest of them are of men whose faces express a secular, worldly power and a kind of urbaneness not found during the earlier periods. The best portrait *huacos* have a sternness and simplicity more akin to the busts of Roman statesmen than to the features of ancient Egyptian and Babylonian priests or the ingrown, stylized, over-decorated products of Chavín and Maya theocratic societies. Furthermore, if we study the drawings on some of the Mochica *huacos,* we find not only priests with their demon masks and other related trappings, but also warriors with their secular chiefs. Indeed, in Fig. 47 we see a number of chiefs being carried on litters before their leading chief, who sits on a kind of throne.

If a growth of secular forces took place during the Mochica Period, a chronological study of the *huacos*

logical verification by extensive stratigraphic excavations. For, as has been pointed out, there are no stratigraphic data on most of the *huacos* in our museums and private collections. Indeed, we generally do not even know from which specific valleys in the Mochica culture complex most of these *huacos* come!

Moreover, such an aesthetic-stylistic sequence in itself does not necessarily tell us much about the evolution of the *social structure* it represents. Since the classification is based on a limited number of specimens, we do not know in which periods of this sequence the "secular type" and in which periods the "priestly type" *huacos* predominate, or whether the percentage of each is about the same in all periods.

One other question concerning Mochica culture arises:

Fig. 39 (above). A group of unusual *huacos* modeled in the forms of potato-shaped human figures. *Chiclín-Kosok* • Fig. 40 (right). The regular and irregular white structures rising out of this modern sugar cane field are the remains of ancient adobe *huacas* that once formed a *huaca* cluster, of which Huaca Campanilla (left center) may have been the principal structure. Connecting walls and houses probably existed here, but if they did they have been plowed under. At the left, not shown in the photograph, are additional *huacas*. *Servicio 171:582.*

might support the theory of such a development. But unfortunately the Mochica style has never been adequately subdivided chronologically. True, Señor Rafael Larco Hoyle (1948) has made an aesthetic-stylistic analysis of Mochica *huacos* and has divided them into a series of periods ranging from the earliest, most primitive forms, through the highest artistic forms to the last stages of decadence. Professor John Rowe, working with archaeological material carefully collected by Uhle, arrived at a division of periods that apparently supports Señor Rafael Larco Hoyle's analysis. While this sequence may have inherent artistic validity, it still awaits chrono-

Why are Mochica ceramics artistically the finest, not only in the Chicama Valley but also in all of the Americas? While it is premature to try to answer such a question at present, it might not be amiss to point out that the integration of the *culminating* power of a priest-dominated society — with its well-established art forms and techniques — and the vigorous, *rising* secular forces — with a tendency toward a new artistic vitality — might have helped to produce the cultural florescence characteristic of the Mochica Period.

Such a situation would not be unique to Peru. In Europe, when the Gothic style reached its highest stage

of development, it represented both the culminating power of the medieval Church and the rising power of the growing towns, whose inhabitants, the merchants and artisans, not only helped to pay for the construction of cathedrals but also, by their increasing activities, gave impetus to the development of this art style into its highest form. Other examples in European and Asian art developments could be cited, but it is impossible to do so here. It is sufficient to indicate that the very duality and ambivalence of Mochica society could be the bases of its high cultural achievements. For a detailed analysis of the relationship of art forms and social structures, see the numerous stimulating publications of the German art historian, Wilhelm Hausenstein.

But if we assume for the time being that secular forces were growing in power within the framework of a theocratic Mochica culture, we are supported by Señor Rafael Larco Hoyle's theory that there actually existed a Mochica political and military *empire* from the Chicama to the Nepeña Valleys inclusive. Priest-dominated social units are generally limited in size, consisting of single communities or groups of communities. Through their knowledge of the movements of the heavenly bodies and the mysteries of this world, the priests can develop a

superior position over their people by threatening them with punishment by the demons that infest both this world and the next. But the achievement of extensive military conquests and political organization requires military and political *specialists,* namely the *secular chiefs.* These, of course, have always existed alongside the priesthood. But when a certain level of material development has been reached in society, the secular chiefs are better equipped to carry on conquests with their tribesmen-soldiers, first for loot and later for regular tribute.

When the secular chiefs are finally successful, they are able to establish a secular state based on a class society, in contrast to the priests, who generally are at best able to produce a kind of proto-class society within a limited area. But there is often a long *transition* stage, during which the priests and the secular chiefs need each other for territorial expansion and to control and consolidate the conquered peoples, at the same time struggling with each other for internal control. Perhaps such a condition existed in the Mochica Period. At certain times the priests may have maintained control; at other times the secular rulers may have won out. Perhaps the Mochica Period represented a kind of theocracy like that of Tibet, where

Fig. 41 (upper left). Portrait of what appears to be a secular Mochica ruler. *Guillen* • Fig. 42 (lower left). A drawing from a Mochica *huaco. Larco Hoyle* • Fig. 43 (below). Mochica huacos that illustrate the kinds of mutilation used as punishment for crimes. One may be shocked at such revelation of man's brutality to man, but we must remember that until very recent times mutilation was also practiced in our own western "civilization." *AMNH.*

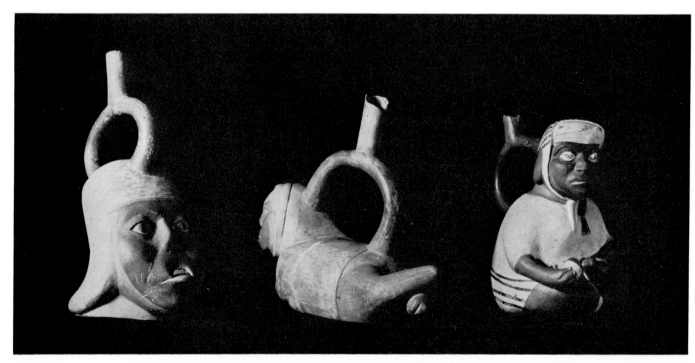

the soldiers fought for the Chief Priest; most likely, at the climax of Mochica political power, the secular rulers were the ones who expanded the Empire.

The findings of the Virú Expedition indicate that there was no gradual infiltration of Mochica cultural forms into Virú. Mochica ceramics appeared suddenly, probably indicating a Mochica military conquest with possibly some Mochica colonization.

Assuming that a Mochica Empire existed for a considerable time, we might conclude that it extended into the so-called Middle Period, during which it expanded southward to the Nepeña Valley, where it came into conflict with the steadily northward-moving Tiahuanaco culture, or Tiahuanaco "Empire." The latter then slowly pushed the Mochicas back, valley after valley, until the Mochica Empire and culture crumbled, even in the Chicama Valley.

This situation may help to explain why the Mochica culture continued so long in the Chicama Valley. The

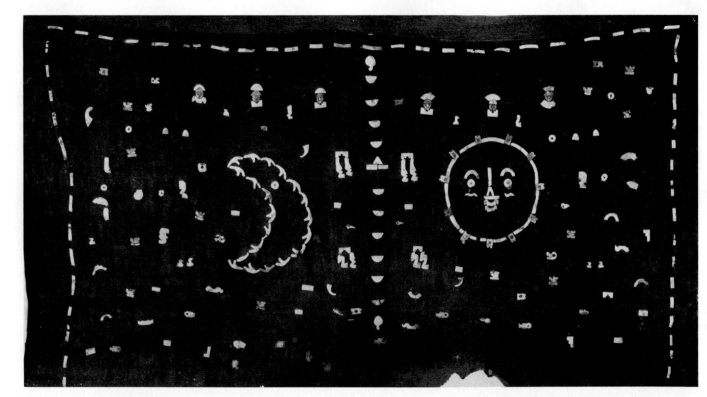

Fig. 44 (upper right). This unique textile from the Peruvian Coast has not been dated archaeologically. The sun and the moon obviously bring it into the category of astronomical-calendrical textiles. Note, in the outer circle of the sun, that there are *eleven* figures. The number was important among many ancient peoples, for it represents the days left over at the end of a year based on a lunar-solar cycle (see Chapter VI). The other figures may refer to the planets, constellations and individual stars, or they may have merely numerical significance. Perhaps some aspiring scientist versed in positional astronomy can solve the mystery of this textile. *AMNH* • Fig. 45 (lower left). Mochica *huaco* decorated with birds and plants. *AMNH-Rein* • Fig. 46 (lower center). A *huaco* showing scenes from ancient Mochica life (see Fig. 47). *AMNH-Rein* • Fig. 47 (bottom). This scene, copied from the *huaco* shown in Fig. 46, shows how local rulers make their obeisance to the chief ruler. Servants or slaves, preceded by runners, carry their masters on litters. The chief ruler is seated on a covered throne on the top of a small pyramid. *Huaco* drawings of this type give us insight into some aspects of the social structure of Mochica society. *AMNH-Mead* • Fig. 48 (lower right). This stern-visaged head, characteristic of many Mochica portrait *huacos*, suggests a strong, secular ruler. The realism and virility expressed in many Mochica *huacos* is generally atypical of the art of a purely priest-dominated society. *Gaffron-Doering.*

Fig. 49. Another stern-visaged head that seems to portray the majesty and power of a Mochica ruler. *Gaffron-Doering.*

fact that many Mochica potsherds are found there at almost every site — a situation unknown in other valleys — seems to confirm this hypothesis. This situation may also explain why so few pure Coastal Tiahuanaco potsherds have been found in the Chicama Valley and why practically no walled compounds, so characteristic of the Coastal Tiahuanaco Period, were built.

We can speculate further that after the rising secular power of the Mochicas had gradually been overthrown by the rising secular power of the Coastal Tiahuanaco culture, the latter was defeated, in turn, by a rising secular power from the Lambayeque region, which expanded through the Chicama Valley into the nearby Moche Valley. Here, the Chimú dynasty established an ever-expanding empire in which the secular power finally became predominant to an extent unknown anywhere else in the Americas.

However, the problem of the social structures of the Mochica, Coastal Tiahuanaco and Late Chimú Periods in the Chicama Valley remains unsolved. Perhaps the attempt to solve it will necessitate a study of the Chicama and nearby Moche Valley as a *unit.* Even though the long Chicama-Moche Canal may have been built only during the Late Chimú Period, the nearness of the two valleys to each other makes it appear likely that what went on in one seriously affected events in the other. But until further serious archaeological excavations are carried on and the results published, we will have to content ourselves with scientific speculations based on the meager amount of material available and with the artistic enjoyment of the many beautiful *huacos* that have come down to us from ancient Mochica times.

XII

Crossroads of Cultures and Empires: The Jequetepeque Valley

T̲HE M̲OCHE-C̲HICAMA unit was the political center of the Chimú Empire — and at an earlier time had been the center of Mochica culture. However, the Northern Zone of the Empire was the economic *hinterland* for it had a much more extensive cultivated area which supported a much larger population than the Moche-Chicama unit.

This Northern Zone, as pointed out in Chapter IX, lies to the north of the Moche-Chicama unit and consists of a geographically distinct group of five valleys, namely, the large Jequetepeque, the small Zaña, the large Lambayeque, the small Leche and the still smaller Motupe. As the result of our field work, described in part in the following chapters, we were able to determine that at one time, probably during the period of the Chimú Empire, if not earlier, all of these valleys had formed a hydrological - economic unit, that is, they had been interconnected by means of irrigation systems. We also established the fact that this complex unit then had embraced almost a third of the cultivated area of the whole Coast and more than half of that of the Chimú Empire!

We know little of the political and military history of this region. There are only a few hints about it in the limited sources we possess. According to native traditions

Fig. 1. A striking example of how the sand and algarroba bushes combine to cover what was once an extensive planned site situated alongside the main ancient highway. This site, called La Pampa, lies to the northwest of Cerro Cañoncillo. The markings at the left have the appearance of abandoned plots irrigated until relatively modern times. *Servicio 170:284.*

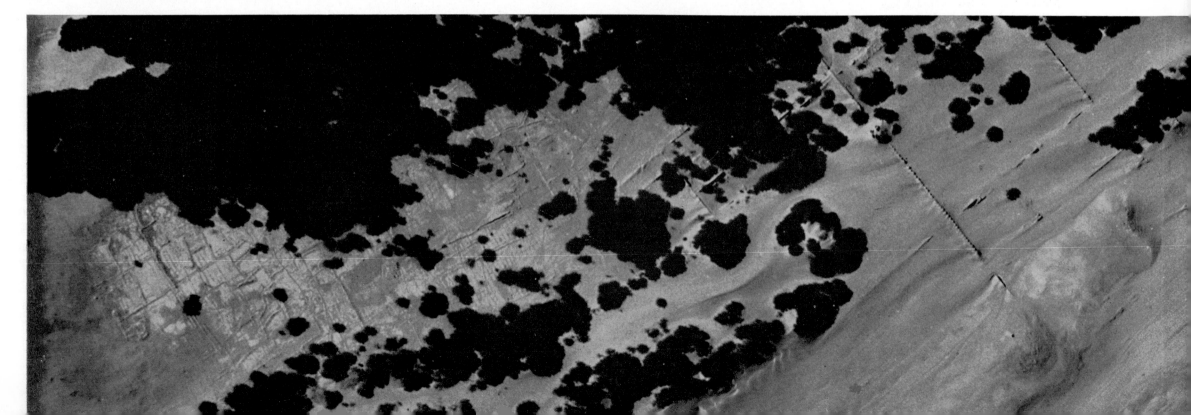

recorded by the Anonymous Trujillano (1614), the Jequetepeque Valley was conquered by Ñançenpinco, the third ruler. This event, if we follow Chart II in Chapter VIII, took place probably around 1300 A.D. Unfortunately, our informant is silent on further northern conquests under the six succeeding rulers. All we learn is that Minchançaman, the last independent Chimú ruler (defeated by the Incas possibly about 1475), was in control of the whole of northern Peru up to the Ecuadorian border.

However, the chronicler Cabello, in his seventeenth century account of the Lambayeque region, tells us that the Chimú ruler from ChanChan had once sent a governor by the name of Pongmassa to rule the Lambayeque Valley, north of the Jequetepeque. According to our chart this event should have taken place some time after 1400. In other words, the military conquest of the greater part of the Northern Zone by the Chimús appears to have been a slow and apparently late process — not at all surprising in view of the size and complexity of this zone. This indicates that the region had a long period of local cultural development, most aspects of which are still unknown.

The story of the political seizure of this Northern Zone by the Incas is even more vague. Apparently there was no real military conquest — at least Cabello mentions none. Possibly after the destruction of the Chimú power the local rulers of the various regions in the Northern Zone submitted voluntarily to the mighty Inca hosts and continued to rule under Inca control.

One of our tasks in Peru was to determine whether the Northern Zone had at any time been connected by canals with the Moche-Chicama unit, and if not, how closely the irrigated areas of the Jequetepeque and the Chicama had approached each other in the past. Trimetrogon aerial photographs made by the United States Armed Forces during World War II included the present desert areas separating these two valleys. But they were taken at such a great height that the details we were interested in were in most cases not clearly delineated. Furthermore, no Servicio aerial photographs were made of this desert, with the exception of the narrow regions bordering the two valleys. Therefore, practically all our findings here were based on extensive ground reconnaissance made with a truck in 1940-41 and with a jeep in 1948-49.

Although we cruised through this desert area on various occasions, we discovered no major ancient canals. Questioning of inhabitants of both adjoining valleys likewise yielded negative results. Only a few minor canals were eventually located; these had once slightly extended

116

the irrigated areas of the Chicama Valley towards the north and of the Jequetepeque Valley towards the south. This absence of canals connecting the two valleys meant, contrary to the first impression we had obtained in 1939 (Kosok, 1940:175), that the Chicama and Jequetepeque Valleys had always been distinct hydrological-economic units in ancient times.

The only connections we could find between the Chicama and Jequetepeque Valleys were the remains of two old roads. The more important and better preserved of the two intersects the present Pan American Highway a few miles beyond the cultivated area of the Chicama Valley. Without much difficulty, we traced its walls and roadbed partly into the Jequetepeque Valley. We found extensions of this same road in other valleys and inter-valley desert areas. As a result, we were able to reconstruct on our maps most of the coastal trunk road all the way from the Chao Valley to the Motupe, a distance of about two hundred miles.

This road, like most other ruins of ancient Peru, is usually designated as "Inca" by the present day inhabitants. Undoubtedly, this trunk road was used and developed by the Incas, but it must have been, at least in part, the transportation backbone of the earlier coastal Chimú Empire. Indeed, parts of it may have been built during the Middle or even the Early (Mochica) Period.

While Dr. Schaedel and I were reconnoitering in the desert area just north of the Chicama Valley, we observed the remains of another road. It ran in a northerly direction, parallel to the main ancient road, and about midway between the latter and the ocean. Though it was late afternoon when we discovered the road we nevertheless decided to see where it would lead. We recount our experiences, not because of the importance of this road, but because they exemplify some of the problems we often encountered in the field. Doubts of the road's antiquity arose when we discovered that parts of it had

been made level by *cutting through* the slight ridges of land that ran in an east-west direction! This was not at all typical of ancient roads, which usually *ran over* the tops of hills and ridges. We also looked in vain for road-side walls, another feature typical of ancient coastal roads. Consequently, we decided that this road might have been an old colonial carriage road, which had been built as level as possible to permit the easy passage of wheeled vehicles.

Nevertheless, we decided to continue to see what would happen. To our disappointment, even the faint traces of the road soon petered out. So, as on previous occasions, we continued in the same direction to see whether we could pick it up again. After a short time we suddenly encountered, on a stretch of flat terrain, the remains of an ancient walled road running in the same northward direction! It soon passed the remains of an old *tambo* (ancient rest house), nestled among three distinctive hillocks. The ruins looked familiar! Soon I recalled them as the same *tambo* and the same section of the road we had encountered and mapped in one of our field explorations of 1940-41 and then later had located on the U. S. trimetrogon photographs! We decided that this road could have been a continuation of our previous road. We surmised that the so-called carriage road may, after all, have been an ancient one, with parts of it leveled off in colonial times to permit the passage of wheeled vehicles.

We did not attempt to follow the road farther north, since it had become quite dark and we were anxious to get out of that desolate region as soon as possible. After cruising for almost an hour in an easterly direction through desert gulleys and around *monte* bushes, lit up garishly by the headlights of the jeep, we were happy when we finally reached the Pan American Highway!

In 1940-41 we had explored the northern extension of this road but found that it soon got lost in the *monte* that grew in the beds of the dry Cupisnique River. When

we studied our map we decided that if this road had continued beyond the river beds — as it undoubtedly did — it would have joined with the westerly and smaller of the two ancient roads that extend through the Jequetepeque Valley farther north.

According to some old maps and the reports of various local people, another ancient "road" exists between the Chicama and Jequetepeque Valleys. Still occasionally used, it runs along the seashore for about fifteen miles from Malabrigo on the northern edge of the Chicama Valley to the southern edge of the Jequetepeque Valley. We had no time to follow this "road." But we followed a well-preserved section of an ancient walled road, several miles long, which extends from the shore to the town of Pacasmayo. This section could well have been a continuation of the shore road. In ancient times, such north-south roads following the coast line appear to have been fairly common because the flat beach was often a natural highway.

Before describing our work in the Jequetepeque Valley proper, a word ought to be said about the Cupisnique Valley. The latter is actually a long, dry *quebrada* running in a northwesterly direction between the Chicama and Jequetepeque Valleys. Only during some exceptionally rainy years in the Sierras does some water flow down this coastal valley.

In 1941 we used one of the sturdier trucks of the Peruvian Road Department to carry on some limited reconnoitering into the parts of the valley directly above the Pan American Highway. It was an extremely rugged trip through a desolate, forbidding area covered by innumerable rocks of all sizes. No ruins of any kind were located.

In 1946, Dr. James Ford, of the American Museum of Natural History, studied the remains of a number of primitive houses farther up the valley. They had apparently been built around a small, now extinct, "lake." This site represented, most probably, a *temporary* settlement built in ancient times during a relatively long period of unusually heavy rains in the mountains. During this period water came down the dry valley, accumulating partly in a small natural depression, thus forming the lake. Later on, with the return of a normal, drier period, the lake and its surrounding settlement disappeared.

When we visited the German agriculturist, Mr. Hämmerle, at his stock farm in the Jequetepeque Valley, he told us that there were some minor canals in the middle part of the Cupisnique Valley, probably somewhere below the general area of Dr. Ford's investigation. Twenty-five

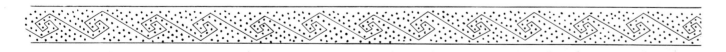

Fig. 2. An oblique aerial view showing the peculiar form of the lower Jequetepeque Valley. The river, while descending to the Coast, passes from (I) obliquely to (B) where it enters the Pacific Ocean. Overhead is a small *loma* cloud. The main parts of the valley are as follows: (A) Town of Jequetepeque; (B) Mouth of the Jequetepeque River; (C) Ruins of Pacatnamú (see Figs. 6 to 8); (D) Ruins of Farfán; (E) Town of Guadalupe; (F) Town of Chepén; (G) Cerro Talambo (see Figs. 14 and 15); (H) Main canals bringing water from the Jequetepeque River at (I) to the large northern side of the valley, past the Río Seco de San Gregorio, to the Pampa de Zaña (both beyond the right edge of the photograph). *U. S. Army 107-R-45.*

years ago, when he had led mule trains from the middle Jequetepeque Valley across the Cupisnique Valley into the Mocan region of the Chicama Valley, he had often come across these minor canals. However, as a result of a number of unfortunate circumstances we were unable to visit these canals and localize them on our map.

Mr. Hämmerle pointed out that these former irrigated habitation sites probably were similar to the *temporales*, which are to be found today at various places on the Coast of Peru. *Temporales* come into being in those rare years or series of years when an exceptional amount of rain in the mountains brings water for a few days or weeks down into some dry coastal valleys or *quebradas*. Then people from neighboring valleys come into these regions *temporarily* and divert the water onto some nearby level ground. If there is sufficient water, a meager crop of corn can be produced. But, during the years when the water does not appear, these plots are abandoned.

Archaeologically the Jequetepeque Valley proper presents a peculiar problem. While the Chicama-Moche to the south and the Lambayeque Complex to the north developed distinct "local" cultural forms, no such distinct forms have thus far been identified by archaeologists for the Jequetepeque! The ceramic collections from this valley at present indicate mainly importations, imitations or influences of Cupisnique, Mochica, Cajamarca, Lambayeque, Chimú and, finally, Inca styles. The valley seems to have been a kind of meeting ground or crossroads of the cultures of the adjacent coastal and Sierra regions.

But the Jequetepeque seems to have been more than just a *cultural* crossroads. There are some indications that at certain times it had also been a *political* crossroads. For the Incas, the Jequetepeque Valley was obviously significant. Their main control center for the northern part of the Peruvian Andes was Cajamarca, where Atahualpa, the last Inca ruler, was defeated and killed by Pizarro. But apparently the Incas had also used Cajamarca as an indirect control center for the related coastal valleys. The controlling armies and administrative officials of the Incas could be dispatched directly down the Jequetepeque to the neighboring coastal valleys to the north and south. In this sense, the Jequetepeque Valley became a local crossroads or nodal point for at least a section of the Inca Empire.

But in earlier (Chimú) times this valley had apparently already played a somewhat similar role. As mentioned above, Ñançenpinco, the third Chimú ruler, had con-

118

quered the valley probably at the end of the thirteenth century. Calancha (1638) tells us a similar story of the conquest of the valley by Pacatnamú, a general who served one of the Chimú rulers. It is not clear whether these accounts deal with the same conquest or two separate conquests. For our present purposes this is immaterial. What is important is the fact that the accounts show early control of the valley by the Chimú Empire. But more important, when later on the Chimú Empire extended its power farther north into the Zaña and Lam-

Fig. 3 (left). This vertical aerial photograph shows a section of one of the two ancient north-south trunk highways where it crosses the Pan American Highway (wide black line at bottom) and part of the vegetation zone of the Jequetepeque Valley (dark section at top). The road is the more westerly and possibly the older of the two highways. Parallel to the road and at some distance from it are the remains of two walls. This arrangement was also found in the Pampa de Tecapa in the Jequetepeque Valley as well as in some other valleys. The purpose of these walls has not yet been determined. Perhaps they were used to zone off state property alongside the road from local village property and to keep state troops and messengers from coming into direct contact with subject local populations. *Servicio, 170: 166.*

Fig. 4 (above). The same road as shown in Fig. 3 photographed at the point where it crosses the Pan American Highway. Note that the road is directed straight towards the lowest notch in the nearby hills. Also note its construction: it is elevated slightly above the level of the land and does not have the customary side walls. The parallel walls cannot be seen here. *Kosok.*

bayeque, the Jequetepeque Valley became a crucial political-military base.

We also know from Cabello de Valboa (III, Chap. XVI) that the last of the Chimú rulers had a military alliance with the ruler of Cajamarca in the Sierras, since apparently neither ruler was strong enough to conquer the other, and both feared the growing power of the Incas. We know also that, when the Inca army attacked Cajamarca, the Chimú ruler sent contingents of troops to the Sierras, though this did not prevent the final victory of the Incas over both. But before the Inca victory, this military alliance tended to make the Jequetepeque important as a crossroads for the two powers, since most troop movements between Coast and Sierra probably went up and down this valley. It is possible to go up to Cajamarca through the Moche or Chicama Valleys, but these routes are much more difficult and time-consuming to negotiate than the one through the Jequetepeque. Even today the quickest bus trip is through the latter valley.

We do not know whether the aforementioned role of the Jequetepeque Valley goes back further than the Chimú Period, for the nature and extent at that time of the relationship of the coastal valleys to one another and to the Sierras is still completely unknown. However, it is very likely that in this general area, trade and tribute routes from the Coast to the Sierras and from coastal valley to coastal valley would have crossed this strategically located Jequetepeque.

The Jequetepeque Valley, one of the larger ones along the Coast, contains a cultivated area about the same size as that of the Chicama to the south. Sugar and rice are today the main commercial crops. We are fortunate in having a brief reference to this valley by Cieza de León, Spanish soldier and outstanding Chronicler of Peru (I, Chap. LXVIII). Writing as early as 1548, less than fifteen years after the Spanish conquest, he found the valley to be the most fertile and populous one he had encountered since landing at Tumbes in the north! Cieza further reports that great quantities of cotton cloth were made in this valley. He saw many flowers and trees, and the branches of the latter were covered with thousands of varieties of birds — a condition hardly characteristic of the valley today.

The Jequetepeque Valley has a rather peculiar shape. While the river flows from the mountains almost in a straight line to the Pacific Ocean, the valley, unlike that of the Moche and Chicama, has no broad coastal plain that spreads fan-like down towards the sea. To the south

of the river there stretches for a distance a plateau which is too high to have been reached by ancient canals, thus limiting considerably the area that could be irrigated. To the north of the river a chain of coastal hills near the sea prevents cultivation in this region. The only place level and low enough to permit the extensive development of irrigation is a plain wedged in between the coastal hills and the foothills of the Andes. Since, however, the land here slopes slightly downward all the way to the Zaña Valley in the north, the cultivated area could be extended as far as the latter valley. Our study showed that this extension was actually achieved, probably in Chimú times, if not earlier. The main canals crossed, as many still do, the bed of the small and generally dry "river" of San Gregorio, called in its lower section Río Chamán (see Fig. 2 and map, p. 146).

In the middle of the wide irrigated plain to the north of the Jequetepeque River lies Guadalupe, the main town of this area. Established in the sixteenth century by the Spaniards, apparently near an old Indian site, it soon became an important pilgrimage center, a position which it still maintains. Here, during the seventeenth century, the Jesuit priest, Calancha, wrote an account of the still extant folk traditions and customs of the ancient Indians of this region (1638: II, Chap. III). To this day, his description has remained one of the few valuable sources we possess concerning these people. A good English summary can be found in Means (1931).

Calancha tells us among other things that the Indians of the Jequetepeque Valley worshipped the moon as their deity and that her temple was then called Signan (Fig. 18). They also worshipped the three belt stars of the constellation Orion, which the Spaniards called *los tres Marías*. To the Indians, two of the stars were officers of the law chasing the third, a thief. Apparently legal enforcement of property rights was held to be a reflection of eternal heavenly relationships! These Indians — as well as other coastal peoples — calculated their year (and probably their calendar) by the Pleiades, which they called Fur. This is not surprising, since in the Southern Hemisphere, in regions with seasonal rains, the annual disappearance of the Pleiades marks the beginning of the rains, the coming of the waters in the rivers, the beginning of the annual agricultural cycle — food!

Calancha says that the ancients believed mankind had descended from four stars. Two of them gave rise to kings, chiefs and nobles, while the other two were the progenitors of the workers! This would indicate that class

distinctions had become so set that the two main classes of society even had separate divine creations! That Calancha does not mention the priests in his social classification may be an accidental omission. But it also might indicate that the priesthood no longer played an important role as a part of the upper class. This would further substantiate our previous statements concerning the growth, towards the end of the pre-Spanish period, of a secular upper class at the expense of the priesthood.

Calancha also gives us this interesting admonition of

Fig. 5. Market day in the main square of Guadalupe. *Kosok.*

119

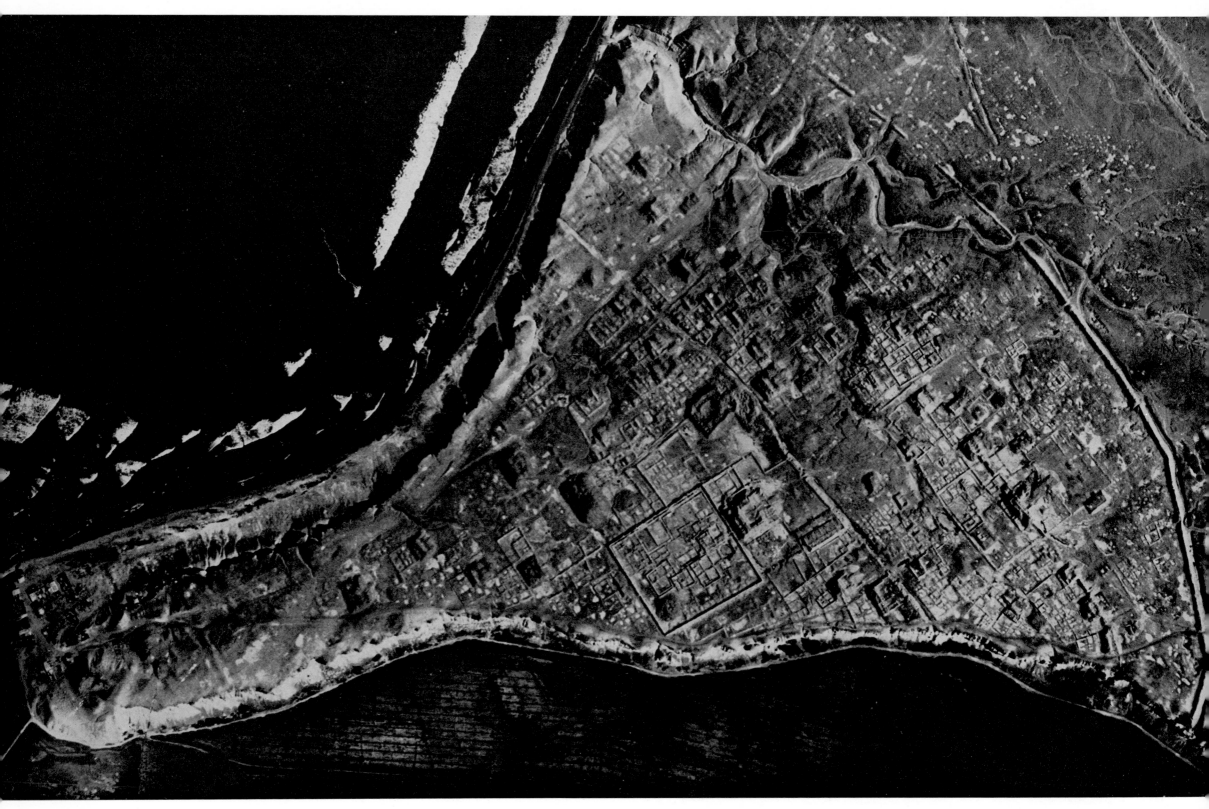

the official marriage sponsor to a bridal couple: "Now you are married, but bear in mind that you must always be equally industrious and equally ardent in love, for you must always be equals in the state into which you are entering." Does this mean that despite the rise of a secular class society, generally accompanied by a rise of patriarchy, this marriage admonition indicates that women still had maintained some of the rights which they had possessed in an earlier matriarchal stage? This democratic admonition is at variance with the low social status which women are supposed to have had in ancient Peru. Or was the status of women not so low as is generally assumed?

Calancha devoted only a few pages to this folklore, but he did somewhat better than Cieza, who wrote laconically during his stay in 1548: "The natives tell some traditions of their fathers, which being fables, I shall not write down." What a pity that Cieza was so contemptuous of the culture of the "heathens."

Not far from Guadalupe lies the old town of Chepén, the market center of the northern part of the valley. Other smaller settlements and several minor *haciendas* dot this northern region. The only large *haciendas* of the valley are those of Talambo and Limoncarro, the latter owned by Casa Grande Hacienda in the Chicama Valley.

Fig. 6 (left). The land mass shown in this dramatic vertical aerial photograph appears, at first sight, to be a peninsula. Actually it is a peculiarly shaped plateau (*barranca*) with the waves of the Pacific beating at its western side, and sugar cane fields bordering its southeastern side. The ruin, called Pacatnamú or Barranca, is one of the largest and most important on the Coast. On the western side of the site are a large number of adobe pyramids that possibly comprised an ancient ceremonial center. Their weather-beaten condition indicates that they represent the older part of the site and probably date back to the Middle or even Early Period. The major part of the site is covered by numerous compounds that apparently were living quarters; their better preserved state tends to indicate a Late Period construction. The largest walled compound (center of photograph) with a more clearly defined and more complex pyramid in front of it, may have been the "palace" of General Pacatnamú, who was sent from ChanChan by the Grand Chimú to conquer the valley of Jequetepeque. Note at the right of the photograph the curved defensive wall paralleled by a dry ditch or "moat." Probably the ditch was produced when the soil was excavated for building the wall. Another "moat" cuts across the middle of the ruins. To the right of the picture several large canals were found but no remains of cultivated fields could be located in the canal region. At the foot of the *barranca* (extreme left of the photograph) a small modern settlement can be seen. *Servicio 170:36*.

Fig. 8. A close oblique aerial view of the "palace" shown in Figs. 6 and 7. Note the size and structure of the flat-topped pyramid which dominates the surrounding rectangular structures. *Kosok.*

On the southern side there are fewer *haciendas* and settlements, for here the cultivated area is smaller. The two most important colonial and probably pre-colonial towns are Jequetepeque and San Pedro de Lloc. But the development of coastal and foreign trade in the nineteenth and twentieth centuries has now made the colonial port of Pacasmayo, situated some six miles to the south of the mouth of the Jequetepeque River, the leading town of the valley.

Unlike Chimbote in the Santa Valley region, Pacasmayo has no natural harbor. Ships anchor alongside or near the large modern steel pier that juts far out into the ocean. The distinctive feature of Pacasmayo is a wide boardwalk along the ocean front, which is a popular promenade center in the evening. It runs from the Hotel Ferrocarríl (Railroad Hotel) to the spacious and rather pleasant *Club* where the leading citizens of the town

Fig. 7. This oblique aerial view, which we caught from a low-flying Faucett plane, shows part of the ruins of Pacatnamú at a closer range than in Fig. 6. Note how the walls and pyramids as well as the *quebrada* at the right of the main ruin stand in sharper relief than in Fig. 6. At the left center of the photograph can be observed part of what might have been the "palace" of General Pacatnamú (see Fig. 6). *Kosok.*

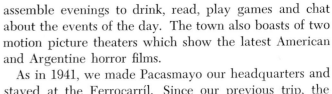

assemble evenings to drink, read, play games and chat about the events of the day. The town also boasts of two motion picture theaters which show the latest American and Argentine horror films.

As in 1941, we made Pacasmayo our headquarters and stayed at the Ferrocarríl. Since our previous trip, the Peruvian government had taken it over, renovated it and put it in the hands of a competent Italian-Swiss hosteler. From the balcony of our pleasant room we looked out over the town square and the expanse of the Pacific.

Once settled there we made the usual rounds of the government offices. We were fortunate in also meeting the editor of the local paper, Señor Carlos Rios, and his son, who spoke English fluently. They showed a real interest in ancient Peru, and had reprinted some portions of Calancha's work in their paper. We were warmly welcomed by them and were introduced to a number of people who aided us in our field work.

From Pacasmayo we also visited the nearby home of

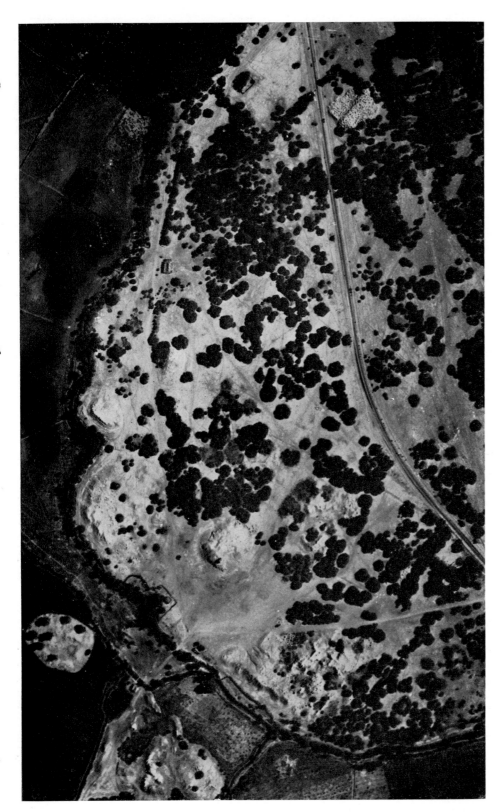

Fig. 9. Adobe ruins of Moro Viejo as seen from the air. At the bottom, middle, just above the dark irrigated area, is the main pyramid with its complex of walls. Here the significant potsherds discussed in the text were found. Above and to the left of the main pyramid are a number of other structures which are in a much poorer state of preservation than the main pyramid. At the right the Pan American Highway cuts through part of the site. *Servicio 170: 264* • Fig. 10 (margin and center). Potsherds from Moro Viejo. *Kosok-Wrynn.*

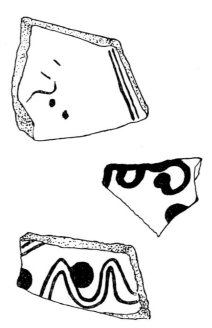

Señor Hämmerle. He and his family greeted us heartily and invited us to *Kaffee und Kuchen.* During later visits, we enjoyed some fine German dinners which Mrs. Hämmerle and her daughters prepared. I was very surprised when Mrs. Hämmerle handed me a small book of field notes which I had unknowingly left there in 1941 and had given up for lost! But most important, Mr. Hämmerle's intimate knowledge of the valley, gained over several decades of active life, aided us materially in our investigations.

The valley contains rather extensive and fairly well preserved remains of several "Inca" (probably pre-Inca) roads, including the former main coastal trunk road. The present Pan American Highway cuts these at several points and they can be seen without leaving the highway (Figs. 3 and 4). Those parts that run through the present day cultivated areas are difficult to locate because, in many cases, they have been ploughed under by the cultivators.

122

Only by lining up all the aerial photographs of this valley could we trace the former courses of the roads.

But, of most importance, the valley of Jequetepeque is littered with a great variety of ruins along the desert edges as well as within the cultivated areas. More than forty distinct sites were located, visited, and mapped.

The larger northern side of the valley contains the greater number of sites. Outstanding among these is ancient Pacatnamú (Figs. 6 to 8). Dramatically situated on a desert bluff overlooking the blue Pacific as well as the green fields of the Jequepeteque Valley, this magnificent site is one of the largest and best preserved ruins of ancient Peru. Apparently it had been an extensive ceremonial site containing many small and medium-sized pyramids, dating from the Mochica and the Middle Periods. It also contains what seems to be a more recent Chimú type compound, situated in the eastern part of the settlement. This compound is very likely the palace referred to by Calancha as having been built by General

Fig. 13. Ground view of the adobe Huaca Estacas showing side platforms, taken from a position near the lower left corner of Fig. 12. The vertical erosion lines on the sides of the *huaca* were caused by rains that fell occasionally during the centuries. *Kosok.*

Pacatnamú after he had been sent by his Chimú sovereign from ChanChan to rule over the Jequepeteque Valley.

A smaller, but nevertheless significant, companion ceremonial center lies across the river just south of Pacatnamú. Here are the tall Huaca de las Dos Cabezas (Two Heads) — badly destroyed by many treasure hunters — and many extensive but unexplored structures. General sketch plans of both sites have been made by Professor Kroeber (1930), while Professor Doering (1952) has excavated some Mochica graves at Pacatnamú and is making further excavations in the Jequepeteque Valley.

About eight miles east of Pacatnamú lie the extensive ruins of Farfán. This is a large and important prehistoric *urban* site which stretches along the present Pan American Highway somewhat to the north of the river. The ancient north-south trunk road runs right through this settlement, paralleling for a few miles the present Pan American Highway. The unexcavated ruin consists of many walled structures and a few minor pyramids. During several visits to the site, Señor Oscar Lostaunau of Guadalupe found and collected ceramics of many periods, from the Mochica to the Inca.

Talambo, with nearby Huachaco, is the third large ruin on this bank of the river (Figs. 14 and 15). The site consists of habitation terraces, stone-walled fortifications, walled compounds and pyramids and once must have controlled the entrance and exit to the narrow upper part of the valley. After we had visited Talambo, Dr. Schaedel and his assistants made a ground plan of the main pyramid grouping. Huachaco has been partially explored by Señor Lostaunau.

It was at Guadalupe that we first met Señor Lostaunau, the administrator of the local hospital, Afora, who possesses an intense scientific interest in the culture of the Indians of the past. Señor Lostaunau is a comparatively

Fig. 11 (left). The universal magician, this time at a fair at Guadalupe in the Jequetepeque Valley, exhibits his bag of tricks. The fairs in this region date back to early colonial times and possibly to the pre-Spanish period of Peruvian history. *Kosok* • Fig. 12. The pyramid of Estacas (The Stakes) is surrounded by ill-defined ruins and masses of dark *monte* bushes. Unusual in its form, the pyramid is one of the largest structures on the Dry River of San Gregorio. The approaching front ramp does not lead directly to the summit, but rather to a base platform from which side ramps must be followed to reach the top of the pyramid. *Servicio 170:245.*

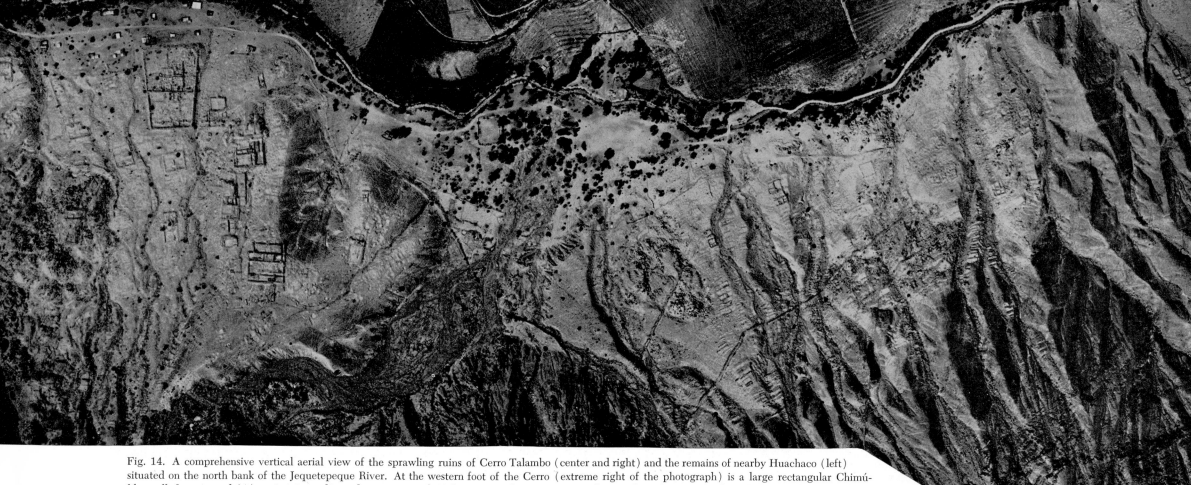

Fig. 14. A comprehensive vertical aerial view of the sprawling ruins of Cerro Talambo (center and right) and the remains of nearby Huachaco (left) situated on the north bank of the Jequetepeque River. At the western foot of the Cerro (extreme right of the photograph) is a large rectangular Chimú-like walled compound (A), containing a dirt and stone pyramid. Other rectangular structures can be noted nearby. Not far from (A) are several badly damaged adobe pyramids (B) of an apparently earlier construction than (A). Between these pyramids are the remains of an ancient canal (C). Beyond the ancient canal the main modern canal can be seen clearly defined by two parallel white lines. The black area above the latter canal represents modern irrigated fields. The irregular white line running past the ruin at (A) is a modern local dirt road to Huachaco. The Cerro itself is covered with many terraces containing stone-walled habitation sites, as well as numerous stone walls built for defensive purposes. Additional structures, not shown, exist in the area adjacent to the region at the right of the photograph. This major site of Cerro Talambo undoubtedly controlled the neck of the Jequetepeque Valley, which here is only about a mile wide. Little is known of ancient Huachaco and nothing of its relationship to Cerro Talambo. Interesting in Huachaco is the trapezoid form of the main structure within which walled subdivisions can be detected. Note also the various rectangular structures further up the *quebrada*. The hill to the right of the *quebrada* contains additional rectangular structures as well as numerous habitation terraces. The peculiar shape of the composite photograph is due partly to the fact that different sections were enlarged at different times and partly to the fact that the Servicio photographs cover only part of the arid hilly regions. *Servicio 170:557*.

Fig. 15. Ground view of a part of the right section of Fig. 14. The main rectangular structure with its earth and stone pyramid (A) can be clearly seen and corresponds to section (A) in Fig. 14. Above (B) are the three older and more damaged adobe pyramids. The ancient canal (C) running through the pyramids and visible in Fig. 14 can barely be seen in Fig. 15. The main modern canal, bordered by trees, and the cultivated fields are in the far background. *Schaedel*.

Fig. 16. Dr. Schaedel crossing the Jequepeteque River near Talambo in an accepted
prehistoric style. *Rodríguez SuySuy.*

young man who devotes all of his free time to archaeology and at present is carrying out a systematic study of the practically neglected archaeological remains of the Jequetepeque Valley.

We spent several very happy and fruitful days with the charming and obliging Señor Lostaunau. He accompanied us on some of our field trips in a valley where he knew almost every foot of the way.

He has visited many ruins in the valley on foot and horseback and has formed a significant collection of textiles and ceramics. But most important, he has drawn accurate ground plans of a number of outstanding sites. He is now making a detailed ground plan of Pacatnamú which he has visited numerous times. A conscientious and persevering worker, he deserves moral and material assistance in his important work.

A trip to Moro Viejo yielded unexpected and valuable results. These ruins are situated on the Río Seco de San Gregorio, just west of the Pan American Highway and about five miles north of the town of Guadalupe. On several previous occasions when passing through on the Highway, we had noticed this rather inconspicuous site. We had ignored it, for local residents had insisted that it dated back only to colonial times. But during one of our return trips to Lima a careful examination of the aerial photographs of this area convinced us that at least part of the ruins must have been of a pre-Spanish pyramid

type. Our subsequent field trip confirmed this (Fig. 9).

The ruins of Moro Viejo consist of one major pyramid-like structure, several smaller mounds, and other ill-defined adobe constructions scattered among the algarroba bushes. These remains, as well as another small pyramid and some badly destroyed structures on the eastern side of the Pan American Highway, indicated the probability that this whole area had once been a major site, possibly the main site, in the valley of the Río Seco de San Gregorio. It is along the "banks" of this "river," which since ancient times were irrigated by water from the Jequetepeque River, that the interesting Huaca Estacas (Figs. 12 and 13) and other significant pyramids, located on our previous trips, are situated.

Another surprise awaited us at Moro Viejo. As we began our usual procedure of picking up potsherds, we found that a good portion of them were of a type we had not encountered in the many surface collections we had so far made in other parts of the Coast. This unusual type consisted of dark brown-to-orange designs on white-to-buff background and appeared strikingly reminiscent of Sierra ceramics. We learned from Dr. Schaedel that the nearest affinity to this type of ware is to be found in the so-called Cajamarca cursive. Nevertheless there were significant differences, especially in the kind of paste. The Moro Viejo type of ware, found sporadically as far north as Motupe and as far south as Moche, indicates a definite and specific Sierra influence. According to Señor Rondón of Chiclayo, this ware is particularly common to the Nancho region in the upper Zaña Valley, a site which can be reached at present directly from Moro Viejo by a path that very likely dates back to ancient times.

The southern side of the Jequetepeque Valley, though smaller than the northern, showed an abundance of inter-

esting and unexplored sites, a few of which we shall mention. The *monte* and sand-covered area to the south and southwest of the present town of San Pedro de Lloc, in the region labeled with the old Mochica word Sincape on the Army map, attracted our attention. After some ground reconnaissance and discussions later with Dr. Schaedel, we surmised that there were some remains of an old settlement in this area. Archaeological exploration of the area which is just below the present limits of cultivation of the southern bank of the river should bring much unknown material to light, material that should also reveal aspects of the relationship in the past of this valley and the Chicama to the south.

During one of our sojourns at Pacasmayo, when we were without transportation, the local SCIPA engineer lent us his jeep and chauffeur for several days. As a result we were able to make an extensive trip up the valley as far as Tembladera, which for our purposes could be considered the terminus of the coastal part of the valley.

On the way up, we stopped at several Chinese *haciendas* which we had visited in 1941. There are quite a number of Chinese settled in all parts of Peru, many of whom are traders. Some own restaurants where they serve a fine array of real Chinese dishes, creatively adapted to the culinary habits of the Peruvians. Others engage in agriculture, and some even own small *haciendas* where they employ Indian laborers.

Fig. 17 (left). Aerial view of several small *huacas* with surrounding rectangular structures, rising out of the rice fields east of San José. The rice farmers adapt their fields to the more resistant walls of the ruin. *Servicio 170:337* • Fig. 18. According to Father Calancha, the ancients worshipped the moon, which they called Si, and built a "temple" in its honor. Local tradition claims that Huaca Signan (right), situated south of the town of Guadalupe, is this temple. Note that the partly destroyed pyramid is surrounded by an adobe wall. The upper platform is gutted with holes from trial "excavations" made chiefly by *huaqueros*. *Servicio 170:239*.

Fig. 19. This mixed train, on its way to Chilete and Tembladera, is chugging past the four stone and dirt mounds of Monte Grande. This photograph, taken from the top of one of the mounds, shows another mound on the other side of the train. *Kosok.*

Fig. 20. The impressive and extensive ruins of Ventanillas (Little Windows), situated in the narrow part of the valley above Hacienda Tolón, are shown in this vertical aerial photograph. The densely packed structures center about the huge adobe pyramid. Note the large walls on the hills situated on opposite sides of the *quebrada.* Also note how occasional waters, that flowed down the *quebrada* during many centuries, have washed away part of the site. The bank of the Jequetepeque is just below the bottom of the photograph. The curved lines at the left of the photograph are the tracks of the railroad running from Pacasmayo to Chilete. The black spots are algarroba bushes. *Servicio 170:420.*

The first Chinese *hacienda* we stopped at was Hacienda Tecapa. The owner greeted us in a very friendly manner and, to our pleasant surprise, recalled our visit in 1941. After the usual polite preliminary conversation, he took us up to the loft of one of his buildings where he showed us a large number of boxes filled with ceramics that his employees had dug up while working on the *hacienda.* He opened several of these boxes, and a superficial examination showed that the ceramics were representative of various cultural periods, including Inca. But here, as in museum collections, nothing was seen that would indicate the existence of a distinct local style.

After a round of Coca-Colas, which the *hacendado* produced from his electric refrigerator, his two polite but lively sons, born and brought up on the *hacienda* and now attending college, accompanied us on an extensive reconnaisance. Whereas, in 1941, we had been able to find and map only a few canals and sites in the Pampa de Tecapa area, we were now able, through the aid of the excellent Servicio aerial photographs, to make a much more comprehensive and systematic survey. Driving our jeep carefully over the rough terrain, we soon discovered that the whole Pampa de Tecapa was literally covered with canals, furrows, walls, roads, and *tambo*-like structures. We even found a wide ancient road with a double set of walls, similar to the one described on page 118.

Between the *hacienda* and the small Cerro Pitura, on the south bank of the river, in the section north of the present railroad, we encountered a series of walled adobe enclosures and structures as well as a number of small pyramids. Parts of the pyramids were covered by algarroba trees and wind-blown soil.

After bidding farewell to our host, we continued up the valley, which, above Cerro Pitura, suddenly becomes very narrow. Our next stop was at Tolón Hacienda, likewise owned by a Chinese family. After inviting us for lunch and presenting us with a five gallon can of gasoline for our jeep, the owner examined our aerial photographs and maps and pointed to the places where some of the old canals that we had located in 1941 actually terminated.

We then crossed the river to the northern bank and continued on the road to Tembladera. As we drove along, we could see additional ruins directly beside the road as well as along the hillsides. Many of the ruins we had already spotted on the aerial photographs. Most important of the sites were those of Los Leones, and a group of four small rectangular dirt and stone mounds between Monte Grande and Chungál, which we examined (Fig. 19). From Tolón to Tembladera the character of the ruins changed. Stone completely replaced adobe; hillside structures became more numerous, though smaller in size than in the valley below Tolón.

We had now entered the lower reaches of the Sierras. On our aerial photographs, we had located some ruins and canals above Tembladera as far as Chilete, the terminus of the railroad from Pacasmayo. But this region was already somewhat beyond the coastal zone proper to which we had confined our work. So we merely entered these sites on our map and decided to leave them to archaeologists to explore at some future date.

XIII

Cajamarca: Sierra Ally of the Chimús

WE VISITED CAJAMARCA to see the place where a former ally of the Chimús once had flourished and from which later the Incas had wielded their extensive power over the whole northern part of Peru. We also wished to make the trip up the steep, narrow Jequetepeque Valley in order to study there the specific forms of transition from desert coastal zone to rainfall mountain zone. As has been pointed out in Chapter X, these transitional areas are important, so we used every opportunity to ride up and down coastal valleys. In addition, such trips always passed through some of the most imposing mountain scenery in the world!

Three thousand or more years ago, some of the earliest agricultural settlers came down these valleys to the Coast. And ever since then conquering armies have marched through them, dragging their loot along. On more peaceful missions, llama trains have carried a variety of products between Sierra and Coast, thus forging economic as well as cultural links between the two zones. With the coming of the Spaniards these zones were brought closer together. Trade and tribute were increased; llamas were replaced by mules and horses. These, in turn, have now given way to buses, cars, trucks and railroads.

We decided to make the first part of the trip up the Jequetepeque Valley by means of the narrow gauge railroad that runs from Pacasmayo to Chilete, a distance of about fifty miles. We took the fast *autovagón,* a kind of very large motor car equipped with flanged wheels that fit the railroad tracks, instead of the regular, but much slower, "mixed train." The motorman obligingly stopped the overcrowded car at a point not far from the ancient site of Ventanillas so that we could take ground photographs of this important ruin. About noon we reached the terminal at Chilete. From here on, since the valley bottom rises so sharply, the extension of railroad construction into the Sierras would have proved too expensive.

After a quick lunch in a small restaurant at Chilete, we looked around for a bus to take us up into the mountains. But it was Sunday and no buses ran! We finally located a lone truck about to leave for Cajamarca. After making a "deal" with the driver we climbed aboard. Perched on the front seats next to the driver, we had a wonderful time, enjoying to the fullest extent the beautiful and inspiring trip into the Sierras.

Though the Continental Divide here is only 11,000 feet high, while in the Moche and Rimac Valleys, respectively, it is 14,000 and 16,000 feet, the journey nevertheless continually provided new thrills and dramatic vistas as the truck slowly pushed its way up the endless series of hairpin turns along the precipitous mountain sides. We crossed the Continental Divide late in the afternoon and soon were able to discern in the rapidly approaching twi-

Fig. 1 (left). Typical mountainside farms at the upper limits of cultivation in the Andes. Note the narrow road as it winds tortuously back and forth along the terraced slopes, above which tower the rocky, snow-covered mountain peaks. *U. S. Army 112-R-101.*

Fig. 2. Meditation. *Kosok.*

129

Fig. 3. View of Cajamarca with surrounding mountains. Note main square near center of city. *U. S. Army 43-L-115.*

light, the broad green valley of Cajamarca stretched out below. Suddenly the city itself emerged into view!

Darkness had descended when the truck pulled into Cajamarca and parked in the dimly lit main plaza. As we alighted, we saw Indians in their Sierra costumes crossing the square on their way home, while the large loud-speaker of the public radio was filling the entire square with overpowering music that seemed strangely familiar. We listened for a moment spellbound! Yes! It was Stokowski's orchestral arrangement of Bach's powerful "Toccata and Fugue"! As one tremendous chord after another thundered toward a gigantic climax, it seemed as if Bach were expressing in his music the power of the mighty Andes, where peak after peak towers into the endless heavens. During many another evening on the plaza were we to hear some of the world's finest music, while the Indians passed by humming their simple, plaintive songs.

We found a clean and attractive hotel with a balcony looking out over the square. Directly across the square we located a good restaurant with tasty food. And we were pleasantly surprised to find that prices at both hotel and restaurant were much cheaper than those along the Coast. But that which attracted us most to Cajamarca was its wonderful, sunny but cool and energizing mountain climate, together with the calm and peaceful atmosphere that seemed to pervade the town.

Originally, we had planned to stay only a few days and then return to the Coast to write up some of our field notes while the details were still fresh in our minds. Instead, we decided to do our work here in this wonderful place. For the next two months I rewrote most of the first draft of *Water and Life* on the basis of new material I had found. Michael did the typing. He also recalculated the data we had collected on monthly water discharges of the coastal rivers in order to obtain annual averages based on the agricultural year, i.e., from each October to the following September, in place of the calendar year used by the Dirección de Aguas. This brought the results more in line with the actual agricultural process. In his free time, Michael studied with a good local guitar teacher, thereby further increasing his repertoire of Andean songs and dances.

There is practically nothing left at Cajamarca now to remind one of the fact that it was once the capital of an important Andean state. All the old buildings have been destroyed by conquerors. In place of them, a typical Spanish colonial town has been built which consists mainly of red-tiled Spanish type houses surrounding a main plaza and several lesser plazas.

Almost nothing is left of the structures built during the short Inca period. All one can find is a moderate-sized room — the one that Atahualpa, the last of the Inca rulers, is said to have filled with gold and silver vessels in order to pay the ransom exacted by Pizarro. In the suburbs, all one can see are some thermal baths called "Baños de los Incas."

When Alexander von Humboldt (1849:430) visited one of the ruins of Cajamarca, he met Astorpilco, the local Indian cacique, who claimed descent from the ancient Atahualpa! We did not find any living descendants of Astorpilco, though a thorough search might bring some to light. We did, however, ascertain that the various local archives contain valuable records and documents from early colonial times, which should also give insights into some aspects of the pre-Spanish period. A systematic study of the archives, together with archaeological research of the type being done by Dr. Henri Reichlen in various parts of the wide Cajamarca Valley, will eventually enable us to reconstruct something of the nature and extent of the ancient state and society of Cajamarca and its antecedent cultures.

In the nearby mountains is the well-known site of Cumbemayo. Here, incidentally, Dr. Georg Petersen of Zorritos (see Chapter XXIV), had surveyed, as he later informed us, an ancient irrigation canal that led to this site. To his surprise, he found that, as a result of a number of local topographic-hydrological factors, the canal took water from several streams on the "drier" *western* side of the Continental Divide and brought it to Cumbe-

Fig. 4. Inside the garden of a *hacienda* near Cajamarca. *Kosok.*

mayo, located on the "wetter" *eastern* side. This was indeed a unique phenomenon in Peru!

In Cajamarca we were privileged to make the acquaintance of the above-mentioned Dr. Henri Reichlen, a French archaeologist who, together with his wife and fellow worker, Paule, and their sweet little daughter, had been living in Cajamarca for some time. Dr. Reichlen had been carrying on important excavations in the environs of Cajamarca and had made several scientific trips further north in the Sierras and associated lowlands. As a part of his work he was also carrying out a program in the far northern part of Peru which he expects will yield a more solid foundation for our present rather vague theories concerning Ecuadorian-Peruvian interrelations in the ancient past. During one of our visits, he outlined to us a cultural sequence for the Cajamarca area, comparable to a certain extent, with the established coastal sequences. Interestingly enough, the finer of the ceramics, i.e., those of the Cajamarca II period, appear to have developed during the time that the artistically rich Mochica culture was progressing on the Coast.

In his house, which was filled with pottery, skulls, and stone carvings, he showed us two distinctly Nazca type *huacos*, apparently trade pieces, which he had excavated near Cajamarca! He also told us of a hilltop that had been terraced in such a way that it resembled a step pyramid — possibly an ancestral form of the coastal pyramid. Or was its form the result of coastal influences?

We lived for several months in Cajamarca, and we soon became part of the whole Andean way of life; it is essentially Indian with a Spanish colonial veneer to which American gadgets have been added. As already indi-

cated in Chapter IV, in Cajamarca and the remainder of the northern Sierras the Spanish influence is stronger than in the Central and South Andes. There are more Spanish-Indian mixtures than pure-blooded Indians, and practically all Indians speak Spanish. Moreover, the llama, faithful servant of the Indian, has completely disappeared, though traditions among a few of the very old inhabitants in Cajamarca indicate that it survived there up to a hundred years ago.

But the evidence of Spanish influence tends to be misleading. Although only a small portion of the Indians still speak Quechua in addition to Spanish, they have on the whole maintained their Indian customs. In other words, the Indian way of life still gives its stamp to the whole region, a fact by which one is increasingly impressed, the longer one stays in Cajamarca.

We often visited the market and took walks out into the countryside. Even as we worked on our balcony, we could see the Indians with their short, rapid strides moving across the square below us. They went to market, took their babies to the nearby churches for baptism, participated in processions, came home in a merry but suppressed mood after drinking their weak *chicha* and strong *aguardiente*. And each day we could see the funeral processions, mostly of the poor, with relatives carrying the coffin and the few friends of the departed straggling on behind, clad in their everyday clothes — for they possessed no others.

For weeks there was an epidemic of measles, and daily we could see the coffins of little children being carried across the square by their parents — whose tearless faces nonetheless revealed the sad story. Despite the epidemic,

the government sent no doctor to help these forgotten children, although a veterinary was available for sick cattle on the large *haciendas*.

Many of the rich lands of the valley plain have been absorbed by large *haciendas* whose owners have turned the old corn-growing lands of the Indians into grazing grounds for their cattle. The Indians live mainly in the

Fig. 7. Entrance to the Colegio de Belén, built in colonial times.

poorer hill lands where they cultivate small plots. But in order to obtain cash, some of them must work part of the time on the *haciendas* in the valley.

Living much closer to the Indians than we had on the Coast, we came to understand them better and to share

131

Fig. 5. Church procession in Cajamarca. *Kosok.*

Fig. 6. One of Cajamarca's main streets. *Kosok.*

their feelings in many ways. Behind their stoic features often lay a mixture of contradictory emotions. The bitterness over their lot has expressed itself partly in resignation, but also partly in a hope and a struggle for a better life in the future. The Indians of the Sierras were once

Fig. 8. Andean musician playing the *quena* with one hand and the drum with the other, a fairly common form of "one-man band". *Kosok.*

132

a great people. They still have great potentialities, not merely in the arts but also in their ability to overcome their miserable conditions and produce a more humane way of life for themselves.

Many an afternoon, while at work on our balcony, we could hear a blind beggar on the square playing the sad mountain songs on his *quena*, a small native wooden flute. Andean music has warmth and an intimate, personal pathos rarely found in folk music of this level of development. Despite its relatively limited emotional range, it nevertheless seems to encompass man's relation to the overpowering Andes around him.

Much has been written and said about "Inca" music of both present and past. But most of this is a product of the imagination. Actually, we know little specifically concerning the music of the ancient Incas or of the other ancient mountain or coastal people. All we possess are *instruments found in ancient graves or pictures of instruments painted on huacos.* Two kinds of melodic instruments existed, the *quena*, a wooden flute, and the *antara*, a kind of panpipe. Both are still in use today, though in a slightly modified form. Drums, cymbals, whistles, bells, rattles and a sort of bugle have also been found (Figs. 8 to 11).

When discussing instruments, scales, rhythms, and melodies we must bear in mind that they had undoubtedly developed differently in the various parts of the Sierras and the Coast. In the latter region, where the ceramic and textile arts had reached much higher levels than they had in the Sierras, it is not unlikely that the art of instrument making, the development of scales, rhythm and melodies had likewise reached much higher levels. Besides this, the instruments used and the music played by the "court" musicians of the Inca and Chimú rulers or the powerful priests were probably more sophisticated than those of the simple farmers and shepherds. These differences doubtless account, in part, for the different conclusions that various writers have drawn con-

Fig. 9 (far left). Ancient Mochica drawing of musicians; one blows a conch shell, the other a horn-shaped bugle. *AMNH* • Fig. 10 (left). Hand carved wooden *quena. AMNH* • Fig. 11 (right). Ancient instruments, (upper left) horn-shaped bugle or "trumpet", (right) *antarra* or panpipes, (lower left) three kinds of *quenas* or flutes, each with a different "scale". *AMNH.*

cerning the music of ancient Peru. To really answer the question of Peruvian musical instruments, it would be necessary to study the musical instruments on the basis of the different associated cultural periods. But this is extremely hard to do at present, since, as has been pointed out, more than 95 per cent of the archaeological material in museums and private collections has no "birth certificate."

Can we at least determine what scale the ancients used? Here we run into the same difficulties. While visiting the Chiclín Museum in the Chicama Valley, I played the various flutes and clay panpipes that Señor Rafael Larco Hoyle had found in Mochica graves. None of them indicated an organized pentatonic scale! Various writers have, however, claimed that they found instruments which produced pentatonic and even diatonic (seven tone) scales. On a coastal *huaco* there is a drawing of two connected panpipes that jointly may have had a complex scale. Professor Wagner of Lima showed me a rarity, a panpipe that could produce our modern *chromatic half tones,* and which he insisted came from an ancient Paracas grave! The existence in ancient times of this modern type of scale is extremely doubtful; the instrument may perhaps have been an early colonial product. As we know, the Indian artisans continued their crafts into colonial times, using however certain Spanish innovations in their work. However, not until most available instruments have been scientifically studied can one deny that some coastal musicians in the pay of high priests or secular rulers may have developed advanced scales and rather complicated instruments. But the musical instruments of the common people were probably quite simple, producing "scales" which at best *fluctuated around the pentatonic.*

What kind of music did the ancients produce on these instruments? What kind of rhythms, what kind of melodies? We do not know! Obviously, the melodies were limited by the generally narrow tonal range of their instruments. They were probably simple, but anyone who has heard a shepherd play on his simple flute must have been surprised at the melodic complexities sometimes achieved. Rhythms were probably also simple, but this cannot be stated definitely, for simple melodies may have utilized complex rhythms. It is likely that some of the coastal melodies, and perhaps rhythms, were more complex than those of the Sierras. We are, however, safe in assuming that *organized harmony and counterpoint did not exist.*

But what happened when the Spaniards came to Peru with their modern diatonic-chromatic scale and their European instruments? The Spaniards gradually introduced into Peru such European instruments as the organ, the guitar, the harp, the violin and later the clarinet. Of these, the guitar became most popular among the Indians. The definite intervals of these instruments very likely

Fig. 12. Andean Woman. *Kosok.*

transformed the various incipient forms of the five-tone scale into the *organized* five-tone scale now found throughout the Andes — that is, if this scale had not already been attained. *Today this scale is the basis of all Andean folk music.* Even on the Coast, where European musical influence is stronger, the pentatonic always forms the basic framework. What happened to possibly more advanced forms of the Indian scale, we do not know. Probably, like many other aspects of coastal culture, they

just atrophied under Spanish domination or were unwittingly absorbed into the new culture. It is only in the Church music and in certain limited "art" music that the European scale and harmonies have been able to maintain themselves as a thin "upper layer" in the musical life of the country.

The chord-forming ability of the guitar resulted in a characteristic Andean harmonization of folk melodies. There are only two *European type* triads (chords of three notes) that can be formed in the pentatonic (five-tone) scale and which *sounded acceptable* to both the conqueror, and — later on — the conquered. One was a minor chord, for instance, A C E based on the A of the A C D E G (A) scale, and the other was a major chord, C E G, based on the second note C. Incidentally, the mode given here is universal in the Andes. The usual cadence achieved has thus been one in which the melody starts with the minor chord, then rises to the major chord and at the end drops back to the minor chord. *Today this is still the fundamental sequence that underlies all Andean music and gives it its inherent and characteristic form of sadness.* Sometimes the melody starts on the major chord, but it almost always ends on the minor. The basic sequence is a peculiar welding of a specific mode of the pentatonic scale with limited harmonic forms based on the diatonic. For a detailed presentation of the evolution of the pentatonic scale and its various harmonic possibilities in terms of *modern* musicology, see the excellent and unique volume of Yasser (1932) on the evolution of tonality.

Fig. 13. An *antarra* (panpipe) made of clay, indicating its coastal origin. *Kosok.*

Fig. 14. An "Amfortas" of the Andes. *Kosok*.

ments has resulted in the present day *Andean* folk music — often mistakenly called Inca music. Of course, other foreign elements have also been absorbed. For instance, we heard an *Inca foxtrot,* popular throughout the Andes! The form and rhythm were those of a foxtrot, the melodic line with harmonic sequences was Andean, i.e., based upon the pentatonic scale.

In 1939, while collecting some Andean folk melodies, we heard a theme that seemed to have been taken from Gilbert and Sullivan's *Mikado!* But our greatest surprise came when a group of mountain Indians, who were then visiting Lima, announced to us that they would play a real Inca song for us. What did we hear? The New York Jewish song "Bei mir bist du schoen" played with Andean trimmings! After our initial astonishment, we realized that its plaintive character was not at all incongruous with the Andean atmosphere. When I mentioned this to an Indian scholar he calmly answered: "We Indians and the Jews are similar in certain ways. We are both oppressed peoples and why should not the music of two oppressed peoples be similar?" Such absorption and remolding of new elements is true of all living music of the people and helps to give folk music its many-sided character.

The instrumental composition of Andean musical groups of today differs from village to village. Besides the ancient *quena*, panpipes and hand drums, one finds guitars, violins, harps and clarinets. In recent times even the easily played saxophone has wheedled itself into this motley assortment of instruments. Some combinations sound better than others, some are better trained, some play more in tune, but all of them produce the same Andean folk music.

The scholar and artist may ask: What is the oldest and most unadulterated form of Andean music that one can hear today? The answer to this question obviously cannot be stated unequivocally. But most likely it is the music performed by the lone *quena* player, in some instances, to the accompaniment of a small hand-beaten drum. The sad melody, in most cases, is characterized by a complex descending line. This is the kind of music one often hears played by the itinerant beggar on the street or the lonely shepherd on the mountainside.

Once a cultural renaissance gets further under way in Peru, as has already happened in Mexico, Brazil and several other Latin American countries, the music of the Andes will undoubtedly play an important role. Its warm, sensitive sadness and its emotional depth, together with its strong but never brutal rhythmic qualities,

possess tremendous potentialities for the future development of a truly great national music.

We wanted to stay longer in Cajamarca in order to absorb more of the Andean life and to complete our manuscript. But our time in Peru was running short and we still had field work to do on the Coast as well as some aerial photographs to study in Lima. We therefore bade goodbye to the friends we had made and boarded the semi-weekly plane for Trujillo on the Coast.

By bus, the trip takes more than a day and a half, by plane, twenty minutes! And the plane trip is both fascinating and informative. After the plane leaves the lush green landscape of the Cajamarca Valley and passes over the Continental Divide, it enters into a region characterized by the growing aridity of the coastal side of the Andes. While some of the higher mountains still support a rainfall crop of wheat and maize, the valleys are completely dry. But soon the mountain tops, too, lose their greenness until finally, as the coastal plains appear, the whole countryside becomes completely arid. But here, on the banks of the rivers, the fertile green irrigated oases, the wonderful products of man's labor, stand out in bold and welcome relief.

Fig. 15. Modern "French horn" made from the horns of cattle. This instrument, made in Huancayo, is in the possession of the author. It has been tested by a musician friend, who succeeded in playing modern symphonic themes on it. *Kosok*.

What the melodic contributions of the Spaniards were, we do not know. It is not unlikely that simple Spanish songs, especially those basically pentatonic in their form, were given the "Andean treatment" and became part of the folk music. The Spaniards obviously also introduced their own rhythms. To what extent some of these paralleled, enriched or simplified the ancient Indian rhythms, we likewise do not know. Today the triple rhythm is used; but the duple one is the more usual. The most common one in the dances is the dactylic form of the duple meter (♩ ♫).

Thus, the integration of these Indian and Spanish ele-

XIV

Hunting Canals on the Pampa de Zaña

Today the large, flat Pampa de Zaña is a desolate and windswept desert plain. It is crossed only by the cars that speed over the Pan American Highway on their way between the Jequetepeque and the Zaña Valleys. But once this barren region was filled with life. In order to ascertain the total area formerly under cultivation, we had to trace the ancient extensions of the present day irrigation system of the Jequetepeque Valley into the Pampa as far north as possible. We also had to trace the irrigation remains from the Zaña Valley as far south as possible. And these roads of inquiry led to the key question: Did these two systems once meet and thus form a Zaña-Jequetepeque hydrological unit?

In 1941, we had discovered some of the extensions of these systems in the Pampa. But with the truck we then had, we were able to enter only part of the Pampa and were thus unable to solve our problem. Horses were difficult to obtain and use in this extensive region.

However, the United States trimetrogon aerial survey of the Pampa de Zaña was now available, and it provided us with a general picture of some of the major canals to the east of the Pan American Highway. But the aerial photographs, while giving us an over-all picture of the Pampa de Zaña, were taken at such a great height that many details essential for our ground survey were not visible.

The aerial photographs of the Servicio also proved of little use, for only short sections of ancient canals were visible on the margins of the cultivated areas of both the Jequetepeque and Zaña Valleys. We were therefore forced to locate practically all of the canals in the Pampa by means of ground surveys.

What we would have given for a helicopter! With it we could have hovered over each canal at will and then slowly and deliberately have followed it to its final disappearance. Before leaving New York we had visited the offices of several helicopter manufacturing companies in order to interest them in our exotic, non-profit making, scientific project. But it seems that the helicopter has not come of age sufficiently to meet the demands of paleo-hydrology, for we would have needed, in addition, a special helicopter crew, special replacement parts and a special service station.

Some more fortunate scientist of the future will make use of the helicopter and thus clarify all the details that our ground survey could not hope to do. And may he have at his disposal a good set of aerial photographs of this region, which undoubtedly will some day be made. But most important, may no unusually heavy rains, like those of 1925, occur again to complete the destruction of the remains of these ancient canals, thus rendering the work of scientific reconstruction impossible.

But, since it is impossible to do the work of the present with the tools of the future, we resigned ourselves to our ground survey methods. In fact, we were happy that such a thing as a jeep had been invented. And we were very thankful that Mr. John Neale was able to lend us a SCIPA jeep for our work.

Canal-hunting is often an exciting experience! The usual method is to cruise around the region where the remains of canals are said to exist until they are actually located — and then follow them. In such desert work, the jeep proves definitely superior to the truck. But the jeep, too, has its limitations. Where the canal winds along the

Fig. 1. Remains of one of the many old stone-lined canals that once brought water to the Pampa de Zaña. Cerro Colorado is in the background. *Kosok.*

135

sides of hills, the only way to do the job is on horseback or on foot.

Even with a jeep, there are often difficulties in following a canal on level ground. For strong sea winds blowing across the region for centuries, together with occasional rains, have, at places, almost leveled off the elevated sides of the canal and filled the canal itself with soil. In such a case, one points the jeep in the general direction of what remains of the canal. Then, as one peers carefully along the ground in front of the jeep, it often becomes possible to follow the vestiges of the canal for many miles; late afternoon or early morning are best for this work because, at those times, even the slightest elevation casts a shadow.

We spent the equivalent of a week in carrying on ground reconnaissance, zigzagging in our jeep back and forth over the Pampa de Zaña. After unsuccessful initial attempts at following major canals, we located one, east of the Pan American Highway near the Jequetepeque Valley, which ran straight north in the direction of the Zaña Valley! Though it often seemed to disappear, we always could see, almost straight ahead, some slight elevation or depression which indicated that we were on the right track. A few times, we seemed to have lost the

canal; but when we climbed on top of the jeep and peered both backwards and forwards we could, figuratively, tie the two ends of the canal together.

We were thrilled when, after many hours of this rather exciting adventure, we found the canal actually entering the Zaña Valley! There, after making a turn to the west, it appeared to have at one time led into one of the ancient canals from the Zaña River itself. The Zaña canal was in a much better state of preservation, indicating that it had been used later than our canal from the Jequetepeque.

We have often been asked: "How do you know, after a canal has disappeared for a distance, that when you later on pick up the trace of a canal it is the same one and not another?" Of course, one can never be *absolutely* certain, especially when there are a number of canals in the same area, and when parts of these canals have been completely obliterated by the elements. But the basic answer must be: "Water always runs downhill." Therefore, in following a canal, one has to train the jeep driver and oneself always to keep moving ahead *at about the same level* as the sloping Pampa. At first, this is a little difficult; but, with some practice, it can be done. In such cases an altimeter does not help much because it is not sufficiently sensitive. However, a good driver can tell by

the response of the motor whether the car is traveling on an upgrade or on a downgrade.

To be sure, at times, one runs into various snags. A common one occurs when a canal, after entering one side of a *quebrada*, disappears (as a result of centuries of periodic washouts) only to reappear on the other side of the *quebrada* in the form of two or three parallel canals! Another type of problem occurs when another canal appears at an angle and cuts across the canal under investigation, indicating that it was part of an earlier or later system of canals. In such instances, knowledge drawn from previous experience, as well as a bit of common sense, is helpful.

Often, when a canal is traced along the hills forming the sides of a valley descending to the coast, *the canal appears to be running uphill!* This optical illusion is caused by the fact that the terrain of the bottom of the valley slopes downhill *more sharply* than does the canal. However, one is unaware of the downward slope of the valley; one notices only that the canal seems to be rising gradually along the side of the hills above the valley bottom. Therefore, one gets the impression that the canal once carried water uphill!

While dealing with this subject we should like to draw attention to an incident that occurred during our 1940-41 trip. At that time, we were in the Santa Valley where an old, unused Inca canal had been cleaned out and repaired by a young engineer from one of the *haciendas*. Together with some villagers, we were excitedly waiting for the water to be released. One of the men shook his head skeptically and said: "The young engineer who is in charge of this work must be crazy. He must have studied too much at college. He is trying to tell us that water is going to run down this canal when actually anyone can see very clearly that the canal is running uphill." But when the water was released, it ran merrily along the canal following the contours of the hill just as the engineer had predicted! The villagers shook their heads with astonishment. Some of them admitted they must have been wrong. One exclaimed: "My goodness, what they learn in college nowadays!" Another remarked: "The Incas were certainly smart people building canals that could lead water uphill." And it must be confessed that it appeared to us as though the water were actually running uphill!

But let us return to the Pampa de Zaña. The job of tracing some of the other canals raised a number of problems. In the general region where we had found the canal

Fig. 2 (left). Stone and dirt pyramid with a partially-destroyed ramp still visible. The pyramid is at the foot of Cerro Colorado and just east of the Pan American Highway. *Kosok* • Fig. 3 (right). Part of the ruins of Chérrepe Antigua, located near the southern limit of Pampa de Zaña, and not far from Cerro Colorado. Since this photograph was taken, part of the site has been placed under cultivation. *Servicio 170:606.*

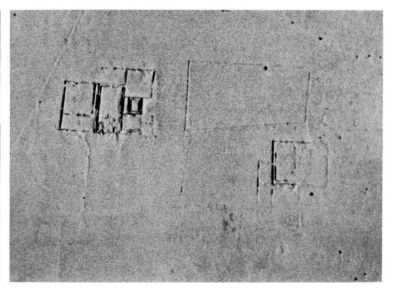

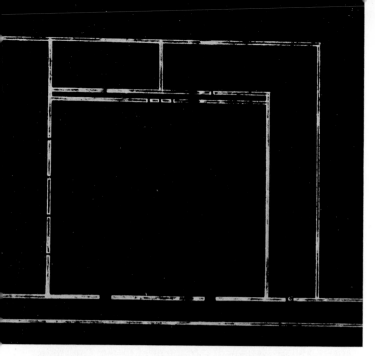

Fig. 4. The main part of a plan of the "Inca" road and *tambo* in the northeastern part of Pampa de Zaña drawn by Martínez de Compañón, Bishop of Trujillo (Pl. 86).

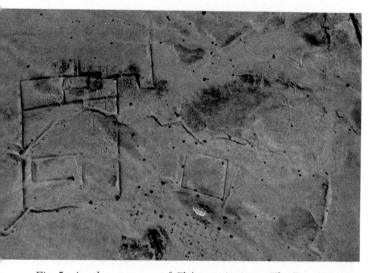

Fig. 5. Another structure of Chérrepe Antigua. The Pan American Highway can be seen in the upper right corner. *Servicio 170:606* • Fig. 6. The "Inca" road that crosses the Pampa de Zaña (see also Fig. 4). *Kosok* • Fig. 7 (right margin). An interesting cactus found on the Pampa de Zaña. *Kosok* • NOTE: The ancient design on p. 138 was unique to Peru and to other parts of ancient America. *Reiss and Stübel.*

described above, we encountered a considerably larger canal at a higher level. In order to extend the canal across an extensive depression of the terrain, the ancients had constructed a *mampuesto*, an elevated aqueduct built of dirt. This aqueduct, the longest we found in Peru, extended for approximately five miles. At certain places it reached an elevation of more than twenty-five feet. The aqueduct itself was obviously easy to follow, but when it approached more elevated ground, the dividing ridge between the Jequetepeque and Zaña Valleys, it ran along the ground and then disappeared. We cruised around for a while and finally found what might once have been an elevated continuation of the aqueduct. But the latter, in turn, suddenly disappeared at the edge of a small *quebrada*.

It did not make sense to us that the ancients should have troubled themselves to build a long, elevated aqueduct merely to dump the water into a *quebrada*. Of course, they could have taken the water out of the *quebrada* further down in order to cultivate the lands of that region; yet, to get the water to the *quebrada* they need not have built a time-consuming aqueduct over the low areas. They could have constructed a much more easily built contour canal which would have brought the water to the *quebrada*, though at a slightly lower level.

With our jeep we then crossed over to the other side of the narrow *quebrada*, and for many hours cruised around in the general direction in which the canal should have continued. But no traces of it could be seen anywhere. Since this region is swept by exceptionally strong winds from the Pacific Ocean, the remaining section of the aqueduct-canal, if it existed at all, may have been destroyed during the past centuries. Or there may have been a war or internal upheaval that prevented completion of this project. Possibly the great rains of 1925 had destroyed the whole canal system here. In any case we could not solve the problem of its termination.

Here was one of the few places where we could not satisfactorily locate the termination of a major canal. Our failure did not discourage us too much, since it affected our end results only to a minor degree. For, to judge by the contour of the land, the amount of additional land that could have been cultivated by an extension of this aqueduct further towards Zaña would have probably amounted to only a few per cent of the total area of the Pampa de Zaña formerly irrigated.

All reconnaissance discussed so far had been made to the east of the Pan American Highway, which cuts right across the Pampa de Zaña. In this region we traced other canals that ran for many miles to the north in the direction of the Zaña Valley. But none of these canals seemed to have continued into the valley itself. We did, however, locate the remains of the main north-south Inca road — which is crossed by the Pan American Highway — and which once led right into the middle part of the Zaña Valley. This road with adjacent *tambos* has been described and mapped in part by Kroeber (1930: 90-91, Pl. xxix); but he did not attempt to trace it further. It is interesting to note that at the end of the eighteenth century Bishop Martínez de Compañón had already made a ground plan of one of these *tambos* (Fig. 4).

The remains of the walled road indicated something we had already noticed in other parts of the Coast, namely, that with rare exceptions, the ancient roads were widest and best constructed where they crossed the cultivated and populated parts of the valley. However, in the desert areas between the valleys the roads became narrower and, finally, both walls and road disappeared altogether. This absence of the road structures today may, of course, be due to their destruction by the desert winds. But there may be another reason. These structures may never have been built! According to some Spanish Chroniclers, the ancients often substituted, in the desert areas, a succession of upright wooden poles. This policy of building the largest and most impressive roads in the regions of densest population is of course characteristic among all peoples, ancient and modern.

Besides the above-mentioned *tambos,* and two minor stone-walled constructions alongside an old canal near the Pan American Highway, the only ruin that we found in the Pampa to the east of the Pan American Highway was a large, low platform *huaca* near the *mampuesto* we have already described. Ironically, a modern telegraph pole of the main north-south telegraph line now stands on the top of the pyramid. Since the pyramid, as far as we knew, had no name, we christened it "Huaca Palo Telégrafo (Telegraph Pole Pyramid) and so entered it on our map.

Not far from the ruin we found several dozen broken water jugs, all typical black Chimú ware, two of which are shown on pp. 135 and 136. The style of the potsherds tended to confirm our previous impression that this whole Pampa had been a region of maximum extension of agriculture during the period of the Chimú Empire. To what extent it was such a region during an earlier period, we could not say. The absence of remains of any real habi-

tation sites on the extensive Pampa seemed to indicate that, in Chimú times, it may have been *state* land, cultivated by people living in villages near the present day population sites or in temporary reed or algarroba huts erected on the Pampa itself.

The Pampa may well have been cultivated also in Inca times and perhaps was tilled to some extent in early colonial times. But it is quite safe to assume that, with the advent of the Spaniards, the main part of the verdant Pampa gradually or suddenly became a desert region. In modern times, on various occasions, very limited parts of the Pampa have been put back under cultivation and then abandoned, as the fresh condition of some of the canals and furrows indicates.

The water jugs that we found had apparently been broken by inexperienced and clumsy *huaqueros*, for some of the *huacos* were still one-half to three-quarters intact. Curiously enough, in 1941, we had come upon a similar collection of broken Chimú jugs near the same place. The condition of the soil indicated that this was the site of an old graveyard. Significantly, it was situated near the holy pyramid, the church of the ancients, whose proximity would impart imaginary blessings to the dead.

The remainder of the Pampa de Zaña, the part *west* of the Pan American Highway, caused us even more trouble. For days we cruised back and forth in this region, which extends almost up to the sea. We were soon convinced that what some of the people in Jequetepeque and Zaña had told us was true: The whole Pampa was once covered with old irrigation remains. Canals were everywhere, and they seemed to run helter-skelter, without rhyme or reason, indicating possibly different construction periods. In some places the canals had been destroyed by the elements, a factor which added to the general confusion. Our problem was one of working out the system and of mapping it without aerial photographs.

Finding the limit of irrigation near the sea proved difficult. We went to the area, just north of the Jequetepeque irrigated area, where a few of the aerial photographs indicated the beginnings of several large canals. Here we cruised around, following each major canal leading north into the Pampa. Señor Lostaunau, who accompanied us on some of the trips, was of great assistance, since he had traversed part of this region on horseback. Eventually, we hit the major canal nearest the sea. To our surprise it continued for many miles in a northwesterly direction, becoming lost, finally, in the unearthly, desolate region at the eastern slope of Cerro Chérrepe. Many fairly well-preserved secondary canals and furrows gave mute evidence of the labor and energy of the Indians in bringing life into these forbidding parts. The well-preserved state of portions of the canals brought up the eternal question: How far into modern times was the system used?

We cruised around further in order to see how the main canals "fitted together." Though the elements had destroyed part of the canal systems, we were, nevertheless, able to determine that the system as a whole extended almost two-thirds of the way to the Zaña. In this entire region we found few potsherds, and these were mainly utilitarian. We found no structures except a very small pyramid on one side of a canal, some three miles from the present zone of vegetation of the Jequetepeque Valley, and an associated small walled compound on the other side of the canal.

A difficult part of our task entailed the entering of the canals on the Army topographical maps. What we did was to judge the length of a canal by the kilometer gauge on the jeep, and determine the general direction with a compass. By following various related canals this way, we could check our results to some extent. Another way of checking some of our main points was a simple triangulation process. We applied this process by relating our position at a particular point on the Pampa to the various hills that were visible on the horizon, hills that were also indicated on the Army topographical maps. Aerial photographs, when made, will undoubtedly modify some parts of our map.

In order to study the Pampa near the Zaña end we drove to the ancient village of Mocupe near the southern border of cultivated land of the Zaña Valley. There we were happy to find some of our friends who had helped us in 1941. We were most fortunate in meeting again an old guide who owned a small farm in the neighboring area, and who again accompanied us on some of our trips. He helped us locate several major ancient canals on the south side of the Zaña Valley. These canals had once marked, as far as we could determine, the maximum southern cultivation zone of the Zaña area, which zone, in some areas, appears to have been close to the canals from the Jequetepeque.

We drove the jeep on a zigzag course over the Pampa in the region between the Jequetepeque and Zaña areas where we found some "odds and ends" of canals. There were some places, however, where for a distance of a few miles, we could find no remains of canals. Our various informants from Mocupe insisted that the rains of 1925, the heaviest and most destructive since ancient times, had destroyed many canals that formerly were visible in this region. We were inclined to accept their statements, inasmuch as these rains had caused similar destruction in other parts of the Northwest Coast of Peru.

On one of our trips across the Pampa, we suddenly came upon faint but clear traces of the walls of a wide road, hitherto unreported. The road ran in a straight line from a point about five miles south of the village of Mocupe in a southwesterly direction and vanished gradually in the region of the former location of the small settlement of Santa Rosa on the lower Chamán River. This river is the continuation of the Río San Gregorio and carries the surplus water to the sea from some of the cultivated areas of the Jequetepeque Valley. Near its mouth is the present small settlement of Caleta Chérrepe.

The unusual nature of this road indicated that it might have been a colonial one that had once connected the Zaña and Chamán Valleys. While preparing the manuscript for this book we re-read Calancha and were surprised to find what was probably a reference to this road. For Calancha relates that since the valley of Zaña did not have its own port, the town of Zaña used the port of Chérrepe. Consequently, all goods coming to and from the town of Zaña and this port *must have passed over this road,* for its course is the only logical one connecting these two places. Since Zaña in early colonial times was an important administrative center, this road must have once been extensively used. This situation possibly explains why this lower section of the Chamán, while being geographically part of the Jequetepeque area, today belongs administratively to the Zaña Valley.

While we thus succeeded in tracing the main irrigation and cultivation interconnections between the Zaña and Jequetepeque Valleys in ancient times, the subject is hardly exhausted. Once aerial photographs of the Pampa are made, the actual courses and connections of the various canals will undoubtedly become clearer to us. And when the helicopter can be used, the problem will come still closer to solution.

In addition, archaeological explorations and studies of local and national archives should yield material that would provide insight both into the practical relations between these valleys and into the character of their domination by the Incas, Chimús and earlier conquerors. Indeed, information may even be obtained of a possible temporary domination of the Pampa at one time — during the Middle Period? — by the Lambayeque-Zaña unit.

XV

The Valley of Zaña: A Connecting Link

THE ZAÑA VALLEY occupied a strategic position in the past. During the Late and possibly the Middle Periods, its irrigated fields were extended up to those of the Jequetepeque to the south and the Lambayeque to the north. At that time, and even before, the valley must have played an economic, political and cultural role greater than its size would seem to warrant. Limited historical records show that this exceptional role continued down into early colonial times.

The Zaña River can be classified as moderately small, with an average annual water content approximately the same as that of the Moche. The valley, itself, which is long and narrow, has three natural divisions. The upper part consists of a somewhat triangular-shaped irrigated pocket which we determined had been considerably larger in ancient times than it is at present. It is administered today by the old town of Oyotún situated near the upper end of the pocket.

The middle part possesses a kind of elongated oval shape and extends from Cerros Motete and Culpón, where the valley is very narrow, to approximately the region of Cerro Guitarras, Hacienda Ucupe and the ancient settlement of Mocupe, a distance of about fifteen miles. Incidentally, the latter places are cut by the Pan American Highway. The administrative center of this main part, as well as of the valley as a whole, is the ancient *pueblo* of Zaña. The economic and political power of this *pueblo*, however, is not great at present since most of this part of the valley and sections of the upper and lower parts are owned or controlled by the large Hacienda Cayalti. This *hacienda* employs several thousand laborers, including many Sierra immigrants and

Fig. 1. The large hillside ruin of Cerro Guitarras in the Zaña Valley, showing the large circumferential wall of stone in the foreground, was photographed from Pardo y Miguel's plane. The wall is the part of the ruin most easily seen from the nearby Pan American Highway which is barely visible in the lower left hand corner of this photograph. The white triangle on one of the hills was made by the Peruvian Geodetic Survey. The Cerro Guitarras region depended mainly upon canals from the Lambayeque River and probably represented an outpost of the expanding Lambayeque (Collique) culture some time before the Chimú occupation. This hillside site is one of the best preserved ruins of coastal Peru (see vertical aerial photograph of this ruin on next page). The name of the site is sometimes spelled Cerro Guitarra. *Kosok.*

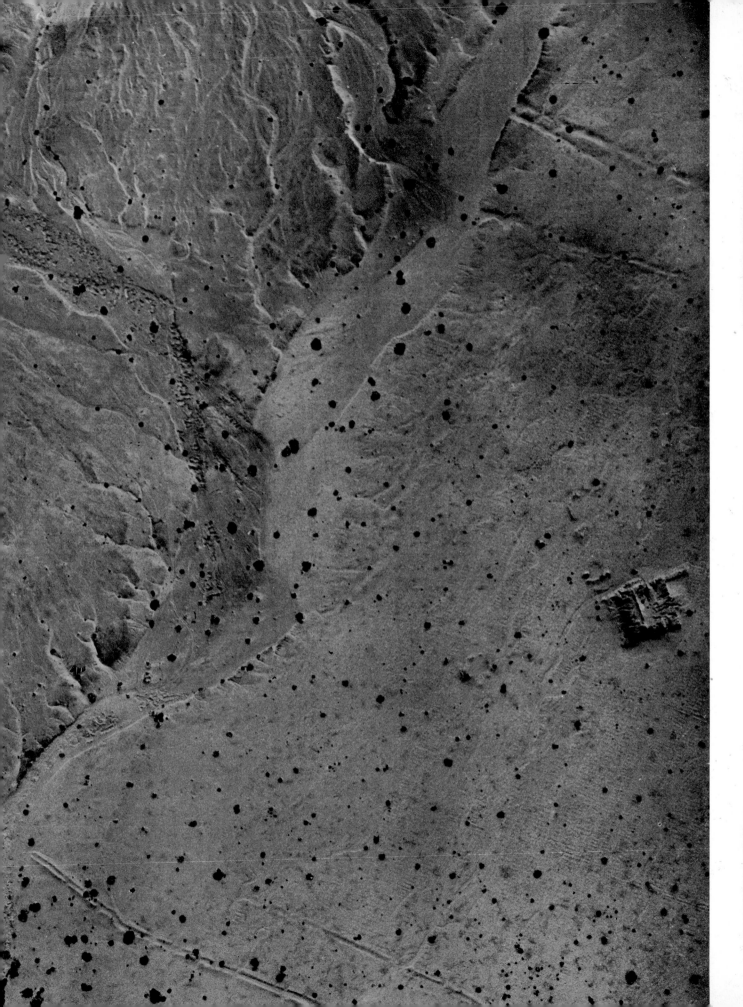

Fig. 2 (left). Part of the ruins of Cerro Guitarras, showing several hills partly covered with the remains of rectangular habitation sites, can be seen in this vertical aerial photograph. Note the large and extensive protective walls around and over the hills. Partly encircling the bottom of the hills is a large, ancient canal (*acequia madre*) which once irrigated the fields below it. Visible at the lower right are sections of smaller canals, probably post-dating the main canal. Farther right stands the lone Huaca Miguelito in a large deserted *pampa* which is covered with many canals and furrows of the past. Only a small portion of the *pampa* can be seen. The wide black line across the left side of the photograph is the Pan American Highway (see Figs. 1, 3 and 4). *Servicio 3330.*

Fig. 3. This photograph was taken from a point near the crest of one of the hills of Cerro Guitarras, looking down upon the terraced, stone-walled structures (see Figs. 1 and 2). Note the cacti, typical of some of the hilly regions of the Zaña-Lambayeque area, growing among the ruins. The Pan American Highway can be seen at the top of the photograph. *Schaedel.*

Fig. 4 (below). Model of the ceremonial Huaca Miguelito. The form of the *huaca* appears to be the prototype of most step-*huacas* of the Coast. It contains two steps, or levels, with a ramp cutting the first and leading to the second, main level. Separating the latter into two sections runs a wall, about six feet high, which contains a doorway connecting the two sections. The lower rear level is not as high as the lower front level. A small formless mass of abodes (not in model), spread on the ground just below the wall, gives the impression that it once was a stairway leading to the front and/or rear top level. The purpose of the long low extension jutting out from the left front level is not clear. *Storck-Kosok.*

some migratory workers. On both desert sides of this section we found extensive remains of ancient canal systems indicating that much more land was cultivated in ancient times than is required for the present sugar crop of the *hacienda*.

The lower part of the valley runs from the Pan American Highway to the sea and consists of a narrow stretch of relatively poor land. But here, as indicated in Chapter XIV, we found extensive canals on the southern side of

known. In fact, Kroeber (1930:91) stated that in crossing the valley on the main highway he had not noticed any ruins, a statement all the more surprising since the highway passes several pyramids and cuts through part of the important site of Cerro Guitarras. Actually, both sides of the valley, from above Oyotún all the way down to the sea, are littered with ruins of ancient canals, roads, walls, pyramids, fortifications and settlement sites! In all, we found and mapped some thirty distinct sites. We took

The *hacienda* had in its possession an aerial mosaic of part of the valley which a private company had made. While this mosaic served the *hacienda* well by showing the size and position of various fields, it was practically useless for our purposes. The mosaic was too small; besides, it did not include any of the adjacent desert areas where most of the ancient sites are located.

When we returned to Peru in 1948, we found that there were still no satisfactory aerial photographs of the

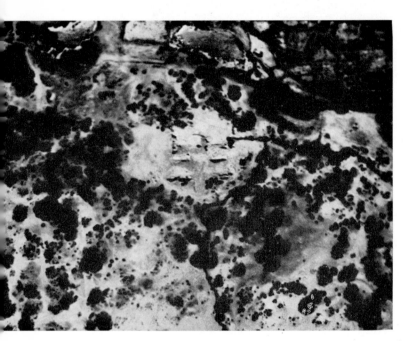
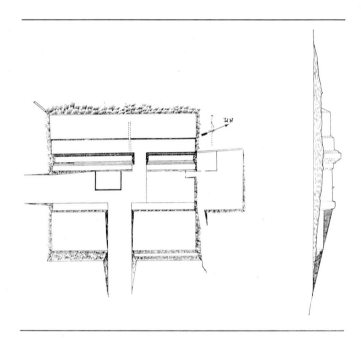

Figs. 5 to 7. Huaca Teodora can be seen in the *monte* bushes south of Mocupe as one drives along the Pan American Highway. The vertical aerial photograph shows how centuries of occasional rains and the roaming of cattle have modified the original shape of this complex structure. *Servicio 3330: 1678* • Dr. Schaedel and Antonio Rodríguez SuySuy were able to make an accurate ground plan of the pyramid after a field trip to Huaca Teodora. The amount of detail, not visible in the aerial photograph but discovered *in situ* and embodied in the ground plan, emphasizes the importance of careful field work. *Schaedel-Rodríguez SuySuy* • On the basis of the ground plan, John Storck made a plaster model of the pyramid. Comparison of this model with that in Fig. 4 shows that Huaca Teodora is a sophisticated form of the simple Huaca Miguelito. Even so, Huaca Teodora is simple in form when compared with the main buildings of El Purgatorio, in the Leche Valley. *Storck-Kosok.*

the valley. On the northern side, we later traced the canals which once came from the Lambayeque Valley and stretched for a considerable distance into the presently desolate desert. After mapping these canal systems, we at once saw clearly that the irrigated parts formerly spread in a wide fan-shaped form in the direction of the sea, thus making this section of the valley larger and more important in ancient times than it is at present.

Archaeologically, the Zaña Valley is practically un-

ground photographs and made some surface potsherd collections which are now at the Institute in Trujillo.

When we first visited the valley in 1941, we had made Hacienda Cayalti the center of our operations. Its administrator, Señor Neumann, very kindly put trucks and horses at our disposal. Since the valley is narrow and contains roads on both sides, it was not difficult to locate some of the archaeological sites and the courses of a number of main canals.

valley. Consequently, we had to rely on field work for our information. But shortly before we left Peru in 1949, when the Servicio made an aerial survey, we checked our own map against the aerial photographs. To this we added a short field trip to confirm some additional sites which we had missed in our previous work.

In 1948 we stayed at Hacienda Cayalti again. It was during one of the periods when we had no jeep, and we were fortunate when Señor Neumann again put the truck and horses of the *hacienda* at our disposal. This time we met Ingeniero Tupac Yupanqui, who had been the field surveyor of the *hacienda* for many years. He accompanied us on most of our trips, and since he knew practically every place in the valley, his guidance was extremely helpful in locating canals and sites. We were struck by his name which was the same as that of one of the great Inca rulers. When questioned about it, he proudly asserted that he was a descendant of that ruler. He was a most engaging person who showed keen interest in the life and works of his ancestors. In his home he had a small, representative collection of water jugs, mainly blackware, which he had found on the land of the *hacienda*.

The whole upper pocket is cluttered with sites that merit attention. One pyramid was built in such a way that the top could be reached by following a spiral road around the perimeter! Was this its original form or a colonial or even a modern modification? Farther up the Río de Tingues, a branch of the Zaña, lies Nancho with its unique ceramics mentioned in Chapter XII. At the lower end of the pocket where the valley is extremely narrow, we climbed up part of the steep slopes of Cerro de Culpón, whose sides contain several levels of very long and extremely high stone walls. Were they part of the defensive system which together with structures on Cerro Motete just across the valley guarded the entrance or exit to the Oyotún pocket?

We noted with interest that at Cerro Campana, an important site in the upper valley, there is a fair-sized *huaca* cluster which might once have been the center of the upper pocket. Surprisingly, one of the *huacas* was built *on the crest* of Cerro Campana, a rather unusual location for a *huaca*. We also found a *huaca* on top of Cerro Songoy further down the river.

Fig. 8. The ruins of Cerro Corbacho form one of the major ancient sites in the Zaña Valley. They constitute a typical terraced hillside settlement of the Late Chimú and Inca periods. This vertical aerial view of a section of the Cerro shows clearly: (a) large rectangular Chimú-like enclosures of adobe at the foot of the hill; (b) terraced platforms of stone on the side of the hill; (c) extensive walls near the summit which continue around the sides of the hill. This crowded settlement is an excellent example of the ancient Peruvian concept of utilizing to the maximum the uncultivated zones for habitation purposes, so that all cultivable ground could be used for agriculture. *Servicio 3330: 1689, 1690.*

Down the valley near the end of the middle section are the major ruins of the valley, namely, the hillside clusters of Cerro Guitarras and Cerro Corbacho. Cerro Guitarras rises above the northern edge of the present irrigated zone just to the east of the Pan American Highway.

Fig. 9. While standing in the middle of this walled road crossing the desert north of Cayalti, we could see in the distance the hills separating the Zaña from the Lambayeque Valley. The unusual width of the road (30 yards) and the fact that it ended at these hills prompted us to classify it tentatively as belonging to the "ceremonial" type (see Chapter VI). *Kosok.*

(Figs. 1 to 4). Cerro Corbacho is situated somewhat further up the valley in the middle of the present irrigated region. (Figs. 8 and 10). Both sites, recently surveyed by Dr. Schaedel, probably dominated the northern part of the valley.

In the lower section, we located a number of partly destroyed small- to medium-sized pyramids and mounds including Huaca Teodora (see next paragraph). Later on we located by air (see Chapter XXIV) an interesting

pyramid-like structure situated on a northern promontory of Cerro Carrizal near the sea. Unfortunately, we were unable to visit this promising site on foot.

While many smaller sites proved to be of considerable interest, no photographs of them are reproduced in this report. The enlargements of the aerial photographs turned out to be rather poor and the ground photographs we took were unimpressive. However, photographs of models of two pyramids are given, one of Huaca Teodora (Figs. 5 to 7) just west of the Pan American Highway and south of Mocupe, the other of an unnamed *huaca* which we called Miguelito (Fig. 4) situated just to the east of Cerro Guitarras.

One of the hydrologically most significant objects that we encountered in exploring the valley was a set of parallel canals that started in the upper part of the valley near Nueva Arica. These we followed in and out of the hills and *quebradas* that flank much of the southern side of the valley. One of them disappeared in the Pampa de Zaña near the old trunk road coming from Jequetepeque (see Chapter XIV). A branch of the second "connected" with the long canal that came from the Jequetepeque while the other branches spread out beyond the Pan American Highway into the Pampa de Zaña where they disappeared in the regions bordering the lower part of the Zaña Valley.

This phenomenon of parallel canals or "double" canals as we called them occurs in a number of valleys. The parallel nature comes out best when they are cut into the side of a hill where one runs at an elevation some distance higher than the other. But when they enter a flat *quebrada* or *pampa*, the distance between them widens until it may be several hundred yards or even more, thus enabling the upper one to irrigate a considerable amount of land between the two canals. We heard many explanations for this method of building canals, but the one that seems most logical is the following: the lower canal was built first; later on when it became necessary to irrigate more of the plains above the first

Fig. 10. Terraced platforms were found at higher levels on the side of Cerro Corbacho (see aerial view, Fig. 8). *Schaedel.*

canal, the second one was built at a higher level.

The most important political-hydrological system of the valley is the one that once brought water from the Lambayeque via Collique to the Zaña (see Chapter XVI). By studying the aerial photographs and by making repeated field trips, we were finally able to disentangle, so to speak, much of this two-valley irrigation complex. We found that water was brought from the *southern* bank of the Lambayeque River to help irrigate the *northern* bank of the Zaña. As a result, more of the water from the latter river was used to extend the irrigated

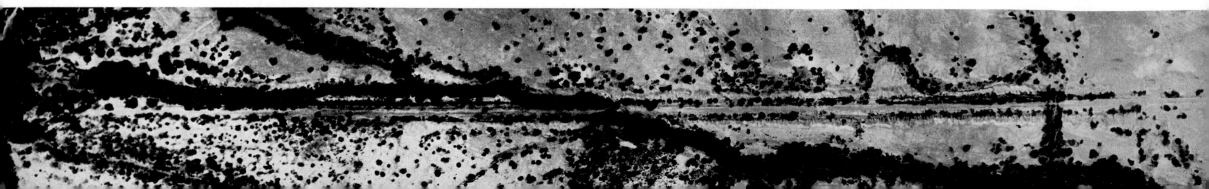

Fig. 11. Part of the ancient north-south trunk road running between the Lambayeque and Zaña Valleys can be clearly discerned in this vertical aerial view. This section o[f] road was traversed by Pizarro on his way to Cajamarca in the Sierras where he encountered Atahualpa, the Emperor of the Incas. Following the road on foot, we f[ound]

areas on its *southern* bank farther into the Pampa de Zaña. As we carefully studied the map of this region, we could see that many economic and political implications had to arise out of the nature of this two-valley complex.

In exploring the valley, we found that while there were a number of large-sized canals, most of the pyramids were of a small or medium size. Does this possibly mean that the *huacas* and *huaca* clusters are older and more typical of the local culture of the valley, while the large canals are products of the later empire-building period when Zaña was dominated from the outside?

There is good reason to assume that in earlier times the economy of the Zaña must have had a certain independence of its own. The question then arises, was there a distinct local Zaña culture? If so, what was it like? Later on, when Mochica expansion took place, how did it affect the Zaña culture? Since Mochica cultural and possibly political influences extended as far as Pampa Grande (see Chapter XVI) in the Lambayeque Valley

they certainly must have penetrated the intervening Zaña. It is true that no Mochica potsherds from this valley have been recorded so far. This is of course not surprising since so few of the Zaña sites have been studied by archaeologists. We found a small potsherd in a former excavated graveyard to the west of Cerro Songoy, which could well have been Mochica; but this find was too insignificant to permit a positive conclusion.

During the so-called Middle Period when there seems to have been a general expansionist movement, the middle and lower Zaña may have come under the control of the probably once powerful principality of Collique in the Lambayeque Valley, for this region is the most direct connecting link between the two valleys. The conquest could have been led by one of the descendants of Naymlap who, according to Cabello de Valboa, became chief of Collique. Was it during this period that the canals linking the two valleys were built? Was it then that the canals in the southern lower side of the Zaña

Valley were expanded? Could not such an expansion have occurred also in the reverse direction: from the Zaña into the Lambayeque?

In a certain way, the Zaña Valley must have played its greatest role when the Pampa de Zaña was under complete cultivation, for then the Zaña was the *connecting link* between the expanding Jequetepeque Valley and the Lambayeque Complex. This link existed during the Chimú and Inca Empires, but may already have been developed during the Middle Period. Of course, this position of Zaña does not mean that the local ruler or rulers of Zaña then played a dominant political role. But in this three-valley complex it probably meant that the wishes of the Zaña rulers, economically strengthened by the expanded canal systems, must have been respected by the Incas, Chimús and such earlier rulers of Lambayeque or even Jequetepeque who may have attempted to establish "local empires" of their own. In fact, during the Middle Period the strategic geographic position of

Fig. 12. While hunting for ancient canals in the upper Zaña Valley, we found this stretch of dense vegetation produced by the sub-soil waters of a nearby modern canal. In the foreground is the station wagon of Hacienda Cayalti. Standing in front of the vehicle, left to right, are Michael, Ingeniero Tupac Yupanqui, the chauffeur and some children of the neighborhood. *Kosok* • Fig. 13 (center). Storage jars, used for corn, beans and chicha, found in the lower Zaña Valley. *Kosok* • Fig. 14 (right). Palms in the desert! Here we see the entrance to Otra Bande, one of the smaller *haciendas* in the middle part of the Zaña Valley. *Kosok*.

section where two canals had once been built, each paralleling an outside wall of the road. Close examination of the photograph will show rows of *monte* bushes ng in these canals. The other irregular dark lines also represent *monte* bushes, here growing in temporary runoffs from modern canals. *Servicio 3330: 2044, 2046.*

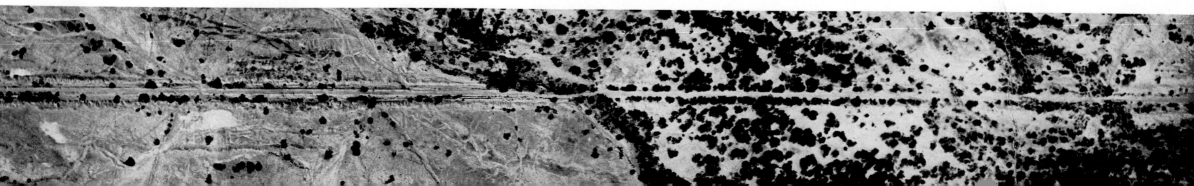

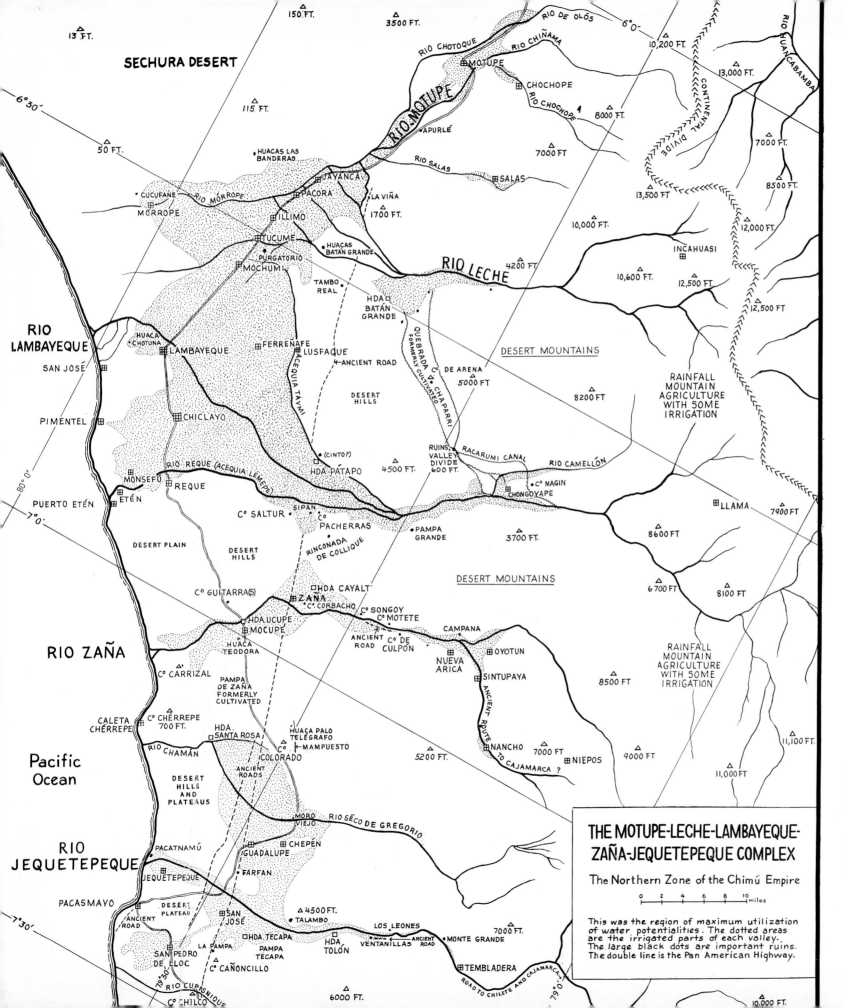

The Northern Zone of the Chimú Empire

Zaña may have given its rulers a very advantageous position in negotiating favorable alliances with sections of Lambayeque and even of Jequetepeque.

The Zaña must also have had important relations with the Sierras. During the period of the Inca Empire, the main road from the large Lambayeque region to Cajamarca in the Sierras passed through the Zaña Valley. A section of this road can still be seen. Quite likely this road had existed in pre-Inca times, and the commerce that passed over it must have helped to strengthen the economic and political power of the Zaña Valley rulers.

Our suspicion that Zaña played an important though yet undefined role in pre-Spanish times is strengthened by our knowledge that in early colonial times the Zaña Valley was of outstanding importance. The colonial town of Zaña, ruined parts of which can still be seen, was built near the present Pueblo Zaña. This colonial town soon became the capital of the new Corregimiento or Departamento de Zaña which was created by detaching the valley of Zaña and the greater part of the Lambayeque region from the original Departamento de Trujillo. Significantly, the new Departamento was named after Zaña and not after Lambayeque or Chiclayo, and the capital was placed in the Zaña Valley and not in the much larger Lambayeque.

As early as 1604, Lizárraga mentioned that Zaña was the richest valley between Jayanca and Trujillo and that the town of Zaña was an important trading center. True, some of its importance in colonial times lay in the fact that it was an exchange center for goods that passed not only between the Sierras and the Northwest Coast but also between northern Peru and Spain. The exports and imports of the latter country were transported by way of the road from Calete Chérrepe, the only port in the Departamento de Zaña (see Chapter XIV). But irrespective of the forces that may have strengthened Zaña during colonial times, this valley must already have been of sufficient importance in pre-colonial times for the Spaniards to have established a political and economic center here. As was pointed out before, the Spaniards did not locate their administrative centers arbitrarily; they took into consideration the location of the already important centers of the conquered Indians.

Archival research and archaeological work, even of a limited nature, should help to reveal some of the past significance of this strategic valley, a valley so far practically unknown!

XVI

Unity and Diversity in the Lambayeque-Leche-Motupe Complex

The Lambayeque-Leche-Motupe Complex is the largest and most complicated irrigation and population unit on the Coast of Peru. Everything related to it is complicated: topography, river systems, canal systems, administrative methods, distribution of population centers, and, we might add, methods of reconstructing its past. There seems to be an amorphous *unity* to this sprawling region, but one is more forcefully struck by the *diversity* of its component parts.

The Lambayeque Complex is larger than the Lambayeque Valley. Owing to differences in valley levels, irrigation canals bring water from the Lambayeque Valley into the Leche Valley (to the north), and, in turn, canals bring water from the latter valley into the Motupe Valley (still farther north). In ancient times, these valleys had more interconnecting irrigation canals than they do today, and the total irrigated area was considerably greater than it is at present.

As indicated in previous chapters, the irrigation system of the Lambayeque Valley at one time also brought water to the Zaña (to the south), and the irrigation system of the latter meshed with that of the Jequetepeque (still farther south). With the coming of the Spaniards, the interconnections of the Lambayeque with the Zaña and the Jequetepeque systems were destroyed. But in ancient times, these interconnections had produced a *unique five-valley complex,* much larger and more significant than the three-valley Lambayeque-Leche-Motupe Complex. Preliminary estimates, based on our investigations, indicate that in ancient times this five-valley system probably accounted for almost *one-third of the total cultivated area* and almost *one-third of the population of the entire*

Coast! In fact, one of the major purposes of our trip to this region was to locate and map the various intricate canal systems that had once united the five valleys.

We have already discussed the Jequetepeque and Zaña Valleys (Chapters XII, XIV and XV). Therefore, we shall confine ourselves here to an examination of the Lambayeque, the Leche and the Motupe Valleys. Archaeologically, this three-valley unit has been one of the least explored regions, although it contains many more remains of ancient pyramids, settlements, walls and roads than any other region on the Coast. Ironically, this very superabundance of ruins, as well as the geographical complexities, has deterred archaeologists from making a systematic study of the region.

Dr. Tello did work at Chongoyape, Batán Grande and several other places in the three valleys, and Professor Kroeber reported on Purgatorio and Huaca Chotuna. Most important, Professor Bennett established a tentative and workable culture sequence, although it is based on limited excavations. Dr. Schaedel visited numerous sites with us and studied some of them in greater detail on other trips. However, a really *comprehensive* investigation of the entire complex still requires the work of a group of archaeologists. Only then will a detailed and continuous cultural sequence for the whole Lambayeque Complex be definitely established. This sequence can then be related to the well established but apparently somewhat different sequence of the Moche-Chicama region.

Although this three-valley unit has been neglected by most archaeologists, one of its important folk legends has been preserved in the writings of Cabello de Valboa. It

Fig. 1. Girl from the ancient Monsefú-Eten region selling typical products of her home area. *Kosok.* NOTE: Initial line-cut is a head from a water jug found by the author in the Rinconada de Collique.

is the legend of Naymlap, a local ruler who, with his chief wife, Ceterni, many concubines, a group of 40 officials, and many other followers came to Lambayeque "with a great fleet of balsas" (rafts), from *"el parte suprema."* The meaning of the latter term has been the subject of some misunderstanding, since it has been confused with the term *el parte alto*. In Peru, *el parte alto* often means *south*, while *el parte bajo* means *north*. Consequently, it has been assumed by some scholars that Naymlap came from the south. But according to Peruvians, *el parte suprema* cannot be equated with *el parte alto*, since the former is a generic term that can be applied equally well in a physical, regional or social sense. However, the reference in the legend to balsa rafts would tend to place the origin of Naymlap in the Guayaquil basin, since, according to the Chroniclers, only in that general region was the balsa raft a common means of transportation. Moreover, we have no representations of balsa rafts on any Peruvian ceramics; only the small, reed *caballitos* are shown (Chapter XVIII).

Cabello tells us that Naymlap and his children and grandchildren throve so well in Lambayeque that they became rulers of a number of the leading communities in the middle and lower regions of the Lambayeque Complex (see Chart 2, Chapter VIII). It may be significant that while Cabello's account lists the names and duties of many of Naymlap's royal retainers such as a conch blower, a chief litter bearer, a drink master, a

Fig. 2 (above). An oblique aerial view of Chiclayo, the principal city of the Lambayeque Complex. In the foreground is the main plaza, flanked at the right by the Cathedral. The photograph portrays vividly the vast extent of flat, irrigated areas that characterize the lower Lambayeque Valley. *Servicio 0:4619* • Fig. 3 (far left). Part of the main plaza in Chiclayo. *Kosok* • Fig. 4 (left). Fragment of an ancient ceremonial spear made of hard, dark-brown wood, Lambayeque area. *Brüning-Doering.*

cook, a bathing master, a chief tailor, and an ointment and powder carrier, he does not mention any priests in his conquering group. Could this mean that a secular-mercantile power had become supreme in Naymlap's original home? Cabello gives many more interesting details in his account, of which there is a good and complete translation in Means (1931).

Cabello lists the names of eleven generations of the direct descendants of Naymlap. According to our Chart 2 in Chapter VIII, this line ruled from about 1050 A.D. to about 1350 A.D., a period corresponding to Professor Bennett's Late Middle Period in archaeology. In other words, it was the period of movement of ruling groups

up and down the Coast. The section dealing with the destruction of the Naymlap line and the rise of a new line of rulers of Lambayeque during Chimú and Inca domination is discussed in the latter part of this chapter.

Unfortunately, we have no traditions or lists of kings covering the long period of more than two thousand years before Naymlap's conquest. The archaeological sequence of most of this period is likewise unknown, or at best covered by very tentative hypotheses. This period corresponds in time roughly with the Cupisnique, the Salinar, the Mochica and the early part of the Middle Period in the Moche-Chicama region.

In 1940-41, we mapped the main canals and some of

the sites of the Lambayeque Complex, but we realized at the time that much more field work was necessary to complete the job. As mentioned in Chapter V, when we returned in 1948 we discovered that much of our data unfortunately had to be obtained by means of field trips. They were conducted at various times between October 1948 and April 1949. After the aerial photographs were completed by the Servicio, we returned to the Lambayeque area in May 1949 and checked some of the sites that we had previously missed.

Michael and I made our first trip to the Lambayeque district with Dr. Schaedel and his chauffeur, arriving at Chiclayo, the leading city of this region, during the latter part of October 1948. We stayed at the Hotel Royal which is situated on the main plaza in the center of the life of the city. Chiclayo is about the same size as Trujillo, but while Trujillo, the cultural center of the Northwest Coast, boasts of an *Universidad,* Chiclayo has only a *Colegio* (high school). However, the *Colegio* is housed in a fine, modernistic building, which was constructed under the supervision of its director, Dr. Karl Weiss. The splendor of the *Colegio* reflects the greater wealth of Chiclayo, which attracts the trade of the whole Lambayeque Complex. In Chiclayo, there are a number of reasonably good eating places, among which the Hotel Europa, operated by a German couple, is by far the best. Besides tasty Peruvian dishes, the Europa's menu contains many German specialties ranging from "Sauerbraten" to "Baumtorte."

Incidentally, a number of friends who read this book in manuscript objected to our repeated references to good hotels and good restaurants. However, anyone who does extensive field work in Peru soon realizes that a clean bed and an appetizing meal are basic tools in archaeological research!

Among Chiclayo's other attractions is the pleasant Plaza de Armas. Here every evening, in the customary manner, the young men and women come for a stroll; the latter walk in a clockwise direction around the square while the former proceed in a counterclockwise direction or watch the young women from the sidelines. Two evenings a week the military band plays popular and folk songs.

On our first day in the city, I went to see the local irrigation officials, while Dr. Schaedel and Michael made a survey of the nearby ruins of Collús. These interesting ruins consist of one set of four *huacas,* each of a different type (Figs. 5 and 6), and another set of four low, adobe

mounds. The Collús site is similar in some ways to the Chotuna site but is located farther inland, about four miles east of Chiclayo. A main pyramid with steep sides and a secondary stepped pyramid with a central ramp that cuts into the first two terraces are grouped around an irregular open space. Plain and white slipped paddle ware, red-on-white slip ware, and a few incised and reed-marked potsherds were found here. On the basis of the description and the potsherd collection, Dr. Schaedel tentatively assumed a Middle to Late occupation at this site.

In Chiclayo, we visited our friend, Señor Jorge Rondón, who, though a business man, has been interested in archaeology for more than twenty-five years. In 1941, he had been most helpful in locating a number of archaeological sites. Now he offered us new information that he had gathered in the meantime. He also accompanied us on a trip to the famous pyramid group of Chotuna, which

Fig. 5 (below). Vertical aerial view of the major part of the ruins of Collús, Lambayeque Valley. Shown here is a cluster of various types of pyramids. At the left are the modern *hacienda* buildings. The well-aligned dark spots are shrubs and trees grown for commercial purposes (see Fig. 6). *Servicio 3330:2118* • Fig. 6 (upper right). A ground view of two of the pyramids of the ruins of Collús (the two pyramids at the upper left in Fig. 5). The structure at the right is a two-platform pyramid with a ramp leading to the top (compare with Fig. 4, p. 141). A chapel has been built on the top of the main pyramid. *Schaedel.*

he had previously visited with Professor Kroeber in 1926. Photographs of the structure can be found on page 10.

Unfortunately, after a week of field reconnaissance Dr. Schaedel was suddenly forced to return to Trujillo with the jeep. However, the local director of the SCIPA took Michael and me in his jeep on a fruitful trip up the Lambayeque Valley as far as Chongoyape, about twenty-five miles from the Coast. En route to Chongoyape, we stopped at Hacienda Pátapo, where our old friend, Señor Pardo y Miguel, and his wife invited us to an excellent lunch. In 1940-41 we had stayed at the *hacienda* several times in order to study the ruins of the important ancient site of Cinto. At that time, Señor Pardo had taken us on three flights in his private plane over the extensive ruins of the Lambayeque Complex. However, this time we concentrated our efforts on mapping lesser known pyramids, canals and population centers in the middle and upper Lambayeque Valley.

After we had returned to Chiclayo, we made contact with the regional office of the Department of Agriculture in the neighboring town of Lambayeque. The office was under the direction of the energetic and affable Ingeniero Victor Baca, who showed us the blueprint of an ambitious plan made some decades earlier by irrigation engineers for an extension of the present Taymi Canal, the main canal on the northern side of the Lambayeque Valley. The blueprint covered the large and complicated region where the Lambayeque and Leche Valleys are joined, and included roughly the area bounded by the towns of Lambayeque, Mórrope and Ferreñafe. Besides existing and proposed canal systems, the blueprint contained the sites and names of numerous pyramids and mounds, some of which were completely unknown to us. Ingeniero Baca obligingly lent us this blueprint, and we used it on many field trips. He also offered us the use of the trucks of the department, which we gladly accepted, because at that time we were without transportation facilities. The truck drivers, intelligent men from the Lambayeque area, were able to help us locate many unknown and out-of-the-way sites.

One day as I was standing on top of a pyramid trying to get bearings on nearby pyramids and ill-defined mounds, I suddenly felt very ill. I returned to Chiclayo for an examination and learned that I had malaria, yellow jaundice and amoebic dysentery, a combination of afflictions quite common in this region. While these diseases can be cured with modern medicines, which fortunately were available in Chiclayo, the sickness, nevertheless,

prevented my doing field work for almost six weeks.

After I had recovered, Michael and I again had the use of the jeeps of Dr. Schaedel and of the SCIPA, which, together with the trucks of Ingeniero Baca, enabled us to complete our field work in the Lambayeque region. Since the details of these trips are too complicated to be presented here, it may suffice to say that the region of the Lambayeque, Leche and Motupe Valleys involved us for a number of months in what seemed an endless task of locating and mapping major and secondary canals, pyramids, fortifications, walls and population sites.

The difficulties of field reconnaissance were accentuated here by the fact that the work could not be carried on from one or two major *haciendas* as it was in most of the other valleys. The area is too large and the terrain too complex. Several large *haciendas* control the best land in the upper and middle parts of the Lambayeque and Leche Valleys. However, in some of the middle and most of the wide lower parts of these two valleys, as well as in the entire Motupe Valley, much of the land is divided into *haciendas* of small and medium size. In addition, in the middle and lower parts of these valleys there are a number of *communidades* and towns, such as Motupe, Jayanca, Pacora, Illimo, Túcume, Mochumí, Ferreñafe, Mórrope, Eten, Monsefú, Reque, San José and Pimentel. Here many families work their own small plots or rent land from *hacendados*. As a matter of fact, throughout Peru the *hacendados* generally cultivate only the best parts of their estates; the poorer lands are rented in small parcels to individual farmers.

The *communidades*, which date back to ancient times, have been only partially successful in holding their lands against the encroachments of the *hacendados*. Moreover, the lands they work are of a poorer quality than those of the *hacendados*, and their water rights are more limited. Furthermore, as a result of their position in the lower parts of the valley, the *communidades* obtain a proportionately smaller amount of water in the years when the rivers are low.

The terrain in these regions is difficult to traverse even with a jeep, since the numerous individual holdings are often surrounded by boundary walls and ditches. The roads are generally in poor condition; indeed, in some places there are no roads at all.

Despite the many obstacles we encountered, we located and mapped over *two hundred and fifty* sites in the three valleys! This large number demonstrates concretely the economic and cultural significance of this enormous valley complex. Although most of the sites are unreported in archaeological literature, only a few interesting and significant ruins will be described here. The rest of the material will be published in *Water and Life*.

In order to make clear to the reader the relative positions of the sites described in the following pages, we are presenting them in the sequence in which they would be visited on a journey from the middle Lambayeque Valley up to Chongoyape in the upper part of the valley, northward across the once cultivated Quebrada Chaparrí to Hacienda Batán Grande in the upper Leche Valley, down the Leche Valley to the region where it meets the Lambayeque and Motupe Valleys, and then both up and down the Motupe Valley, including the lower Motupe-Mórrope section. Finally, some of the sites in the complicated lower Lambayeque Valley itself are described (see map, p. 146).

Let us start with the two dominant population clusters in the middle part of the Lambayeque Valley. Local tradition has it that these settlements are the Collique and

Fig. 7 (p. 150) and Fig. 8 (p. 151). Vertical and oblique aerial photographs, respectively, of the hillside ruins of Saltur. The buildings of Hacienda Saltur are at (C) while at (A) and (B) are some of the Late Period walled compounds that were built on levelled-off slopes of the hill. Between (A) and (C) four square pyramids can be seen built symmetrically around a plaza. These *huacas* probably date from an earlier occupation period. Between these pyramids and (C) are ancient cemeteries. Vertical photograph by *Servicio 3330: 1351;* oblique photograph by *Kosok* • Fig. 9 (margins). Two views of a stirrup spout vessel of the Middle Lambayeque II Period. *AMNH.*

151

Cinto mentioned in Xerez' report of Pizarro's first trip to Cajamarca. Cabello states, in his account of the legend of Naymlap, that Nor, one of the latter's grandsons, became ruler of Cinto, while another, unnamed grandson became chief of Collique. In the volume, *Lambayeque Anuario* (1947:191), Cuntipullec is given as the name of this ancient ruler of Collique, though the source of this information is not cited.

Collique, on the *south* side of the valley, was possibly a collective name for a number of large sites which are situated close to one another. They comprise the fortified walled structures on and around Cerro Pacherras together with the terraced and fortified northeast slopes of the nearby Cerro Saltur. (Figs. 7 and 8). Between the two sites, in a narrow plain, lies the large pyramid grouping of Sipán (Figs. 10 and 11), which consists of more than two dozen *huacas*, some of stone, others of adobe. This grouping, which includes the huge adobe Huaca Rajada de Sipán, may have formed the ceremonial focus of the vast complex — provided the adjacent sites comprising the complex belonged to the same period of construction. In the adjoining Rinconada de Collique, which connects with Pampa Grande (see below) and the Zaña Valley, are extensive masses of walled compounds, irrigation canals, furrows of former cultivated areas and numerous minor structures. Unfortunately, no aerial view of the wide Rinconada exists; consequently, we had to rely entirely on field work in mapping the region.

At various times, the so-called Collique area undoubtedly *controlled the south side of the lower-middle Lambayeque Valley.* It also dominated the narrow area, now only partly cultivated, leading to the nearby Zaña Valley, a portion of whose north side was once irrigated by water from the Lambayeque River (see Chapter XV). Some of the largest canals came from the upper Lambayeque by way of the adjacent, now barren Rinconada de Collique and then passed into the Zaña Valley. The Huaca Rajada

de Sipán has been superficially described, but no archaeologist has attempted to study systematically the tangle of the Collique structures, even though it is *one of the largest in Peru.*

Controlling the north side of the valley opposite Collique is the almost equally large complex of ruins known today as Pátapo, which probably was the aforementioned pre-Spanish Cinto. These ruins stretch for several kilometers along the southeastern slopes of Cerro Pátapo (Figs. 16, 17 and 20). Obviously representing a variety of local types of construction and more than one period of occupation, they consist of walled compounds of adobe; rectangular enclosures with subdivisions of stone; densely-packed, terraced mounds of earth, and some adobe pyramids.

Two parallel canals, which we called Taymi Antigua, and whose remains we traced for many miles above the present large Taymi Canal, passed partly below and partly through these ruins. We determined, after considerable field work, that these two canals once brought water all the way from La Puntilla in the upper Lambayeque Valley, past Pátapo, Cerro Mirador and Lusfaque to the extensive ruins of Cerro Purgatorio in the Leche Valley. Thus these two valleys — or at least portions of them — were linked technologically and possibly politically.

In ancient times, both Cinto and Collique lay astride the strategic main north-south Inca highway whose remains we had traced along much of the Northwest Coast. Dr. Schaedel found considerable evidence of Chimú and Inca occupation of these important sites; proof of an earlier occupation will likely be established once the sites are studied more thoroughly. The highway, to which we referred in previous chapters, we also traced into the Leche Valley, farther north, where there were indications of Inca occupation. A number of elderly informants insisted that they had seen parts of the highway near

Apurlé and Cerro de la Vieja, both in the Motupe Valley farther north. A systematic study of the trunk road from the Chao to the Motupe Valley, together with an archaeological survey of the nearby sites, should throw much light on the history of the road, including the role it played in keeping the various valleys in the control of the Incas, Chimús, and possibly earlier conquerors. In crossing from the Lambayeque Valley to the Leche Valley, this road passes through an extensive, hilly desert region, and thereby avoids the main centers in the lower part of the complex. Did the conquerors merely intend to make the road as short as possible, or did they aim to avoid crossing the dense, hostile population areas of the lower parts of the valleys? Perhaps they had both purposes in mind when they constructed this vital artery.

Fig. 10 (left). The huge pyramid cluster of Sipán, shown in this odd-looking vertical aerial photograph, is situated between Cerro Saltur and Cerro Pacherras, and consists of more than twenty-five structures. At (A) can be seen Huaca Rajada (Torn Pyramid), which is comprised of the large rectangular pyramid and the two irregular-shaped structures just below it on the photograph. At (B) are some of the numerous smaller pyramids of adobe or stone and earth. These and related structures form part of the Sipán Pyramid Complex. (C) marks the location of ancient canals that are still used for cultivation purposes, while (D) indicates ancient canals used at present as run-offs for surplus irrigation water. At (E) is the modern dirt road that connects the Lambayeque and Zaña Valleys. *Servicio 3330:1387* • Fig. 11 (upper right). Oblique aerial view from Señor Pardo y Miguel's plane of Huaca Rajada, the largest structure of the Sipán Complex (see text and Fig. 10). *Schaedel* • Fig. 12 (lower right). Part of a water jug with conical spout and bridge which we found in the Rinconada de Collique. Typical high lustre Lambayeque blackware. *Kosok-Storck.*

Puma head with collar around neck and ring in mouth. Polished blackware.

Llama head with bridle rope. Heavy orange ware.

Part of a mold form for a jar (inside).

Part of the mold form (outside).

Well-modeled head. Smooth blackware.

154

Fig. 13 (margin, p. 154). Ceramics from Rinconada de Collique. *Kosok-Kosofsky* • Fig. 14 (p. 154). Oblique aerial view, taken in the Cerro Guitarras region, looking up the middle and upper sections of the Lambayeque and Zaña Valleys, with the cloud-covered Sierras in the background (see also Fig. 29). The photograph shows clearly the interrelationship of the two valleys and the positions of the main archaeological sites. (A) Ancient canals that once carried water from the Lambayeque Valley (left) to the Zaña Valley (right). (B) Ancient main north-south road (see Fig. 11, pp. 144 and 145). (C) Hacienda Cayalti. (D) Zaña River. (E) Oyotún, the center of the Zaña "pocket." (F) Northernmost point of cultivation of Zaña fields today. (G) Desert *pampa* with ancient canals from both the Zaña and Lambayeque Rivers. (H) Southernmost point of cultivation of Lambayeque fields today. The region between (A), (F), (H) and (M) was formerly cultivated. (I) Part of Cerro Saltur (see Figs. 7 and 8). (J) Large pyramid complex of Sipán (see Figs. 10 and 11). (K) Cerro Pacherras. (L) Lambayeque River. (M) Rinconada de Collique, formerly cultivated. (N) Ruins of Pampa Grande (see Fig. 21). (O) Chongoyape, center of the upper Lambayeque "pocket." (P) Entrance to Quebrada Chaparrí and the Leche Valley to the north. *U. S. Army 42-R-42* • Fig. 15 (below). A view of the sugar refinery, administration buildings, workers' quarters and fields of Hacienda Pátapo, on the north side of the Lambayeque Valley, as seen from one of the many ruins that cover the barren hills near the *hacienda*. An ancient adobe pyramid rises out of the irrigated fields just beyond the refinery. A part of Cerro Pacherras can be seen on the opposite, south side of the Lambayeque Valley, at the extreme left in the photograph. Across the cultivated lowland from Cerro Pacherras, along the nearest slope of the group of hills, lie the ruins of Saltur (not visible in the photograph). See Figs. 7 and 8 for photographs of these ruins. At the foot of Cerro Pacherras and stretching toward Saltur is the large pyramid cluster of Sipán (see Figs. 10 and 11). The ancient north-south highway (not visible in this photograph) ran from the Motupe and Leche Valleys in the north, past Pátapo, across the irrigated fields of the Lambayeque Valley, past Sipán into the Zaña Valley, south of Sipán (see Fig. 10), and from there through the many valleys and deserts still farther south (see map, p. 146). *Kosok* • Fig. 16 (upper left). One of the many rectangular structures of the ruins of Pátapo as seen from a hill above the site. *Schaedel* • Fig. 17 (upper center). One of the stone-walled bastions of the ruins of Pátapo. *Schaedel* • Fig. 18 (upper right). Barren hills near Pátapo. A stone wall can be seen on one of the ridges. *Kosok.*

Fig. 19 (above). The open cockpit plane in which we flew with Señor Pardo y Miguel over many of the sites of the Lambayeque Complex. The author, Señor Pardo and his administrator. *Wyler* • Fig. 20 (next two pages). Ruins of Pátapo. *Servicio 3330:1518, 1520, 1543, 1546, 1572, 1574.*

Fig. 20. The main section of the extensive hill-side ruins of Pátapo (ancient Cinto?) is shown on the page at the right. Ceramics of both Inca and Chimú Periods have been found here; further examination would probably indicate an earlier occupation. Below the ruins are parts of the fields and buildings of the modern Hacienda Pátapo. A Chimú-type walled compound can be seen in the center of the page at the left. At the left of the compound are the ancient Taymi Canal and the main ancient north-south road.

Leaving Collique, we journeyed several miles up the south side of the valley to a wide *quebrada* where there is a large ancient site known as Pampa Grande. Like Pátapo and Saltur, the site consists of the remains of an extensive settlement on the lower slopes of a hill. Below it runs the large double canal that passed through the Rinconada de Collique and continued to the Zaña Valley. Dominating Pampa Grande is a huge pyramid that is probably exceeded in size only by the Huaca del Sol in Moche. Nearby is a small pyramid, which, like the larger structure, is made of rectangular adobes.

Dr. Henri Reichlin, of the French Archaeological Mis-

Fig. 21 (left). The ruins of Pampa Grande on the south bank of the Lambayeque River. In the upper part of the photograph is the huge adobe pyramid that ranks with the Temple of the Sun in the Moche Valley as one of the largest adobe structures on the Peruvian Coast (see Figs. 23 and 24). Below is a smaller pyramid of similar construction. At the left and right are the remains of extensive habitation sites. In the lower left corner of the photograph are some of the buildings of Hacienda Pampa Grande. The white line is the modern road. Crossing it at various points is one of the old irrigation canals that formerly carried water from the upper Lambayeque to the Rinconada de Collique and the Zaña Valley. Below the ancient canal is the modern canal with irrigated fields below it. *Servicio 3330: 1509, 1510, 1566* • Fig. 22 (above). Transplanting rice in the upper Lambayeque Valley. *Kosok* • Fig. 23 (upper middle). Rear view of the main *huaca* at Pampa Grande (see Figs. 21 and 24). *Kosok* • Fig. 24 (lower right). Front view of a section of the main *huaca* at Pampa Grande showing its huge size as well as the extensive damage done to it by centuries of occasional rains (see Figs. 21 and 23). *Schaedel.*

sion, obtained a representative sampling of Mochica potsherds at Pampa Grande in 1948. The presence of Mochica potsherds was also confirmed later by Dr. Schaedel, who was led to conclude that the site is *the northernmost area of Peru in which Mochica ceramics have been found,* and that the area thus represents the point of farthest northern expansion of the Mochica "Empire" or culture. Remains of later Inca occupation were also located on this site. It appears that Inca control was usually concentrated in the upper to middle parts of many of the coastal valleys.

Above Pampa Grande, on the opposite side of the valley, lies the Chongoyape "pocket," which at one time was probably the largest of its kind along the whole Coast (see Chapter IX). At present, Chongoyape, a town of about 8000 people, is the administrative center of this large pocket. In ancient times, the area under cultivation was considerably larger than it is today, a fact that is indicated by the large number of unused ancient canals. The numerous remains of pyramids and fortifications suggest that the pocket once supported a larger population. A number of fortified sites are strategically located in the pocket, the most important being on Cerro Chongoyape and Cerro Magin, on the north bank of the river, as well as on smaller hills on the nearby south bank (Fig. 25). Control of the *upper* valley had probably once been exercised by means of these fortifications. On the western slopes of Cerro Magin, just above the ruins of the ancient Racarumi Canal, lies a very extensive, partially destroyed, adobe pyramid grouping which *probably was the chief ceremonial center of the pocket.* Although Tello, Reichlin, and others have studied some of the sites in the region,

the archaeological sequences have not yet been clearly established. The problem is complicated by the fact that Sierra influences have been constantly active.

In the Chongoyape region, we traced in detail the course of the famous Racarumi Canal, *one of the largest canals in prehistoric America.* It had its intake some miles above the town of Chongoyape and carried water along the north bank of the Lambayeque until it entered the broad and long Quebrada Chaparrí, which is part of the Leche Valley to the north. The canal then divided into several branches that completely irrigated both sides of the *quebrada* before combining with the canals on the north side of the Leche Valley.

Unfortunately, aerial photographs do not cover the entire area traversed by the canal. Therefore, most of our conclusions were based on field work, which was done by jeep, on horseback and on foot. The canal seems to have been comprised of *two different systems, partly superimposed and apparently of two distinct periods.* It is possible that one system dates from the Chimú, the other from the Inca Period, or one from the Chimú-Inca and the other from the pre-Chimú Period. The dating cannot be established until the basic archaeological sequence of this desert region has been determined.

In June 1949, when we made our last trip through this region, we were greatly surprised to find the whole Quebrada Chaparrí and the surrounding hills carpeted with grass and blooming with many-colored flowers! The

few adobe pyramids were covered with dried grass, which gave them the peculiar appearance of having suddenly grown a good crop of light brown hair. Rain — so infrequent in this region — had fallen during the previous March, and within a short time had completely changed the appearance of the landscape. As a result, our quest for additional canals proved futile.

The Quebrada Chaparrí contains a group of pyramids at its *upper,* i.e., south, end at the valley divide. In the *middle* of the *quebrada* rises the important fortified hill, Cerro de Arena (Sand Hill). At the foot of the hill, we located remains of a small settlement which contained adobe walls and several very small adobe *huacas.* The site is referred to locally as Ferreñafe Viejo. If this designation is correct, then it might mean that in colonial times, after the Racarumi Canal stopped bringing water to this region, the inhabitants were moved to the present Ferreñafe, situated on the Lambayeque-Leche plain. A study of local archives may clear up this problem.

Near the *lower,* i.e., north, end of the *quebrada,* we found several small pyramids and a small fortified hill with associated structures, while on the hills to the east we saw other unexplored structures, which we later located on the Servicio aerial photographs.

While exploring Quebrada Chaparrí, we were astonished to find a long stone wall which extends from Río Camellón, a branch of the Lambayeque River, through Quebrada Chaparrí, on the upper east side of the Racarumi Canal, into the Leche Valley. The wall then crosses the latter valley, and seems to disappear in the hills on the northern side. Its length we estimated as about thirty miles, thus making it *the longest wall on the Coast of Peru, outside of the Santa Wall discovered by the Shippee-Johnson expedition.* At the places where we inspected it, the wall ranged from 6 to 10 feet in height.

Whether it was a defensive or a boundary wall, and whether it was pre-Spanish or colonial, could not be determined.

On leaving the wide Quebrada Chaparrí, we entered the upper Leche Valley, which is dominated today by Hacienda Batán Grande (Large Milling Stone) and the subsidiary Hacienda Mayascón. As in 1940-41, we made Hacienda Batán Grande our center of operations. The estate is owned by the Aurich brothers, who, with their mother, Señora Aurich, greeted us warmly on our arrival and offered us the full hospitality of their home which we gladly accepted. We remained for about a week and returned later for a shorter visit. During our stay, we located a considerable number of hitherto archaeologically unknown small pyramids, mounds, fortified sites and canals that are scattered throughout the upper part of the Leche Valley, and which were probably related to some of the sites in the adjoining Quebrada Chaparrí (see above).

Fig. 25 (upper left). Hilltop, surrounded by large concentric walls, near Hacienda Huaca Blanca buildings on the south bank of the Lambayeque River opposite Chongoyape. Note the large wall trailing off to the top of the photograph. A small sub-divided rectangle, partly covered by vegetation, can be seen at the upper left. *Servicio 3330: 2351* • Fig. 26 (lower left). The faithful burro, still a common means of transporting goods in the roadless regions of Peru. *Kosok* • Fig. 27 (lower center). Owing to the light but somewhat frequent rains in the upper Lambayeque Valley, large cacti like these are common. *Kosok* • Fig. 28 (above). A scene in the upper Lambayeque Valley. *Kosok.*

One day, two of the Aurich brothers took us to an interesting and archaeologically unknown site at the foot of Cerro Tambo Real (Royal Road Station Hill) on the south side of the Leche Valley. The site consists of remains of habitation structures and a group of adobe pyramids, parts of which are covered with rough stone facings. A complex ancient canal system runs through part of the site, while nearby is a section of the north-south trunk highway. Our attention was attracted to the main pyramid, which is built in the form of a "U", with the open end toward the lower northern entrance of the ruin. One of the brothers took us inside the "U" and showed us the remains of some low adobe relief work in the form of a series of angular spirals on one of the walls. On a later reconnaissance, Dr. Schaedel found that the frieze had in the meantime been destroyed. Potsherds collected in the area indicate that the site may be one of the earliest yet found in the Leche Valley.

In the middle part of the Leche Valley, the descending river "divides" into what appear to be a number of natural "channels" that are very wide and, in places, have cut about twenty to thirty feet deep into the soil. However, after discussing the matter with irrigation engineers, we concluded that these "channels" had probably *originally* been irrigation canals, built in ancient times. Apparently owing to the rapid drop in terrain and the

Fig. 29 (left). An oblique aerial view of the Lambayeque Valley and part of the Zaña Valley. Much of the same region as that in Fig. 14 can be seen here. However, this photograph, taken near Chongoyape, in the upper Lambayeque Valley, shows the Lambayeque and Zaña Rivers flowing westward into the Pacific Ocean. (A) Lambayeque River. (B) Modern road to Chongoyape. (C) Sections of the ancient Racarumi Canal. (D) Quebrada Chaparrí. (E) Ruins of Pampa Grande. (F) Pampa de Burros. (G) Ruins of Pátapo. (H) Lower Lambayeque Valley, in the region of Chiclayo. (I) Rinconada de Collique. (J) Ruins of Sipán. (K) Cerro Guitarras (L) Lower Zaña Valley. *U. S. Army 61-R-29* • Fig. 30 (below). One of the many petroglyphs that can be found on Cerro Mulato near Chongoyape. *Kosok.*

softness of the soil, the canals had dug deep troughs that now appear to be natural channels. This theory was later strengthened when we studied two other large ancient canals on the north side of the Leche Valley that ran to Apurlé (see below) and which for a short distance had produced similar deep cuts.

Four of the channel-like canals in the middle part of the Leche Valley carry water in a west-northwest direction. They pass below the Pan American Highway and finally enter the small Motupe River, which comes from the north. This system, built in ancient times and still in use, increases the cultivated area of the Motupe Valley and combines the two valleys into a hydrological unit.

Another channel-like canal carries water of the Leche River north of the huge ancient site of Cerro Purgatorio (see below) in a southwesterly direction, meshing with branches of the "modern" Taymi Canal, while a dry sixth branch runs south of the site. The extensions of this dry branch at one time undoubtedly connected with some of the canals of the *lower* Lambayeque River that drew water from that river. In ancient times, Cerro Purgatorio was also serviced by the "modern" Taymi Canal and the now unused Taymi Antigua, both coming from the Lambayeque Valley, and hence must have once occupied a powerful and strategic position. It should be added that the two above-mentioned channel-like canals of the lower Leche River may have been the original beds of the lower Leche River.

The land between several of the channel-like canals of the Leche Valley is not cultivated now, for it is about twenty-five feet above the water in the canals, but due to underground seepage it has a dense growth of an algarroba forest, a kind of "desert jungle," as Michael called it. On this "high" land, we found sections of other ancient canals indicating that this area was once cultivated.

Rising out of this dense algarroba forest, which grows on formerly cultivated land, are *some of the largest and most dramatic-looking pyramids in northern Peru*, called the Huacas of Batán Grande, since they are situated on the lands of Hacienda Batán Grande. Brüning claims that the ancient name for this site was Sicán.

The individual pyramids are La Rodillona (The Kneel-

ing Woman), which is the largest; El Oro (The Gold One), where gold treasures are purported to have been found; La Ventana (The Window), where Dr. Tello reported finding a sequence of coastal cultural periods; El Horno (The Oven, or The Colored One); and Santillo (Little Saint). On the south bank of the river, two pyramids known respectively as La Merced (Mercy) and La Cruz (The Cross) complete the principal cluster. To the east is an extensive, possibly older, badly damaged group of smaller *huacas*, the most important of which is known locally as Huaca de los Ingenieros (The Engineers' Huaca). The name is derived from the *huaca's* use as a triangulation monument in recent times (Fig. 38).

Like many others on the Coast of Peru, these names are

Fig. 33 (above). Bullock cart in the upper Lambayeque Valley. *Kosok* • Fig. 34 (below). Houses near Chongoyape. *Kosok*.

Fig. 31 (upper left). Ancient canal, part of the Taymi Antigua, in the middle Lambayeque Valley. *Kosok* • Fig. 32 (left). The deepest cut made by the ancient Racarumi Canal as it passes from the Lambayeque Valley through the valley divide to Quebrada Chaparrí, in the Leche Valley. *Kosok*.

Spanish, the original nomenclature having been forgotten. However, Señor Zevallos Quiñones has shown that the original names can often be found by studying ancient land titles in local governmental, church and *hacienda* archives. More difficult is the task of connecting these ancient names with the actual *huacas*.

The main *huaca* group obviously was one of the powerful centers that at one time controlled an important part of the Lambayeque-Leche-Motupe Complex. Although at least four investigators (Brüning, Tello, Bennett, Kroeber) have mentioned these pyramids, none has given a plan or sketch of their positions. Therefore, we include in this report an aerial photograph and some ground photographs of the ruins (Figs. 38, 39, 42, 44 and 47). Although we had no time to make surface collections, Dr. Schaedel, in a subsequent reconnaissance, found interesting potsherd material that indicates a relatively early period of occupation of the complex. Drawings of several of the potsherds are reproduced here (Fig. 46). On his reconnaissance, Dr. Schaedel also saw and photographed fragments of a polychrome frieze on Huaca del Oro. Subsequently, Señor Mario Florian, an inspector of ruins, completely cleared this frieze, which is illustrated in his report published in 1951 (Fig. 42).

The ruins of Cerro Purgatorio, mentioned above, are situated near Túcume (Figs. 49, 52, 54 to 57), where, according to Cabello, Cala, one of Naymlap's sons, made himself the ruler. These ruins, consisting of many steep adobe pyramids and walled compounds constructed on the sides of a lone hill arising out of the plains of the Leche Valley, represent *the most impressive architectural group of pyramids in the Lambayeque Complex*. The site has been sketched by Professor Kroeber, but Dr. Schaedel and his staff have produced the first authentic ground plan for the site as a whole. This plan was printed in the August 1951 issue of the *Scientific American*.

The *huacas* are all very steep, and some have narrow terrace ledges. The approaches are long ramps, although some of the pyramids have the circumferential form of approach found at Chotuna and Collús. Dr. Schaedel states:

Several of the elevated compounds present a new

and apparently local urban unit. It shares the principle of numerous room divisions with the Chan-Chan compound, but in place of the high circumferential walls as the delimiting and defending element, the Purgatorio compound is elevated some fifty feet with a sheer drop to the ground level, and has no exterior wall. As in the ChanChan compound the entrances are few.

Its potsherds and its general layout indicate that the site was occupied in the Late Chimú Period. In fact, it may well have been one of the leading Chimú strongholds in this valley, if not the leading one. Professor Bennett, who excavated a number of graves at the site, also found some Inca material, which indicates Inca occupation at one time.

We located a smaller ruin across the canal a short distance northeast of Cerro Purgatorio. This site, which is called Túcume Viejo, is comprised of very dilapidated mounds and other adobe structures, and it seems to be an archaeological mystery. Was it the ancient site of the present town of Túcume? Or was it an antecedent of the Cerro Purgatorio site?

Cabello relates that when Pizarro reached the general area of Túcume he found that Jayanca, situated to the north, had just concluded a war with Túcume, which, at the time, was an ally of the Chimús farther south! The Túcume mentioned by Cabello may well have been the site we know as Purgatorio. The local conflict indicates clearly that the Incas at that time exercised either very limited control or no control whatsoever over this coastal area, which they had conquered only some fifty to sixty years earlier.

In addition to the six channel-like canals described above, we located, on the north side of the Leche Valley, two other large ancient canals that were no longer in use. They once carried water for a great distance, turning north through the ruins of La Viña and adjacent open plains and terminating in the very large ancient center of Apurlé, near the Motupe River. Thus, while the Racarumi Canal carried water from the north side of the Lambayeque Valley to the south side of the Leche Valley, these canals and the others mentioned above, carried water

from the Leche Valley still farther north and west into the Motupe Valley. Because of the strategically important position of the Leche Valley, both of the huge pyramid sites of Cerro Purgatorio and Batán Grande probably played a political and economic role far beyond that warranted by the small size of the Leche River.

We visited the ancient settlement of La Viña (Figs. 61 and 62), which is comprised of regular, well-aligned rectangular structures indicating a Late Period urban center. Extensive reconnaissance could not be made because a large part of the site had been converted into fenced-in pastures where bulls were being raised for the Lima bullfights. However, we were able to see enough of the ruin to realize that it was considerably destroyed and

Fig. 38 (left). This group of ruins, situated amidst an algarroba "forest" on the Leche River, is known as the Huacas of Batán Grande (see text, pp. 162-163). Near the center of the photograph, an open plaza can be seen, faced on each of three sides by a large *huaca*. At the left is El Oro; at the right is La Ventana; at the top is El Horno. The arrangement of these *huacas* around an open area is similar to the Mochica pyramid groupings and in this setting has a curious Mayoid cast. Although occupied as late as Chimú times, this group probably had its greatest development sometime before 1000 A.D. In the upper left of the photograph is La Rodillona, while in the lower part are the remains of La Merced and La Cruz. At the right are a number of semi-destroyed pyramids, of which Los Ingenieros is the most important. *Servicio 3330:751* • Fig. 39 (right). Ground photograph of Huaca del Oro. On an inner wall of the upper part of the adobe pyramid, a painted frieze was found by Dr. Schaedel in 1948 (see Fig. 42). The foreground is part of the plaza bounded on two other sides by Huaca Ventana and Huaca del Horno (see Fig. 38). *Schaedel* • Fig. 40 (p. 164, margin). Gold Chimú vase found at Batán Grande. *Guillen* • Fig. 41 (below). An intricately-wrought Chimú gold knife from the ruins of Batán Grande. *Guillen* • Fig. 42 (right center). Drawing of the painted frieze on Huaca del Oro. The frieze is about two yards high; the colors are red, yellow and dark blue. A similar frieze was discovered 20 years ago in the Huaca Pintada, near Túcume, but it has been destroyed. *Florian.*

that much labor would be required in order to explore it systematically. The modern road and the ancient trunk road cut through the heart of the settlement.

The only reference to La Viña in archaeological litera-

ture is made by Brüning, who suggests that the site may have been the ancient Jayanca mentioned by Cabello, since it lay on the main Inca Road. Cabello states that Llapchillulli, one of Naymlap's many grandsons, assumed the chieftainship here and that one of his descendants still ruled Jayanca at the time of the Spanish conquests, over 400 years later. The present Jayanca lies some distance farther west, on the Pan American Highway. The Spaniards, it appears, moved some of the old settlements to a secondary, more western, north-south, pre-colonial or colonial road that ran from Motupe through Chiclayo to the Zaña and Jequetepeque Valleys, and that has now become, with some modification, part of the Pan American Highway. It is possible that Jayanca-La Viña was one of these towns, but archival investigations will be necessary to settle the question.

Apurlé excited our curiosity, for there seemed to be no reason why this large center should have developed in the small Motupe Valley. The site consists of a spaciously planned urban complex with the high adobe walls built at the foot of the small Cerro Apurlé, a lone hill in a large plain. Surrounding the complex are several dozen adobe pyramids and mounds, of small to medium size, that seem to be in a kind of regular alignment (see frontispiece and Fig. 58). The complex canal system, together with thousands of furrows, can still be clearly

traced in the broad plain surrounding Apurlé, as well as within the site itself. Limited surface collections and the general nature of the ground plan of the site indicate a Middle to Late Period of occupation.

Apurlé is situated near the small Motupe River, from which it received water. However, since the Motupe contains water during only part of the year, the two large canals that passed through La Viña were extended as far as Apurlé and thus brought a great amount of addi-

165

centers with one another. This leads to further speculation concerning possible relationships of these centers with El Purgatorio, since these four leading sites were dependent upon the waters of the relatively small Leche River. Archaeological knowledge is at present much too limited even to attempt to answer these speculative questions. All that stands out clearly in this case is the necessity for studying the close interrelationship of political-military power and the control of large-scale irrigation systems.

Although Apurlé is one of the largest sites in Peru, it has been practically ignored by professional archaeologists; Brüning and Rossell alone mention Apurlé, but they say little about it. In 1941, my assistant, Verne Grant, visited the site and made a rough but accurate ground plan of it; in 1948-49, Dr. Schaedel, Michael and I visited it twice. Let us hope that in the near future some enterprising archaeologist will solve the mystery of this lone site.

While trying to work out the complex system of irrigation canals on the great plain east of Apurlé, we "cruised" in our jeep as far as Salas. This small settlement, which is situated on the "river" of the same name, boasts of several small but interesting ruins. More intriguing, however, is the fact that Salas in the past was known as one of the leading centers of witchcraft (brujería)! Here, the ancient witch doctors gathered and by means of magic and medicine drove out devils and cured people of sicknesses and mental complexes.

Even more amazing is the fact that this knowledge has been passed down from generation to generation, so that today some of the descendants of the ancient witch doctors still practice their magic arts. In fact, Salas has a kind of witchcraft "school" to which "students" from various parts of the Northwest Coast go for study and to which persons afflicted with physical and mental ailments go for a cure. Since the government considers people engaged in witchcraft to be illegal medical practitioners, all practices and teaching are carried on in secrecy. Therefore, it is difficult to obtain information about the present day ideas and practices of brujería. Gillin, however, in his interesting sociological study on Moche (1945), has collected some fascinating material on the subject.

Salas is visited not merely by the ignorant, but also by the educated. In one instance that came to our notice, a lawyer had developed a high state of nervous tension because he felt that his own failures and the successes of one of his colleagues were caused by the fact that the latter had put the "evil eye" on him. In desperation, he finally yielded to the urging of friends and went to Salas for treatment. This apparently included such standard practices as casting out the devil, destroying doll images of his hated rival, and drinking magic potions. After participating for some time in these ceremonies, the lawyer eventually felt assured that his rival could never harm him again, and he returned to his home full of confidence in his own abilities. Before one smiles at this story, one must remember that in some regions of our own country people believe that they have been "hexed" while others in their nervous conditions wander off to psychoanalysts to be "unhexed."

Salas and Apurlé did not become the northernmost points of our reconnaissance, for we decided to follow the Motupe Valley farther north to see what we could find. We set out from Chiclayo one day and, after checking on various minor sites along the road, we arrived late in the evening at the town of Motupe. We scouted around

Paddle ware design.

Unfired clay pot (function unknown).

tional water all the way from the upper part of the Leche River, a distance of almost twenty-five miles! This would indicate that Apurlé, when it was built, must have exercised control over the north side of the Leche Valley! Indeed, the loss of this control may have been an important factor leading to the downfall of Apurlé. Since the two large canals that once fed Apurlé first passed through La Viña (Figs. 58, 61 and 62), some cooperation must have developed between these two centers, provided both existed at the same time. The large center of Batán Grande could likewise have controlled the two canals mentioned above, thus giving rise to interesting speculations concerning the possible interrelations of these three

166

Fig. 43 (upper left). Señor Portugal, Dr. Schaedel and the author in front of the SCIPA jeep amidst some of the "desert jungle." Vivas • Fig. 44 (left). Huaca Ventana, of the Batán Grande pyramid group (see Fig. 38). The algarroba forest in the foreground conceals most of this large pyramid. Schaedel • Fig. 45 (left margin). Ceramics from Huaca Ventana. Schaedel-Cacho • Fig. 46 (below and bottom of next page). Ceramics from Huaca de los Ingenieros. Schaedel-Cacho.

Circular base, white slip ware.   Paddle ware, triangle and bar design.   Puma head, thick orange ware.   Leg of tripod or tetropod.   Part of the inside of a corn grater.   Polished Chimú blackware.

for food and lodging, but all we could obtain was a miserable supper and a miserable room in a miserable hotel. We partly overcame our misery that night by drinking a bottle of *pisco* (an excellent and cheap Peruvian form of cognac).

Early the next morning, we left Motupe and drove up the small Chochope Valley, a branch of the Motupe Valley.

The Peruvian Army map indicated that there were ruins in this valley, and a number of people in Lambayeque agreed. No one, however, seemed to know what the ruins were like, and this aroused our curiosity. We arrived at about nine o'clock in the morning at the pleasant little village of Chochope. Here, in one of the large huts built of algarroba posts and covered with matting, the pleasant

and hospitable wife of the owner prepared us a fine breakfast. Cheered by the meal and the friendly atmosphere, we set off to hunt for ruins. Our first discovery included a large stone wall, several miles long, and several structures on nearby hills. More important, however, were a number of adobe *huacas* and other ruins at Cerro de la Virgen, in the region where the Chochope Valley enters the Motupe. This weather-beaten site may once have been *the ceremonial center of the whole Motupe-Chochope area.* It yielded some interesting local ceramics, some of which may have belonged to the Middle Period.

Considerably farther down the Motupe Valley, on the north bank of the river, we investigated another interesting site. Listed on the Army map under the picturesque name of Huacas de la Bandera (The Banner), it had long posed a tantalizing question for us. It was in a zone beyond the limit of vegetation of the Motupe Valley, on the southern edge of the large Sechura Desert. What could it be? Was it really a ruin or a series of natural hills? In colloquial language, the word *huaca* means not only pyramid, or *artificial* mound, but also *natural* mound. This usage is understandable because the word *huaca* meant "sacred" to the ancients. It appears that certain natural hills were considered sacred, but the fact that natural hills were rare in the coastal plains led the ancients to build artificial mounds or pyramids. This confusion of terminology sent us on many a wild goose chase. More than once did we check on a reported *huaca grande*, only to find it to be a natural mound. On the other hand, we were sometimes told that a certain small "hill" was only a natural mound, but upon investigation we discovered that the structure was a man-made *huaca*.

We visited La Bandera aided by a guide from Pacora who accompanied us on an arduous two-hour ride over hardened furrows and canals. Finally, a series of ruins loomed upon the horizon in a completely desert zone. There were three adobe pyramids, of average dimensions, which formed an extended complex containing a network of canals and subsidiary enclosure walls linking the pyramids with lesser structures. An abundance of potsherds, with a great variety of motifs, littered the extensive site and gave a reddish hue to the soil. The potsherds consisted almost exclusively of paddle ware. (Figs. 65 and 67).

We later heard reports of additional ruins still farther down the Motupe Valley in the direction of the sea. One of these reports came to us at the Lambayeque Office of the Agricultural Department. A man from the town of

Fig. 47 (below, left). A side view of Huaca Rodillona. The extensive damage done to the adobe structure by periodic rains is strikingly obvious in this view. Emilio González, one of the anthropology students at the Institute, is at the summit. *Schaedel* • Fig. 48 (below, center). Ceramics from Huaca Rodillona. *Schaedel-Cacho.*

Small unfired clay pot (function unknown).

Modeled red ware, unpolished.

Small unfired clay pot (function unknown).

ge ware potsherd, relief of face

Orange ware potsherd with incised designs.

Orange ware potsherd with relief of face.

Orange ware potsherd with incised designs.

Lambayeque polished blackware.

Unfired clay paddle, showing four designs, used for making impressions on pots.

Mórrope, an ancient settlement on the Mórrope River, one of the lower channels of the Motupe River and some six miles from the ocean, told us of a Huaca Cucufane not far from his home town. Since we had never heard of this ruin — and neither had anyone else in the office —, we decided to go to Mórrope at once to investigate. We arrived at the town during the early afternoon after a strenuous trip over the desert in the SCIPA jeep. The settlement seemed unusually forlorn and remote from modern forms of life. However, we found that it contained an interesting colonial church. In fact, a manuscript written by Padre Rubiños (1782) and published in 1936 by Carlos Romero indicates that at one time the town had been of some importance.

We drove along the streets questioning people, but no one had heard of Huaca Cucufane. Finally, an elderly man admitted he knew about the pyramid, but he claimed that a friend of his who lived some distance outside the town was the only person familiar with the compli-

Fig. 49 (above). An unusually comprehensive oblique aerial photograph showing a number of important sites arising out of the cultivated fields of the Leche-Lambayeque region. In the foreground is the village of Túcume; immediately behind it and to the right is the large Huaca Pueblo de Túcume (see Figs. 50 and 51), while farther behind it and to the right is the northern part of the important site of Purgatorio. At the left rear is the isolated hill, Sapamé, where many ancient graves have been found; directly behind it is Huaca Rodillona of the Batán Grande group; to the right of Rodillona, the summits of the other huacas of the Batán Grande cluster are barely visible. *Servicio 0: 1051* • Fig. 50 (upper right). Huaca Pueblo Túcume as seen from the air (see Figs. 49 and 51). *Servicio 3330:1009* • Fig. 51 (lower right). Ground view of Huaca Pueblo Túcume (see Figs. 49 and 50). *Kosok.*

168

Fig. 52 (above). Oblique aerial view of the north end of the ruins of Purgatorio. This cluster of pyramids and plazas is densely packed around the sides of one of the few hills in the Lambayeque plain and commands an excellent view of the entire countryside. The photograph reveals, in a striking manner, how the ancients utilized the hills for their administrative centers, both for economy (non-cultivable areas) and for strategic (greater height) reasons. The village of Mochumí is visible in the background. Note the encroaching fences of the present agriculturalists in the lower left. *Servicio 0: 1053* • Fig. 53 (lower margin). Jaguar, chased and soldered gold, found in Lambayeque region. *Mayrock-Doering.*

that extends into the extensive Sechura Desert to the north.

After returning to Mórrope, we were told that local counterfeiters of "antique" water jugs often bury their wares in this *huaca* for a year or so in order to make them look genuine before selling them in Chiclayo. Perhaps that is why people were reluctant to direct us outsiders to the ruin! Incidentally, while the production of "antique" water jugs is a minor industry in Mórrope, it is a major one in Catacaos in the Piura Valley, farther north.

The trip to Mórrope produced many other important results. On our long trip to the town, we had passed through areas that appeared utterly desolate, though here and there the ground bore traces of past habitation. This aroused our interest, and we decided to investigate these remains. While making several trips to this region and after having studied enlargements of International Petroleum Company photographs of this extensive area, we were astounded to find the remains of many small pyramids and formless mounds. As we crawled over some of the latter, we discovered that they were covered with what seemed to be millions of potsherds — all crude ware!

But, more important to our study, we encountered many large ancient canals whose extent and direction indicated that the waters of the Lambayeque had once been carried a considerable distance north of the Chotuna-Chornancap area. Indeed, we even found vestiges of canals that had formerly carried water still farther north and west to regions below the town of Mórrope. This was indeed a find, for no one with whom we had discussed this desolate region had mentioned the existence of these canals. We also located a long, high stone wall, running from north to south and cutting across the canals. It may date from late Indian or early colonial times.

We also tried to unravel the mystery of the complex of canals in the less desolate eastern part of this zone which borders on the present day irrigated area. Individual canals were difficult to trace for any distance in this region, even by means of the photographs, for here, more than twenty-five years ago, Ingeniero Carlos Sutton had built a large number of modern canals across the remains of old canals that were to have been part of an extensive irrigation project. Water from the Amazon side of the Andes was to have been tunneled through the mountains and spread over the entire Olmos-Motupe-Leche-Lambayeque region. However, following a change of government, the project was dropped. It has been under discussion ever since, but nothing has been done about

cated route to the site. Our elderly informant took us to his home for a good meal and then accompanied us to the home of his friend, who after some persuasion, both spiritual and financial, finally joined our "safari." Directed by our guide, we drove for several miles into the desert until we suddenly came upon our *huaca* dramatically silhouetted by the setting sun!

There is a possibility that this *huaca*, a small, intensively excavated adobe structure with walled enclosures, was a roomed temple like Huaca el Dragón in the Moche Valley — in other words not a pyramid. But whatever Cucufane's structure may have been, its geographical position is unique, for it appears to have been the last outpost of that part of the lower Lambayeque Complex

169

it. Nevertheless, the modern canals remain in the midst of the old, and since the two systems often cross and intertwine they were difficult to untangle. Fortunately, Ingeniero Sutton, before his death, had given us some indication of the nature and direction of his canals. We were finally able to determine that the ancient canals extended considerably farther west into the desert than did the modern ones. By integrating our findings in this zone with those in the zone nearer the sea, we were able to establish the fact that the limits of ancient cultivation in this vast and unexplored area had been much more extensive than we had originally assumed.

We likewise carried on intensive reconnaissance in the region between Mórrope, Túcume, Ferreñafe and the town of Lambayeque. Here we located and mapped many previously unknown pyramids and made surface

collections from some of them. Of the many interesting sites located, the small *huaca* site called Arbusto (Bush), just west of the Pan American Highway and about four miles north of Lambayeque, can be mentioned. There, some unusual pieces of orange-on-white ceramics were found by our SCIPA mechanic, Señor Portugal. They were discovered in some adobe material that had been dug out of the bottom of the *huaca* by the present owner, who had been excavating for gold. This discovery points to a local style of Lambayeque ceramics, as yet unstudied and possibly as old as the Mochica or even older.

At Hacienda Sasape, in this general area, we came upon evidence of an interesting cultural phenomenon. The obliging *hacendado* showed us some fine pieces of black Chimú *style* ceramics he had dug up. While examining them, we noticed that one of them had a distinctly Span-

Fig. 54 (left). The site of Purgatorio on the Leche River was part of the Lambayeque culture that flourished during the Middle Period, although it continued to be occupied until the time of the Spanish Conquest. The old ceremonial center out of which it apparently grew is visible on the north and northwest sides of the hill. The large concentration of pyramids on the north end was built during the Middle Period and continued into Chimú times. *Servicio 3330:9790* • Fig. 55 (above). A view of one of the larger pyramids on the north side of Purgatorio showing the layers of logs and matting used to keep the successive levels of the adobe platforms regular. *Schaedel* • Fig. 56 (right). Oblique aerial view of the ruins of Cerro Purgatorio. This view shows many of the structures seen in Fig. 54. The significance of both vertical and oblique photographs is clearly indicated when the two are brought into juxtaposition. The large main structure in the foreground is approximately four hundred yards long and is an "elevated" type of urban compound. It has a single entrance, visible at the front. *Servicio 0: 1053* • Fig. 57 (below). Ross Christensen, a North American student and member of the Trujillo Institute group, on his way to the top of one of the large pyramids on Cerro Purgatorio. Note the remains of part of the free ramp approaching the *huaca* and continuing along the side of it. *Schaedel.*

Bright orange on white slip ware.

Fragment of a thick storage or *chicha* jar with incised concentric circles.

Fig. 58 (both pages, above). Vertical aerial view of the ruins of Apurlé (left side of this page) shown in relationship to the canals that once brought water to the site from the Leche River (beyond the right of the photograph on the next page). These canals also passed through La Viña, which is on the lower slopes of one of the desert hills (lower center of the next page). Note the ancient furrows that still exist near Apurlé. The white line cutting through the site is the Pan American Highway. For an enlarged view of Apurlé see the photograph opposite the title page of this volume. *Servicio 1626:2135, 2137, 2139, 2141* • Fig. 59 (left). Fields, formerly cultivated, between La Viña and Apurlé. In the foreground is the Pan American Highway • Fig. 60 (opposite page, lower left). Riding through one of the large canals that once brought water to Apurlé. *Kosok* • Fig. 61 (opposite page, lower middle). Vertical aerial photograph of a part of the hillside settlement of La Viña showing some of the canals and buildings and the ancient north-south highway. Note the rectangular enclosures. Compare this view of La Viña with that presented in Figs. 58 and 62. *Servicio 3330:618, 650* • Fig. 62 (opposite page, lower right). The dark lines in this oblique aerial photograph are canals that brought water to Apurlé and passed through ancient La Viña, the remains of which can be seen on the lower sides of the hill (see Figs. 58 and 61). *Kosok* • Fig. 63 (margins). Ceramics from Apurlé. *Schaedel-Cacho.*

An "engraved" pot-
sherd of brown ware.
The design stands out
in deep relief.

Paddle ware.

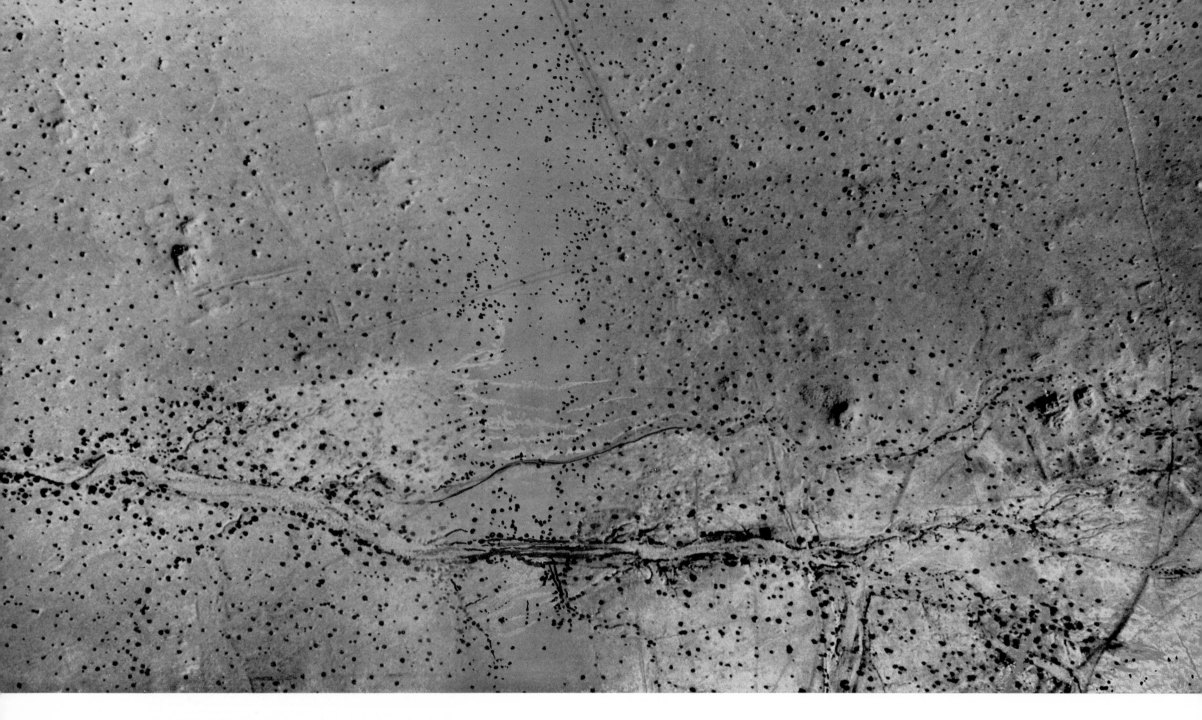

ish medallion type of design! Further examination seemed to indicate that the vessel was not a forgery but merely an early colonial product. After the Spanish conquest, as pointed out before, Indian artisans continued for some time to make their products in the same way they had previously done, utilizing new designs that appealed to them. Thus, it is sometimes difficult to determine whether certain archaeological material is of late Indian or early Spanish times.

The rest of the lower Lambayeque region, from Ferreñafe to the coast of Pimentel, and to the southwest as far as Eten and Monsefú, we likewise covered by truck and jeep until, bit by bit, each known and unknown site that we encountered had been mapped.

The southwestern section of the Lambayeque area is often considered the "oldest," because there, especially in the two old towns of Eten and Monsefú, the ancient Mochica language held out longest against the overwhelming tide of Spanish. In Chapter VII, we discussed this problem and described our interview in Trujillo with Señora Manuela Millones de Carillo from Eten. The Mochica words we obtained from her are given in the Appendix.

After we had left Peru, we were informed by Señor Rodríguez SuySuy that an old man in Monsefú was said to have a list of more than a hundred Mochica words that he had collected. At our request, Señor Rodríguez went to Monsefú where, after some difficulties, he obtained the list and sent a copy of it to us. This list, with the original Spanish translation, as well as an English translation made by Dr. Schaedel, is given in the Appendix. Señor Rodríguez also wrote us that the only man in Monsefú who supposedly could still speak Mochica fluently had died three years previously. However, the local padre informed our friend that if he came to the next big local fiesta and joined in the general *borrachera* (drinking bout), he would hear the tongues of some of the people begin to loosen and use Mochica words still current!

The Lambayeque region contains still other verbal vestiges from the ancient past, for many folk legends come to us from the early colonial as well as the pre-colonial past.

The myths, of which a representative sample has been chosen and translated from the volume of A. Léon Barandiarán entitled *Mytos leyendas y tradiciones lambayecanas*, are interesting for several reasons. Besides their intrinsic literary merit, they preserve the flavor of North Coast traditions which, despite anachronisms and the reembroidery of four centuries of retelling, reflect the outlook and values of the virtually unrecorded Chimú culture which antedated that of the much better-known Incas. Among other items, one notices the sacred references to the adobe pyramids (huacas) and the reverence for moon worship and for the characteristic desert animals. Finally, the myths are important in that they preserve, however imperfectly, the proper names and place names of the Chimús and their contemporaries of the North Coast, providing (as in the example cited here of the Huaca Pintada and Pacatnamu) important clues relating to the function of these known archaeological sites.

THE MUMMY OF THE CACIQUE (CHIEFTAIN)

A century before the Spanish arrived on our coasts, Inca Huyna Capac was already terminating the conquest and subjugation of the Yungas and Mochicas, a task which his forefathers had begun.

With 40,000 men of an army which he personally commanded, this Inca and his brother Cussi Hualpa defeated the Penachis, a fierce warrior tribe whose principal city was the actual hamlet Penachi, and this was the only tribe which resisted losing its independence.

When he made his first attempt of advancing towards the highlands, before defeating the Penachis, General Cussi Hualpa, owing to the rising of the rivers, was not able to continue his advance and returned to where he had started from. He established his headquarters in Jayanca where he married the daughter of the chieftain of this village called Falloshuli, a direct descendant of Llapchillulli founder and first governor of said village.

As things turned out, Falloshuli was involved in the resistance which the Penachis had offered to the Incas; and once the total subjection of the Penachis had been accomplished, his transfer to Cuzco from Jayanca was ordered and he was sent there as a prisoner for some years until, through the influence of his own daughter, the wife of Cussi Hualpa, he obtained his liberty and the corresponding authorization to return to his people. He left from Cuzco with a large group of attendants, constituting among others Puinconsoli, Fontam, Chumbi, Manallulli, Pillacup and Monlotum who were his distinguished servants and principal chieftains and who also had suffered imprisonment in the capital of the empire since the time they, together with their chief, had fallen prisoners of the Incas.

Old age, defeat, prison, sadness and humiliation had undermined the health of the old chieftain who died in the sanctuary of Pácatnamu when he was returning to his people. His servants made a solemn pyre and mummified

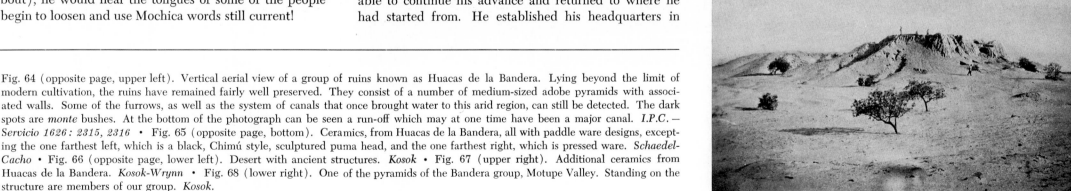

Fig. 64 (opposite page, upper left). Vertical aerial view of a group of ruins known as Huacas de la Bandera. Lying beyond the limit of modern cultivation, the ruins have remained fairly well preserved. They consist of a number of medium-sized adobe pyramids with associated walls. Some of the furrows, as well as the system of canals that once brought water to this arid region, can still be detected. The dark spots are *monte* bushes. At the bottom of the photograph can be seen a run-off which may at one time have been a major canal. *I.P.C.* — *Servicio 1626: 2315, 2316* • Fig. 65 (opposite page, bottom). Ceramics, from Huacas de la Bandera, all with paddle ware designs, excepting the one farthest left, which is a black, Chimú style, sculptured puma head, and the one farthest right, which is pressed ware. *Schaedel-Cacho* • Fig. 66 (opposite page, lower left). Desert with ancient structures. *Kosok* • Fig. 67 (upper right). Additional ceramics from Huacas de la Bandera. *Kosok-Wrynn* • Fig. 68 (lower right). One of the pyramids of the Bandera group, Motupe Valley. Standing on the structure are members of our group. *Kosok.*

Fig. 69 (above). The fishing village of San José. The complete isolation of the village from the agricultural life of the Lambayeque Valley is graphically evident in this oblique aerial photograph. The oval mound at the right is an ancient *huaca* which is now used as the village graveyard. The other mounds, in the foreground, are apparently also the remains of ancient *huacas*. Villages like San José have existed along the west coast of South America since the earliest pre-ceramic times. Compared with the evolution of the agricultural communities, they have always been of slow development, and even today, except where they have been converted into modern ports, retain a primitive and conservative cast that reflects their time-honored role. The last vestiges of the old coastal Indian populations are concentrated for the most part in San José and villages of the same general type. *Servicio 0:1022*

the cadaver of their chief. Entering into their own lands, they buried the corpse on the slopes of the hill which is found to the east of the actual hacienda house of the La Viña estate near which the prehistoric town of Jayanca was located.

Before he had begun his adventure of resisting the Inca's forces, this chieftain had consulted with the "ichuris" or professional diviners who, after having practiced their accustomed rites such as sacrificing a ram of brown color to make studies of the viscera, said (symbolizing the future things that were to take place), "You chieftain will leave on your own feet and you will return on those of others." Falloshuli, misinterpreting these words to mean he would go to war and return victorious in a royal litter, decided to embrace openly the project of rebellion and suffered the consequent defeat.

And the prediction was fulfilled because the rebel chieftain of Jayanca did indeed return to his village, albeit as a corpse, borne by his retainers. And there lies his mummified body awaiting his ancient servants and subjects that they may return his powers and his lost lands.

THE LEGEND OF THE PAINTED TEMPLE OF ILLIMO

The Huaca Pintada or the painted temple which is found at about a kilometer south of the village of Illimo was originally a sanctuary or religious temple dedicated to the worship of the moon, the rivers, the rains, the lizards and spiders. It was constructed totally of large adobes without a single decoration or painting on the inside or out. Prior to the government of Inca Pachacutec, that is, when the conquest of the Yungas had still not been accomplished by the Incas, the priest who directed the activities of that sanctuary and whose name was Anto Tunpa dreamt that the sun had come close to him, totally burning the sanctuary, and that he had had left impressed upon his face the aspect and the color of that celestial body as though to remind him that he was obliged to render tribute to its cult. But the old priest refusing to heed the warning continued offering sacrifices, libations, prayers and vows to the moon, the waters, and the animals disdaining the premonition. But, when in the early morning he awoke and was making preparations to cook maize for the sacred chicha with which he was accustomed to propitiate his gods, he found that the sanctuary was totally colored with red on the outside and on the inside that the walls were decorated in three colors: red (the sun), blue (the sky), and yellow (gold). And he felt in his face that devastating fire of the sun which was burning into him the night before and he soon fell dead, but still showing on his face as a sign of the power of the celestial body, a mask of gold.

The painted temple of Illimo was decorated by the sun itself. And the mask of gold found in the temple at the beginning of the present century was that of Anto Tunga, punished thus by the celestial body because of his refusal to worship the sun since he did not want to establish the cult of the Incas in the villages. And also it was a sure warning of the forthcoming triumph of the conquerors from Cuzco.

Of course, there is no way of verifying the truth of any of these legends, which have come down to us during a period of more than four centuries. Nevertheless, collectively they give us an insight into the social structure of ancient Peruvian society and serve as records of a semi-historical character which archaeological work by itself cannot furnish. The publication of Señor León Barandiarán's volume should also focus the attention of young Spanish-speaking ethnologists upon collecting these valuable but rapidly disappearing relics of the past, not only in the Lambayeque Complex but also in other regions of Peru. They are exactly the materials necessary for connecting old Spanish records with some of the discoveries of modern archaeologists!

When we had "finished" our work in the Lambayeque Complex — at least to the extent we found necessary for our study —, we heaved a collective sigh of relief! At the same time, while musing over some of our findings, we arrived at a tentative answer to a question that had pursued us throughout our work: Was the Lambayeque Complex ever politically unified from within? We con-

Fig. 71 (right). The lower Lambayeque Valley and the shores of the Pacific Ocean. Characteristic of this area are the many small fields. Also characteristic is the non-cultivation of the land near the sea. This is due to a number of factors, chief of which is the lack of sufficient water. The many thin black lines are plants growing in the run-offs that carry surplus irrigation water to the sea. This general condition also exists in the lower Chicama Valley. The many white spots in the photograph are small mounds, both natural and artificial, which are above the level of cultivation. At (A) is the town of Lambayeque. At the left of the town is the road that runs to Chiclayo. At (B) is the port of Pimentel (see Fig. 78). At (C) is the fishing village of San José (see Fig. 69). *U.S. Army 41-L-20.*

177

cluded that it probably was not. A number of large-scale, *regional* key areas had been organized around important administrative and population centers, some of which had even entered the stage of urbanization. It appears that some centers were dominant during certain periods, some during other periods. However, if they existed contemporaneously they probably formed temporary alliances or carried on wars of conquest against one another. But, whatever the situation may have been, none of these *regional key areas* apparently ever became strong enough to achieve a *centralized control over the whole Lambayeque Complex!* A kind of *cultural* unity of the whole complex existed, developing, however, probably diverse

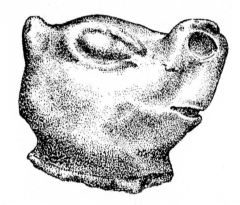

regional forms. But politically there was probably *more diversity than unity!*

Even the presence of unusually long canal systems in these valleys did not necessarily mean that the valleys were united politically, for a large canal system could have been used by politically distinct but geographically adjacent groups that had formed some kind of economic agreement concerning the distribution of the water in

the canal system. The group controlling the *toma* (intake) of the canal water generally would have possessed greater power over the water than the other groups. As a result, the former would have been tempted to transform its economic power into political power and control over the others. Of course, the reverse may have taken place. The possessors of the intake may have been conquered by the other groups! But each unified canal "government" serviced only one large section of a valley and probably one or two large centers at a time.

Even though complete *intravalley* political control may not have been achieved, some form of *intervalley* political control must have arisen in connection with the growth of *intervalley* canal systems. For example, the Taymi Canal carried water from the Lambayeque to the lower Leche. Even more important, the Racarumi Canal brought water from the upper Lambayeque to the upper and middle Leche, with its important sites of Batán Grande and Purgatorio, while several canals brought water from the Leche to La Viña and Apurlé in the Motupe Valley. But there was *no unifying canal system* for the whole Lambayeque Complex whose upkeep would have required a *single* political control center! Furthermore, as already stated, there are no indications that any of the key economic centers was able to conquer the entire Lambayeque Complex.

There are likewise no legends or traditions that would indicate the former existence of an independent, politically unified state embracing the whole Lambayeque Complex. On the contrary, the existing legends indicate a diversity of centers. The Naymlap legend refers at best only to a kind of kinship-dominated "federation" of local "states" over parts of the middle and lower Lambayeque Complex in which the local ruler of Lambayeque was looked upon as a kind of senior partner or leading chief. The accounts of early Chroniclers and the legends collected by Señor León Barandiarán give us the same general impression.

To summarize: This area, because of its size and geographical-topographical complexity, gave rise to many conflicting elements. Consequently, *in terms of the general level of the existing productive forces,* social relationships could not evolve that were sufficiently developed to have produced a centralized political state of the kind the Chimús created in the Moche Valley (see Chapter VIII).

Only when the Lambayeque Complex was conquered in the latter part of its prehistoric period by the Chimús, and later by the Incas, was some kind of administrative

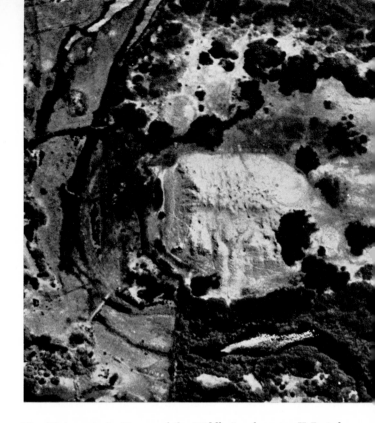

Fig. 72 (margins). *Huacos* of the Middle Lambayeque II Period. *AMNH* • Fig. 73 (upper left). Figure of a Peruvian bear from a jar found at Huaca Arbusto, near the town of Lambayeque. Plain orange ware. *Kosok* • Fig. 74 (above). The pyramid of Chornancap in the *monte* of the lower Lambayeque Valley. With Chotuna, it is linked by legend with the founding of the Naymlap dynasty in Lambayeque. Chotuna (the temple of Chot) was allegedly built by Naymlap, while his wife, Ciurnancacum, is said to have had Chornancap erected for her greater glory. Note the remains of a ramp on the front side of the *huaca*, which so far has been unreported by archaeologists. *Servicio 3330-863* • Fig. 75 (lower left). Cursive-like decoration on light background from the interior of a bowl found at Huaca Arbusto. This design is suggestive of a pre-Chimú pottery style in the Lambayeque zone (as yet unreported). The dark ring was caused by a stain that partly destroyed the design. *Kosok-Storck* • Fig. 76 (below) and Fig. 77 (lower left, opposite page). Polished blackware found by the author in the Lambayeque area. *Kosofsky.*

"unity" achieved. But it was a *mechanical unity, enforced from the outside.* It was not designed to satisfy the needs of the people living within the area but to provide more loot and tribute for the foreign conquerors!

Little is known of the Chimú conquest of this region. According to Cabello, a Chimú governor by the name of Pongmassa was sent to rule over Lambayeque, and he was succeeded by two other Chimú governors. Undoubtedly, the Chimús established some kind of military-administrative control of this area, but how centralized it was and how effective it was, we do not know. We can only guess that a firm, centralized administrative control over such a large and complex area must have been impossible to establish, especially since it was one that was antagonistic to the interests of the people of the area.

Of the Inca conquest of Lambayeque, we know even less; in fact, Cabello does not even mention it. From the change in the name forms of the later rulers of Lambayeque, we can deduce that possibly a local ruling house was put in control, undoubtedly under an Inca "Gauleiter." Archaeological remains so far indicate Inca control of only a few focal points. But the nature and extent of the administrative control of the Incas is still a moot question. It is significant that in Xerez' account of Pizarro's march through northern Peru from Tumbes through Lambayeque to Zaña, *there is no mention of contact with any Inca troops or even Inca officials.* The contact seems to have been made solely with local rulers! Only when Pizarro marched into the highlands towards Cajamarca did he make direct contact with the Incas. The fact that Pizarro did not encounter Inca officials and troops until he entered the highlands may be explained by the coincidence of the civil war between Atahualpa and his half brother, Huascar; nevertheless, it throws light on the

Fig. 78 (above). The town of Pimentel, one of the harbors of the Lambayeque region. Note the steel pier that juts out into the ocean. Freight is carried by railroad cars to the end of the pier where it is loaded on barges and transferred to the ocean-going vessels anchored some distance from the shore. Because of its sandy shore, Pimentel is used as a summer resort by people from Chiclayo. In the foreground of the photograph are a number of reed *caballitos* drying in the sun. As mentioned before, these boats that can hold one or two men have been used for fishing purposes since ancient times. Note the arid region behind Pimentel. In the far distance, the cultivated fields of Lambayeque can be seen. The irregular dark line is vegetation growing in one of the many run-offs used for irrigation water (see Fig. 71 and map. p. 146). *Servicio 0: 4613.*

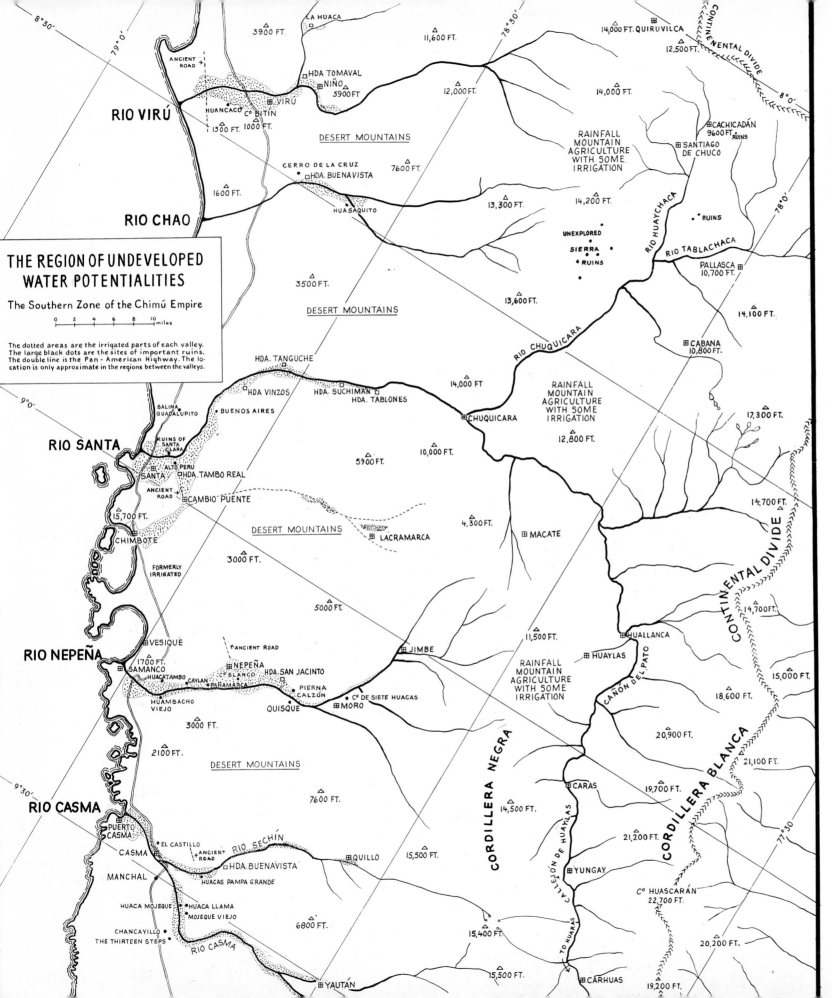

THE REGION OF UNDEVELOPED
WATER POTENTIALITIES

The Southern Zone of the Chimú Empire

0 2 4 6 8 10 miles

The dotted areas are the irrigated parts of each valley.
The large black dots are the sites of important ruins.
The double line is the Pan - American Highway. The lo-
cation is only approximate in the regions between the valleys.

tenuous nature of Inca control over this whole coastal region. Some of the first Chroniclers do mention previous punitive expeditions by Inca troops that had annihilated rebellious coastal settlements in order to maintain Inca "control" of the Coast, but this merely confirms our previous statement that the Inca Empire had a weak hold on an important part of the Coast.

The decentralized nature of the Lambayeque Complex throughout its history did not necessarily prevent some of the key economic and political centers of this amorphous region from expanding culturally and perhaps even politically towards the Zaña and Jequetepeque Valleys to the south and to some of the valleys farther north. In fact, it would be surprising if such expansions had not taken place. But, as yet, we have no proofs supporting such a hypothesis.

While discussing interrelations, another important question arises. A great deal of Chimú type blackware has been found in the Lambayeque region; this would tend to indicate a longer period of Chimú *cultural* occupation of this region than the short period of Chimú *political* control over Lambayeque would logically permit. Moreover, since the Anonymous Trujillano states that Taycanamu, the founder of the Chimú Empire, came from the north, it is possible to assume that he *could have come from the Lambayeque region.* Can we, therefore, look for some of the roots of the Chimú Empire, especially its culture, not only in the local Moche-Chicama area and in the so-called Coastal Tiahuanaco influences, but also *in Lambayeque itself?*

As pointed out previously, the Chimú Empire had extensions north of the Lambayeque Valley which included the Piura, Chira and Tumbes Valleys and perhaps even part of coastal Ecuador. However, this Northern Extension of the Chimú Empire was undoubtedly of very short duration; consequently, Chimú culture had exercised only a superficial influence in this region. Therefore, only cursory reference to it is made in Chapter XXIV of this report.

If, however, these valleys are to be studied as a unit, attention must be paid not only to the Chimús and Incas, but also to the neighboring Sierra peoples and, most important, to the peoples of the adjacent Guayaquil Bay Complex with their unusual social structures and cultural forms. For the far northern region of Peru was a transition zone where various forces coming from south, east and north intermingled with the indigenous cultures that had evolved during several thousands of years.

XVII

The Viru and Chao Valleys: Small Isolates

IN OUR STUDY of the various parts of the Chimú Empire, we first described the Moche-Chicama Valley Complex, the core of the earlier Mochica culture and also of the later Chimú Empire. We next considered the problems of the Northern Zone. Here, we noted that the Jequetepeque Valley apparently was a crossroads of various adjacent cultures and "empires." According to the tradition presented by the Anonymous Trujillano, this valley must have been conquered by the third Chimú ruler, Ñançenpinco, possibly around 1300 A.D. We then showed how this valley was once linked with the large Zaña-Lambayeque-Leche-Motupe Complex which came under the control of the Chimús, presumably at the beginning of the fifteenth century. The rule of the Chimús ended there during the latter part of the century when the Incas took over.

Probably soon after the conquest of the Lambayeque region, the Chimús extended their power further north to the Piura, Chira and Tumbes Rivers. Possibly, even part of the Guayaquil area, as far as the present Puerto Viejo in Ecuador, was temporarily conquered by the Chimús.

Fig. 1. The nature of the Chao Valley is shown in this unusual oblique aerial photograph. Note the small amount of irrigated land, the large regions covered with *monte* bushes produced by ground water and short annual floods, and the vast stretches of desert soil bordering both sides of the valley. In the background are *loma* clouds hovering over the coast line and the nearby Pacific Ocean. *U. S. Army 130-L-96* • Fig. 2 (right margin). Negative and modeled potsherds from the Virú Valley. *Strong and Evans* • NOTE: Line cut above. Part of a molded jar, Virú Valley.

When we turn to the southern limits of the Chimú Empire, the information becomes even more vague. The Anonymous Trujillano informs us that the same Ñançenpinco, who conquered the area as far north as the Jequetepeque, also extended his power as far south as the Santa. After that, we are left in the dark until we hear from the same author that Minchançaman, the last independent ruler who controlled the area as far as Tumbes to the north, also had extended his domain as far south as Carabayllo, the present Chillón Valley, just to the north of the Rimac.

This southern extension is confirmed by Calancha (1638:Bk. III, Chap. 4), who states that the Chimús, after having won three battles at Carabayllo (Chillón), were finally defeated by the army of the ruler of the Rimac Confederation. We do not know how far back to the north the Chimús were then driven, nor do we know how strong was their control, while it lasted, in the southern extension of the Empire. We merely know that when the Incas conquered this region, the Rimac Confederacy, consisting of the Chillón, Rimac and Lurín Valleys, probably had some kind of federation with at least the Chancay Valley, while the Chimús held Paramonga in the Pativilca Complex farther north (Garcilaso).

The Anonymous Trujillano says that, at the time of the Inca conquest, Chumuncaur, a son of the last independent Chimú ruler, Minchançaman, was staying with his mother, a ruler (*señora*) of the Huaura Valley, which is situated between the above-mentioned Chancay Valley and the Pativilca Complex. Perhaps it was by such marriages with women rulers or with female relatives of local rulers that the Chimús tried to maintain their power over the distant parts of the realm.

It appears that the Chimús may even have made temporary conquests and raids below the Rimac area. Thus, Garcilaso, in his *Royal Commentaries* (Bk. VI, Chap. XXXII), states that in the war of the Incas against the Chimús, among the most bitter enemies of the latter were the rulers of Pachacamac and Runahuánac (the upper Cañete) — both south of the Rimac — because in a previous period the Chimús had waged a cruel war against them and had enslaved many of their people. The Quipucamayocs state that Chimú conquests extended even as far as Nazca!

This complicated region south of the Moche can be divided roughly into several sections: (1) the Southern Zone of the Chimú Empire consisting of the southern part of the Northwest Coast running from south of the Moche to the Pativilca Complex; (2) the Southern Extensions of the Chimú Empire consisting of the Central Coast running from the Pativilca Complex to the Rimac group, and of the South Coast (more correctly South Central Coast) running from below the Rimac group to the Nazca area; (3) the region below Nazca which, as yet, has not been linked in any way with the Chimú Empire.

The Southern Zone of the Chimú Empire consists of a number of small and even diminutive valleys, each separated by a fairly wide stretch of desert. From north to south, they are as follows: the quite small Virú, the diminutive Chao, the small (in ancient times almost medium-sized) Santa, the small Nepeña, the small Casma and the diminutive Culebra and Huarmey. Because of the small size of the rivers (except the Santa) and the large distances and natural barriers between them, no multi-valley irrigation complexes were ever established in this region. As a result of these factors, it must not have been difficult for the Chimú Empire, once it was organized, to take over this zone rapidly, valley by valley — a fact in part confirmed by the Anonymous Trujillano.

Just below the Moche, but separated from it by a large

desert, is the Virú. Both river and valley are smaller than the Moche, and the ancient peoples of this region never played a dominant role in the history of the Coast. Nevertheless, this valley has received more attention from archaeologists in the past two decades than any other valley in Peru. There are several reasons for this. In the first place, previous findings indicated the existence in this valley of all the major periods of the past. Secondly, the valley is small enough to permit a group of scientists to cover all its essential parts in a reasonable time and thus obtain an over-all picture of its development. Its nearness to the larger key Moche Valley would also help to throw light upon the development of the latter.

As a result, the Virú Expedition sponsored by various organizations spent 1946 and 1947 excavating and mapping the Virú Valley intensively. The Expedition consisted of the following North American Peruvianists: Duncan Strong, Wendell Bennett, Gordon Willey, Junius Bird, James Ford, Donald Collier, Clifford Evans, Allan Holmberg, and Webster McBryde. Some of their tentative results were presented in 1948 in the previously mentioned *Reappraisal of Peruvian Archaeology*. Detailed accounts of their work have been published by Ford (1949,

with a map by McBryde), Bennett (1950), Strong and Evans (1952), and Willey (1953). Other studies are in the process of publication.

In 1940-41 we covered most of the valley, mapping its major canals and sites. In 1948-49 we spent little time in this valley inasmuch as the findings of the Virú Expedition would yield far more detailed results than were necessary for our own study. We therefore concentrated our efforts on some unsolved canal problems. The aerial photographs of the Servicio showed what appeared to be an impossibility: namely, a large canal, beyond the present border of cultivation of the lower part of the southern bank, which appeared to run, at its eastern end, *up* the side of Cerro Bitín! Professor Gordon Willey had previously mentioned this problem to me. It is clear, since water cannot run uphill, and since Cerro Bitín is much too low a hill to have been the recipient of rainfall, that the answer had to be found in another direction. During the latter part of our stay in Peru, Señor Emilio González, one of Dr. Schaedel's archaeology students at the Trujillo Institute, made a two-day trip on horseback following the canal. He came to the conclusion that there had been no canal. The apparently elevated borders of the "canal"

had been a double wall! The structure was produced by digging a wide trench and throwing dirt and sand on both sides, thus producing two walls. The winds of the centuries had covered parts of the structure with sand and dirt in such a way that it looked like a canal on the photograph. The walls were probably built to ward off raids from the Santa Valley to the south and seem similar to the dirt and sand walls just north of the latter valley.

We also clarified one other canal problem. In 1941 we had been informed that the large canal which runs at quite an elevation along the hills of the upper southern side of the Virú Valley had once carried water over the small divide into the Chao Valley just to the south. We were able, on our last trip, to determine that the elevation of the divide is too high for this canal to have done so. This fact would prove that the two valleys had never been a hydrological unit, as we had tentatively supposed as the result of our first visit.

The aerial photographs of this valley turned out far less impressive than those of other valleys. We therefore reproduce only two of them (Figs. 3 and 6). Many of the sites, moreover, are being reproduced as ground plans by the members of the Virú Expedition.

Fig. 3. The hilly region between Tomaval and Niño, situated on the north side of the Virú Valley, is shown in this sharply focused vertical aerial photograph. The density of the ruins is illustrated by the many white spots, which are the floors of rooms, and by the many habitation terraces. Note the stone walls along the hills. The dark area at the bottom of the photograph represents modern irrigated fields. *Servicio 104: 1225 and 1227.*
Fig. 4 (left margin). One of the rare bearded men of Mochica times portrayed in the form of a ceremonial water jug. Virú Valley. *AMNH.* • Fig. 5 (right margin). Mochica style figurine, Huaca de la Cruz, Virú Valley. *AMNH.*

hills on the west side of Quebrada Chaparrí connecting the Lambayeque and Leche Valleys, bears have been shot in recent times. In fact, on our last visit at the Hacienda Batán Grande in the Leche Valley, the owners showed us a live black bear cub they had caught in the region.

In 1941, while traversing the flat semi-*monte* area just below the Cupisnique Valley plains, not ten miles from the sea, our truck driver suddenly espied a fox! He shouted at once, "Let's go fox hunting!" He raced the truck back and forth over the desert and around *monte* bushes until in less than fifteen minutes he had winded the fox so much that he was able to run over him and kill him. He threw the dead animal into the back of the truck and exclaimed joyfully, "A nice fur for my wife!"

In valleys like the Chao, which have a short water period, it is customary to build many long, wide canals so as to be able to use the sudden rush of water for a few months, following the height of the rainy season in the Sierras, and distribute it over as much land as possible to assure a large crop. In rivers where there is water for the greater part or all of the year such a procedure is unnecessary. Here, to one's surprise, the major canals are

often relatively smaller, since enough water is available during the major part of the year. In ancient times, this may have led, in favorable areas, to two corn crops a year (a crop can be raised in four months on the Coast).

In all valleys, during the period of high waters, much of the water rushes unused into the ocean. This waste of water has led to various private proposals for building concrete dams across side *quebradas* to store up water for the dry season. But the expense has so far proved too great. Whether the ancients built dirt dams for such purposes is doubtful. At least we found none in our wanderings along the Coast. Only small ones built of rocks and sod were encountered in our travels in the Sierras. The ancient dam in the Nepeña Valley which Squier mentions had probably been a *mampuesto* (aqueduct) leading water over a dry *quebrada*.

Buena Vista is the only large *hacienda* in this valley today. It has a swimming pool and, ironically, grows water-consuming rice for commercial purposes. We had visited this valley in 1941 and mapped the remains of a canal on the north side. During the 1949 trip, with the aid of aerial photographs and a jeep, we were able to make

Fig. 6. Ruins of Huancaco, situated on top of a hill on the southern side of the lower Virú Valley. The black spots at the top are *monte* bushes. *Servicio 104: 852* • Fig. 7 (left). Negative type of ceramics of unusual shapes; place of origin unknown. *Kosok-Rein* • Fig. 8 (right). Typical Virú modeled ceramics. *AMNH-Rein.*

Just south of the Virú lies the Chao Valley (Fig. 1). For about three months each year it contains water which rushes down and often floods the wide flat banks, producing an extensive and heavy *monte* of bushes and even small desert trees. This *monte*-covered valley is probably a good example of what many valleys looked like in their natural state when, in early times, they were traversed by small bands of hunters who sought rabbits, foxes, deer, pumas and bears. Even today such animals are occasionally found and hunted in parts of the coastal valleys!

When we were in the middle Casma, we encountered a man who was hunting deer which had eaten some of his crops. In the Chongoyape pocket in the upper part of the Lambayeque Valley, pumas occasionally come down from nearby mountains to attack calves and colts. In the

184

Fig. 9. The remains of ancient stone terraces that cover one side of Cerro de la Cruz can be discerned in this ground photograph (see Fig. 10). The structures consist of many small rooms. *Kosok.*

Fig. 10 (right). The nature of the extensive ruins of Cerro de la Cruz, the largest hillside site in the tiny Chao Valley, is clearly shown in this vertical aerial photograph. The main structures seem to be inside the natural semicircular basin that is part of the hill. Note that half of the outer side of the hill is completely covered by terraced stone units (see Fig. 9). Farther down are concentric stone defense walls, while on the plain below are remains of ancient canals. Not far from this site is Hacienda Buena Vista, the only *hacienda* in the valley. *Servicio 104: 1170* • Fig. 11 (right margin). Virú negative and modeled ware. *Strong and Evans.*

a much more comprehensive survey. As a result, an additional series of canals was found on the north side. Whether this meant that more land was cultivated in ancient times than at present or that the area of cultivation was merely shifted in modern times is difficult to decide. Probably both explanations are partly correct. No major old canals were found on the south side.

Surprisingly enough, this small valley contains two major ruins, one on Cerro de la Cruz (Hill of the Cross), near the present day *hacienda* building (Figs. 9 and 10), and the other near Huasaquito (Fig. 13) on the southern bank. We had visited both sites in 1941; in 1949 we revisited them and took additional notes.

After returning to Trujillo, we met Señor Enrique Jacobs, a long-time resident of this city and an expert in ancient ceramics and burial sites of the neighboring valleys. He had assumed the management of a small *hacienda* in the hilly middle part of the Chao Valley and had explored this region. As a result, he was able to enter on my map a number of sites in the upper part of the valley which we had not been able to visit. He also confirmed the results we had obtained in our own work on the lower part of the valley.

The Virú and Chao Valleys—as well as the Santa just to the south—have yielded extensive Mochica remains indicating that they were once a long-lived part of the Mochica culture complex—and empire, if one existed. The Anonymous Trujillano notes that the conquest of these three valleys had been accomplished by Ñançenpinco, the third of the Chimú rulers. This would indicate that the valleys were under Chimú rule and cultural influence for almost two centuries. Once control of the Moche-Chicama Complex was established, conquest of the valleys directly to the south was easy to achieve.

Fig. 12. Mochica portrait *huaco*, supposedly found in the Virú Valley. *AMNH* • Fig. 13. Huasaquito is the second major hillside ruin in the Chao Valley. This vertical aerial view indicates that, like the ruin of Cerro de la Cruz, it consists of closely packed stone structures in concentric rows. The site is on the south side of the valley, somewhat further up than Cerro de la Cruz. *Servicio 104: 1256.*

XVIII

A Potential Giant: The Santa River

THE SANTA is Nature's big tragedy on the Coast of Peru. It is by far the largest coastal river, but only a very small portion of its water has ever been used to irrigate the land, owing to the narrowness of the valley, which is hemmed in by the Andean foothills that extend almost down to the sea. Thus it was in ancient times, and thus it is today.

These topographical limitations were overcome by the ancient Indians to the fullest extent possible at their level of technological-social development. On the north bank, canals carried the water around the foothills of the Andes near the sea and distributed it as far north as possible on to the *pampa*, outside the valley proper. On the south bank, the water was carried over the low ridge, Cambio Puente, by a very long canal that continued for many miles in a southerly direction over the immense wind-swept *pampa*, stretching between the Santa and the Nepeña. These two canal systems increased the area of cultivation of the Santa Valley and helped to make it in ancient times the largest cultivated unit between the Moche Valley to the north and the Pativilca system to the south. But, despite their most intensive efforts, the ancient Indians could never utilize more than a mere fraction of the water of the Santa.

Today, ironically, even less land is cultivated than formerly. Indeed, the Santa is used to irrigate only slightly more land than the Nepeña, south of it, even though the Santa contains about *sixty times as much water!* Old canals lie disrupted, old fields abandoned. Why? Conflicting property and water rights, as well as lack of capital, provide the answer!

But the real problem is not restoration of the limited cultivated areas of the past; it is rather the utilization of the complete water potentialities of the Santa! Modern engineering techniques can readily overcome the natural handicaps and use *all* the water in the Santa to produce a continuous irrigated area from the Chicama in the north to the Nepeña Valley in the south. Such a unit, comprising six valleys, would rival and even surpass the ancient five-valley Lambayeque-Jequetepeque Complex! The late Ingeniero Carlos Sutton actually worked out in detail a project of this type. He proposed to cut an irrigation tunnel through the hills on the north bank of the Santa, in order to carry water by canals and river underpasses to the dry areas of the valleys of Chao, Virú, Moche and even Chicama, thereby putting 75,000 additional acres under cultivation and improving another 150,000 acres! He proposed that the newly irrigated land be sold in small plots to prospective small farmers. But a lack of funds has caused the project to remain in the drawing board stage. Opposition from large *hacendados* to some of the social implications involved in Señor Sutton's plans has also arisen.

The valley today contains only one small village, also named Santa, possibly a continuation of an old Indian settlement. The village lies near the sea, just east of the Pan American Highway. Two other population centers are the large Hacienda Tambo Real (Royal Road Station) and the smaller Hacienda Santa Clara. Both *haciendas* furnished us with transportation and guides.

The main center for the valley, however, is the port of Chimbote just south of the valley proper. This town lies on a partially enclosed bay and possesses one of the best natural harbors found along the whole Coast of

Fig. 1. Mochica *huaco*, probably representing a llama and rider crossing a river. To lighten the weight the rider lies on a bag of inflated skins. The use of this method of crossing the Santa River has been described by Spanish Chroniclers. *AMNH* • Fig. 2 (margin). Mochica animal *huaco. Chiclín-Kosok.*

Peru. It was at this town of Chimbote that we made our headquarters in 1948-49. There are several passable hotels besides the excellent Hotel Chimú owned by the Peruvian Government. The town also has some Chinese restaurants which serve delicious meals.

For the ancient Indians, the significance of the Chimbote region probably lay in the fact that it was — as it still is — a fishing center of some importance. Ruins of a large number of irrigation canals, pyramids, and other sites in the vicinity would indicate that, even in ancient times, an important population center had existed here.

Just south of Chimbote lies a fairly large group of apparently small regular-shaped mounds covered with green shrubs. Dr. Schaedel suggested that the mounds may have constituted the ancient Chimbote. We spent an afternoon examining this windswept region by the sea, but failed to locate any artificial structures. The mounds and their regular forms seem to have been produced by the action of the rather strong ocean wind, which blows continually over the loose soil. But our conclusions do not obviate the possibility that excavations here may yield positive results.

In 1941 while following one of the long branches of the main southern canal, we had encountered several interesting adobe pyramids on the hills just east of Chimbote. During our 1948 trip, Señores Garrido and Rodríguez SuySuy, who accompanied us, made a more detailed survey of these interesting pyramids. A surface potsherd collection indicates that they had been occupied during the Mochica period. Until recently they were relatively unscathed, protected by high-piled sand. In recent years, the boom-town enterprises of Chimbote claimed them, and several are in the process of being dismantled. It is a shame that these pyramids, which have survived relatively undamaged for a thousand years or more, should face such a fate!

North of Chimbote and just west of the Pan American Highway, one is greeted by a peculiar archaeological landmark. It is a large cat-demon head made of rocks embedded in the side of an isolated hill. The site is near the end of a series of long canals, which can be seen winding around the hills that encircle the plains of Chimbote. Most likely, this cat-demon head was used in a ceremonial cult of the ancients. Although the cat-demon is a common figure in Peru, the particular form found near Chimbote is unique.

The valley of the Santa itself contains an unusual number of ruins. Yet this is not surprising if we consider the

Fig. 3. This view shows clearly the coastal hills extending directly into the Pacific Ocean. In the foreground can be seen a small part of the lower Santa Valley, crossed by the Pan American Highway. In the background are the town and bay of Chimbote. *Servicio 0: 1168* • Fig. 4. Fish designs from Mochica *huacos*. Note the remarkable attention paid to specific characteristics. *Larco Hoyle.*

188

nature of the valley. Since the river always had an over-abundance of water available throughout the year, it permitted a maximum annual harvest — possibly even a second crop. This situation encouraged a maximum population on the limited amount of land, which in turn made necessary the cultivation of every bit of land in the limited terrain. As a result, many population sites and ceremonial centers were apparently pushed into the adjoining desert *quebradas* and hills situated at a level above the highest irrigation canals. Since, in modern times, cultivation has not been extended to these *quebradas* and hills, the ruins of these sites continue to litter both sides of the valley. Each hilly outcropping within the irrigated plain is likewise covered with ruins of some type. In all, we were able to locate and map about forty sites.

Although a few of the sites were mentioned by Middendorf more than fifty years ago, practically none has been studied by modern archaeologists. In 1947, however, Dr. James Ford made surface ceramic collections from numerous sites and burial grounds. Unfortunately, he has not yet published the results of his findings.

When we studied the aerial photographs of this valley, we discovered that we had succeeded, by means of our ground surveys of 1940-41, in mapping most of the important canals and archaeological sites. However, the aerial photographs did show some additional ruins, which we had missed. These included a number of fort-like sites with accompanying structures on the top or the sides of the hills that bordered the valley from Hacienda Tanguche to Hacienda Tablones. The existence of a series of secondary canals in this region was also definitely established by means of aerial photographs.

In this volume we do not have the space to describe the many interesting sites we found in the Santa Valley. However, we reproduce photographs of some of the typical sites of the valley in this chapter. But it may not be amiss

to draw attention to the ruins of Alto Peru and nearby Cantagallo, which we visited in the company of Señores José Garrido and Rodríguez SuySuy, who later presented a report of their findings to the Institute at Trujillo. Alto Peru consists of a series of partly destroyed small pyramids and walled structures built on a slight elevation of ground in the central part of the valley. Señor Rodríguez SuySuy made a ground plan of one of the better preserved groups. We also collected some potsherds; a few examples are reproduced here (Figs. 13 and 13a).

High walls apparently connected this site with nearby Cantagallo (The Cock Crows), which is likewise built upon a natural elevation and is comprised of a series of walled adobe enclosures with a pyramid-like adobe structure at the summit. The site is known also as Huaca Panteón, since a present day cemetery has been built into part of the adobe structure. At the bottom, Middendorf (1894:329) found a rectangular structure with 54 pillars of adobe on each side, each pillar about two and a half meters from the other! And pillars are rare on the Coast.

We had hoped to obtain more information about the famous Santa wall found by Shippee and Johnson during one of their many flights. They had assumed that it continued along or near the crest of the hills east of the Santa Valley as far as the upper Sierras. In 1934 C. v. S. Roosevelt followed it for a short distance on foot. In studying the Servicio photographs, we found that they covered only the lower part of the valley, where sections of the wall could be seen. United States Army photographs include the whole area covered by the Shippee-Johnson Expedition, but since they were taken at great heights, only sections of the wall could be discerned, and these were in the lower valley. Because of these results and because the Shippee-Johnson Expedition was not able

to follow the wall continuously — cloud formations interfered — we suspected that this supposedly long and continuous wall might consist of *a series of disconnected local walls.* The lower section, from which the irrigated areas of the Santa Valley could be defended, would be the most important part, and it is the section which Roosevelt examined. We questioned people throughout the valley, but no one seemed to know much about the wall. The only way to establish the nature and terminus of the wall

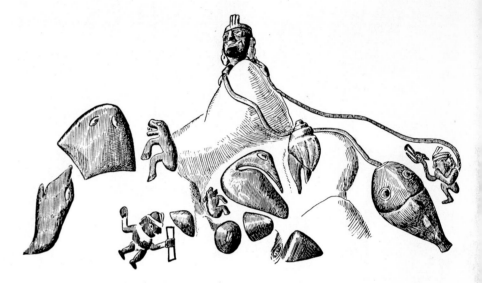

would be to fly over it on a cloudless day and then follow this by a field trip on muleback. We had neither the facilities nor the time to do either and therefore had to content ourselves with speculations.

The wall was probably built as protection against raids or invasions from the *north* by the Chimús or possibly even the Mochicas. We also wondered whether the wall played a role in the gallant defense against the Inca by the Chimús and their Santa allies so eloquently described by Garcilaso. This heroic stand of the Santa peoples is

Fig. 5. An unusual, wind-blown sand dune on the desert coastal plains north of the Santa Valley. The huge size of the dune becomes apparent when we realize that the thin, vertical lines in front of it are telephone poles. *Kosok* • Fig. 6 (above). Drawings of an aquatic scene on a Mochica *huaco*. *Baessler* • Figs. 6a to 6c (margin). High quality Mochica animal *huacos*. Animals and plants were favorite subjects of Mochica artists. *Chiclín-Kosok.*

Fig. 7. The extensive ruins of Buena Vista, on the south side of the middle Santa Valley, have not been studied archaeologically. Defensive needs as well as population pressure made necessary the building of extensive habitation terraces. The main center of the community was at the base of the hill, below which ran an ancient canal. While riding and climbing over the site, we noticed that it was still fairly well preserved. *Shippee-Johnson.*

Fig. 8 (below). View of the main northern Santa canal as it winds along the hills of the coastal *pampa*, north of the Santa Valley. *Kosok* • Fig. 9 (left margin). Two Mochica *huacos,* one showing a corn god, the other showing a victim awaiting sentence by a judge or priest. *Baessler* • Fig. 10 (lower right, pp. 190 and 191). Details from a *huaco* of an ancient fishing scene showing, right, a special ceremonial reed *caballito* (see Chapter IX). *Baessler.*

also mentioned by Cieza (I: Chap. LXX). The latter incidentally refers to the almost depopulated condition of the Santa Valley and the ruined sites on the sides of the hills. Cieza mentions this depopulation in numerous other valleys. Was this the result only of the Spanish conquest, or did the previous Inca conquest initiate this decline?

In addition to mapping sites, we used our aerial photographs and field trips to extend our knowledge of the main ancient canal systems. In 1941, we had traced and mapped the two principal canals already mentioned above. The large canal on the northern bank, which runs through the important Santa Clara ruins (Fig. 11), was traced in 1941, as far as the narrow coastal plain, where it continued in a northerly direction (Fig. 8) as far as the small modern salt works, Guadalupito, near the end of the great Santa Wall. Here the canal seemed to disappear. On our recent trip, we revisited Guadalupito to look for a possible continuation of the canal further north.

After reaching these salt works, we were fortunate in meeting the intelligent and well-informed manager of this enterprise. He showed us what appeared to be ruins of a very small settlement hidden behind an adjacent hillock, where remains of underground rooms were found. Both the site and the position of the rooms may have been chosen to avoid the powerful coastal winds that blow over this desolate region every afternoon. Unfortunately, the salty nature of the soil had so destroyed the potsherds that cultural identification was impossible.

The manager informed us that the main canal did continue in a northerly direction along the side of the nearby hills. He claimed to have seen traces of it where it crossed the Pan American Highway at some distance to the north. We found the canal and followed it for several miles; then it seemed to disappear in the desert. We cruised around for several hours in our jeep, but we could not pick up any further traces of the canal.

On another trip, we tried to obtain additional data

about canals and ruins on the *central northern* bank, in the region of Tanguche. The only way we could approach this area was by means of a primitive road that left the Pan American Highway just south of the Chao Valley. This road, which led into the Río Seco (Dry River), took us through one of the most desolate regions of the whole Coast.

We arrived at Hacienda Tanguche fairly early in the morning. There the very hospitable daughter of the owner of this isolated estate prepared an excellent breakfast, which included a bottle of wine and half a dozen bottles of ice-cold Coca-Cola that were proudly produced from a modern, recently acquired electric refrigerator. Our hostess called in the well-informed manager of the estate, who possessed a small collection of water jugs he had found — mostly Mochica style. He went over our map,

Fig. 11 (below). Ruins of Santa Clara, Santa Valley. This photograph, taken by the author from a Faucett plane in 1941, shows the largest ruin on the north bank of the Santa River. Mr. Verne Grant and the author visited the site in 1941 and followed the large wall, upper part of photograph, to its end on top of a nearby mountain. To the right of the central hill, partly covered by habitation terraces, are two smaller hills. Actually, they are pyramids built of stone and rubble. A long walled corridor may be seen leading from the pyramid on the left to the smaller pyramid. Small house foundations are densely clustered at the base of the central hill in the foreground. A complicated network of long walls and canals crosses behind the two pyramids. *Kosok* • Fig. 12 (right). The author riding up the bleak desert *quebrada* above the ruins of Santa Clara in search of part of the main wall that runs to the north of these ruins (see Fig. 11). *Rosas.*

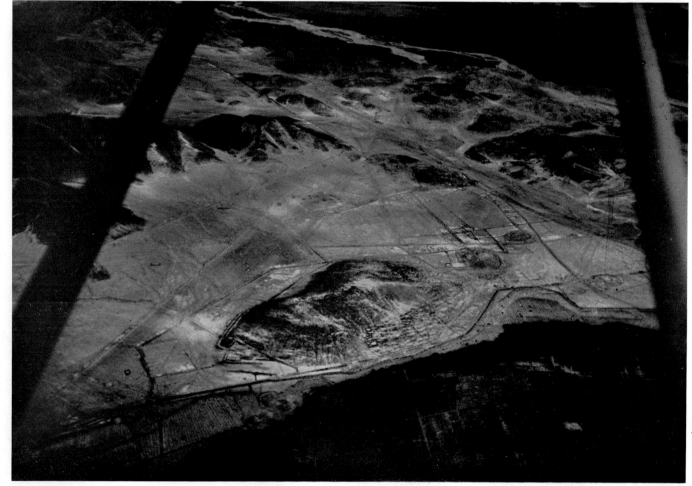

carefully explaining details of the canals and ruins of this entire region. Finally, he joined us in our jeep and we visited some of these sites, which we then entered on our map. Unfortunately, the road farther up the valley was flooded, preventing field survey of that region. Nevertheless, we were able to confirm, through conversations with the administrator, what our aerial photographs had indicated: the existence of a sequence of relatively smaller ancient canals and related ruins in this part of the valley.

The manager suggested that we return to the Pan American Highway by way of the Quebrada Palo Redondo (Round Stick). This "short cut" went through even more desolate regions than those we had passed in the Río Seco area. In some cases, the road was almost non-existent, and only after cruising for many hours through this no-man's

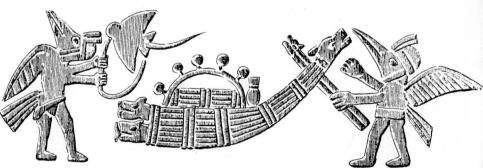

191

Fig. 13. The ruins of Alto Peru. Each unit contains a few rooms with adjoining courtyards and the site is probably an elaborate component of a more extensive settlement. The walls to the left lead to the nearby ruins of Cantagallo • Fig. 13a. Potsherds from Alto Peru. *Rodríguez SuySuy* • Fig. 14 (below). Drawing of a *huaco* showing the decapitated victim after the sacrifice. *Baessler.*

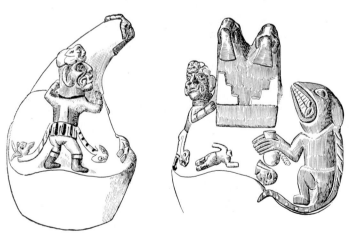

192

land did we finally reach the Pan American Highway again. Luckily, the jeep broke down only once!

On the larger, *upper southern* side of the valley, we determined that the remains of the ancient irrigation system running from Vinzos to Hacienda Tablones, the upper limit of cultivation in the valley, did not consist of just one long canal, as most people of the neighborhood had told us. On the contrary, it "resolved itself" into a number of independent shorter canals, each cultivating a limited area. The "breaking up" of a so-called "very long" canal into a series of shorter ones was observed in a number of other valleys.

The main canal on the southern side, starting below Vinzos, required little new field work. We had followed it in 1941 as far as Cambio Puente, up to which point it is still in use. From there, we had traced it for many miles into the extensive windswept desert plains between the Santa and Nepeña Valleys to a point about two-thirds of the distance to the latter valley and just east of the Pan American Highway. Near this place we had also found a short stretch of a walled road, which did not seem to relate to the sections of the main ancient road located in the Santa and Nepeña Valleys.

On our present trip, we returned to this place hoping

Fig. 15. An oblique aerial view of an important section of the unexplored maze of ruins that stretches along the south bank of the Santa River. This is probably the most extensive site on this bank of the river. Compare with the vertical aerial photograph, Fig. 16. The (A), (B) and (C) in both photographs will serve as guides. *Shippee-Johnson.*

that we might find further extensions of the canal. But we had practically no success, for all traces of the canal soon disappeared in a rocky *pampa*. Though disappointed, we concluded that, in view of the nature of the terrain, the canal could not have gone much further.

Furthermore, we established the fact that the level of the terrain between the "end" of the canal and the nearby Nepeña Valley, which is only some five to six miles distant, is too high to have permitted the canal to have been continued by the Indians into the latter valley. Thus it had been impossible to construct a bi-valley irrigation unit of the Santa and Nepeña Valleys. With modern en-

gineering methods, however, the problem of bringing water to the Nepeña Valley can easily be solved.

We have only two references concerning the relationship of the Santa Valley to the Chimú Empire. The Anonymous Trujillano informs us that the third Chimú ruler (according to our chart, shortly after 1300 A.D.) conquered the valleys as far south as the Santa. This would mean that the Chimú rule here had lasted more than 150 years! We can assume that the Chimús must have had a firm foothold here and a strong alliance with the local Santa rulers in order to have staged a conquest of the valleys to the south. For it would have been impossible

Fig. 17. Two parallel contour canals, above Vinzos, built of adobe and "cemented" against the sides of the hills. *Kosok.*

Fig. 16. A more extensive vertical aerial photograph of the site shown in Fig. 15. At the right, in the photograph, may be seen what appears to be a hillside site surrounded by many habitation terraces. Note the numerous defensive walls that run over hills and across *quebradas*. At the left are the remains of an ancient irrigation system that once brought water to this region. These are possibly the ruins mentioned by Squier. Apparently he did what other investigators, including ourselves, have since done; being overwhelmed by the amount of remains, he decided to leave their study to other scientists. *Servicio 172:33.*

for the Chimús to have maintained a foothold in the Pativilca Complex without safeguarding their very narrow "lifeline" by means of a secure control of the strongest intermediate point, the Santa! That they had succeeded in forming such an alliance is indicated by Garcilaso's account of the bravery with which the Santa allies fought alongside the Chimús against the Incas.

Considerable amounts of Early Chimú (Mochica) ceramics have been found in the Santa Valley, indicating strong and extensive domination by the Mochica culture coming from the Moche-Chicama area further north. What went on in the Middle Period is not clear. Likewise, the existence of a Very Early Coastal Chavín Period has not been clearly established. Again, an intriguing valley without archaeological excavations and archival research!

Fig. 18 (margin). Sleeping man. Mochica style *huaco* from Tanguche Hacienda. *Kosok-Rein* • Fig. 19 (upper right). An interesting, but archaeologically unknown, site on the north bank of the Santa River, south of Tanguche and opposite Vinzos. The ruin is centered about two main groups, each with a sunken plaza. Around them are what appear to be the remains of stone houses. The hillsides have been made habitable by the construction of numerous terraces. *Servicio 172: 211* • Fig. 20 (lower right). An oblique aerial photograph of a portion of the ruin shown in the vertical photograph, Fig. 19. The advantage of having both vertical and oblique photographs is clearly demonstrated here. In the vertical view the ground plan becomes clear at once, while in the horizontal view the three-dimensional relations of the different parts of the ruins are dramatically presented. *Shippee-Johnson.*

194

XIX

Through Canyons and Fields in the Upper Santa

WHEN WORKING in the coastal section of the Santa Valley, one hardly suspects that the larger Sierra section of this valley encompasses some of the most spectacular mountain scenery in the world. Few people visit this region for its beauty, even though it can be reached easily by highway and partly by railroad. Another hidden treasure of Peru!

In this region, the Santa River has created a long, relatively narrow valley basin, the so-called Callejón de Huaylas, running from south to north and dropping from 12,000 to 6000 feet in elevation. It is surrounded on both sides by high mountain ranges, of which the eastern, the Cordillera Blanca, is covered with perpetual snow and ice. This range contains the highest mountain of Peru, the Huascarán, which towers to a height of more than 22,000 feet. At the northern end of the Callejón, the Santa River breaks through towering mountain masses, creating spectacular chasms in its ceaseless rush to the Coast.

We hoped to take a Christmas holiday in the Callejón, but Christmas Eve found Michael sick in the hospital at Chimbote. However, the fine treatment he received in that modern institution made it possible for us to leave by New Year's Eve. We left early in the morning on a quaint and crowded little train. As the train chugged slowly up the valley it passed near a series of ruins on the edge of the cultivated areas. Its slow pace and frequent stops made it possible for us to check some of the notes we had made during our previous trips up the valley by jeep and truck. The train route, incidentally, is the one that Middendorf described some fifty years ago.

At Hacienda Tablones, some thirty-five miles up the valley from Chimbote, the cultivated zone ends. Here

Fig. 1. A view of the upper middle section of the coastal zone of the Santa River. The Sierras are in the far background. At the lower center is a part of the famous Santa Wall, which — like the Great Wall of China — runs over hills and valleys. *Shippee-Johnson* • NOTE: Drawing at upper left is a Chavín stone head. *John Wise.*

At Chuquicara, almost fifteen miles up the canyon from Tablones, there is a slight pocket where the Chuquicara (Tablachaca) River enters the Santa. This branch and its tributaries reach as far north as Santiago de Chuco and Cachicadán, described in Chapter X, and thus act as an important link between this region and the Callejón. Chuquicara is also a railroad junction point, for a spur of the main line runs up part of the Chuquicara Valley. As we stood in the streets of this town and looked up the steep semi-arid mountainsides to the south, we could distinguish small objects moving slowly down the narrow, dizzy mountain path. As we watched intently, we discovered that they were pack mules carrying goods to our junction point. During the short stop here, we bought a box of the grapes that were being shipped in large quantities both to the Sierras and to the Coast. The grapes looked and tasted so delicious that we ate them without observing our standard rule of not eating unwashed fruit.

The train slowly continued its dramatic journey up the

Fig. 2 (margin). Recuay style *huacos* from the Callejón de Huaylas. *Bennett (Handbook, II)* • Fig. 3 (lower left). Part of an automobile road that winds in a series of hairpin turns up the mountainside. *Kosok* • Fig. 4 (below). Gold figurine from Chavín de Huantar. *John Wise* • Fig. 5 (above, left). Looking into the narrow Cañón del Pato, with its precipitous walls rising above the foaming Santa River. Note the automobile road at the left. *Servicio 0:8580* • Fig. 6 (above, right). Bus stop in a mountain town. *Kosok* • Fig. 7 (p. 197). A view across the Cañón showing houses of engineers and workers who were building a hydroelectric plant in the area. *Kosok.*

the train entered the long, narrow and precipitous gorge of the Santa, which continues, almost without interruption, as far as the relatively wider Callejón de Huaylas. The valley floor itself is so narrow that in some places the bed of the railroad had to be cut directly into the rocky walls of the chasm before the tracks could be laid.

narrow gorge, providing an ever-changing vista of overhanging cliffs; then suddenly the train came to a dead stop. We wondered why, for we could see no settlement. The conductor finally came along to inform us that the train could go no further because the large bridge that had to be crossed was being repaired and could not support the weight of the train. So we took our suitcases and, together with the other passengers, walked across the bridge. A fleet of trucks was waiting on the other side to take us to Huallanca, the terminus of the railroad.

At Huallanca, a typical small mountain town, we and some of our fellow travelers soon found a restaurant. Here we ordered double portions of *churrasco con arroz* (beefsteak with rice), a common dish, which always tasted good to us. Our appetites satisfied, we wandered through the streets looking at the displays of merchandise in the various shops. In one of these shops, we bought some dried coca leaves, the source of the drug cocaine. The Indians chew these leaves continually, since the bodily numbness produced by the drug counteracts the fatigue caused by working and climbing in high mountain altitudes. To extract the cocaine completely, the Indians add small bits of lime as they chew the leaves. The use of these leaves dates back to very early times; indeed, the Inca rulers tried to establish a monopoly in them. We chewed our leaves here as we had done in other

Sierra places. The numbness, which is created first in the mouth and then to a lesser extent in the body, gives one a feeling of relaxation and creates a rather pleasant mood. Since there is no narcotics squad in Peru, the leaves are sold everywhere and are very cheap. A handful could be bought for the equivalent of about one cent in American money! Nonetheless, we did not become addicts.

At Huallanca, numerous trucks were standing ready to take passengers and goods to various parts of the still higher Callejón de Huaylas. After hunting and bargaining, we found an open truck which would take us to our destination, the town of Carás in the lower part of the Callejón. Two of the passengers were fortunate enough to obtain the two seats next to the driver; the rest of us had to sit on top of the accumulated baggage and freight that filled the greater part of the open truck. While this method of traveling transmits all the bumps in the road to the passengers, it nevertheless has one definite advantage; it affords a continuous, comprehensive and unobstructed view of the beautiful and ever-changing mountain landscape.

Leaving the town, the loaded truck began to crawl up the ascending road with its innumerable sharp, hairpin turns cut into the steep sides of the mountains. While the landscape was becoming increasingly impressive we, in turn, were becoming increasingly dizzy as the truck went higher and higher along the narrow road that nowhere had any guard rails. Indeed, guard rails are unknown in the Sierras!

When the road leveled off somewhat, we entered the so-called Cañón del Pato (Duck Canyon). The rocky walls here rise precipitously above both sides of the Santa, producing the narrowest and steepest canyon of the Andes (Figs. 5 and 7). Some time ago, a roadbed for the railroad had been cut into one side of the sheer walls of the chasm, necessitating the construction of dozens of short tunnels. As a result of a lack of funds, the railroad was never completed and the surfaced roadbed is now used instead by cars and trucks.

We had probably the most thrilling and unusual experience of our entire stay in Peru riding along this road, in and out of tunnels, with the foaming Santa River a few thousand feet below, and the steep cliffs towering far above! While ascending this road, we discovered that cables had been recently strung at a number of places across the deep, narrow canyon. By means of attached pulleys and baskets, supplies and workers were being shipped to the other side of the canyon to be used for the

Fig. 8. A group of Sierra musicians playing some of their native music while riding with us on a truck to Huarás. Today many Serranos wear modern clothes instead of the traditional costumes. *Kosok* • Fig. 9. Snow-covered Huascarán, with temperate and subtropic vegetation in the foreground. *Servicio 0:8556.*

and bracing in contrast to the hot and often dust-laden atmosphere that we had left behind on the Coast.

Evening had already descended when we arrived in Carás, a quaint little Sierra town. Its white houses, with their Spanish red-tiled roofs, which flank the straight but hilly streets, give it an atmosphere quite at variance from the drabness of many coastal towns. The Plaza de Armas in the center of town was especially handsome with its abundance of multicolored flowers and beautiful trees. And everywhere were the stolid but friendly Indians moving along in the pursuit of their daily tasks. Off the main square, we found a small, clean hotel with good food. We lay down on comfortable beds and talked about our wonder-filled trip, a trip that had cost us less than five 'dollars!

Weeks later, after our return to the Coast, we learned that a very dangerous fever, called *verruga*, is prevalent in the Carás region. This mysterious disease exists only in a few valleys on the Coast and only within certain ranges of elevation. Moreover, it seems to strike the victim only when he stays overnight in these areas. Most disconcerting is the fact that the fever is often fatal.

Having luckily escaped this disease, we took another *camión* (truck) further up the Callejón as far as Huarás, the chief city in the Callejón and the capital of the Department of Ancash. Among the passengers was a group of Indian musicians (Fig. 8) who entertained us the first part of the way with a repertoire of Andean songs and dances. But during the early afternoon rain set in and we put on our Indian ponchos. Since the rain kept up, we were forced to squat under the huge tarpaulin which the driver finally pulled over the top of the truck. Thus we rode for hours in the semi-dark enclosure, occasion-

Fig. 10. A small section of the Callejón de Huaylas showing the town of Carás with its surrounding fields. The winding bed of the Santa River and the road that leads to other towns in the Callejón are clearly visible. *Servicio 0: 1952* • Fig. 11 (margins). Sculptured stone heads from the Callejón de Huaylas. *Tello* • Fig. 12 (right). The main plaza in Carás. *Kosok.*

construction of a number of hydroelectric plants that were to furnish electricity to a considerable part of the Santa Valley. One of these places remained particularly memorable to us. While holding tight to the sides of our truck to overcome our own dizziness, we saw a lone worker sitting on a single plank attached to a pulley, his legs dangling in mid-air as he was being pulled across the abyss by a rope! Our fellow passengers — mostly Indians — seemed, however, unimpressed.

As we left the Cañón del Pato, the valley widened and the truck entered a refreshing countryside of grass, cactus plants and trees. The mountain air felt wonderfully cool ally peeking out at the rain-soaked and dismal landscape.

The Callejón, as already pointed out, is flanked on the east by the extensive and majestic ranges of snow- and ice-capped mountains, called the Cordillera Blanca (White Range), containing the highest mountain of Peru, the Huascarán. It has been scaled only once. During our 1941 tour, we made a three-day horseback trip around the base of this huge massif, during which we encountered the most glorious scenery we had seen in all of South America, with vegetation ranging from subtropic to arctic (Figs. 13 and 16).

The mountains on the western side of the upper Santa are considerably lower and since they are not covered by ice and snow are called the Cordillera Negra (Black Range). The western sides of the latter Cordillera furnish the rather limited headwaters of the small coastal rivers of the Nepeña, Casma, Culebra and Huarmey (see Chapters XX and XXI). It is very probable that these valleys were originally populated by peoples from the Callejón who entered them by crossing the passes of the Cordillera. In fact, the late Dr. Julio Tello was able to find, in the lower coastal section of the Nepeña and Casma Valleys, extensive ruins which he could definitely relate to the very early site of Chavín de Huantar just

across the eastern divide of the Callejón de Huaylas.

The bottom and lower sides of the Callejón contain a sufficient amount of cultivated land to support a moderate-sized population. Apparently, there is sufficient rainfall to permit agriculture without irrigation. Nevertheless, irrigation canals exist to supplement the rainfall by bringing water to the land during the dry season.

The upper, southern part of the Callejón has the characteristics of the treeless *puna* of the southern *altiplano* of Peru. Since this area is above the maize line, the main crops are similar to those of the *puna*. In ancient times, llamas grazed here; today they have disappeared.

Fig. 13. The mighty Huascarán, the loftiest peak in the Peruvian Andes, as viewed before sunset from a pass more than 17,000 feet in height. The peak itself reaches an altitude of more than 22,000 feet. *Kosok.*

Fig. 17 (above). At the foot of the Huascarán. Primitive methods for extracting the syrup from sugar cane. *Kosok* • Fig. 18 (below). Subtropic landscape amongst snow-capped mountains. *Kosok*.

Fig. 14 (margin). Recuay style stone statues of the Early Period. *Bennett and Bird* • Fig. 15 (far left). At the base of the Huascarán. *Kosok* • Fig. 16 (left). On our trip around the Huascarán we had to proceed through a pass more than 17,000 feet high. The horses and the guide can be seen on the path, which is cut into the rock. The outlines of the Huascarán can be seen faintly in the background. *Kosok*.

Huarás, the geographic, economic and administrative center of the Callejón, is a larger but less attractive town than Carás. Since our stopover there in 1941 a tragedy had befallen the town. A glacial lake had overflowed suddenly, causing a huge flood, which rushed down the mountainside and destroyed part of the town, killing many of its inhabitants.

We arrived toward evening in a drizzling rain and, after having eaten a hot meal, looked for a "movie". We wandered around for a while, finally yielding ourselves to *Tarzan,* in which Johnny Weissmuller and his fellow actors babbled their nonsense in Spanish to a partly amused and partly bored audience.

The town possesses a local museum, which houses a representative archaeological collection. The museum is under the able direction of Dr. Augusto Soriano Infante, who, for many years, has made trips all over the Callejón, often on foot, collecting valuable material (Fig. 23). Unfortunately, little of his work has been published. In 1941 Dr. Soriano Infante had shown us his unusual collection and had also taken us on an interesting field trip. Professor Wendell Bennett has also conducted pioneer excavations in this region, the results of which were published in 1944.

The ancient peoples of the Callejón had produced a type of realistic ceramics, which, though rather crude, is quite distinctive and easily recognizable (Figs. 2 and 19). Dr. Schaedel's characterization of it as "Mickey Mouse" ceramics is rather appropriate. Thanks to Professor Bennett's investigations, a continuous culture sequence has been established for the earliest times up to the so-called Middle Period (Tiahuanacoid). However, what little is known of the Late Period, which corresponds in time to the Late Chimú-Inca Period on the Coast, and the Inca in the Sierras, is insufficient to give an idea of settlement size and distribution of population centers. We were, ourselves, unable to find anything to indicate whether a unified political federation had once existed throughout the length of the valley or whether local tribal rule predominated until the conquest by the Incas. The local archives are most likely to yield some information on this and related matters. Just recently, Dr. Augusto Soriano Infante discovered in an archive a list of names of local rulers of the Inca Period.

We returned to the Coast by means of a road that led over the Cordillera Negra down the Casma Valley. This "short cut" to the Coast is about sixty miles long, but because of the mountainous terrain through which the road passes, almost a whole day is required for the trip! It was Sunday when we decided to go. The regular trucks were not operating and the only transportation we could find was a dilapidated old truck. Contrary to our better judgment, we took passage on this vehicle and, to our grief, about every half hour we had to stop because the motor, the brakes, or the clutch refused to function.

Our chauffeur, a cheerful soul, insisted that only its four wheels and "faith" kept the truck running!

The long, serpentine road up to the crest of the Cordillera Negra affords a series of increasingly comprehensive and inspiring views of the vast, snow- and ice-covered Cordillera Blanca on the opposite side of the valley. Indeed it is impossible to go anywhere in the Callejón without being surrounded by the majesty and beauty of the landscape. It compares favorably with the finest in the world. But it is practically unknown to tourists, even though there is a direct bus from Lima that takes only one day!

Fig. 19 (top, left). Recuay style pottery of soldier with llama. *AMNH* • Fig. 20 (top, right). Gold plaque of a highly stylized god head expressing terror and vengeance, typical of the Very Early, priest-dominated Chavín de Huantar culture. The rectangular plaque (below) is of the same character and period • Fig. 21 (above, left). Stone wall of part of an ancient site, showing construction details. *Kosok* • Fig. 22 (above, right). Ancient stone carvings from Aija of once venerated gods or rulers, now degraded into fence posts! *Soriano Infante* • Fig. 23 (below, left). Part of a huge ancient stone wall. At the base of the wall is Padre Soriano Infante, Director of the Huarás Archaeological Museum. *Kosok.*

The ride down the Casma Valley was a fitting end to our exciting trip. In many places, the dirt road is so narrow that, when two vehicles try to pass each other, one of them must back up to a slightly wider spot to enable the other to squeeze by. The real thrill in this procedure comes from the fact that, in many cases, the road is cut into the side of the mountain and, at times, hangs several thousand feet above the floor of the valley! To make matters more dangerous for us, a slight but steady

drizzle set in, with the result that the narrow, tortuous road soon became slippery! Naturally, there were no guard rails! Add to this the fact that the truck had to stop every so often to have its brakes adjusted or the clutch tightened and it can be easily understood why, to us, this trip was the most nerve-wracking and best-remembered one in Peru.

We still had about three or four hours to drive when darkness came; and it comes rapidly in these latitudes. Since we could see nothing and had no lights to read by, Michael began to recite from memory the names of all the chemical elements in the order of their atomic numbers. Then he decided that his father, a college professor, should know at least as much as his son. So he forced me to participate in this memory drill. By the time the trip ended, we both could recite the table, backwards as well as forwards, and separate the elements by periods and groups!

We reached the coastal town of Casma late that night in a state of complete exhaustion. We went to bed at once at the Hotel Royal, for we were expecting our driver to arrive with the jeep early next morning to take us on a canal-hunting trip to the nearby Nepeña Valley. Before falling asleep, we reviewed the day's experiences, feeling thankful for having survived the hazardous trip, which is just an everyday experience for the people who live in this region.

Fig. 24. Flying over the snow-capped Andes. *U. S. Army 112-R-89.*

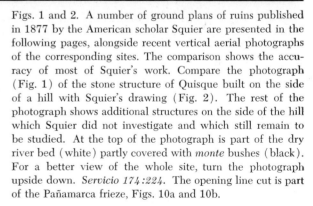

XX

The Nepeña Valley: Southern Limit of Mochica Culture

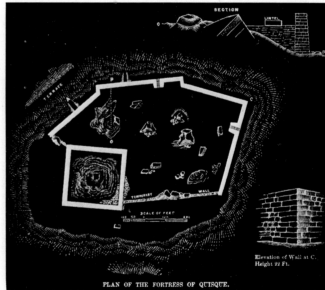

PLAN OF THE FORTRESS OF QUISQUE.

THE NEPEÑA RIVER and the Casma, Culebra, and Huarmey Rivers farther south have a common characteristic: their headwaters are in the rain-scarce Cordillera Negra instead of in the wetter Continental Divide. These rivers, therefore, suffer from annual water shortages. Nevertheless, the small Nepeña insures the cultivation of nearly as much land as the large Santa because almost every drop of its water is utilized.

A large part of this long narrow valley, which lacks a fan-shaped coastal plain, is controlled by the sugar-growing Hacienda San Jacinto, which is owned and operated by English interests. The port of Samanco, the village of Huambacho in the lower, the town of Nepeña in the middle, as well as Moro and Quimbe in the upper, pocket section of the valley, are the only communities of ancient times that have survived to the present day.

While working in this valley, we were able to establish our headquarters at San Jacinto Hacienda as we had done in 1940-41. At that time we made several trips through the valley, and a former assistant of mine, Mr. Verne Grant, proved of great help. On our first trip into the valley in 1949, we were startled by peculiar rumblings all around us; but we were too tired to be concerned. When we reached the *hacienda* buildings everyone was talking excitedly. And no wonder! The rumblings we had heard had come from a slight earthquake tremor felt throughout the whole valley.

At the *hacienda*, we were cordially received by the new administrator, Mr. MacMillan, who put his house at our disposal. When we reached our quarters we were greatly delighted to discover a huge English bathtub full of hot water — the first hot bath we had encountered

Figs. 1 and 2. A number of ground plans of ruins published in 1877 by the American scholar Squier are presented in the following pages, alongside recent vertical aerial photographs of the corresponding sites. The comparison shows the accuracy of most of Squier's work. Compare the photograph (Fig. 1) of the stone structure of Quisque built on the side of a hill with Squier's drawing (Fig. 2). The rest of the photograph shows additional structures on the side of the hill which Squier did not investigate and which still remain to be studied. At the top of the photograph is part of the dry river bed (white) partly covered with *monte* bushes (black). For a better view of the whole site, turn the photograph upside down. *Servicio 174:224.* The opening line cut is part of the Pañamarca frieze, Figs. 10a and 10b.

203

Fig. 3. This rectangular stone structure is the (B) in Fig. 6. The round crater-like structure inside the lower part of the compound appears to be an excavated small pyramid or "palace." *Schaedel.*

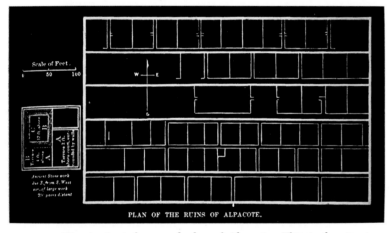

PLAN OF THE RUINS OF ALPACOTE.

Fig. 4. Squier's ground plan of Alpacote. This is the structure below (D) in Fig. 6 and shows details not visible in the aerial photograph. Possibly it was a way station for llama trains en route to and from the Sierras. To this day pack trains pass through Alpacote on their way to the Callejón de Huaylas. *Squier.*

Fig. 5 (below). Here we see how river cobblestones and earth were used to build the walls of Alpacote; the (D) in Fig. 6 is the northern boundary of the series of room divisions described and drawn by Squier. The wall is about five feet high. *Schaedel.*

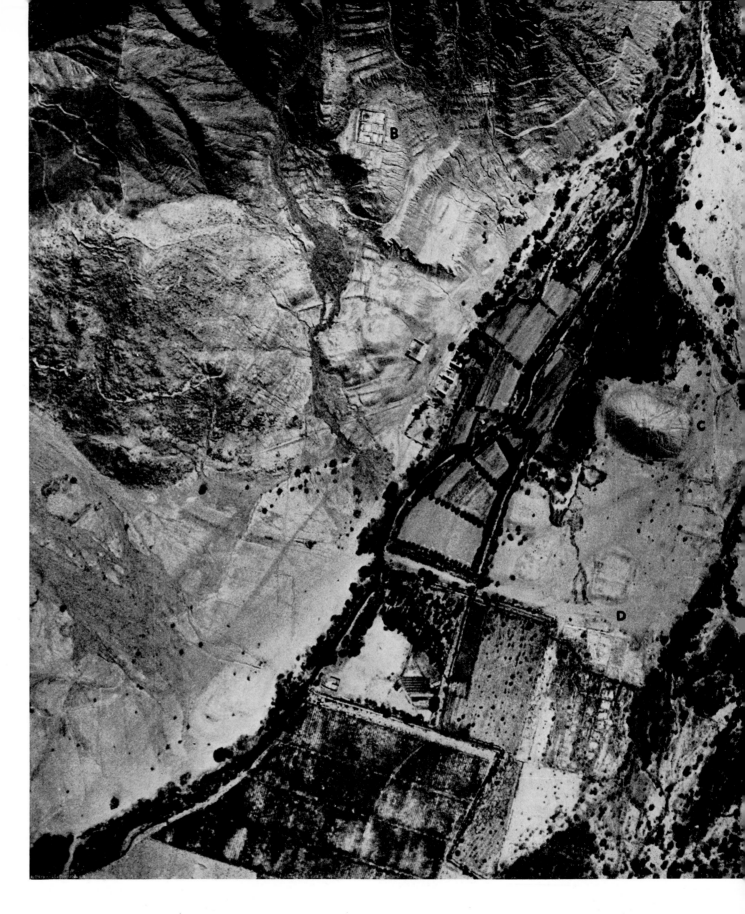

in a long time. The following morning another bath was ready; the same evening, a third. At that point Michael rebelled. "What's the idea, three baths within 24 hours. That's unheard of! I'd rather be a Chimú!" To his dismay, he soon discovered that the Chimús, like other peoples, had their *baños*.

In the course of the dinner conversation we were pleased to learn that, although Mr. MacMillan had been in charge of this *hacienda* for less than a year, he was well acquainted with most of the ruins of the valley. He was even able to give us information about some sites we had only recently discovered on our aerial photographs.

We started off early the next morning to check the character of some of the ancient canals and sites previously entered on our maps and to locate new ones. By the time our work in the valley was completed we had found some fifty distinct sites. Owing to the nature of the terrain, the location of the canals presented some difficulties. However, once we had located the canals, we realized that in ancient times the amount of irrigated land had not been much greater than at present.

In our survey of the valley we revisited all but one of the ruins described by Ephraim George Squier, the American surveyor, archaeologist, diplomat and traveler, who had visited a large part of Peru and in 1877 had published his findings in a volume entitled *Peru; Incidents of Travel and Exploration in the Land of the Incas.* In this work he gave more attention to the valley of Nepeña than to some of its larger neighbors. To this day, his study is valued for the careful descriptions and accurate ground plans of the ruins. The striking correspondence between Squier's ground plans of these Nepeña ruins and the aerial photographs of them can be seen in plates on the adjoining pages (Figs. 1 to 13). The one basic error in Squier's plans lies in his assumption that adjacent walls of rectangular-like structures were built at perfect right angles to each other. Actually they generally formed slightly oblique angles. This was true even of the large walled compounds of ChanChan.

The sites of which he drew ground plans were those of a part of Pierna Calzón and Alpacote, of Siete Huacas, Huacatambo, El Padrejón and Quisque. We did not visit the fortress of Quisque which is perched on the side of a steep mountain since it had no special significance for our study. Squier also visited Pañamarca, but the structures were too complicated to permit the drawing of a ground plan in the short time he had at his disposal. However he did provide a picture of the site.

The ruins of Pierna Calzón (The Trousered Leg), consist of the extensive remains of an ancient walled settlement on the eastern slopes of the hill Pierna Calzón. The area here is also called "Máquina Vieja," named after an old machine, once located nearby! The site includes a number of terraced earth mounds at the base of the

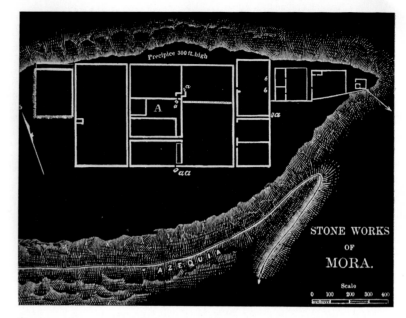

Figs. 8 and 9. A comparison of the vertical aerial photographs of the ruins of Siete Huacas, situated on a small plateau, with Squier's ground plan of the site, which he calls Stone Works of Mora, shows that Squier succeeded in establishing the important features of the structure. His error of failing to realize that the apparent rectangles composing the structure were not true rectangles was made by many other scientists; aerial photography quickly exposed the error. The white line at the top of the photograph is the road from the village of Moro (spelled Mora by Squier). *Servicio 173:393.*

Fig. 6 (left). A vertical aerial photograph of a region studded with numerous ruins, apparently dating from different periods. The most important ones are the extensive hillside structures of Pierna Calzón (Trousered Leg), on the northern side of the Nepeña Valley. Note in Pierna Calzón: the large irrigation canal (A) cutting through the ruin; the rectangular stone compound (B — see also Fig. 3) and the terraced earth and stone habitation platforms above and below the stone compound. At the upper left of the photograph, a series of walls continue for some distance around part of the hill. The dark narrow area cutting diagonally across the photograph represents a stretch of irrigated fields. Below these fields are two small pyramids and a large pyramid (C). Below (D) is the Alpacote of Squier, a rectangular structure with many subdivisions, now partially overgrown with scrub vegetation (see Figs. 4 and 5). *Servicio 173:212* • Fig. 7 (above and below). Potsherds from Pierna Calzón. The color ranges from brown to orange. *Schaedel-Cacho.*

hill, a series of stone-lined terraced mounds further up, and a well-defined rectangular stone edifice with many inter-connecting rooms. The mounds at the base were originally of adobe construction and later were covered with earth. The stone edifices appear to represent a later occupation of the site, although no evidence from potsherds so far confirms this supposition.

At the bottom of the hill, below the terraced earth mounds, is a second unit composed of one rather steep, oval-shaped adobe pyramid, two small rectangular pyramids, and a stone edifice divided into cubicles. This edifice Squier investigated (Fig. 5) and assigned the name of Alpacote to it. Like the upper parts of the ruin, the section at the base presents an archaeological problem since both adobe and stone ruins, of apparently quite

Fig. 10. Mochica polychrome mural painting at Pañamarca. This thirty-foot-long frieze of warriors and priests, lines the inner wall of the central plaza. The small figures are valets or attendants hel[p?] their masters enrobe. The figures with "knee-plates" appear to be warriors; the central figure probably is that of a priest. *Schaedel-Azabache* • Figs. 10a and 10b (margins). Line cuts of parts of another [

distinct traditions, are in juxtaposition (Figs. 3 to 6).

From Pierna Calzón we were able to trace, farther than Squier had done, the large ancient canal which runs through the site. The canal continues north of this ruin, up to the large Quebrada Solivín, east of the buildings of San Jacinto. In this *quebrada* the occasional washes of past centuries destroyed the old canal, but traces of it reappear on the other side of the *quebrada* where it breaks into two branches. One branch continues into the present day cemetery behind the *hacienda* building, while

Figs. 11 and 12. The modern photograph (left) of Pañamarca, the largest and most imposing pyramid site of the Nepeña Valley, was taken by Schaedel from the place where Squier made his drawing (right). For a description and plan of this important Mochica center see *Archaeology,* No. 3, 1951 • Fig. 12a (above). Petroglyphs at Pañamarca, probably from a pre-Mochica period. Redrawn from *Schaedel* • Fig. 13 (p. 207, lower left). In viewing the top part of the main pyramid of Pañamarca from an elevated level to the south of the pyramid, one notices that the core of the structure consists of a rectangular U-shaped ceremonial chamber. This "open" form is characteristic of a number of pyramids that we located in other valleys. *Kosok.*

the other branch ends at the rear of the building itself.

We next paid a visit to Cerro de Siete Huacas (Hill of Seven Mounds). Although the site contains many ruins, we could not establish the reason for the use of the number "seven." To reach this place, which lies farther up the valley, we had to go by way of the town of Moro. This is the center of an agricultural pocket similar to pockets found in Moche, Zaña and Lambayeque. Even today, this pocket has its own local officials including an agent of the Irrigation Department. We soon be-

206

at first meaningless and very time-consuming. But in a pre-industrial society where little happens, any incident is sufficient excuse to "celebrate" and thus escape the boredom of everyday life. Like other foreigners who come to Peru to do a job as rapidly as possible we were at first somewhat disturbed by the amount of time we had to devote to such social activities. But after we had lived among the people long enough to absorb some of their mode of working and living we really welcomed such celebrations, for they enabled us to observe many facets of the Peruvian way of life which are so often lost to the self-centered traveler and scientist.

The following day we went down the valley to check other sites. We revisited Pañamarca, the largest pyramid site in the valley, in which the main pyramid consists of

...olychrome mural painting at Pañamarca. Note in left margin that the plume contains *three* "feathers" growing out of another plume of *thirteen* "feathers," i.e. the same *three-thirteen calendrical* ...ionship mentioned in Chapters VI and XXI. In the figure in the right margin note the *nine* feathers, the *nine* (or *eleven*) toes and the "bulbs" at the top of the head. See Chapter VI. *Schaedel-Azabache.*

came acquainted with these officials as well as the local schoolmaster, a man well-informed on the archaeological sites of this region.

After lunch, four of these gentlemen decided to join our party, thereby turning it, according to local custom, into an "expedition." The officials locked up their respective offices and the schoolmaster locked up his school. All piled into the jeep which, with the chauffeur, Michael and myself, now contained seven persons. Good sturdy old jeep! At our *amigos'* suggestion, we drove over to

Cerro de Siete Huacas which most of them had not seen.

The site is unusual in that it is situated on a small flat plateau rising several hundred feet above the valley. It consists of fairly well preserved ruins of a large stone-walled compound with numerous subdivisions (Figs. 8 and 9). On one side of this compound are many excavations made by *huaqueros,* where we found only crude ware which unfortunately told us nothing of the probable cultural affiliations of the builders. North of this plateau lies another one, likewise covered with ruins. Unfortunately, we were unable to visit them. More important for us was our ability to localize a small but intricate irrigation system which ran alongside of these plateaus and the neighboring hills, and whose existence had been indicated by the aerial photographs.

We then returned to Moro to "celebrate" the results of our "expedition" with some beer. Later, we packed ourselves into the jeep again and went off on a shorter trip, this time to visit Squier's El Padrejón and also to clarify the nature of a number of minor ruins in the neighborhood of Moro which had appeared on the aerial photographs merely as small white spots! Afterwards we again "celebrated" and then returned to the Hacienda San Jacinto for a good supper and yet another "celebration."

To an urbane North American these various "celebrations," in which we participated in many places, may seem

an open U-shaped structure (Figs. 11 to 13). In one of the many adjoining courts we found parts of two polychrome paintings on the walls — one of them covered over by another wall. Mochica type warriors seemed to be represented on one of them. When later on we informed Dr. Schaedel about our find, he investigated the area more thoroughly and uncovered two additional and much larger painted friezes (Figs. 10, 10a, 10b). One of the friezes was the largest and best preserved Mochica wall painting found so far. Dr. Schaedel had these friezes

Fig. 14. The ancient road which we followed from the Nepeña Valley northwards is still used in part today. The horizontal dark line is an ancient wall. Farther in the rear is the Nepeña Valley.

copied, life size and in color, by Señor Azabache, an artist from Moche. These friezes, as well as certain architectural characteristics, identify this as a Mochica site, though there are definite indications of later occupation. What is important is not only the size of the Pañamarca structure but the fact that it appears to have been the *southern outpost of Mochica power or influence!*

We decided to visit another ruin still further down the valley on the north bank of the river. Our attention had been drawn to it by its peculiar appearance on the aerial photograph. It seemed to consist of a large number of white rectangles, of various sizes and shapes, surrounded by walls. It looked like a kind of primitive salt works in

which the white areas were salt! But this was impossible, since there are no known salt deposits in the neighborhood. The ruin, which is called Caylán by the nearby inhabitants, appeared to us at first to be merely the remains of an old "settlement" consisting of innumerable stone walls and containing several small stone pyramids. The walls surrounded enclosures within which we found a whitish soil — the white spots we had seen on the photographs! The ruin was much smaller but similar in certain ways to Pueblo Mojeque in Casma (see Chapter XXI). But there were no streets! Were these enclosures habitation sites, like others we had seen, where the former inhabitants walked along the tops of the walls? Or were

Fig. 15 (upper left). Part of Huaca Cerro Blanco, located in the center of the Nepeña Valley. The colors of the design on the *huaca* are greenish-yellow and brick-red. The excavation of this site was made by Dr. Tello, who found proof of the existence of a Very Early Chavín culture on the Coast. *Tello* • Fig. 16 (above). The ruin of Punkurí Alto, near the Coastal Chavín site, Punkurí Bajo, studied by Tello, is that of a palace-like edifice with many courtyards, rooms and corridors. *Schaedel* • Fig. 17 (left margin, top). Low relief ware, Punkurí Alto; (bottom). Incised ware, Punkurí Alto. *Schaedel* • Fig. 18 (lower center). Excavations made at Punkurí Bajo by Dr. Tello led to the discovery of this jaguar figure, made of hardened clay and covered with paint. The style is characteristic of the Very Early or Coastal Chavín culture. *Tello* • Fig. 19. Mochica designs of birds and snakes. *Larco Hoyle.*

Fig. 20. Some of the stone-lined "basins" of Caylán can be seen in the foreground (see Fig. 21). The hillside terraces, used for dwelling sites, are barely visible on part of Pan de Azucar (upper left of photograph). *Schaedel* • Fig. 21 (p. 209). A dramatic and unsolved riddle of the past! Caylán, on the north side of the Nepeña Valley consists of a complex of stone-lined cubicles (left side of photograph). Possibly they were habitation sites, possibly garden plots. Note several very small stone mounds inside the ruins. The large dark lines crossing the site are stone boundary walls of later origin. To the right is Cerro Pan de Azucar (Sugar Loaf Hill) with its terraces and fortification walls; while the light squares, barely visible to the right of the Cerro, are adobe pyramids called Huacas Carbonera. The dark spots at the bottom of the picture are algarroba bushes growing in formerly irrigated areas. *Servicio 173 :145.*

the enclosures possibly gardens associated with the pyramids? So far the ruin is a mystery (Figs. 20 and 21).

One site we had planned to visit, especially after we had seen the aerial photograph, is called Huambacho Viejo. Although it is identified locally as a colonial ruin, on the photograph it looked like a small but typical Chimú compound. But we had no time to examine the place. Later we found that Dr. Augusto Soriano Infante (1941:267) refers to a document indicating that it was once a provincial Chimú center (*señorío*)! Situated on the old north-south highway it may have been the control center for the Chimú Empire in the lower Nepeña Valley.

Just recently Dr. Schaedel informed us that he investi-

gated the hillside site of Agua de Onda, near the sea and just to the west of the Pan American Highway. On the basis of the aerial photograph which we had ordered for him, he found, as he had anticipated, a Middle Period site analogous to Galindo in the Moche Valley, though on a smaller scale.

We also visited the site of Cerro Blanco in the center of the valley. Dr. Tello, as a result of his previous excavations, concluded that this site belonged to the Very Early or Coastal Chavín Period. This, together with similar discoveries of his in the Casma Valley to the south, gave definite proof to his theory that the ancient Chavín culture of the Sierra had spread at an early period to the Coast.

After having completed our work in the Nepeña Valley (we visited it three times in 1948-49), we tried to pick up additional traces of the ancient road which was supposed to have run from the village of Nepeña to the Santa Valley (see Chapter XVIII). In 1941, we had found a small section of an old road with adobe walls, in the Santa Valley near Cambio Puente, already referred to by Middendorf, as well as another small strip lined with stones, leaving the Nepeña Valley. The latter road headed in a northerly direction, indicating that it might have connected with the Santa section.

During the 1949 trip we followed the road in our jeep for a number of miles from Nepeña to the north, where

the road is flanked by the modern telegraph line (Fig. 14). But alas, after several more miles the walls of the road became completely lost in the desert sands! We cruised around for some additional miles alongside the present telegraph line, in the general direction of the road, but we were unable to pick up any traces again. Eventually, the ruggedness of the terrain made it impossible for us to continue any further, even with the jeep.

We were thus unable to determine whether this ancient road actually continued directly to Cambio Puente in the Santa Valley or whether it turned west in the direction of the Pacific and then north up to Chimbote, somewhat in the manner of the present day road. But even if the ancient road had taken the latter direction, it is probable that some kind of *path* with wooden guide posts had existed in ancient times, paralleling more or less the telegraph line. For such a path would have been the *shortest walking distance between the most important irrigated areas of the Nepeña and Santa Valleys.* Indeed, the Peruvian Army maps show such a path, but we were informed that it is no longer in use.

Our knowledge of the relationship of the Nepeña Valley to the Chimú Empire is almost nil. We do not know when it was conquered or how it was ruled. Huambacho Viejo may well have been the seat of a Chimú *"Gauleiter."* Garcilaso refers to the Valley of Guambacho as one of the valleys where the Chimús fought rear guard battles against the Incas. There our written information ends. Archaeological sites are mainly those of the Very Early Coastal Chavín, the Mochica and the Middle Period. What we need is a unified story of this attractive little valley!

210

XXI

Puzzling Ruins of the Casma Valley

THE CASMA VALLEY, like the Nepeña, suffers from a perennial water shortage. However, the water content of the Casma River is greater than that of the Nepeña River and irrigates more land. The Casma also has a large branch, the Sechín, which empties into it a short distance above the town of Casma. But this branch manifests tremendous fluctuations in its annual water discharges; as a result, only in "wet" years is there a good harvest in the Sechín and in the lower Casma.

The Casma is a relatively isolated valley. Although it is only some fifteen miles from the Nepeña to the north it is about eighty-five miles from the Pativilca Complex to the south, a condition which must have affected its prehistoric development. But of this we know practically nothing. None of the Chroniclers, with the exception of Cieza, even mentions the valley, and he merely makes a brief reference to its good port (I, Chap. IV).

Since we know that the Chimú Empire once extended south beyond the Casma we must assume that this valley

Fig. 1 (left). In the lonesome desert region between the Casma River and the Pan American Highway lies the intriguing ruin of Chancayillo, known also as El Castillo or Calaveras. This ruin, and that of the thirteen "moon steps" to the left, have excited much speculation concerning their original function (see text). *Kosok* • Fig. 2 (right). Squier's ground plan of Chancayillo, from his volume on Peru, illustrates the complex nature of this stone construction. Note the five entrances in the outer wall, an unusual feature for a "fortress" (see Fig. 1 and text). *Squier* • Fig. 3 (margins). Figures cut in stone monoliths. Cerro Sechín, Casma Valley. *Tello.*

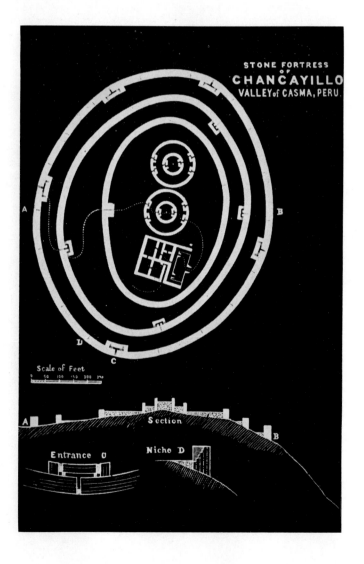

STONE FORTRESS OF CHANCAYILLO VALLEY of CASMA, PERU.

Scale of Feet

Section

Entrance O   Niche D

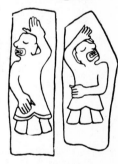

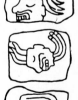

was once part of the Empire. But that is all we can say for the time being. Garcilaso in his description of the Inca coastal campaign northwards against the Chimús discusses the fighting in the very small Huarmey Valley to the south, and in the Nepeña and Santa Valleys to the north, but does not even mention the Casma Valley. Was it of no significance at that time? Or did he and others confuse the Huarmey with the Casma?

Archaeologically, likewise, little is known of the Casma. So far no Mochica ceramics have been reported here, thus leading to the tentative conclusion that Mochica influence never reached this valley. The most significant work has been done by Dr. Tello, who made important discoveries at Cerro Sechín and Huaca Mojeque indicating the existence of a very early Coastal Chavín culture. However, Middendorf, at a much earlier date (1894:307), had already pointed out the probable relationship of some of the Casma ruins to those of Chavín de Huantar in the Sierras. But no complete cultural sequence has yet been established for the valley.

In 1941 we made only a cursory survey of the Casma Valley. One of the sites we encountered was the unique ruin named Chancayillo (little Chancay) or El Castillo situated on the south side of the Casma not far from the Pan American Highway. It has been visited by numerous archaeologists who have, however, been unable to establish its archaeological date. This site (Figs. 1 and 2), has generally been called a "fort" because three sturdy concentric outer stone walls, oval in form, comprise the main part of the structure. But if it had been built primarily as a fort, its size and form are rather unusual for

such a structure on the Coast of Peru. On the Coast — outside of the later Chimú walled compounds — the common type of fortification was a hill with a series of parallel stone walls encircling it at various levels. We found such a fortified hill, called locally El Castillo, on the north side of the Casma just east of the Pan American Highway. But what is most peculiar about Chancayillo is that the outer wall contains *five* entrances. (In his plan, Squier shows *five*, but in his description he says there are *four!*) In addition the second, inner wall shows *four* entrances! This large number is most unusual, for forts are generally built with *one* well-protected entrance. Could this "fort" have been built originally as a ceremonial structure?

We can best understand the nature of Chancayillo by first studying the *thirteen* stone structures in the form of "steps" which were built on a small nearby ridge. Middendorf (1894:310) mistakenly counted only twelve steps but came to the partially correct conclusion that the number of steps referred to the number of months in the year. Kroeber (1944:52), who also visited the ruin, counted the number of steps correctly, but incorrectly concluded that this ruin could therefore have no reference to the number of months in the year. But as has already been pointed out in Chapter VI, *thirteen was a common calendrical number throughout the world in early times.* The number refers to the *thirteenth* lunar month that was interpolated every *third* solar year, thereby producing the common thirty-seven month lunar-solar cycle! This interpolation brought the lunar and solar count into approximately correct relationship, since there are 12⅓ lunar months in a solar year. The fact that the "fort" contains *three* walls may have reference to the three solar years of this cycle.

Within the inner third wall are the remains of two towers, each with two sets of concentric stone walls which form the highest part of the whole structure. Next to one of these towers is a rectangular structure of *seven* rooms. The number seven likewise often had calendrical-astronomical significance. These rooms may have been the place where astronomer priests had once lived and carried on their activities. We might add that if Tello can throw doubt upon the generally accepted "fortress" nature of Paramonga in the Pativilca Complex further south and suggest that it had really been a "temple", we can, with more reason, conjecture that Chancayillo may not have been built originally as a fort, but rather for use in an astronomical-calendrical cult. This function, however, did not prevent its massive walls from being used at various times for defensive purposes.

In 1949 we tried to make a complete survey of the rest of the ruins as well as of the canals of the Casma and Sechín Valleys. But here we at once ran into difficulty, for the Casma is the only valley on the Northwest Coast of which the Servicio had taken no aerial photographs. Only some photographs made by the United States Army Air Force during World War II were available. As a result of the great height at which they were taken, they showed insufficient details to be useful for our work. However, one unusual print (Fig. 4) shows the position of some of the main ruins in relationship to the valley. The remains of old canal systems and the various archaeological sites, consequently, had to be determined and mapped almost entirely by ground reconnaissance. In all, we located several main canals and more than fifteen archaeological sites, some of major importance.

During our 1948-49 trip, we visited the valley twice. Arriving from Trujillo, we settled down in the town of Casma at the Hotel Royal, which apparently had not changed since 1941. We visited the Chief Engineer of the Irrigation Office who gave us detailed information about current agricultural and irrigation conditions in Casma and in two very small valleys southward, the Culebra and the Huarmey. He also introduced us to Señor Luna, who was one of the most reliable and well-informed guides we met in all of Peru. With Señor Luna's help, we were able to find and map, with a fair amount of detail, most of the major ancient canals in both the Sechín and Casma Valleys. We discovered that even in these two narrow valleys, the amount of land under cultivation in ancient times had been greater than it is today.

Señor Luna also helped us locate a number of major ruins, so far not described by archaeologists. He directed us first along the north bank of the Casma River to the interesting dirt and stone pyramid, Huaca Pampa Llama, with a large rectangular sunken "tank" in front of it. This may have been either a "pool", a sunken garden, or a ceremonial meeting place; or it may have served a combination of functions (see B in Fig. 4).

Then Señor Luna guided our jeep toward the well-preserved remains of an ancient town, the largest one of the valley. This urban site, about seven miles from the town of Casma, we named "Pueblo Mojeque", to distinguish it from Huaca Mojeque (see D in Fig. 4), a few miles away, which had previously been visited and studied by Middendorf and Tello. Later on we found that our site is sometimes called El Purgatorio, though most people had no name for it. Bordered by the main ancient canal we had located, Pueblo Mojeque is situated on a small *pampa* at the foot of one of the hills that juts out into the plain. It is a large, well-planned *urban* settlement. The buildings are small and grouped in compounds and clusters, separated by streets, plazas, courts and canals. Some rectangular walled enclosures are made of stone, others of adobe, and the settlement stretches about one-half mile in each direction. Unusual for such a site are

Figs. 5 and 6. Hanging-type *huacos* which have characteristic decorative designs of the Coastal Tiahuanaco Period. *AMNH; Kosok.*

Fig. 4 (left). The Casma Valley dramatically illustrates the contrast between the extensive desert foothills of the Andes and the limited valley areas irrigated by man. In this oblique aerial photograph the Casma Valley is directly in front, with the Sechín branch at the right. Farther right (not visible in the photograph) lies the town of Casma, beyond which stretches the Pacific Ocean. The region shown here includes some of the major ruins of the valley. The group of pyramids known as Huacas Pampa Grande can be seen at (A). To the left of (B) is Huaca Pampa Llama; above (C) is Pueblo Mojeque, while between them are extensive remains of walls, roads, and canals. On the opposite side of the valley lie the ruins of Chancayillo which, in this photograph, cannot be distinguished from the desert background. In the irrigated area, to the left of (D), is Huaca Mojeque, a ruin studied by many archaeologists in the past. *U. S. Army 121-R-20.*

its numerous arabesques or niche-like friezes. In our short survey we found one small stone *huaca* situated at the western end, below which was a large stone-lined "tank" divided into three compartments. In general *the layout reminded us of a miniature ChanChan*. It is one of the most perfectly preserved settlements in Peru, with many wooden posts still standing atop the buildings (see Fig. 10, also C in Fig. 4).

While wandering around these hitherto unknown remains of a dead past, we assembled a surface collection of potsherds consisting mainly of local reed-punched and incised ware. Later, Dr. Schaedel spent a day at this ruin making a more detailed survey and a plan of one of the building clusters. Since writing this manuscript we learned that Dr. Donald Collier, Jr. had also explored the general region that encompassed the sites mentioned above and had made a rough ground plan of it. As yet the results of these two surveys have not been published.

One day, late in the afternoon, Señor Luna insisted upon showing us *"una huaca muy grande"*. Although fatigued, we obeyed the call of duty and followed him to a site known locally as Las Huacas de Monte Grande, just off the main road in the Sechín Valley and some five miles

Fig. 7 (above). The ruins of Manchal, on the southern edge of the Casma Valley, can be seen in this oblique aerial view taken by the author from a Faucett plane in 1941. Since the Servicio has so far made no aerial survey of the valley, this photograph is probably the only one of the site in existence. It was taken before the building of the Pan American Highway, which now cuts through the site (see Fig. 8). *Kosok* • Fig. 8 (left). Ground view of a part of Manchal as seen from the main adobe structure on a small hill. The lower part of the site consists of a series of rectangular stone-lined enclosures situated on descending levels. These enclosures may have been the terraced gardens below the residence of the ruler. The black line running across the middle of the picture just beyond the telephone pole is the Pan American Highway as it cuts across the ruins. In the background are the ransacked cemeteries where we collected many potsherds (see Fig. 7). *Schaedel* • Fig. 9 (right). Some of the ceramics that we found at Manchal. This ruin is sometimes called Manchán. *Schaedel-Cacho*.

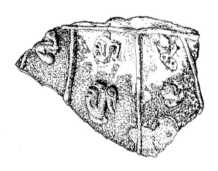

Low relief blackware with bird design.

from the town of Casma. We approached what, at first, appeared to be a huge natural mound of stones and dirt. But after climbing to the top, we found it to be a fairly well-preserved artificial mound! It had a semi-amphitheatre type of arrangement within the top, which was partly hollowed out on one side. We had found pyramids of this type in other valleys, but were astonished to find so large a mound in such a small valley. Directly south of it was a similar mound, but in a poorer state of preservation.

As we were about to leave, Señor Luna pointed to an enormous adjacent mass of stones and dirt and said, "But, Señor, this is the main *huaca*." At first we refused to believe him for it seemed incredible that so huge a hill could be man-made! Our curiosity again aroused, we dragged ourselves up the mound in a rather skeptical and tired frame of mind. But after climbing up and down its many platforms constructed on different levels, we finally became convinced that Señor Luna uttered an understatement when he said, "*una huaca muy grande*".

This pyramid is one of the largest and most complicated mounds on the entire Coast; in fact, *it is the largest stone and dirt pyramid we ever encountered!* According to local estimates, it covers a ground area exceeding one *fanegada* (7¼ acres)! This is about the same base area as that of the Huaca del Sol in the Moche Valley, which is generally assumed to be the largest pyramid in Peru. And what is most astounding is that such a huge structure should have been built in one of the smaller valleys of the Coast. What social and political driving forces could have led to the building of such a gargantuan structure?

Originally, its core might have been a natural mound, but its sides have been so completely faced with well built stone walls from top to bottom, its top so remodelled with fifteen to twenty stone platforms at various levels, that, for all practical purposes, it may be considered to

be an artificial mound. Only the boring of a tunnel through its base would definitely settle the issue. In a wide cut in one of the main platforms, we discovered a curiosity: a part of a structure faced with *exceptionally large conical adobes*. Conical adobes are typical of an early period. But there were no other indications that the pyramid belonged to such a period. No potsherds were found on the mound or in the ploughed fields which surrounded it; therefore approximate dating was impossible.

While standing on this huge mound, we could see, clearly stretched out before us to the west, three much smaller but better preserved mounds, each of which seems to have the semi-amphitheatre form of construction. We could not examine them, for darkness was setting in rapidly (A in Fig. 4 shows the whole group of *huacas*).

Some months later we returned to Casma with the SCIPA jeep. This time Dr. Schaedel was with us. Though he was tired from a day's field trip, we wanted to get his reaction to these ruins. In spite of his vociferous protests we dragged him up to the top of the huge mound and over its many terraces until he was exhausted. He too stood aghast at the size of this monstrosity. At first he could not place it archaeologically; after some deliberation, he felt that it probably belonged not to the Early, but rather to the Middle or Late Period. That evening we returned to Casma town and in a local Chinese restaurant "celebrated" with beer and a Peruvian version of American chop suey.

The third large "unknown" site which we decided to investigate was the extensive and impressive ruin of Manchal (Figs. 7 to 9). "Unknown" is a poor word for this interesting ruin because it straddles the Pan American Highway alongside the vegetation zone just south of the Casma River! For some inexplicable reason, this ruin has never been explored. Indeed, it has rarely been mentioned by archaeologists despite the fact that one

cannot miss seeing it as one rides along the highway.

Located on a slight elevation between two natural hills, the Manchal ruins consist of a major edifice of *adobónes*, below which is spread, at a slightly lower level, an intricate network of rectangular stone-lined terraces, which probably once served as gardens. The remains of the canal that once brought water to this site from the nearby Casma River can clearly be seen passing through the main structure and continuing along the hills to the south. All of these structures are of one occupation period and probably were the seat of a local ruler. Or could they have been the seat of a provincial Chimú administrator whose control extended chiefly over the lower valley?

Northwest of the site is a very small, partially-destroyed mound of rectangular adobes. The nature of its structure and the fact that its walls were painted a brownish-red would indicate that it was of a different and possibly earlier period than the main ruin.

Further west are extensive burial areas and refuse heaps from which we made a large surface collection of ceramics. According to Dr. Schaedel, the potsherds date back to various periods on the Northwest Coast, from Coastal Chavín to Chimú, and contain a great deal of what was apparently local monochrome ware whose chronological position in the generally accepted sequence of coastal cultures is, as yet, undetermined.

In addition to these three large sites, we visited all the smaller ones of whose existence we had heard and entered their positions on our map.

We also investigated the remains of an ancient road which we had seen in 1941. The road leaves the valley near the old airport and extends in a northerly direction towards Nepeña. We followed it, but, as in the case of the Nepeña-Santa road, it just faded out after a few miles. We inquired about any possible remains of an ancient

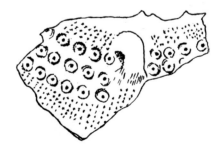

Part of cooking pot decorated with punch marks and incisions.

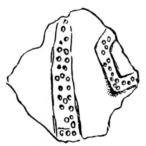

Incised ware, cream colored.

Part of cooking pot, pressed ware.

Part of cooking pot, pressed ware.

Part of cooking pot, decorated with punch marks and incisions.

Appliqué designs on local pottery.

Pressed ware, Chimú type design.

very small Culebra River and the slightly larger Huarmey, each irrigating only a few thousand acres. While we crossed these valleys many times by bus and plane, we spent little time in them because they were of minor importance to our study. No aerial photographs by which we might have located previously unknown sites were available for these two valleys. Our limited ground investigation yielded little important information.

Attention should be drawn, however, to a possibly important site in the Culebra Valley. While flying over this region in 1940-41, we noticed that there appeared to be a fair-sized ruin near the valley, several miles from the sea. One of the Faucett pilots, who knew this stretch well, confirmed our observation. We had planned to visit this intriguing but inaccessible place, but we found no time to do so.

Huarmey has likewise been neglected by archaeologists, with the exception of Professor Wendell Bennett, who studied the site called Burro Corral (1938). While flying across this valley, we noticed various ruins on both of its sides which we never found time to locate and describe. Here, as elsewhere, a survey and excavations are in order — especially since there are indications in the Chroniclers that, in ancient times, this valley was an important way station between the Casma and Fortaleza Valleys, as well as between the Coast and the Sierras.

Fig. 10. Pueblo Mojeque, the largest ancient urban center in the Casma Valley, is shown in part in this ground view. The rectangular compounds and connecting streets are indicative of the planned type of urban center of the Middle and Late Periods. The small size of the pyramids within such an urban site is also typical of these periods. *Schaedel* • Fig. 11 (below, left). Modelled face from exterior of clay jar • Fig. 12 (below, right). Punch marked and incised orange ware from the surface of Pueblo Mojeque. *Schaedel-Cacho.*

Fig. 13. Fine specimen of a typical Inca jar found in the Huarmey Valley. The upper part has been broken off. *Reiss and Stübel.*

road running from the Casma Valley southward towards the Culebra Valley. But no one seemed to know anything about such a road.

To the south of the Casma begins a long and rough desert area in which the foothills of the Andes come right down to the sea. This desolate region extends for about eighty-five miles up to the Fortaleza-Pativilca-Supe Valley Complex, which is regarded as the beginning of the Central Coast. This transition zone is cut only by the

216

XXII

The Patívilca Complex and the Unknown Sites in the Middle Supe Valley

WE HAVE NOW COMPLETED our account of the valleys of the Northwest Coast — the main area of the Chimú Empire. All that remains to be presented is a short survey of some of our findings in the valleys of the North Central Coast, into which the Chimús, at least temporarily, extended their empire (see Chapter XVII). The valleys of the North Central Coast, running from north to south, are as follows: the Fortaleza-Patívilca-Supe Complex, the nearby Huaura, the isolated Chancay, the Chillón (Carabayllo)-Rimac Complex containing the present day capital, Lima, and the nearby Lurín, with the great ancient religious shrine of Pachacamac. Chimú raids apparently extended even into the South Central valleys, possibly as far as Nazca.

It appears that of all the Central Coast valleys only the Fortaleza-Patívilca-Supe Complex may have been under more than transitory control of the Chimús. Here, on the northern edge of the Fortaleza Valley, stands the so-called Fortress of Paramonga, built, or at least held, by the Chimús. Garcilaso gives a description of the fierce defensive battle of the Chimús against the Incas and their coastal allies which took place here. Villar Córdova (1935:250) refers to a similar present day local legend concerning this battle at Paramonga, a legend which adds that the nearby mountains to the east were defended as fiercely as Paramonga itself.

In fact, Paramonga, together with the nearby structures at La Horca (the Gallows) and a former settlement situated between them, which existed when Estete visited the site in 1537, probably formed the southern bastion of the Chimú Empire. By possession of this bastion, the Chimús could not only prevent raids into the northern valleys but

Fig. 1. This natural pattern is known as a dendritic (tree-like) formation. The dark "branches" were formed when, in the course of thousands of years, rivulets of water, resulting from the rare coastal rains, washed away the whitish topsoil inside the many small *quebradas*. The photograph was taken from a Faucett plane as it approached the Fortaleza Valley (upper right of photograph). *Kosok.*

charge of the order of the Chicama and Jequetepeque. The river runs due west through a long narrow valley until it reaches a narrow coastal plain. Northward lies the much smaller Fortaleza River, which courses its way down from the mountains in a southwesterly direction until it reaches the same coastal plain about six miles to the north of the Pativilca. To the south of the Pativilca is the Supe River, which is also very small and runs northwesterly from the mountains to the same coastal plain, approximately ten miles south of the Pativilca.

The Fortaleza and the Supe have water for only a few months each year, but the Pativilca has so much water that it can completely irrigate the joint coastal plain of these three rivers throughout most of the year. Thus, the Pativilca is the hydrological core of this area, as it was in pre-Columbian times.

In 1940-41, we spent some time in this region and made our headquarters at Paramonga Hacienda. Owned by W. R. Grace and Company, this *hacienda* has gradually absorbed the best lands of this valley complex and has become one of the largest sugar plantations on the entire Coast. With the aid of guides from the *hacienda*, we located three major ancient canals in the Pativilca region.

During our 1948-49 trip, we carefully examined all the aerial photographs of much of the Pativilca Valley and, to our surprise, found no indications of major ruins except the canals mentioned above. Only a few minor sites were located. We went over the photographs several times but each time with the same results. Why were there no large sites in the valley of the large Pativilca River?

Fig. 2 (left). Aerial view of the Fortress of Paramonga, with the Pan American Highway alongside it. As the highway continues, it crosses the fields of sugar cane that cover the coastal plain of the Fortaleza Valley. Note that the nearby hills are also occupied by buildings that, together with the fortress and other structures near the sea, probably formed a single large center in ancient times. Paramonga is said to have once been in the possession of the Chimús, who consequently were able to control the northern entrance to the Central Coast. Later, after a bitterly-contested battle, the Incas captured the fortress. *Servicio 0: 839* • Fig. 3 (p. 219, left). Ground view of Paramonga taken from the nearby sugar cane fields. *Kosok* • Fig. 4 (p. 219, right). This fortified hill is situated on the coastal plain of the Supe Valley between Hacienda San Nicolás and the town of Supe. The site is mentioned by Garcilaso, who stated that the hill had three sets of walls, which can be clearly seen on the vertical aerial photograph. *Servicio 125:283.*

could also control the Pativilca Complex, and with that the northern entrance to the remaining Central Coast valleys. The discovery of a fair amount of Chimú potsherds at Paramonga, as well as at San Nicolás in the nearby lower Supe Valley, provides some archaeological indications of extended Chimú control or influence in this valley complex. But as already pointed out, such archaeological evidence does not necessarily mean political control. In this particular case, however, Chimú political control is confirmed by the accounts of several Chroniclers.

The Pativilca Valley Complex consists geographically of a narrow strip of coastal land watered jointly by three rivers. The center river, and by far the largest of the three, is the Pativilca, which has an annual water dis-

Finally the answer became clear to us. As with the Santa and Chira Rivers, the nearby hills prevented the formation of wide valley plains. The narrow valley could not, as a result, sustain a population of any significant size and therefore no important population centers developed here. Minor sites probably existed. If so, their remains were destroyed by the machines of the modern sugar economy. Significant sites might be found on those hilltops and in those *quebradas* that are some distance from the river, in areas not covered by photographs. But to find such sites, we would have had to make extensive field surveys, a task beyond the scope of our own project.

Aerial photographs of the Fortaleza Valley indicated the existence of only relatively minor ruins. Field work may establish the presence of larger sites.

However, when we began to study the aerial photographs of the middle section of the Supe Valley we found a wealth of ruins. This was all the more astounding because this middle section of the valley had not been considered of importance archaeologically. And no wonder. No professional archaeologist had ever visited it!

One day while we were working in Lima on the aerial photographs of this part of the valley, Michael excitedly ran over to my table, pushed a print before me and exclaimed: "Look at the peculiar ruins I've found." Yes, the forms of these ruins were certainly peculiar! They bore no resemblance to any of the hundreds of other archaeological structures that had been localized by means of aerial photographs.

On a desert *quebrada,* adjoining the irrigated southern part of the valley, we could make out a number of peculiar dark rectangular mounds that appeared to be man-made. Most important, each of two mounds had a circular structure attached to it, thereby producing a form we had never encountered in any of the coastal valleys! However, this was not all that aroused our interest. Stretching for miles along the desert edges of the valley to the east and west of these peculiar structures were many walls, compounds, and other structures. Here was certainly an unexpected find! One of the photographic technicians in the office suggested that the round structures might be colonial ruins, while others contented themselves with the noncommittal observation that they were just "*muy, muy antigua, seguro*" (surely very, very old).

Later, when we showed these photographs to Dr. Schaedel, his curiosity was likewise aroused.

When we located the extensive site on our map, we saw that it was some fifteen miles up the south side of the valley, near a place called Hacienda Chupa Cigarro Grande. This name, freely translated, would be "Large Cigar Sucker's Hacienda." Later on, it was suggested to us that the name Chupa Cigarro might be a corruption of the Quechua word *Chuquicara.* However, after reading the section in Calancha (1638:627-632) that deals with witchcraft in the lower Supe Valley, it appeared to us that Chupa Cigarro might be a corruption of some ancient coastal names. Incidentally, Calancha relates an additional number of interesting details about the

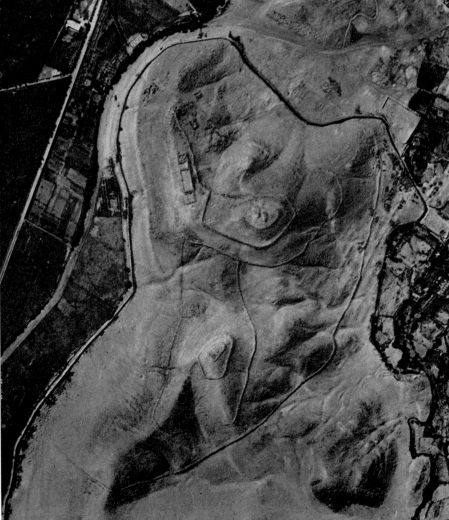

Fig. 5. Guest house at Hacienda Paramonga. *Kosok* • Fig. 5a (below). Blackened gourd bowl inlaid with shells and malachite-green stones. Probably from Early Period, Paramonga area. *Doering.*

Central Coast that so far have not been utilized by scientists.

But we had not finished. By further study of aerial photographs of adjacent areas, we found extensive ruins, though not as striking, in another wide *quebrada* on the north side of the valley just across the river from our circular structures. At once we surmised that these two sites once must have been the "capital" of the central part of the valley. We could trace on our photographs additional minor ruins all the way from Hacienda Llama

220

Huaca to Hacienda Peñica, a distance of about ten miles. Thus, as a result of less than an hour's study of aerial photographs, we had "discovered" the most extensive set of ruins of the whole Pativilca Complex — with the possible exception of the Paramonga area. And, surprisingly, no archaeologist had apparently heard of them!

Our curiosity became so great that we decided to visit Chupa Cigarro, even though our time was limited. We were able to use the SCIPA jeep, which Mr. John Neale kindly put at our disposal. The party consisted of Ingeniero Vivas, the mechanic Señor Portugal, both of the SCIPA, Dr. Schaedel and myself. Michael in the meantime had been sent on a trip into the Sierras to gather necessary information from local agricultural and irrigation engineers.

Excitedly, we drove up the Supe Valley, hoping to spend several hours examining the major ruins. However, the road turned out to be a poor one, and it was late afternoon when we arrived at Hacienda Llama Huaca, the most important *hacienda* in the general neighborhood of the ruins. The manager and his wife told us that we could not get to the ruins, on the other side of the river, before dark. When they saw our consternation, they generously invited our party to stay overnight. We gladly accepted.

Following an excellent supper, the manager told us interesting tales about the many ruins that cluttered up this middle part of the valley. He revealed, among other things, that the owner of Hacienda Peñica, farther up the river, was supposed to have dug over four million *soles* worth of gold and silver ornaments out of the ruins on his own estate, a sum equivalent to several hundred thousand dollars in U. S. money.

He also told us where we could locate some of the ancient burial sites in the neighborhood of his own *hacienda*. Local inhabitants were constantly digging into these sites in order to secure old pots and other artifacts. When he saw how keen our interest was, he sent us, although it was near midnight, with one of his servants, to a site on a nearby hill. There, under the faint glimmer of the stars, and aided by our weak flashlights, we stumbled in and out of ancient graves, which had been freshly dug up, until each of us had collected an armload of pots and potsherds. A macabre sight we must have been! Later on, when we examined the ceramics in our quarters, we saw that all of them were of a utilitarian type with interesting pressed designs.

The next morning we rose early. We forded the river

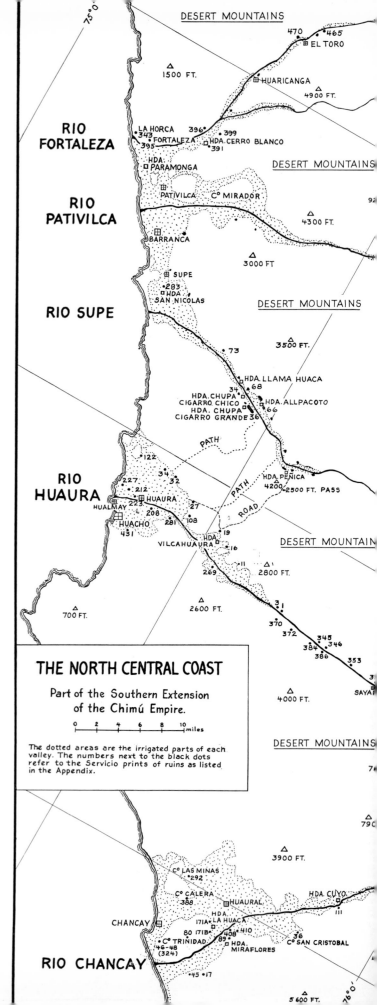

THE NORTH CENTRAL COAST

Part of the Southern Extension of the Chimú Empire.

0 2 4 6 8 10 miles

The dotted areas are the irrigated parts of each valley. The numbers next to the black dots refer to the Servicio prints of ruins as listed in the Appendix.

in the jeep and crossed over to the south side of the valley, where we hoped to find the site we had discovered on the photographs. But before arriving at that place, we stumbled upon a huge ancient cemetery at the nearby Hacienda Chupa Cigarro Chico. It had been extensively excavated by the present day inhabitants of the area for the sake of obtaining crude cooking pots (*ollas*) for use in their homes. Literally thousands of potsherds, including many vessels that were almost intact, covered the ground. A great number of bones and skulls also littered the surface (Figs. 6 and 7). A gruesome sight, but a joy for any archaeologist! The abundance and high quality of the ceramics offered ample indication that few commercial grave diggers and probably no archaeologist had visited this site. In addition to the great mass of pressed utility ware, a considerable amount of ceramics of the Coastal Tiahuanaco type, characteristic of the Middle Period, was in evidence. We remained long enough to fill half the jeep with a representative collection of pottery! Then we proceeded, not without regrets, to the main object of our trip (Figs. 8 to 13).

A mile or so further up the river, we crossed some much-leveled ancient adobe walled structures until we reached the curious ruins we had seen in the aerial photographs. The main group consisted of a number of man-made mounds facing what might have been a plaza. The two largest mounds were high square structures, built of rough stones in a sandy mortar, with retaining walls of large, aligned stones. They were situated at the west end of the plaza. Two smaller mounds, which were at the eastern end, were of similar form and construction. Still smaller mounds were located nearby.

Two complex edifices, one larger than the other, bounded the plaza on the north and south sides. The larger of the two, situated on the northern side, consisted of a high square stone and dirt mound with two lower wings, one on each side. A design of small stones could be faintly discerned on top of the mound. It seemed to be a "stone drawing" of an animal, possibly a bird. On the west platform wing lay two large broken grinding stones, one with three holes in it, both apparently testimony to some ancient agricultural ceremony (Fig. 10).

But most important, just below us and directly in front of the edifice, we suddenly espied the unique *circular structure* that we had spotted on the photograph! We climbed down to the structure and examined it carefully. Finally we decided that it probably had been an amphitheatre, perhaps used by the priests for ceremonial pur-

poses. A row of large monoliths and the remains of a narrow road separated the amphitheatre from the main mound (Fig. 9).

The photographic mystery had been solved. But the archaeological mystery had only been glimpsed!

The smaller edifice situated on the southern side of the plaza also contained a similar circular amphitheatre. Three consecutive rows of stones lined the inside of this amphitheatre at rising levels and may have served the dual function of retaining walls and of seats for an audi-

ence. A large monolith — for phallic worship? — had been set up near the center. On the south end of the amphitheatre, a series of ascending terraces led to two adjoining rooms, which crowned the edifice.

The aerial photographs indicated that, at some distance to the northwest of this site, there was a third amphitheatre, but it appeared to be almost completely buried in the sand, and since we had no time to visit it, we left the investigation of it to other scientists.

The impression given by the ruins was that they had

Fig. 6 (below, right). At the large ancient graveyard of Hacienda Chupa Cigarro Chico, we found thousands of potsherds and hundreds of elaborately decorated but partly broken cooking jars (*ollas*). These ceramics had been left on the surface by the local people who excavate the graves of their ancestors in order to obtain unbroken jars for present day cooking purposes. Here, and later in Allpacoto, we found mainly this kind of local ware (period undetermined) and Middle Period (Tiahuanacoid) ware. *No Late Chimú potsherds were discovered. Schaedel · Fig. 7.* Ceramics from Chupa Cigarro Chico, Supe Valley. (a) to (d) Orange pressed ware. (a) and (b) *Kosok-Wrynn*, (c), (d) and (e) *Kosok-Storck*.

(a) Exterior of an *olla*.

(b) Exterior of an open bowl.

(c) Exterior of an open bowl.

(d) Interior of bowl (c), white and red on orange, showing lower part of a face.

(e) Design (flattened out) on the exterior of an open bowl, black, white and red style.

Fig. 8 (above, left). View of the Late Period structures at the right of the older main ceremonial group shown in Fig. 13. Note the boundary wall of stone in the foreground and the irrigated fields of the Supe Valley in the background. *Schaedel* • Fig. 9 (above, right). One of the circular structures as viewed from the main pyramid. Since the desert soil has covered part of the construction, and since the photograph was none too clear, the top of the circular structure has been darkened in the photograph. *Schaedel*.

Fig. 10 (left). The author, seated upon a ceremonial grinding stone found on the right wing of the main pyramid. In the stone, now broken, were three holes, in one of which was found a pestle, indicating that probably some seed-grinding ceremony once took place here. The two sand-covered stone mounds to the left are man-made and form part of the ceremonial complex. *Schaedel* • Fig. 11 (above). Potsherd from Chupa Cigarro Chico, white slip ware. *Kosok-Okun* • Fig. 12 (right). Detail of one of the principal dark, stone-covered mounds seen from atop the main pyramid. Before the mound are a number of pits excavated a long time ago, with poor results, to judge by the few undecorated potsherds that we found in the area. *Schaedel*.

Fig. 13. While viewing the vertical aerial photographs of the middle Supe Valley, we suddenly came upon this maze of unknown ruins situated in a wide *quebrada,* on the south side of the valley, just east of Hacienda Chupa Cigarro Grande. A visit to this site convinced us that the ruins could be separated into two construction periods. Those belonging to the Early or Middle Periods are in the center of the photograph. They form a "ceremonial complex," bounded both on the north (main pyramid) and on the south by a rectangular structure, each with a circular amphitheatre attached, and bounded on the west by one large dark square mound and on the east by a similar large mound and two smaller ones (see text). The two sets of ruins to the right are of the Middle-Late Period. Other ruins (extreme right and left of the photograph) we left for future explorers. The dark areas are the modern irrigated fields. *Servicio 125:36* • Fig. 14 (right). Pressed orange ware from Chupa Cigarro Chico. Note the glyph-like dots and lines reminiscent of Maya counting devices. *Kosok-Storck.*

once been a complex ceremonial center, though different, both in form and arrangement, from other such centers on the Peruvian Coast. The *virtual absence of potsherds at this site* made any accurate calculations as to its relative age impossible (Fig. 13).

However, we could make some tentative assumptions on the basis of other indirect evidence. Across the eastern mound ran a rather well-preserved boundary wall, made of adobe, that connected with a group of *adobón* constructions further off (Fig. 8). *Adobónes,* as pointed out before, are large blocks of adobe mud, typical of Cen-

tral Coast constructions. Potsherds picked up among these constructions appeared to belong partly to the Middle but mostly to the Late Period. This would indicate that the main center belonged to at least the Middle or possibly the Early Period.

Leaving our jeep behind, we tramped further up the valley to an adjoining site, where we found another set of *adobón* ruins — though better preserved. On the basis of surface collections, this site also appears to date back to the Middle to Late Periods.

By this time, we had become exceedingly hungry. For-

Fig. 15 (left). Part of a cooking jar (*olla*) found in the cemetery of Allpacoto, Supe Valley. Pressed orange ware with mythological, puma-like figures. *Kosok-Okun* • Fig. 16 (above). Sunken rectangle, one of the many constructions at Allpacoto. *Schaedel.*

Fig. 17. Ceramics from Allpacoto, Supe Valley.

Left to right: Part of a jug, black on red on white. *Kosok-Storck* • Outside of small bowl, black on white, Chancay style. *Kosok-Okun* • Part of goblet-shaped cup, black, red and white on orange, Coastal Tiahuanaco style. *Kosok-Okun.*

tunately, when we arrived at the ruins earlier in the day, we found a family living nearby who agreed to prepare lunch for us. When we returned, a tasty meal of chicken with rice, which was served with some good *chicha*, was ready. As we sat eating our meal under the shady trees in front of the house, near which flowed the refreshing waters of an *acequia*, the thought came to us that, although the four of us had spent less than a day in this

area, we had definitely established the existence of a hitherto unknown ancient valley culture, together with some rough estimates of period sequences. In view of the many archaeologically unexplored valleys in Peru, rapid results can undoubtedly also be attained in some of these valleys by means of similarly limited but planned explorations.

After lunch, we jumped into our jeep in order to return

to the northern side of the valley and visit the other large site indicated on our photographs. On the way, we found, west of the ruins we had just examined, another group of similar rectangular stone and dirt mounds though, as far as we could determine, without circular amphitheatres. At the site, we encountered an alignment of stone monoliths (Figs. 18 and 19).

A re-examination of the aerial photographs after our

return to Lima revealed similar square and rectangular mounds in those parts of the valley which we had not explored. One of the aerial photographs (Fig. 20) shows a dramatic group in the region of Cerro los Taros, which consists not only of rectangular mounds but also of circular structures apparently similar to those we had visited. Other photographs show that the Fortaleza Valley also contains several groups of rectangular mounds, though no circular structures could be noticed. Unfortunately, lack of time prevented us from visiting these unexplored sites.

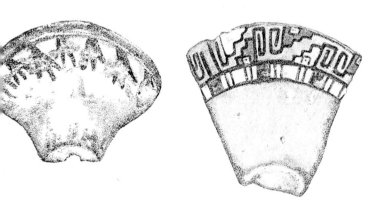

Fig. 18 (left). Vertical aerial photograph of a group of dark mounds similar to those in Fig. 8 but without circular structures. *Servicio 125:34* • Fig. 19 (above). Remains of monolithic uprights that line a quadrangle in the ruins west of Chupa Cigarro Chico (see Fig. 18). This type of stone construction is reminiscent of the Kalasasaya at Tiahuanaco. *Schaedel.*

But let us return to our trip. We followed the road up the north side of the valley and found the region covered by a motley array of ruins including a medium-sized *adobón* pyramid. At the small village of Allpacoto, we turned off into the flat *quebrada* of the same name. This stretches out just across the river from the large *quebrada* which contains the ruins of Chupa Cigarro Grande. First, we encountered an excavated graveyard containing many ceramics very similar to those of Chupa Cigarro Chico (Figs. 15 and 17). Farther up the *quebrada,* beyond the region covered by the aerial photos, we found a large clustering of adobe ruins whose construction forms indicated a Middle and Late occupation (Fig. 16). *No distinctive Chimú ceramics were picked up anywhere;* in contrast, Uhle found many of them at San Nicolás, near the Pacific Ocean. Perhaps the hold of the Chimús was confined to the immediate coastal zone, while the people of the hinterland either remained unconquered or, after a conquest, retained local autonomy. On the other hand they may have been slaughtered or exiled.

We were anxious to follow the ruins farther up the valley, but lack of time prevented our going there and investigating these unknown sites. Indeed, we realized that we had done more than we had planned, for we had dis-

Fig. 20 (right). While restudying the aerial photographs of the north side of the Supe Valley, we found this group of ruins near Cerro los Taros, about nine miles from the sea. Note especially the circular structures, which appear similar to those found at Chupa Cigarro Grande (Fig. 13).

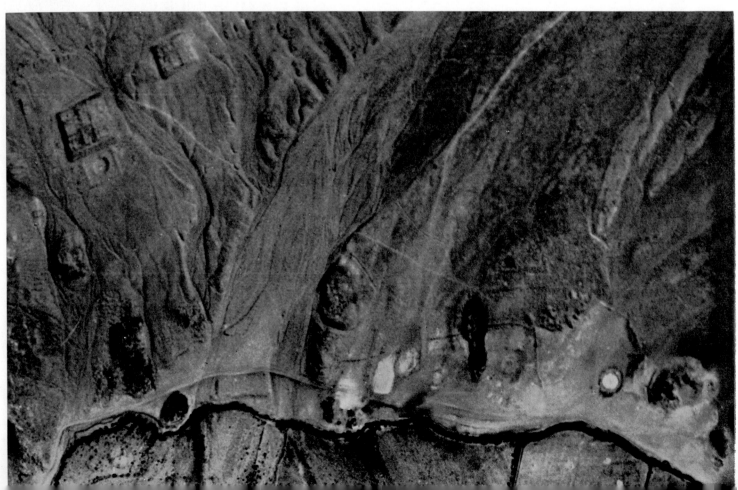

covered in the middle Supe Valley a hitherto unknown culture distinct from that of the lower Supe Valley.

On the basis of the aerial photographs and our limited ground survey, it appeared to us that, while the middle Supe Valley culture extended from the region of Hacienda Llama Huaca to that beyond Hacienda Peñica, it was probably centered mainly in the Chupa Cigarro-Allpacoto region. There may have been a good reason for this. Here, the irrigated part of the valley is somewhat wider than in the regions above or below, and, therefore, has greater economic significance. Moreover, the large size and flat nature of the two opposite desert *quebradas* in this region provided an exceptionally large area for developing extensive ceremonial and living centers. While the political and ceremonial center of the middle Supe Valley, during the Middle Period at least, may have been located in this region, the lower part of the valley near the sea may have led its own independent existence. But the whole valley will have to be explored before this hypothesis can be accepted.

We were studying our maps when we were struck by a thought concerning the "foreign relations" of the middle part of the Supe Valley. This part probably had closer ties with the Huaura Valley to the south than with the Pativilca to the north or even with the lower part of the Supe itself. The distance between the Supe and the Pativilca Rivers at this point is about sixteen miles, and the region between them consists of high mountains without any important paths connecting the two valleys. On the other hand, the distance from the Supe to the Huaura River is less than ten miles. Furthermore, the low terrain between them permits easy communication and transportation (see map, p. 220).

At present, this latter desert region contains two paths and one road connecting the two valleys. One of these paths leaves the Supe Valley near the ruin site of Chupa Cigarro and runs to the lower Huaura Valley; another one runs from a point somewhat farther up the Supe to a different part of the lower Huaura; the road leads from Hacienda Peñica, with its many unvisited ruins, and reaches the Huaura Valley near the large ruins of Vilcahuaura discussed in Chapter XXIII. If these three short connecting links originated in pre-Spanish times — which is not unlikely — it would reinforce our hypothesis of the close relationship of the middle Supe and lower Huaura Valleys in ancient times. A joint survey of these two valleys and their connecting links should, therefore, yield significant results.

226

XXIII

Additional Monuments of the Past: The Huaura and the Valleys to the South

ANOTHER VALLEY that has not been studied archaeologically is the Huaura. Villar Córdova (1935:248) mentions a few sites in this valley but gives no details about them. Through the examination of aerial photographs, we were able to discover the existence of more than twenty-five sites, which we entered on the Peruvian Army map (see p. 220).

The aerial photographs indicated no major ancient canals that are now in disuse. This hardly surprised us since the Huaura River is a fair-sized one and the cotton economy that dominates most of the valleys from the Huaura to Nazca in the south requires as little water per acre as that of the corn economy of the ancient Indians. Consequently, in these valleys, practically all fields and canals of the ancients have been put back into use. In fact, as the result of recent government irrigation projects, there is probably more land under cultivation at present than there was in pre-Spanish times.

Something unique, nonetheless, attracted our attention on the aerial photographs. We noted a series of ground markings similar to the "lines" we had found covering the deserts of the Nazca area far to the south. These were found on print 1008:10 and were localized on our map as being in a wide *quebrada* on the south bank of the

river, about fifteen miles from the sea. The main markings appeared as sets of parallel lines, which rather disturbed us, since no such phenomenon had been encountered anywhere else in Peru.

Although pressed for time, we decided to visit this site and make a ground survey of the "lines." But even with our aerial photographs in hand we had difficulty in localizing the site. And no wonder. The *quebrada* that contained the "lines" had, to our great disappointment, been put under cultivation and all our "lines" destroyed!

A greater scientific disappointment, however, awaited us when one of the older inhabitants who had often seen these lines explained their nature and origin. For cotton growing, the long furrows are drawn as straight as possible. In fact, there are "specialists" in each valley who pride themselves on the straightness with which they can plow these furrows with their oxen. What had happened was that some decades ago this flat *quebrada* had been used as a "practice" ground, possibly in a competition, for drawing straight furrows. The double nature of these lines resulted from the fact that after the initial line had been made going up the *quebrada*, another adjacent, parallel line had been ploughed on the return trip.

This explanation seemed incredible, but after ques-

tioning other persons in the neighborhood, who confirmed it, we had to accept this statement. It was one of the few times that our aerial photographs had steered us completely wrong! But our experience did emphasize the need of a ground survey to confirm aerial observation.

Returning to the Coast, we found that we had a few hours left before dark. We decided to visit an extensive

Fig. 1 (left). Drawing of part of a blue and white textile which we found at Vilcahuaura Antigua. *Kosok-Okun* • Fig. 2. One of the rare — and hitherto unreported — examples of a fortified hill site with walls containing salient and recessive angles. This fort is situated on top of Cerro Centinela near the Huaura River at the point where it enters the sea. The two best known examples of this type of walled construction are Paramonga on the Coast and Sacsahuamán, near Cuzco, in the Sierras. *Servicio 1008:22.*

227

and archaeologically unknown ruin near the present Hacienda Vilcahuaura in the lower part of the valley, about eleven miles from the sea. To reach the site, we crossed the large Pampa Afuera, just then being prepared for cultivation under a government irrigation project.

The ruin, a large one, consisted of a series of connected buildings situated on a slight natural outcropping. The buildings and the surrounding walls were constructed of huge blocks of *adobónes*. The principal edifice consisted of a courtyard and platforms connected by a ramp and was suggestive of a Chimú palace structure.

On the basis of the extensive surface collection of ceramics that we gathered, Dr. Schaedel established analogies between the material from this site and the ceramic styles of the Central Peruvian Coast (Chancay and Ancón) of the Middle and Late Periods (Coastal Tiahuanaco through Inca). Possibly Vilcahuaura Antigua, as we called this place, had been a local political capi-

Fig. 3. Valley of Huaura. This aerial photograph shows part of the site of Vilcahuaura Antigua, which is described in the text. Especially striking is the well-aligned nature of the rectangular structures; some were apparently large residences; others probably served as courts and places of assembly. Forming the core of the large rectangle is the main pyramid, right, which can be identified only by the three terraces in front (see Fig. 8 and map on p. 220). The dark areas at the top of the photograph are the present cultivated lands. *Servicio 1008:16* • Fig. 4 (left). Potsherds from Vilcahuaura Antigua. Central Coast styles of the Middle and Late Period are represented. Drawn after *Schaedel*.

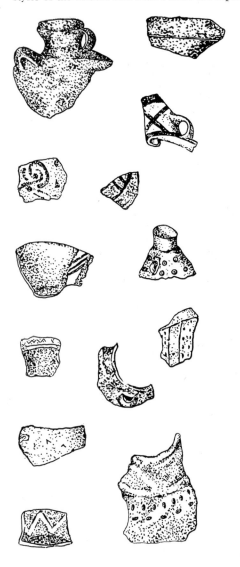

tal or center during part of this time. Was it perhaps at one time the Chimú control center in the lower part of the valley? Was it perhaps even the "palace" of Chanquirguanguan, one of the wives of Minchançaman, the last independent Chimú ruler? It was her son, Chumuncaur, who was placed by the Incas on the Chimú throne after his father had been deposed and taken as a hostage to Cuzco (Figs. 3 to 10).

We had no time to visit the other sites in this valley that we had discovered on the Servicio photographs. However, there are so many sites and they look so impressive, that we hope archaeologists will be induced

to explore them and then make a report on their findings.

Between the Huaura and the Chillón-Rimac Valley Complex, and some distance from both of them, lies the relatively isolated valley of Chancay. Unlike the Huaura, at least some of the sites of the lower parts of this valley have been studied archaeologically and reported upon by several archaeologists (Willey, Uhle). We had visited a few of the sites in 1941 while tracing the remains of an old canal on the south side of this valley.

A careful study of the aerial photographs in 1949 disclosed no additional canals in this valley. We were, however, able to locate nine archaeological sites — some

Fig. 5 (upper left). Part of a walled compound next to the pyramid at Vilcahuaura Antigua (see Fig. 3). *Schaedel* • Fig. 6 (left center). Black-on-orange plate, Vilcahuaura or Allpacoto. *Kosok-Storck* • Fig. 7 (lower left). Part of a well-preserved wall of *adobón* blocks in one of the many rectangular structures at Vilcahuaura (see Fig. 3). *Schaedel* • Fig. 8 (above). A frontal ground view of the "step" pyramid at Vilcahuaura Antigua. Three levels are clearly visible despite the heavy destruction this site has suffered recently. *Schaedel* • Fig. 9 (upper right). Design on exterior of bowl. Pressed ware with white slip, Vilcahuaura Antigua. *Kosok-Okun* • Fig. 10 (lower right). Black-on-red design on a fragment of a jug, Vilcahuaura Antigua. *Kosok-Kosofsky.*

not yet explored by scientists. Although we were unable to visit any of the sites on our last trip, we are reproducing photographs of some of them because of their scientific interest (Figs. 11, 12, 13, 19 and 20). In addition, we counted approximately a dozen "spots" on the prints which may prove to be minor sites.

The ruins of the Rimac-Chillón Valley Complex and of the Lurín Valley have already been discussed in Chapters IV and V. It may not be amiss to repeat that, aside from the few well-known sites, many of these ruins appear exceedingly interesting and *beg for archaeological exploration*. Mr. Stumer and Dr. Schaedel have com-

Fig. 11. A well-aligned site, hitherto unreported, on the south side of the Chancay Valley, near La Huaca Hacienda and also near the site shown in Fig. 20. *Servicio 1002:89.*

Fig. 12 (below). Another unexplored and well-preserved town of the Chancay Valley, near Hacienda Cuyo approximately nineteen miles from the sea. *Servicio 1002:111.*

Fig. 13. A heavily populated, prehistoric center on the south bank of the Chancay River near Cerro Cristóbal, about thirteen miles from the sea. The main walls of the buildings are of adobe, although stone foundations can be seen at the right. Note the large excavated area of ancient graves at the rear of the settlement. *Servicio 1002:36* • Fig. 14 (upper right). Typical Chancay ware. *AMNH* • Fig. 15 (lower right). An unusual landing method used at various ports on the Coast of Peru. Passengers are transported from the steamer, which is anchored outside of the shallow harbor, to the side of the dock by motorboat; then they climb on a platform in the motorboat which is lifted by a crane onto the dock. While this method of landing might appear to be dangerous, actually it is quite safe. *Kosok.*

menced explorations here that have already yielded some significant results (*New York Times,* Jan. 20, 1953).

We also studied the limited number of aerial photographs of the valleys south of the Lurín. We located two sites in the Chilca, three in the Asia, nine in the Chincha, and one each in the Mala and Sihuas Valleys. No aerial photographs were available for the important valleys of Cañete and Pisco. The sites we found on the aerial photographs could not be mapped accurately since no Army maps for the southern region were available. The road maps of this region published by the Ministerio de Fomento, while serving their purpose excellently, are on a small scale (1:500,000) and contain no contour lines. They were, therefore, of little help to us. All we were able to do was to make a list of the sites, together with their calculated distances from the Pacific (see Appendix).

Fig. 16 (left). Loading cotton for export from the Chancay Valley. *Kosok* • Fig. 17 (below, left). Typical Chancay ware. *AMNH* • Fig. 18 (below, right). A piece of black-on-red interlocking ware, which we found in a large ancient garbage mound cut by the Pan American Highway as it passes near the ruins of Cerro Trinidad in the Chancay Valley. *Kosok-Okun* • Fig. 19 (above). Photograph of the ruins of Cerro Trinidad, situated alongside the Pan American Highway. This site was excavated around the turn of the century by Max Uhle, who found wall paintings of a very early (interlocking) period (see Fig. 22). The site was excavated more recently by Professor Gordon Willey. *Servicio 324:46, 48.*

Another purpose in presenting the impressive aerial views of some of the large sites in the Central Coast valleys of Huaura, Chancay and the Chillón-Rimac-Lurín Complex, is to indicate the existence of an interesting phenomenon heretofore unnoticed. These photographs reveal that large *urban* settlements were built in these Central Coast valleys! On the basis of what is known of

Fig. 20. Chancay Valley, south side. A settlement as yet unexplored, with walls that are unusually well defined and apparently in a good state of preservation. This site is about nine miles from the sea, near La Huaca Hacienda and the site shown in Fig. 11. Burial sites are nearby. *Servicio 1002:408* • Fig. 21 (lower right). Typical Chancay ware. *AMNH-Rein* • Fig. 22 (margins). Segments of a conventionalized interlocking fish design found on adobe walls at Cerro Trinidad by Max Uhle.

similar settlements on the Northwest Coast, we should assume that they represent *Late Period developments.* Without detracting from the significance of the Northwest Coast trends toward urbanization, it appears that the Central Coast was undergoing a somewhat similar process.

That period is past in Peruvian archaeology when *origins* loomed as *the major problem.* We hope now that the period of *interpretation of the social significance* of archaeological material is imminent and that the highly significant role that the Central Coast played in Late prehistoric times will be investigated. What new clues will these towns of the Central Coast reveal? Like veiled statues, the ruins in these photographs arouse our intense curiosity. The archaeologist must remove the veil!

XXIV

A Last Look at Peru

Before returning to the United States, I decided to attend the Second International Congress of Indigenists which, after several postponements, was finally held in Cuzco, the ancient capital of the Incas. When I visited Cuzco in 1939, the overland trip from Lima took six days: four by bus and car, and two on horseback. Now, however, ten years later, I made the trip by means of a Faucett plane in about two and a half hours!

While the overland trip provided an intimate insight into the life of the peoples of the Sierras, the plane trip, on which we reached heights up to 18,000 feet, offered a view of the majesty and complexity of the Sierras themselves. Particularly inspiring was the view of the enormous massif, composed of dozens of snow- and ice-capped mountains, that spreads to the north and east of Cuzco.

On the way, the plane flew somewhat south of its regular course, passing rather low over the lakes of Choclococha that dot the grassy, windswept and mountainous plateau (*puna*) located about halfway between Cuzco and the Pacific Ocean. While carefully scanning the landscape below us, I suddenly saw the extensive remains of a huge, and apparently ancient, irrigation canal meandering northward from some of these lakes towards several narrow, inhabited valleys. I had never encountered any reference to this canal, unless it is assumed to be part of one of the two supposedly giant canals which Garcilaso

mentions. But for reasons to be explained in our study, *Water and Life,* this assumption can hardly hold. The pilot, who had flown this trip many times, could not enlighten me about the extent or the antiquity of this canal.

Michael met me at the Cuzco airport. He had completed a two-week trip through the Sierras, collecting information on rainfall, irrigation and crops from local agents of the SCIPA and the Department of Agriculture, information which had not been available at Lima. We settled down in an old-fashioned hotel in Cuzco and immediately began some sightseeing. We greatly enjoyed our stay in this fascinating ancient mountain capital of the Incas, especially after having lived for months on the hot, dry, dusty Coast. We attended the various meetings of the Congress. At one of these meetings I read a paper on the ancient road systems of coastal Peru, as well as a paper by Maria Reiche in which she described some of her Nazca discoveries.

The Congress over, I returned by plane to Lima, and Michael made his way there by train and bus via Puno, Arequipa and the southern Coast of Peru. Along the way he obtained additional local hydrological information.

Our stay in Peru ended, as it had started, with the study of aerial photographs in the offices of the Servicio. During the last few weeks we completed our study of the photographs of those valleys of the Central and South

Fig. 1 (left). In a "sea" of majestic Andean mountain tops lies the ancient site of Machu Picchu, accessible only by means of the serpentine path from the valley below. *Servicio, unnumbered series* • Fig. 2 (right). A descendant of the Incas. *Kosok.*

235

Fig. 3. Part of an old Inca stone structure with post-conquest mortar formation above it. Note the ancient two-serpent motif on the lintel above the entrance. The two women exchanging the latest gossip are probably descendants of the ancient builders of this stone structure. *Kosok.*

Figs. 4 and 4a. People of the Andes. *Kosok* • Fig. 5 (right). View of Huayna Picchu with Machu Picchu in the foreground. *Kosok.*

Coast that had been surveyed, listing all visible ruins which we hoped someone would some day explore.

We bought souvenirs, packed our trunks, said goodbye to our friends, and left Lima not by plane or boat but by a night bus to Trujillo. Arriving at Trujillo soon after dawn, we met the Schaedels, who served us a large and tasty breakfast. Señor Garrido soon joined us, and we spent part of the morning examining a new set of aerial photographs which I had brought from Lima. Then we rushed off to the airport, where we barely made the plane for Tumbes near the Ecuadorian border. Saying farewell to the Schaedels was a somewhat sad affair. During the nine months we had worked together we had become close professional and personal friends.

As the Faucett plane left the ground and flew over parts of ChanChan, our thoughts reverted to the many Indians of the past who had slaved to build this metropolis, the largest and richest of the Americas, humans who now were gone and forgotten except where some curious *huaquero* or archaeologist might excavate their remains in order to sell their trinkets, measure their skulls, or present their beloved water jugs to museums. Today, the descendants of these ancient Indians are still working the same fields and living under conditions not too different from those which existed under former Chimú and Inca masters.

The plane winged its way north along the Coast over the many fields and the very ruins which we had studied on the ground. As the plane flew over the northern edges of the Chicama Valley, near the present port of Malabrigo, we were able to see clearly the large extent of the unknown and unexplored ruin, Malabrigo Viejo, with its many pyramids and related structures (see Chapter XI).

Passing over the Jequetepeque Valley, we cast one last look at the extensive and impressive ruins of Pacatnamú, spread on a plateau alongside the Pacific Ocean. When we approached the Zaña Valley, we were on the lookout for a ruin about which a Faucett pilot had told us, and which I vaguely recalled from one of my flights in 1941. Suddenly it appeared below us. It seemed to consist of a medium-sized flat-topped pyramid either surrounded by a rectangular wall or nesting on the base of a broad platform, set clearly on a promontory along the north side of Cerro Carrizal. I tried to photograph it, but the elaborate ventilating gadget in the middle of each window pane of the Faucett DC-3 airplanes made it impossible to do so. I mailed my information to Dr. Schaedel, who sent one of his assistants there; but the assistant became ill on the way and never reached his destination.

We stopped at Chiclayo for a few minutes — the city which had been our headquarters during our months of work in the Lambayeque region. Then off to Piura farther north. We eagerly anticipated the first part of this trip, since the plane was to pass over a whole series of ruins which we had recently visited by jeep. But clouds suddenly surrounded us, and the ground remained invisible until we entered the extensive but archaeologically empty Sechura Desert.

Soon we approached the narrow green band of vegetation watered by the small Piura River that forms the northern edge of the Sechura Desert. The Piura Valley,

Fig. 6 (right). A close-up of ancient Machu Picchu showing the habitation sites in the foreground and cultivation terraces in the center and background. On the right is one of the heavily forested slopes on which Machu Picchu was built; on the left are the black shadows that cover the deep valley that drops down from this idyllic site. *Servicio, unnumbered series* • Fig. 6a (above). Drawings of llamas. *Mead.*

the Chira Valley just to the north of it, and the Tumbes Valley near the Ecuadorian border, were conquered, according to tradition, by the Chimús. These valleys thus were once the far northern outpost of the Chimú Empire. In fact, the Chimús, as mentioned in Chapter XVI, are supposed to have extended their conquests as far north as the present Puerto Viejo in Ecuador. But this conquest took place only a short time before the Chimús themselves were conquered by the Incas.

We had explored the Piura Valley fairly thoroughly in 1940-41, and no further investigations seemed necessary for our irrigation study. Furthermore, examination of the aerial photographs of the International Petroleum Company showed no important archaeological sites not previously encountered by us on the ground.

A few minutes out of the Piura Valley, our plane approached the nearby Chira Valley. There, also, we had completed our hydrological ground work in 1940-41. At

that time we had also examined the rambling ruins east of the present town of Amotape on the lower north bank of the Chira River. These are apparently remains of the ancient town of Amotape mentioned by the Spanish Chroniclers. In 1949, after study of the aerial photographs of the International Petroleum Company, we were able to obtain a photograph of this site which is reproduced here (Fig. 14).

The extensive flat plateau stretching between the Chira and Piura Rivers represents another important region of undeveloped agricultural potentialities. The Chira is the second largest river on the Coast and thus might have produced one of the major irrigated areas in the past. But as in the case of the Santa, only a very small portion of the annual water discharge could be used for irrigation purposes. The Chira runs through a relatively deep chasm; as a result, the ancient Indians of this region, with their limited productive forces, could not lead the water

Fig. 7 (above). This ruin is on a high mountain above the village of Pisac, not far from Cuzco, former capital of the Inca Empire. It represents one of the finest stone remains of any ancient Andean civilization. The stones are evenly cut and polished. No cement was used to hold them together, but some of the blocks fit so tightly that it is impossible to insert a piece of paper between them. *Kosok* • Fig. 8 (below). Part of a stone wall of a Cuzco house built in Inca times. The Incas, who had no iron tools, quarried these blocks by using tools fashioned from harder types of stone. Despite this difficulty, all joints fit perfectly and contain no mortar. Nevertheless, the attempt to achieve regularity in the thickness of the layers of cut stones was only partly successful here, in contrast to the structure shown in Fig. 7. *Kosok.*

Fig. 9. Aerial view of the ancient Inca fortress of Sacsahuamán, which defended the Inca capital of Cuzco (see upper right corner of photograph as well as Fig. 10). The fortress, the largest and most powerful in ancient Peru, was built on a steep hill above Cuzco. To make the fortress impregnable on the exposed side (left in photograph), three tiers of defensive walls with salient and recessive angles were constructed. The walls are built of enormous cut stones; it has been estimated that the heaviest weighs more than one hundred and fifty tons! These stones supposedly came from a pit about four miles away and were probably pulled over rollers to the fort site by large numbers of men harnessed together with fiber rope. The purpose of the circular structure within the fort is unknown. The present restoration of the ruins was made by Dr. Valcárcel of Lima. The small dots on the left side of the picture are people visiting the fortress. *Sercicio 0:1425* • Fig. 10 (right). Cuzco, the largest city in the Sierras today, nestling among the rolling hills of the southern Andes. *Servicio, unnumbered series.*

the nearby town of Zorritos, whom we had first met in 1941 while we were surveying the canals and ruins of Tumbes. Zorritos, the seat of the government-owned Peruvian Oil Company, had undergone a tremendous change in eight years: the streets and sidewalks were paved; trees, flowering bushes and flowers were everywhere. At night electric street lamps illuminated the streets. It presented quite a contrast to dreary Talara.

Dr. Petersen took us to his home where with his wife and fourteen-year-old son we soon sat down to a German supper which included *Rinderbraten, Kartoffelsalat und Bier!* After supper, while Michael and our host's son went to see a western film, Dr. Petersen showed me his manuscripts and his archaeological finds. This last night in Peru turned out to be one of the most pleasant and instructive I had spent in that country.

Dr. Petersen, a German geologist, has worked many years for the Peruvian Government Petroleum Company. When we met him in 1941, he was spending his free time making archaeological surveys of the Tumbes region. He had kept up his field work, and by the time we returned in 1949 he had collected a great mass of material. He had mapped the whole Tumbes area, made an excellent ground plan of what now remains of the core of the ancient settlement of Tumbes, found more than a hundred archaeological sites in the Tumbes Valley, and meticulously kept and catalogued a collection of archaeological artifacts

---

of the Chira onto the very extensive plateau between the Chira and Piura Rivers by means of canals. Modern techniques could solve the problem without difficulty, but lack of funds as well as conflicting property rights, until recently, have prevented any further exploitation of the waters of the Chira River. Limited projects are under way which are designed to utilize, at least in the Quiroz area, some of the waters of the Chira that have been flowing unused into the Pacific since ancient times.

This entire northern region, including the Sechura Desert and even parts of the Lambayeque Valley Complex as far south as the Leche, receives a limited amount of rain in those rare years when the warm equatorial current, the Niño, is especially strong and reaches farther south than usual. When this happens, there is sometimes sufficient rain to grow a scant cotton or corn crop in the

Chira-Piura area. And then, too, the dormant life in the Sechura Desert blossoms forth. When I flew over this area in 1940-41 — a wet year — I could see the immense desert, covered with a carpet of soft green grasses and flowers of many hues!

From the Chira Valley the plane flew to Talara, oil port of the International Petroleum Company, which is owned by Canadian and United States interests. Here the landscape is covered by a maze of oil derricks and interconnecting oil pipes. No agriculture is carried on, and all water has to be imported or drawn from artesian wells. The whole scene is extremely depressing.

The final stretch of the trip in Peru brought us to the town of Tumbes situated on the river of the same name, the last important river on the northern Coast of Peru. There we were greeted by an old friend, Dr. Petersen of

Fig. 11. A typical suspension bridge of the Andes. *Kosok* • Fig. 12 (margin). Pisac Indian with an exceptionally fine poncho. *Kosok* • Fig. 12a (margins). Glyph-like figures, Tiahuanaco area. *Mead.*

labeled with their places of origin. He had also made a ground plan of the ruins of Los Organos, a settlement of some hundred and thirty houses located in one of the *quebradas* between Tumbes and Talara. There, among other things, he had found interesting gold trinkets.

Dr. Petersen had also written a manuscript of more than four hundred pages dealing with his finds. The uniqueness and high calibre of all of Dr. Petersen's work make it imperative that some archaeological institute take cognizance of his remarkable accomplishments and publish his manuscripts.

The following day we left Peru, having stayed there a year less one day. We took the bus to Zarumilla on the Ecuadorian border, where, after lengthy personal and baggage inspection, we were permitted to enter Ecuador.

Here we boarded a gaudily painted bus which by late afternoon brought us as far as the town of Santa Rosa. It was fascinating to see how in the course of the day the landscape changed. At Tumbes, we had left a tropical desert landscape, though with sufficient rainfall to produce cacti and mesquite bushes and trees, but as the bus rolled on, the effects of a greater annual rainfall became evident. The cacti became larger; gradually grasses and trees appeared, until finally, as we approached Santa Rosa itself, we were traveling through thick tropical jungle that contained large banyan trees! Part of the foliage in this jungle region was dead, since it was the dry season of the year.

At Santa Rosa, we boarded a typical small river boat for Guayaquil, one which carried both passengers and freight. Soon the boat pushed off and wound its way slowly down the narrow river, its top and sides often scraped by the overhanging branches of trees. We might well have been floating down some tributary of the tropical Amazon on the other side of the Andes! As the

Fig. 13 (left). A group of workers engaged in cleaning out one of the huge ancient canals used today by Hacienda Pabur, situated in the upper Piura Valley. The laborious method, by which each worker throws a shovelful of earth to the worker above him, probably dates back to ancient times. Annual canal-cleaning then was an important form of social activity and was accompanied by processions and ceremonies. Allan Holmberg found that in the Virú Valley, as late as 35 years ago, similar canal-cleaning processions were still popular. Indeed, according to our informants in Ferreñafe in the Lambayeque region, canal-cleaning processions and ceremonies — now directed by the local Catholic priest — are practiced in the town to this day. *Kosok.*

Fig. 14. This photograph shows the largest ancient site in the Chira Valley. Located on the north bank of the river next to the modern town of Amotape, it consists of two parts. Just to the left of the town are a number of considerably disintegrated adobe mounds, dating back possibly to the Middle, or even the Early Period. In the center and just left of center are two better-preserved clusters of pyramids and walled enclosures suggesting a Late Period construction. The site, which we visited in 1941, is mentioned by the earliest Chroniclers. *International Petroleum Company* • Fig. 15 (left). Fields south of Pabur in the upper part of the Piura Valley which, in many years, get sufficient rain for growing stock feed. The slight elevations at the right are remains of small ancient mounds. *Kosok* • Fig. 16 (left center). This dramatic method is used to warn drivers to be careful in the hilly section of the Pan American Highway north of the Chira Valley. The legend reads: "Rotary Club of Piura. Go slowly and you will go far." *Kosok* • Fig. 17 (lower left). Street in the village of Catacaos, Piura Valley, known among other things for its production of "ancient" *huacos*. *Kosok* • Fig. 18 (right margin). Peruvian boy. *Kosok*.

boat nosed its way down the river, dolphins appeared and began to play around the vessel.

The river gradually widened and we witnessed a beautiful sunset as the boat approached the harbor of Puerto Bolivar. The latter is the port for the town of Machála and is at the end of two short railroad lines that connect with the towns in the hinterland. Our boat stopped at this settlement for an hour to take on more passengers and freight. While sauntering along the piers, we were attracted to some of the small eating stands where vendors were selling huge fried shrimp, the largest we had ever seen. They tasted so delicious that we ate all our stomachs could hold.

After the boat left for the trip to Guayaquil, we found that the sleeping accommodations consisted mainly of hammocks strung in rows along the covered deck. For a while we sat with some of the passengers chatting, drinking and playing cards, but by midnight most of the ship was a sleeping, snoring mass of humanity.

The next morning found us approaching Guayaquil, largest and richest city of Ecuador. Situated on the Bay of Guayaquil, it is a modern international trading port, the main center for exporting bananas and other products of both the tropics and the Sierras, and for the importing of industrial products.

The whole Guayaquil bay and river system probably always has been the center of some kind of trading economy — even in ancient times. We have no detailed description of the economy or society of those times, but we have various references which indicate that trade had once played an important role here (see John Murra in *Handbook*, Vol. II). It was only here that large balsa rafts were built in pre-Spanish times. They were made of large logs of the very light balsa wood which grows in this region. The logs were lashed together with fiber rope, and they had rudders, oars, sails and even a "cabin" (see Fig. 25). Heyerdahl's raft of recent fame was built in imitation of these ancient craft. Some of them were even large enough, according to early Spanish records, to carry horses and men. The rafts sailed the intricate network of rivers that flow into the Gulf of Guayaquil. They also sailed to the nearby Coast of Peru, to Tumbes, to Payta and, on rare occasions, even further south. We are not informed about the extent of their operations along the coast of Ecuador, but it is not im-

possible that they went up along the Manabí Coast.

The extreme geographical limits of their voyages are, however, of secondary importance to us; basic are the social and material conditions that produced such large units of transportation and the specific functions the latter played in the society of this region. From the limited information we have of the ancient balsas, we gather that they probably were not merely used for fishing purposes or for pleasure trips by rulers, but were also used to transport goods and men from one part of this maritime complex to another. Since we have no indications that there existed in the Guayaquil Complex a large agrarian empire which, like the Inca, had transformed trade into transportation of tribute, we may infer with a certain degree of assurance that some kind of free commerce had existed which was managed by a special group of traders.

This would mean that in certain respects a qualitatively different type of society from that of Peru had developed here. No centralized agricultural empire had emerged, but rather a decentralized society, held together by relatively independent trading groups. In a certain sense it might be considered similar to the germinal forms of early eastern Mediterranean semi-trading civilizations. The Spanish conquerors, unfortunately, paid little attention to the social structure of the Indians living in the Guayaquil river system. However, an archaeological and historical reconstruction of this whole area, including the Tumbes region in Peru, should throw light on the true nature of their society.

Such a study may also help connect this region more closely with the original home of the legendary Naymlap who is supposed to have conquered the Lambayeque area

in Peru, possibly around 1100 A.D., and established an important dynasty there. If he came *with balsas* from "de la parte suprema," as the legend goes, he is most likely to have come from the Guayaquil region, for it is only here that balsa rafts were built and used.

Our main purpose in coming to Guayaquil, however, was to acquaint ourselves a little more with the nature of the climatic conditions in the region between Guayaquil and the Pacific Ocean. According to the meterological reports of the Ecuadorian government, there are places here with as low an annual rainfall as that of the Northwest Coast of Peru just across the Bay of Guayaquil. Our aim was, if possible, to find the limits of this "dry" region in Ecuador and to see if there were any indications here of irrigation in ancient times.

After visiting a number of government offices, we were fortunate in obtaining a fine, large map of the area, as well as a letter of introduction to officials in Santa Elena, a town situated in the center of the area in question, near the coast of Ecuador.

Early the next morning, Michael and I left for Santa Elena by means of an *autovagón*. As we progressed from Guayaquil the vegetation gradually became sparser and sparser until after about an hour's ride it took on a semi-desert character. We knew we had now entered the so-called "dry" zone.

At Santa Elena we met the mayor of the town. This intelligent, energetic man called in his assistants and all the members of the regional council that he could locate. Then with our map spread on the large council table, we presented our problem. The Mayor asked each one present whether his village was in a "dry" or a "wet" zone. As the answers were given, we checked off each village on the map. About some villages we obtained contradictory answers. Further inquiry revealed that these villages were in the transition zone; during some years there was enough rain for agriculture, during other years there was an insufficient amount. Within an hour we had the necessary answers and were able to draw a line across the map separating the two zones! To minimize errors,

Fig. 21. Crossing the Chira River. *Kosok* • Fig. 22 (right). Mouth of the Tumbes River as it empties into the Guayaquil Bay region. The dark area is a mango swamp, while the striped area at the left was produced by strong winds sweeping over the earth and sand, the white stripes being bare soil and the dark stripes bushes thriving on subsoil water. *Servicio 220:46.*

we carefully repeated the whole questioning process. This was the fastest and, in many ways, the most reliable method we had come upon for making a detailed hydrological survey of a critical area.

At present there is no irrigation in the dry area; only a little animal husbandry is carried on there. The greater part of the population works for a petroleum company which has drilled oil wells on the southern coastal part of the dry terrain. But there are indications that some of this area was probably cultivated in ancient times. At various places across the beds of the small streams that are dry most of the year, remains of small dams have been found and, in a number of cases, pottery finds have been associated with them. According to the current general explanation, these dams were once used to impound some of the water during the short rainy season when the swollen "rivers" rushed down the dry stream beds from the nearby hills The amount of water thus impounded, together with the limited amount of rain that fell annually, was generally sufficient to furnish a limited crop of maize for small population clusters.

After our return to Guayaquil by bus, we obtained reli-

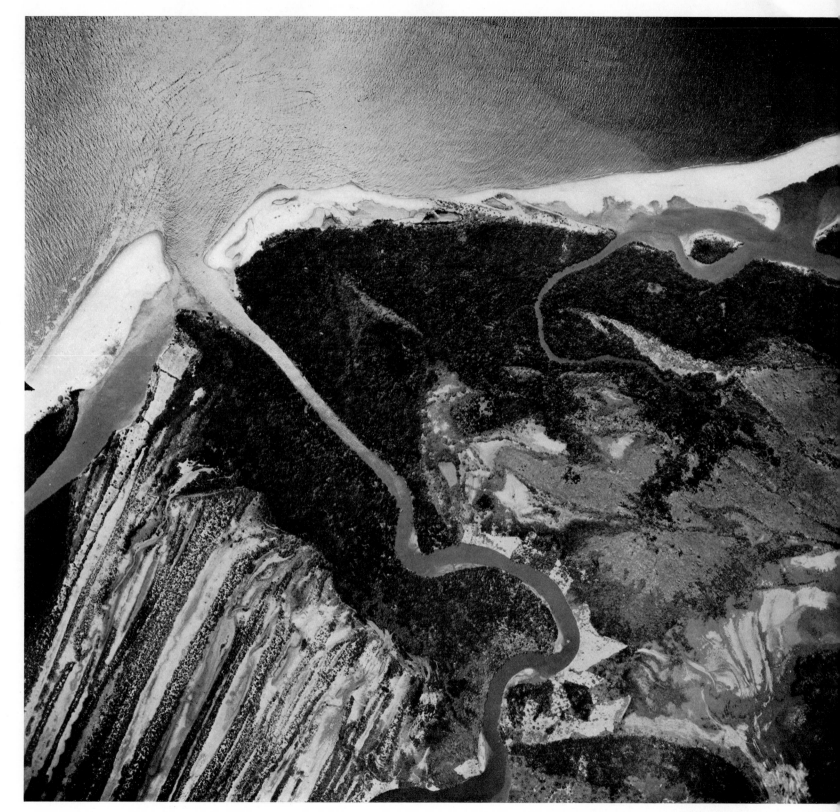

243

able information indicating that on the large island of Puna, which lies in the Gulf of Guayaquil between Ecuador and Peru, a western dry zone and an eastern wet zone can be distinguished. Piecing together this information with that which we had obtained for Peru, we were able to establish *a continuous line from Ecuador to southern Peru separating the dry area from the wet one.* The line runs across the lower tip of Ecuador, across the island of Puna, touches the mainland just beyond Zarumilla, then goes up the Andes to a height of about 9000 feet in the neighborhood of the upper Lambayeque Valley. Then it rises slowly until it reaches 11,000 to 12,000 feet near the southern border of Peru.

Our work in South America was done! At midnight, we left Guayaquil on a Panagra plane that was equipped with many luxury gadgets. I settled down in my extremely comfortable seat and dozed off. After what seemed like a few minutes, I woke up. The plane was bouncing up and down and I heard the stewardess say: "Put on your safety belts!" Peering quickly out of the window, I was surprised to see the bright lights of Panama City sparkling below us. It was not long before the plane approached the runway and gently deposited us at this attractive metropolis, just as the dawn of the new day was lighting up the skies. The first part of our journey home was over!

Fig. 23 (upper left). Loading bananas onto a steamer by means of a combination of hand labor and machinery. *Kosok* • Fig. 24 (left center). Women and children workers sorting coffee beans on the streets of Guayaquil. *Kosok* • Fig. 25 (lower left). A balsa raft of the seventeenth century, similar to the rafts used when the Spanish arrived. According to the Chroniclers, one raft was encountered carrying 30 tons of native cargo, plus 20 men; another, used by the Spaniards, carried 50 men and 3 horses (see also Heyerdahl, 1952). *Juan and Ulloa, 1748* • Fig. 26 (below). The Bay of Guayaquil, with solitary Cerro Masvale in the background. The dark spots in the foreground and the dark line parallel to the shore are small "islands" of soil and grass that move up and down the bay with each change of the tide. *Kosok.*

XXV

Meditations on Ancient Beginnings

Oᴜʀ ᴡᴏʀᴋ in Peru was done! We had completed mapping — as far as we knew — all still existing but unused canal systems and irrigated areas of the Northwest Coast of Peru, the largest and most important section of desert Peru. We further had indicated on our large maps the present day irrigated areas. Since in almost all cases the latter areas were also irrigated in ancient times, a glance at the maps shows us the total irrigated areas of the past at the maximum stages of development.

Some 300 ruin sites had also been entered on the maps, sites which we had found as the result of thorough field work and systematic study of thousands of aerial photographs. To make these entries more intelligible we had prepared a "key" of each of the sites, which gives the name and a short description and in such cases as is possible, a reference to archeological literature. In some cases, we were able to relate major ruin sites to major canal systems.

Finally, we completed most of the second draft of the manuscript of "Water and Life in Ancient Peru" which describes the irrigation systems of each of the thirteen valleys from the Tumbes in the north, near the Ecuadorian border, to the Casma further south. We also surveyed all the valleys south of the Casma as far as Nazca. But, with some exceptions, most of the ancient irrigation systems here are still, or again, in use. To give some social impact to this somewhat technical volume, we added chapters which attempted to interpret the various aspects of the irrigation economy of the whole of Peru.

Our work in Peru thus had resulted in giving us a more concrete foundation for understanding the changing economic, social and political structure of ancient coastal Peru. But each question that was answered obviously produced new questions and problems that required new answers and solutions. In such a way all science progresses. And these new questions and problems dealt not only with the irrigation societies of coastal Peru, but also with the relationship of the coastal to the ancestral Sierra societies, and comparisons and contrasts to similar societies in other parts of the world.

Returning by plane to the United States, we stopped over at the well known Maya centers at Copán in Honduras and at Chichén Itzá and Uxmál in Yucatan, Mexico. Since I had not seen these sites before, I was interested in comparing and contrasting them *in situ* with similar sites I had found in Peru. We flew first from Panama to Tegucigalpa, the capital of Honduras. The latter part of the trip proved especially interesting to us since some of the vegetation of the hills and mountains as we approached Tegucigalpa was of a semi-arid nature! It seemed as though we were in some parts of the hills and mountains of coastal Peru. A *detailed* investigation of the still largely unknown climatology of this country, as well as that of neighboring Guatemala and Yucatan, should provide a new and more detailed insight into the relationship of the various vegetation zones of this area to the rise, development, and spread of the early Maya and related civilizations.

Unfortunately, the meteorological data of this whole zone is still very spotty and limited in area, and, as was already stated in the case of the Peruvian Sierras, unless detailed data exists, not merely from valley to valley, but *within each valley*, no worthwhile conclusions can be drawn. However, from the facts so far gathered, by zoologists and botanists, it can be stated here that there are tremendous varieties of flora and fauna, within the small area of this Central American region. This fact in itself indicates considerable differentiations of climate within the area and must have affected the nature and growth of the economy and society of the regions inhabited by the Maya and related peoples. This may be the key approach in attempting to explain the many complex problems which haunt the scholar of Maya history and culture. It *may* indicate that the proto-Maya cultures evolved in the moderate rainfall areas. Later expansions did not go to non-existent desert areas, as was the case on the coast of Peru. Instead the expansions became, so to speak, *intrusions* into the richer jungle areas where, later on, the highest forms of Maya culture evolved.

From Tegucigalpa, a charming mountain town, quite distinct from the capitals of the other Central American states, we visited the Maya ruin of Copán. This famous site dates back to the Early Period, more or less contemporaneous with the same period in Peru. The flight was a fascinating one over hilly country which at places also showed the same semi-arid vegetation we had seen south of Tegucigalpa. After a two hour trip over the mountain tops, our plane descended into a small valley and after some cruising, landed successfully on the small grass covered airfield situated between the present village of Copán and the ancient ruins of the same name.

The ruins, which have been largely cleared of jungle growth and are fairly well restored, were our first sight of a major Maya ruin. It was this ruin, which its dis-

245

coverer Stevenson — who also wrote about Peru — bought for fifty dollars! Its discovery and the significance of the whole area intrigued Lewis H. Morgan, the American anthropologist, sufficiently to write a letter to Washington, D. C., urging the United States government to spend $10,000 for the purchase of an extensive strip in Honduras before treasure hunters would carry off or destroy much of its most significant archaelogical treasure.

As we climbed over the various pyramids and structures we soon realized that this did not represent the remains of an urban site, but rather those of a large *ceremonial center* containing pyramids and associated structures built around several plazas, undoubtedly controlled by the local priesthood — possibly in conjunction with the secular chief who held secondary powers.

Our impression was that ancient Copán probably had the same general architectural layout, and the associated population had evolved a similar type of social structure, as had been characteristic of at least part of the Mochica period in ancient Peru. Both societies consisted of local habitation units clustered around a priestly-controlled ceremonial site. No urban centers, no real political states, no "empires" existed. At best, temporary federations of theocratic units could have prevailed. The houses of the habitation units probably were built largely of mud walls with thatched roofs, like those still being erected today.

The pyramids themselves, built of stone-faced rubble and now reconstructed by archaeologists, are in many ways more impressive than the partly destroyed adobe pyramids of the coast of Peru. This impressiveness is increased by the fact that while the bases of the Mayan pyramids are not larger, and are, in many instances, smaller than those of the larger pyramids of Peru, the nature of the stone building material permitted the Maya pyramid to be much steeper. On the other hand, the nature of adobe bricks used in most of the Peruvian pyramids, does not permit the heights of pyramids to exceed one third the width of the base, a limitation which does not apply to stone structures. Moreover, the accompanying stone buildings, walls and *stellae* of the Maya that still stand in place or have been reconstructed in part, give one a much more concrete picture of the relationship in ancient times of all the parts to the whole than is generally possible in the case of Peru. There the perishable adobe walls and other secondary structures have often been destroyed by centuries of steady winds, as well as by modern farming methods, with their bulldozers and other mechanical equipment.

After having completed our visit to Copán we flew to Yucatan. We had Morley's archaeological map with us and tried to imagine this country as it once had been at the height of its development. This proved to be extremely difficult since much of the country is now, as it had been in earlier times, covered by dense vegetation. But it was this very denseness of vegetation which tended to confirm our opinion of the role of nature in helping to maintain the decentralized form of Maya society.

As we approached the town of Merida, we noticed that some of the vegetation became scantier. Here the rainfall is somewhat less than in the central and southern regions. Moreover, the subsoil consists of porous limestone rock, which still further lowers the effectiveness of rainfall. This is another aspect which must be taken into consideration in evaluating not only the nature of the later Maya period but also its development in this particular region.

Our time was running short and so we confined our excursions to the ruins of Chichén Itzá and Uxmál. These Maya ruins, which date from the later period of Maya culture, have been described many times and in great detail and are by now a typical tourist attraction. Suffice to say that an inspection of both places confirmed the impressions we had obtained at Copán of the local nature and the ceremonial function of the ruins and the theocratic or theocratically-colored type of decentralized society that produced them. The only "centralization" we hear of in the Late Period is the League of Mayapan, apparently a very loose federation that lasted a short time, and which had only traces of secularization in its social and political structure.

In Mexico proper, which I covered on three separate visits, before and after this Peru trip, the early developments indicate similar "demon-infested, priest-dominated" societies. Only the later Aztec Empire indicated the evolution of a secular state and society, though this Empire never quite reached the level of secularization of the Chimú and Inca empires in Peru. Further archaeological and archival research will undoubtedly bring out more clearly the characteristics mentioned. At the same time unknown aspects and specific "variations" will begin to reveal themselves in the theocratic transition form from late tribal societies to early secular class societies.

I sent my son, Michael, to Mexico proper, which he had not yet visited, and I flew on to New Orleans and then returned to New York by train. While traveling through parts of the South, I thought about what I had read of

its pre-history. It became clearer to me than it ever had been before that the many earth mounds and mound clusters, so far discovered in the Mississippi Valley undoubtedly represented *early forms* of the same type of pyramids and pyramid clusters we had located in Peru and had just seen in Yucatan. In terms of construction, they probably are a product of a social structure similar to that of the very Early Cupisnique Period in Peru, while the group of some 25 Cahokia mounds, near St. Louis, may even parallel the Salinar and Gallinazo periods. It must be remembered that the largest of the pyramids of the Cahokia group is comparable in volume to the largest ones in Peru and Mexico and these in turn to the large ones in Egypt and China.

If we can reconstruct more clearly the society of the ancient Mississippi Valley Mound Builder cultures — which apparently had existed until a few centuries before the Spanish conquest, and whose pyramids were not enlarged or destroyed by an additional two thousand years of development, as was the case in Coastal Peru, we can get a better understanding of the still somewhat nebulous character of the Cupisnique and Salinar cultures of Peru and parallel cultures of Mexico.

Thus, as was pointed out in Chapter I, while the most advanced developments of Peruvian Coastal societies undoubtedly can help clarify certain aspects of the early forms of Afrasian irrigation societies, in turn certain basic aspects of the Mississippi Valley cultures — though not based on an irrigation economy — can be used to help us better understand the Very Early Coastal Chavín (Cupisnique) culture and perhaps some of its antecedents in the Sierras.

We can, of course, go even further and study the early stage of the Mississippi Mound Builders in terms of such semi-agricultural, semi-food-gathering and hunting societies that existed when the Europeans first came here — and in turn study the early stages of the latter societies in terms of the completely pre-agricultural hunting and food-collecting societies. (Specifically fishing societies we omit here for, while they date back to the very early times of man's existence, they develop a *special* evolutionary aspect of a *sedentary* and often stagnant society with special forms of social relationship which are different from both the hunting and the agricultural societies.)

Thus, by studying a series of interlocking cultures with overlapping characteristics from different parts of the world, we can reconstruct a continuous story of the development of man in the New World. Of course, corresponding early developments in Afrasia and Europe must be considered. But, as pointed out in Chapter I, the transformation from a hunting and food-collecting societies to early agricultural societies, and from these to the rise of early civilizations in Afrasia is more difficult to trace than it is on the American continent where the transformation came some four to five thousand years later and where the remains of this period have not been so destroyed or covered up as in the Eastern Hemisphere.

Comparative archaeology is necessary, but not only on an American scale, which has already been carried on by a number of scholars. It is even more necessary on a world-wide scale, not merely in terms of *cultural forms* or in terms of *prehistoric sequences,* but in terms of *similarity of social structures.* Then an examination of the irrigation coastal cultures of Peru can hardly be considered complete if careful comparisons are not made with cultures of similar early irrigation societies of Egypt, the Indus Valley, and that of the early Yellow River in China. In our present stage of knowledge, ancient Babylonia seems most promising in yielding results. Not to be forgotten must be such an irrigation culture as that of ancient Khorezm, south of the Aral Sea, excavated by Professor S. P. Tolstov. Drawings of the rectangular walled compounds found there are very reminiscent of a great number of the late Chimú compounds.

But *broader* aspects must also be studied in such a comparative world archaeology. Thus the Peruvian Sierra and the Coastal cultures, while distinct in many ways, were nevertheless *interrelated* in many others. Indeed, one can assume for the present that the first maize agriculture and with it the establishment of a basically agricultural economy, as distinct from the much earlier fishing cultures with some subsidiary bean and other plant proto-agriculture, came mainly from the Sierras with small priest-dominated clans of the Chavín or pre-Chavín Period. The Serranos undoubtedly brought limited irrigation techniques with them which they had evolved in "dry" years. Many reasons may have brought them to the coast, including military defeat by their more successful rivals who remained in the rainfall and semi-rainfall agriculture areas of the Sierras. Moreover, once established on the Coast, the coastal peoples and those of the Sierras undoubtedly developed trade in one another of mutually necessary natural products and manufactured goods.

This development of an agricultural irrigation economy from a semi-irrigation economy in the Sierra, and the latter from a rainfall economy where the original *grains* first grew and were first domesticated, does not appear to be peculiar to the Peruvian Sierra-Coastal complex. Perhaps it also developed in the Mexico-Mesoamerica complex where, however, this interrelationship appears to have been on a smaller scale and more complex in its forms. Most important, a similar mountain-desert valley complex seems to have existed in the region consisting of desert Babylonia and the neighboring mountains of Persia and Asia Minor, in the Egypt-Ethiopia complex, in the complex of the Indus valley and the mountains of Northwest India and Baluchistan, and possibly in the Middle Yellow River and nearby mountain areas. In other words, comparative world archaeology and corresponding world pre- and proto-history become important integrative factors that show that below the diversity of cultural forms there exist important topographic-climatic and social-economic *similarities.*

It is relatively easy to discover differences. It requires, however, a greater knowledge and a deeper and more mature insight into the problems concerned to see *common* basic characteristics and processes of development. Therefore, it becomes imperative for us to find among the multitude of concrete forms and processes, those basic factors and processes which have been *common* to *all* peoples of the world as they evolved from primitive tribal societies through the transitional priest-dominated societies into the agriculturally-rooted early class societies with their state apparatuses and their "empire" building potentialities.

All studies of the complex and often "exotic" aspects of the past must always bring to the forefront the basic *unity* of mankind!

Epílogue

Professor Paul Kosok's untimely death (October 1959) cut short a plan of publications of a lifetime of fruitful research in various fields, ranging from the history of science to Peruvian irrigation and music. In this volume some of his erudition in these several fields is revealed. He was working on the final touches of this volume when he died, and half of the volume was already printed. Those of us who collaborated with him as researchers and editors experience great satisfaction in seeing this volume at last emerging in the light of day, and we look forward to the forthcoming publication of the remainder of his manuscripts. The oft-referred-to title of *Water and Life in Ancient Peru* was to be the sequel to this book. Since its title is so similar to the one this volume bears, we should like it known that while plans still exist for publishing Kosok's detailed study on Peruvian irrigation, the title of that work will be altered to avoid confusion.

Professor Kosok had fully intended that this book be dedicated to the memory of his close associate and friend the late Tristram Walker Metcalfe, President of Long Island University from 1931 through 1951. It was he who made the expeditions to Peru possible and encouraged publication of the findings in their present form.

Yet, subsequent important help from Chancellor John H. G. Pell has been essential to the completion of this effort. The cooperation of Chancellor R. Gordon Hoxie has made the issuance of the volume at this time possible.

LIST I OF MOCHICA WORDS AND PHRASES

These words and phrases were copied by Señor Antonio Rodríguez SuySuy in July 1951, from a list of Señor Simon Quezquen in the village of Eten. The list was originally taken from "some papers which his [Señor Quezquen's] grandparents left and which he copied because these papers were already deteriorating and as a result now no longer exist." In copying the list Señor Rodríguez SuySuy had the following to say: "As he was dictating to me, I copied down everything with great care and exactness, but, I noticed that there are some letters which do not represent the actual pronunciations. For example, there are words like NE HIC which, as Señor Quezquen pronounced it, I put down erroneously NEQUIC, but on hearing him pronounce it again, I noted that his pronunciation was smoother. This pronunciation I cannot write, but I can pronounce it. For this reason I proceeded to copy them [the words] just as they were [on the original list] and they are all that I am sending." According to Señor Rodríguez SuySuy's report, Señor Quezquen said that "in Eten there remain but very few persons who speak or remember three or four words, but within this list are all these words now spoken."

Mochica	English	Spanish
WORDS		
1. achecone	1. agreeable	1. agradable
2. auy	2. listen!	2. oye
3. cateníc	3. female sex organ	3. naturaleza de mujer
4. cojpan	4. black	4. negro
5. consiche	5. cold	5. frío
6. costape	6. pubic hair	6. pendejos (bellos)
7. cuchis	7. Trujillo	7. Trujillo
8. cunti	8. tied	8. atado
9. chafca	9. dirty	9. sucio
10. chanc	10. wet	10. mojado
11. chaypi	11. Chiclayo	11. Chiclayo
12. Chéjemer	12. drunk	12. borracho
13. cheméteque	13. earrings	13. aretes
14. chichi	14. pants	14. pantalón
15. chichuy	15. meat	15. carne
16. Chijape	16. dry	16. seco
17. chumay	17. chicha	17. chicha
18. chupetes	18. highlander	18. serrano
19. Etin	19. Eten	19. Eten
20. fac	20. bull	20. toro
21. facch	21. brushwood	21. leña
22. fanun (or yanun)	22. dog	22. perro
23. fellum	23. duck	23. pato
24. fone	24. nose	24. nariz
25. grelis	25. concealing	25. disimulando
26. hem	26. rapid	26. ligero
27. hemoyac	27. girdle, band	27. faja
28. her	28. yucca	28. yuca
29. hot	29. eye	29. ojo
30. huy	30. to fall down	30. caerse
31. ja	31. water	31. agua
32. jacse	32. head	32. cabeza
33. jarmensap	33. liar	33. mentiroso
34. jax pulem	34. braggart	34. palangana
35. jechis	35. binding clay	35. barro ligoso
36. jédeñet	36. duck dung	36. excremento de pato
37. jelu (see fellum)	37. duck	37. pato
38. jiac	38. fish	38. pescado
39. jiad	39. to sleep	39. dormir
40. jiam	40. sun	40. sol
41. jiamud	41. hairy	41. peludo
42. jiay	42. money	42. dinero
43. joc (or jocce)	43. foot	43. pié
44. jujuna	44. tablecloth	44. mantel
45. man	45. take (eat)	45. tomar
46. manes postap	46. dry	46. secco
47. mecherque	47. woman	47. mujer
48. mellús	48. eggs	48. huevos
49. metse	49. hand	49. mano
50. mish (or mis)	50. cat	50. gato
51. mo	51. that	51. ese
52. mob	52. cachema (a fish)	52. cachema (pescado)
53. murrup	53. iguana	53. iguana
54. ne hec	54. mantle (wrapped up)	54. manto (envuelto)
55. neis	55. night	55. noche
56. niñecosque	56. Lambayeque	56. Lambayeque
57. Ñancaipe	57. hen	57. gallina
58. ñañe	58. husband	58. marido
59. ñau	59. child	59. criatura
60. ñess	60. liar	60. mentiroso
61. ñetasapec	61. liquor	61. licor
62. ñiech	62. ?	62. ?
63. ñoven	63. youth (young man)	63. jóven
64. opene	64. sweet potato	64. camote
65. pucheque	65. disappeared	65. desvanecido
66. quismique	66. old	66. viejo
67. Recpaneque	67. Reque	67. Reque
68. rometec	68. crazy	68. loco
69. Siúrrepe	69. Monsefú	69. Monsefú
70. teb	70. male sex organ?	70. organo masculino?
71. up	71. salt	71. sal
72. usap	72. pepper	72. ají
73. usenic	73. small farm	73. chacra
74. vellus	74. drink container	74. poto
75. yémeque (or lléméc)	75. stew	75. espesado
76. zápete	76. one	76. uno
77. zarcillas	77. rings	77. sortijas
78. zúpete	78. three	78. tres
PHRASES		
1. acan mo mish	1. look at that cat!	1. vea ese gato!
2. acan mo ñess	2. look at that child!	2. vea ese criatura!
3. acan mo ñetesapéc	3. look at that nut! (crazy man)	3. vea ese loco!
4. acan mo rometec	4. look at that liar!	4. vea ese mentiroso
5. ajpe fone	5. big nose (person)	5. narigon
6. ajpe pott	6. beautiful . . .	6. hermosa . . .
7. amoch fénun	7. let's eat	7. vamos a comer
8. amoch miquer	8. let's go soon	8. vamos pronto
9. amoch jiad	9. let's go to sleep	9. vamos a dormir
10. ap pesen	10. big neck (person)	10. pescuezón
11. ayena moyi	11. fine, thanks!	11. bien gracias
12. coss tap tote cap	12. "bottoms up!"	12. boca abajo
13. chanque de cap	13. the weaving is going bad	13. tejido va malo
14. chep chep	14. ashamed	14. avergonzado
15. chipe de mot	15. corn husk	15. hollejo del maiz
16. chuchepe fone	16. flattened nose	16. nariz ñata
17. chucho rometec	17. crazy boy	17. muchacho loco
18. eches suy	18. I have served myself	18. me he servido
19. emes unam (or unanche)	19. how did you get up?	19. cómo has amaneci
20. fenequit	20. last child	20. niño ultimo
21. hecha guara	21. it's elegant	21. está elegante
22. hich	22. what does it have?	22. ¿qué tiene?
23. iches tem	23. what do you want?	23. ¿que es lo que qui
24. ich teme	24. who is that?	24. ¿quien es eso?
25. jay	25. take another	25. toma otro
26. kiche	26. child on back	26. niño a la espalda (or cargado el n
27. manan tut coch	27. take your chicha	27. toma tu chicha
28. manan tut llemec	28. have a little stew	28. come un poco de espesado (de c
29. mesjepeque	29. pray to God	29. implorar a Díos
30. metantate tut caten	30. lend me your rear	30. préstame tu culo
31. midam cap	31. stingy	31. caranganoso
32. misanchimo	32. he is a thief	32. este es ladrón

Mochica	English	Spanish	Mochica	English	Spanish	Mochica	English	Spanish
33. mitan (or minan) cuchis	33. my chicha	33. mi chicha	40. pelam chemoy	40. sit down, sir	40. sientese, Señor	47. tates tu cuchis	47. take your chicha	47. toma tu chicha
34. móymene	34. just like you	34. igual a tí	41. pomete cauchimo	41. this one is crazy	41. este está loco	48. tep tep	48. bad taste	48. mal gusto
35. ñespe toc	35. ugly face	35. fea cara	42. réquepot	42. raised rump	42. trasero levantado	49. tillipe	49. defecating without feeling (it)	49. defecando sin sentir
36. peinas nenh	36. crazy-head	36. cabeza loco	43. roj pepot	43. nude rump	43. trasero desnudo	50. tote cape	50. cup upside down	50. copa volteada
37. peinas nerrem	37. good afternoon	37. buenos tardes	44. sappi jappi	44. long bearded man	44. barbón	51. tu cap	51. get out! (jealous one)	51. véte celoso
38. peinas nerrem séquemoi	38. good afternoon, sir	38. buenos tardes, Señor	45. sec secfane	45. pregnant (or irritable)	45. embarazada (or colérico)	52. yarnanloc	52. shut up!	52. cállate la boca
39. peinas unan séquemoi	39. good day, sir	39. buenos dias, Señor	46. taschep tumanacupu	46. they will say that we are drunk	46. dirán que estamos borrachos	53. ych teme	53. who is that?	53. ¿quien es eso?

LIST 2 OF MOCHICA WORDS AND PHRASES

These words and phrases were obtained 1948 in Trujillo by Señor Antonio Rodríguez SuySuy and the author, from Señora Manuela Millones de Carillo, resident of Etén (see Chapter IX). The English translation of both word lists was done by Dr. Schaedel.

Mochica	English	Spanish	Mochica	English	Spanish	Mochica	English	Spanish
WORDS			21. joch	21. eyes	21. ojos	**PHRASES**		
			22. jocke	22. foot	22. pié			
1. acan!	1. look!	1. vea!	23. jujuna	23. tablecloth	23. mantel	1. acan ñieshon	1. look at your son!	1. vea a su hijo!
2. ajpe	2. large, big	2. grande	24. man	24. eat	24. comer	2. ajpe fome	2. big nose (person)	2. narigón
3. amoch	3. let's go	3. vamos	25. mecherka	25. woman	25. mujer	3. ajpe jech	3. big head (person)	3. cabezón
4. apúte	4. two	4. dos	26. meden	26. ear	26. oreja	4. ajpe joch	4. big eyes (person)	4. ojón
5. ayen!	5. good!	5. bien!	27. nópete	27. four	27. quatro	5. ajpe jocken	5. big foot (person)	5. patón
6. catenique	6. female sex organ	6. naturaleza de mujer	28. ñan	28. husband	28. marido	6. ajpe meden	6. big ear (person)	6. orejón
7. conch	7. meat	7. carne	29. ñieshon	29. your son	29. su hijo	7. ajpe sapa	7. big mouth (person)	7. bocón
8. cucho	8. chicha, a mild drink made of fermented corn	8. chicha	30. ñiest	30. small child	30. criatura	8. amísinam	8. how did you get up?	8. ¿como ha amanecido?
			31. onek	31. one	31. uno	9. amoch jía	9. let's go to sleep	9. vamos a dormir
9. cujo pemey	9. male sex organ	9. naturaleza de hombre	32. ópeno	32. sweet potato	32. camote	10. amoch manan	10. let's eat	10. vamos a comer
10. cuyupe	10. colored, red	10. colorado	33. palla	33. cooking pot	33. olla	11. amoch micar	11. let's go soon	11. vamos pronto
11. eigmeche	11. five	11. cinco	34. sai	34. cooked corn	34. mote (maiz cocido)	12. emesenama	12. good day!	12. buenos días!
12. épen	12. a strong pepper	12. aji	35. sape	35. mouth	35. boca	13. fac pepotes	13. black bottom	13. poto negro
13. ers	13. yucca, sweet manioc	13. yuca	36. secúye	36. white	36. blanco	14. jarmen sape	14. loudmouth (gossiper)	14. hablador
14. fano	14. dog	14. perro	37. sech	37. ten	37. diez	15. manan	15. that (you) are eating	15. que come
15. fone	15. nose	15. nariz	38. sópete	38. three	38. tres	16. manang ñiete	16. like nothing (at all)!	16. como nada!
16. já	16. water	16. agua	39. terco	39. lazy	39. ocioso	17. ñiete sape	17. liar	17. mentiroso
17. jech	17. head	17. cabeza	40. upe	40. salt	40. sal	18. ñasanchi	18. is it good?	18. ¿esta rico? (food)
18. jía	18. sleep	18. dormir	41. usa	41. stick for spinning	41. palo para hilar	19. tastem conch	19. to make a present of a piece of ...	19. regalar un pedazo de
19. jiak	19. fish	19. pescado	42. velloso	42. gourd, pot	42. poto	20. tastem man	20. (he) wants to eat meat	20. quiere comer carne
20. jime	20. spoon	20. cuchara	43. yemeke	43. a sort of corn goulash	43. pepían de choclo (mazamorra de maiz)	21. terco fano	21. lazy as a dog	21. ocioso como un perro

Glossary

acequia — irrigation canal

acequia madre (mother canal) — main feeder canal of an irrigation system

adabones — large blocks of pressed earth made from a mold.

adobe — sun-baked brick

aguardiente — a strong alcoholic beverage made from grain

altiplano — literally high plateau. In Peru, the plateau in the southern part where the Andes widen out.

camión — truck

carro — car

cerro — hill or mountain

costa — the coastal region, a desert

fortaleza — fortress

hacienda — plantation

haciendado — plantation owner

huaca — general term, any structure or burial ground considered to have been built in ancient (prehistoric) times.
specific term, a ceremonial or burial mound or pyramid.

huaco — an ancient water jug of high quality

lomas — clouds that settle along the coast during the winter that produce no rain but merely an occasional cold mist. Where they "rest" on the side of the mountain, they condense into moisture that produces some vegetation.

montaña — the jungle, beyond the Andes, area of heavy rainfall

monte — a natural growth of grasses, shrubs, bushes and even small trees growing in the desert near the rivers or irrigated areas. These plants get the necessary moisture from subsoil seepage and occasional rains. In some places, this growth is quite heavy and difficult to penetrate, and becomes a kind of "desert jungle".

pampa — Peruvian usage — plain on the coast; it has a desert character.

potsherds — broken pieces of pottery

puna — flat cold highlands of the Peruvian Sierra

quebrada — a small dry valley, generally leading to a "wet" valley with a river in it. Also sometimes a "wash".

quipu — A series of knotted cords of different size and color by which the Inca kept statistical records of flocks, supplies, population, taxes, and possibly also of astronomical-calendrical and historical data. Still used by some of the Peruvian-Bolivian shepherds.

río-seco — dry river, similar to *quebrada*

sherds — broken pieces of pottery

sierra — the mountains, i.e., the Andes, moderate but fluctuating rains.

sol — Peruvian dollar — Its value has dropped considerably during the post war years. In the year of our stay it fluctuated from five to seven American cents per sol. Now (1964) its exchange rate is about 30 soles to one U.S. dollar.

tambo — ancient roadhouse

temporales — dry valleys, or parts of them, which in occasional years have water in the rivers, and which are then cultivated temporarily by people from the main valley during that year.

English Translation of the Key to the 1793 map made by Joséf Juan of Pachacamac (see page 40)

Horizontal Sketch of the Pachacamac Ruins found at the southernmost tip of a sand strip two and one half leagues long called the Tablada de Lurin, to the north of the river of this name and near the coast.

1. Ruins of a castle or, according to the Indians, of the Temple of the Great Pachacamac, wherein the pagans worshipped the creator of the sun. It is composed of four walls making it a rectangle, some built on top of others in the form of large staircases, each 15 ft. thick and with larger bases than summits, so that they form equal down grades and quite sufficient for their firmness. On the southwest side, it has two pillars 2, 3, in the form of four other staircases: it is made of mud-wall brick and is all bulk filled with earth, sand and portions of the very bricks from its walls and ruined outer walls: at the very top one finds the ditch 4 which crosses it, but not very deeply, and at its sides there are various mud-walls as though they came out of foundations, indicating some divisions, and the whole of this building is located to the southwest on a hill of stone and some earth, and the rest is covered with sand. This hill dominates the rest of the terrain included in this sketch. 5. Ruins of another building just as solid but not so high and smaller than the previous one, whose wall is circular and of stone with round columns. 6. Mud-walls or portions of adobe walls of two, three and more feet thick provide the outlines of very straight streets, divisions of city blocks, patios and reveal the existence of smaller rooms with numerous niches, or square recesses as little as two palm lengths high and wide and one palm length deep that have also been completely conserved in the outlined walls and done in squares as though they had been made to-day.

7. . . . Heavy mud-wall whose direction and thickness indicate it was the defense or place of refuge for the inhabitants of the village.

6. . . . the same as buildings 1 and 5. 8. . . . Sand hills which slope gently down towards the coastal beach, covering a portion of the ruins, since the walls indicate by their direction that they continue towards the big wall.

10. Places where there are parts of bones and skulls of human beings.

11. Sand hills, some earth and stone, at the bottom of which begins the beautiful Lurin valley.

12. Four stone slabs made recently to support a draw-bridge.

13. Lurin River and its valley. 14. Rough road along the Tablada.

15. to go to Lurin. 16. A ranch house or hut inhabited by an Indian.

Written by Josef Juan, year 1793.

Bibliography

Adachi, Kiroku (1933)
Chóan Shiseki no Kenkyū (Study of Historical Remains at Ch'ang-an), Tokyo Oriental Library, 1933.

Anonymous Trujillano (ms. 1614)
Two pages published by Rubén Vargas Ugarte in "La feche de la fundación de Trujillo". See: Vargas Ugarte, below.

Baessler, Arthur (1902)
Ancient Peruvian art; contributions to the archaeology of the empire of the Incas, from his collections, by Arthur Baessler; tr. by A. H. Keane . . . Berlin, A. Asher & Co.; New York, Dodd, Mead & Co., 1902-1903. 4 vols.

Bandelier, Adolph Francis Alphonse (ms. maps)
American Museum of Natural History. Archives.

Bennett, Wendell Clark (1938)
. . . *Archaeology of the north coast of Peru; an account of exploration and excavation in Virú and Lambayeque valleys.* (Anthropological papers. v. 37, pt. 1). New York, The American Museum of Natural History, 1939. 153 p.

Bennett, Wendell Clark (1944)
The north highlands of Peru; excavations in the Callejón de Huaylas and at Chavín de Huántar. (*Anthropological papers.* V. 39, pt. 1). New York, The American Museum of Natural History, 1944. 114 p.

Bennett, Wendell Clark (1950)
The Gallinazo group, Virú Valley, Peru. (Yale University Publications in Anthropology, No. 43.) New Haven, Published for the Department of Anthropology, Yale University, by the Yale University Press, 1950. 127 p.

Bennett, Wendell Clark and Bird, Junius Bouton (1949)
Andean culture history. (Handbook series, no. 15). New York, American Museum of Natural History, 1949. 319 p.

Bird, Junius Bouton (1948)
"Preceramic Cultures in Chicama and Virú". (*In: A Reappraisal of Peruvian Archaeology*). Memoirs of the Society for American Archaeology, Supplement to *American Antiquity*, April, 1948. V. 13, No. 4, Part 2, pp. 21-28.

Bird, Junius Bouton (1951)
"South American Radiocarbon Dates". (*In:* Memoirs of the Society for American Archaeology). *American Antiquity*, July, 1951. V. 17, No. 1, Part 2, pp. 37-49.

Brüning, Enriqué (1923)
Lambayeque Reglamentacion de las Aguas del Taimi. (Estudios monograficos del Departamento de Lambayeque. Fasciculo I and

IV.) Chiclayo, Peru. Dionisio Mendoza, Libreria y Casa Editoria. No. 165, Parque Principal. 1922, 1923. 36, 44 p.

Buck, Fritz (1937)
El Calendario Maya en el Cultura de Tiahuanacu. La Paz, Bolivia. Lit. e. imp. Unidas, 1937. 210 p.

Cabello de Valboa (or Balboa), Father Miguel [ms. 1586] (1951)
Miscelánea antártica y origen de los Indios y de los Incas del Perú (ms. 1586 [published 1951]). Ms. in the New York Public Library.

Calancha, Father Antonio de la (1638)
Coronica moralizada del Orden de San Augustin en el Perú, con sucesos egenplares en esta monarquis . . . Compuesta por el muy reverendo padre maestro fray Antonio de la Calancha . . . Dividese este primer tomo en quatro libros; lleva tablas de capitulos, i lugares de la Sagrada Escritura . . . Barcelona, P. Lacavalleria, 1638. 922 p.
"A second . . . volume of this work was printed at Lima in 1653 [or 1654] . . ."

Carrera, Fernando de la [1644] (1933)
. . . *Arte de la lengua yunga* (1644). Reedición con introducción y notas por Radames A. Altieri. (Universidad nacional de Tucumán Publicación no. 256. Departamento de investigaciones regionales. Publicaciones especiales del Instituto de . . . [no. 3]) Tucumán: Instituto de antropología, 1939. xxvi, 117 p.

Casa Vilca, Alberto (1939)
"La Ciudad Muerta de Cajamarquilla," *Boletín de la Sociedad Geográfica de Lima.* v. 56, 100-110. 1939.
The above refers to an expedition to Cajamarquilla led by Albert Giesecke.

Cieza de León, Pedro de [1553] (1924)
La Cronica General del Peru (1553). Lima, Publica de Urteaga, 1924.

Cieza de León, Pedro de (1554)
Parte primera de la Chronica del Peru, que tracta la demarcacion de sus prouincias, la descripcion dellas, las fundaciones de las nueuvas ciudades, los ritos y costumbres de los Indios, y otras cosas estrañas dignas de ser sabidas . . . Anvers, En casa de I. Steelsio, 1554 [Seville, 1553].

Collier, Donald, Jr. (1955)
Cultural chronology and change as reflected in the ceramics of the Viru Valley, Peru. [Chicago] Chicago Natural History Museum, 1955. 226 p.

Cruz, Padre de la [ms., ca. 1545]
This manuscript may still be in existence (See: Chapter VIII of this volume).

Deevey, Edward S., Jr. (1952)
"Radiocarbon Dating". *Scientific American.* V. 186, Feb., 1952, pp. 24-28.

Doering, Heinrich U. (1952)
The art of ancient Peru. New York, Frederick A. Praeger [1952] 240 p.

Estete, Miguel de [1533-1552] (1918)
El descubrimento y la conquista del Peru; [ms. of 1533 to 1552] relacion inedita de Miguel de Estete; la publica con una introduccion y notas Carlos M. Larrea. Quito, Ecuador, Impr. de la Universidad Central, 1918. 51 p.

Evans, Clifford. *See:* Strong, William Duncan

Feyjóo de Sosa, Miguel (1763)
Relacion descriptiva de la ciudad y provincia de Truxillo del Peru, con noticas exactas de su estado politico . . . Escrita por del doctor don Miguel Feyjóo . . . Madrid, Impr. del Real, y supremo consejo de las Indias, 1763. 164 p.

Florian, Mario (1951)
Un icono mural en Batan Grande. Lima, Impr. Amanta, 1951.

Ford, James Alfred and Willey, Gordon Randolph (1949)
Surface Survey of the Virú Valley, Peru. 1. Virú Valley; background and problems [by] James Alfred Ford and Gordon R. Willey. 2. Cultural dating of prehistoric sites in Virú Valley, Peru [by] James Alfred Ford. (*Anthropological papers.* V. 43, pt. 1) New York, The American Museum of Natural History, 1949. 89 p.

Garcilaso de la Vega, el Inca [1601] (1918-1920)
Los comentarios reales de los Incas por Garcilaso de la Vega . . . [ms. 1601] Anotaciones y concordancias con las Crónicas de Indias, por Horacio H. Urteaga. Elogia del Inca Garcilaso, por el doctor José de la Riva Agüera. Lima, Imp. y Libreria Sanmarti y ca., 1918-20. 6 v.

Giesecke, Alberto (1939)
"Las Ruinas de Paramonga". *Boletín de la Sociedad Geografica de Lima*, V. 56, No. 2, 1939. pp. 116-123.

Gillin, John Phillip (1945)
Moche, a Peruvian coastal community. (Smithsonian Institution. Institute of Social Anthropology. Publication no. 3). Washington, U. S. Government Printing Office [1945] 166 p.

Hagar, Stansbury (1909)
Elements of the Maya and Mexican zodiacs. Wien, A. Martleben, 1909.

Handbook of South American Indians. (1946-1950) Edited by Julian Haynes Steward. (Smithsonian Institution. Bureau of American Ethnology. Bulletin 143). Washington, U. S. Government Printing Office, 1946-50. 6 v.

Heyerdahl, Thor (1952)
American Indians in the Pacific; the theory behind the Kon-Tiki expedition. London, Allen, 1952. xv, 821 p.

Holstein, Otto (1927)
"Chan-Chan: Capital of the great Chimu". *Geographical Review*, Jan., 1927. V. 17, pp. 36-61.

Horkheimer, Hans (1943)
Historia del Peru: época prehispánica. Trujillo, Impr. Gamarra, 1943. 193 p.

Horkheimer, Hans (1944)
Vistas arqueologicas del noroeste del Perú. Trujillo, Libreria e imprenta Moreno, 1944. 83 p.

Horkheimer, Hans (1947)
"Breve bibliografía sobre el Peru prehispánico". *Revista de la Biblioteca Nacional de Lima.* No. 5, 1947. pp. [200] -282.

Horkheimer, Hans (1947)
"Las plazoletas, rayas y figuras prehispánicas en las pampas y crestas de la hoya del Río Grande". *Revista de la Universidad Nacional de Trujillo.* época II, no. 1, 1947. pp. 45-63.

Horkheimer, Hans (1950)
El Perú prehispánico: intento de un manual. Lima, Editorial Cultura Antartica, 1950.

Humboldt, Alexander von (1814)
Researches concerning the institutions and monuments of the ancient inhabitants of America . . . London, Longman, 1814. 2 v. (*See:* Vol. I, p. 379 for Mexican calendar; Vol. II, p. 130 for calendar of the Chibchas).

Humboldt, Alexander von (1877)
Sitios de las Cordilleras y Monumentos de los pueblos indígenas de América. Traduccion de Bernardo Ginex, Madrid, Imprenta y Liberia de Gaspar, 1878. viii, 439 p.

Jijón y Caamaño, Jacinto (1949)
Maranga; contribución al conocimiento de los aborígines del Valle del Rimac, Perú. Quito, Ecuador, "La Prensa Católica", 1949. 511 p.

Johnson, George R. (1930)
Peru from the air . . . with text and notes by Raye R. Platt. (American Geographical Society. Special Publication No. 12). New York, American Geographical Society. 1930. 159 p.

Juan, Joséf (1793)
Ms. map of Pachacamac, 1793. (*See:* Chapter V).

Kosok, Paul (1940)
"The Role of Irrigation in Ancient Peru". (*In: Eighth American Scientific Congress Proceedings.* Vol. II: Anthropological Sciences. pp. 169-178 + map. Washington, D. C., 1940). Washington, U. S. Department of State, 1940.

Kosok, Paul (1947)
"Desert Puzzle of Peru". *Science Illustrated.* Sept., 1947, V. 2, No. 9, pp. 60-61, 92.

Kosok, Paul (1947)
"Pre-Inca Markings in Peru". *Life*, July 28, 1947. V. 23, pp. 75-76.

Kosok, Paul and Reiche, Maria (1947)
"The Mysterious Markings of Nazca". *Natural History.* May, 1947. V. 56, No. 5, pp. 200-207, 237-238.

Kosok, Paul and Reiche, Maria (1949)
"Ancient Drawings on the Desert of Peru". *Archaeology*, Dec., 1949, V. 2, No. 4, pp. 206-215.

Kroeber, Alfred Louis (1926)
Archaeological explorations in Peru. Pt. II: The Northern Coast. (Anthropological Memoirs, Field Museum of Natural History. V. 2, No. 4). Chicago, Field Museum of Natural History, 1926.

Kroeber, Alfred Louis (1944)
Peruvian Archaeology in 1942. (Viking Fund Publications in Anthropology, No. 4). New York, The Viking Fund, 1944. 151 p.

Lambayeque Anuario. (1947) published in Chiclayo [?] Peru.

Larco Hoyle, Rafael (1938)
Los Mochicas. Lima, 1938-39. 2 v.

Larco Hoyle, Rafael (1941)
Los Cupisniques. Trabajo presentada al Congreso internacional de americanistas de Lima, XXVII sesion. Lima, Casa editoria "La Crónica" y "Variedades", s.a. ltda., 1941. 259 p.

Larco Hoyle, Rafael (1948)
Cronologia arqueologica del norte del Peru. Trujillo, 1948.

Léon-Barandiarán, Augusto D. (1934)
A golpe de arpa; folk-lore lambayecano de humorismo y costumbres, por Augusto D. Léon-Barandiarán y Rómulo Paredes . . . Lima, 1934. 397 p.

Léon-Barandiarán, Augusto D. (1938)
Mitos leyendas y tradiciones lambayecanas [*por*] Augusto D. Léon-Barandiarán. [Lima? 1938?] 312 p.

Locke, Leslie Leland (1923)
The ancient quipu or Peruvian knot record. New York., The American Museum of Natural History. 1923. 84 p.

Lockyer, Sir Joseph Norman (1906)
Stonehenge and other British stone monuments astronomically considered. London, Macmillan and Co., 1906. 340 p.

Martínez Compañón, Baltasar Jaime, archbishop
. . . Trujillo del Perú a fines del siglo XVIII, dibujos y acuarelas que mandó hacer el obispo d. Baltasar Jaime Martínez Compañón; edición prologo de Jesús Domínquez Bordona, Madrid, 1936. 22 p.

Mead, Charles Williams (1916)
Conventionalized figures in ancient Peruvian art. N. Y., The Trustees [American Museum of Natural History] 1916. p. 193-217 (Anthropological Papers of the American museum of natural history. Vol. XII, pt. V.)

Means, Philip Ainsworth (1931)
Ancient civilizations of the Andes. New York, Scribner, 1931. 586 p.

Means, Philip Ainsworth (1932)
Fall of the Inca empire and the Spanish rule in Peru; 1530-1780. New York, Scribner, 1932. 351 p.

Mejía Xesspe, M. T.
"Acueductos y caminos antiquos de la hoya del Rio Grande de Nasca". *Actos y Trobajes Cientificos.* pp. 559-570. 27th International Conference of Americanists. Lima, 1938. Vol. I.

Meneses, Padre (ms., ca. 1545)
Ms. may still be in existence. (*See:* Chapter VIII).

Middendorf, E. W. (1892)
Das Muchik oder die Chimu-Sprache . . . Mit einer einleitung über die culturvölker, die gleichzeitig mit den Inkas und Aimaràs in Südamerika lebten, und einem anhang über die Chibchasprache. Leipzig, F. A. Brockhaus, 1892. 222 p.

Middendorf, E. W. (1893-1895)
Peru; beobachtungen und studien über das land und seine bewohner während eines 25 jährigen aufenthalts. Berlin, R. Oppenheim (G. Schmidt), 1893-1895. 3 v.

Modesto de Rubiños, Justo (1936)
"Un manuscrito interesante: sucesión cronológica de los curas de Morrope y Pacora". *Revista histórica,* Lima, 1936. Tomo 10, pp. 289-363.

Montesinos, Fernando de [ms. 1644] (1920)
Memorias antiguas historiales del Peru. Translated and edited by Philip Ainsworth Means, with an introduction by the late Sir Clements R. Markham. London, Printed for the Hakluyt Society, 1920. 132 p.

Morley, Sylvanus Griswold (1915)
An introduction to the study of Maya hieroglyphs. (Smithsonian Institution. Bureau of American Ethnology, Bulletin 57). Washington, U. S. Government Printing Office, 1915. 284 p.

Muelle, Jorge C. (1943)
"Concerning the middle Chimu style". *American Archaeology and Ethnology.* Vol. 39, no. 3, 1943. pp. 203-16.

Murra, John (1946)
"The Historic Tribes of Ecuador". (*In: Handbook of South American Indians.* Smithsonian Institution. Bureau of American Ethnology. Bulletin 143. Vol. II, pp. 785-807). Washington, U. S. Government Printing Office, 1946.

Nordenskiöld, Erland (1925)
"Calculations with years and months in the Peruvian quipus". *Comparative Ethnographical Studies.* V. 6, pt. 2. New York, Oxford University Press, 1925. 36 p.

Nordenskiöld, Erland (1925)
"Secret of the Peruvian quipus". *Comparative Ethnographical Studies,* v. 6, pt. 1. New York, Oxford University Press, 1925. 38 p.

Nuttall, Mrs. Zelia (1901)
. . . The fundamental principles of Old and New world civilizations: a comparative research based on a study of the ancient Mexican religious, sociological and calendrical systems. By Zelia Nuttall . . . Cambridge, Mass., Peabody Museum of American archaeology and ethnology, 1901. 602 p. (Archaeological and ethnological papers of the Peabody museum, Harvard University, Vol. II).

Pacheco, Julio Victor (1922)
"Historia de los Valles de Chicama, Virú y Santa: *La Industria,* Trujillo, Peru, March 8 and 25, 1922.

Pacheco, Julio Victor (1926)
"Los Yungas, Prehistoria y Origen de los Primeros Pobladores de las Costas del Peru". *Ciudad y Campo,* Trujillo, Peru, Jan., 1926.

Peru, Republica del. Ministerio de Hacienda y Commercio. Dirección Nacional de Estadistica. (1944)
Censo Nacional de Poblacion y Ocupacion, 1940. Lima, 1944.

Posnansky, Arthur (1945)
Tihuanacu, the Cradle of American Man. New York, J. J. Augustin [1945]

Quipucamayocs (ca. 1541-1544)
Discurso sobre la descencia y gobierno de los Incas. Edited by Drs. Horacio H. Urteaga and Carlos A. Romero.

A Reappraisal of Peruvian Archaeology (1948)
Memoirs of the Society for American Archaeology. Supplement to *American Antiquity,* published jointly by the Society for American Archaeology and the Institute of Andean Research. April, 1948. V. 13, No. 4, part 2.

Reiche, Maria (1949)
Mystery on the desert; a study of the ancient figures and strange delineated surfaces seen from the air near Nazca, Peru. With 25 aerial photos from the archives of the Peruvian Air Ministry and 34 ground views by the author. Lima, 1949. 66 p. (Also published in Spanish).

Reichlen, Henry and Paule (1949)
"Recherches Archaeologiques dans les Andes de Cajamarca". *Journal de la Société des Américanistes,* n.s., V. 38, pp. 137-174. 1949.

Reiss, Wilhelm und Stübel, Alfons (1880)
The necropolis of Ancon in Peru; a contribution to our knowledge of the culture and industries of the empire of the Incas; being the results of excavations made on the spot by W. Reiss and A. Stübel; tr. by Professor A. H. Keane . . . with the aid of the general administration of the Royal museums of Berlin . . . Berlin, A. Asher & Co., 1880-87. 3 v.

Roosevelt, Cornelius Van S. (1935)
"Ancient Civilizations of the Santa Valley and Chavín," *Geographical Review,* XXV, 1935. pp. 21-42.

Rowe, John Howland (1945)
"Absolute Chronology in the Andean area". *American Antiquity,* Jan., 1945. V. 10, pp. 265-84.

Rowe, John Howland (1948)
"On Absolute Dating and North Coast History". (*In: A reappraisal of Peruvian Archaeology*). Memoirs of the Society for American Archaeology. Supplement to *American Antiquity.* April, 1948. V. 13, No. 4, Part 2, pp. 51-52.

Rowe, John Howland (1948)
"The Kingdom of Chimor", *Acta Americana* (Inter-American Society of Anthropology, Washington, D. C.) V. 6, No. 1-2, Ann Arbor, Mich., 1948.

Sarmiento de Gamboa, Pedro [ms. 1571] (1907)
History of the Incas, by Pedro Sarmiento de Gamboa, and the execution of the Inca Tupac Amaru by Captain Baltasar de Ocampo; translated and edited, with notes and introduction, by Sir Clements Markham. Cambridge, Printed for the Hakluyt Society, 1907. 395 p. (Original manuscript in the University of Göttingen Library).

Schaedel, Richard Paul (1949)
"Uncovering a Frieze on the Peruvian Coast". *Archaeology,* June, 1949. V. 2, No. 2, pp. 73-75.

Schaedel, Richard Paul (1951)
"The Lost Cities of Peru". *Scientific American,* August, 1951. V. 185, No. 2. pp. 18-23.

Schaedel, Richard Paul (1951)
"Mochica Murals at Panamarca". *Archaeology,* Sept., 1951. V. 4, pp. 145-154.

Schaedel, Richard Paul (1951)
"Wooden Idols from Peru". *Archaeology,* March, 1951. V. 4, No. 1, pp. 16-22.

Squier, Ephraim George and Davis, Edwin Hamilton (1848)
Ancient Monuments of the Mississippi Valley. New York, Bartlett and Wadford, 1848. xxxix, 306 p. 48 pl. (*In:* Smithsonian Contributions to Knowledge, Vol. I).

Squier, Ephraim George (1877)
Peru, incidents of travel and exploration in the land of the Incas. New York, Harper, 1877. 599 p.

Strong, William Duncan, Gordon R. Willey, and John M. Corbett (1943)
Archaeological studies in Peru, 1941-1942. (Columbia Studies in Archaeology and Ethnology, Vol. I). New York, Columbia University Press, 1943, viii, 222 p.

Strong, William Duncan and Evans, Clifford (1952)
Cultural stratigraphy in the Virú valley, northern Peru; the formative and florescent epochs. (Columbia Studies in Archaeology and Ethnology, Vol. 4). New York, Columbia University Press, 1952.

Tello, Julio César (1929)
Antiguo Peru, primera epoca. Lima, 1929. 183 p.

Thompson, John Eric (1927)
Civilization of the Mayas. (Field Museum. Anthropology Leaflet 25). Chicago, Field Museum of Natural History, 1927. 110 p.

Thompson, John Eric (1950)
Maya hieroglyphic writing; introduction. Washington, 1950. 347 p. (Carnegie Institution of Washington. Publication 589).

Uhle, Max (1903)
Pachacamac, report of the William Pepper . . . Peruvian expedition of 1896; plan of the city and twenty-one plates in phototype. Philadelphia, The Department of Archaeology of the University of Pennsylvania, 1903. 103 p.

Uhle, Max (1913)
"Die Ruinen von Moche." *Société des américanistes de Paris, Journal,* n.s., 10, pp. 95-117. 1913.

Vargas Ugarte, Rubén (1935)
Biblioteca peruana; manuscritos peruanas. Lima [Talleres tipográficos de la Empressa periodística, s.a., La Prensa] 1935. 3 v.

Vargas Ugarte, Rubén (1936)
"La feche de la fundación de Trujillo". Instituto histórico del Peru, *Revista histórica,* V. 10, pp. 229-39. Lima, 1936. (Contains the 2 page ms. of the Anonymous Trujillano).

Vargas Ugarte, Rubén (1939)
"Los Mochicas y el cacicazgo de Lambayeque". (*In: International Congress of Americanists,* 27th, Mexico and Lima 1939. Actas y trabajos científics. Vol. 2, pp. 475-482. Lima, 1940-43.

Villar Córdova, Pedro Eduardo (1935)
. . . *Las culturas pre-hispánicas del departamento de Lima . . .*

ed. Auspiciado por la h. municipalidad de Lima (Homenaje al IV centario de la fundación de Lima: o antigua "Ciudad de los Reyes") Lima, Perú [Talleres gráficos de la Escuela de la guardia civil y policía] 1935. 423 p.

Villareal, Federico (1921)
La lengua yunga o mochica. Segun el Arte oublicado en Lima en 1644 por el licenciado d. Fernando del la Carrera. Lima, Imprenta peruana de E. Z. Casanova, 1921. 126 p.

Willey, Gordon Randolph (1945)
"Horizon Styles and Pottery Traditions in Peruvian Archaeology", *American Antiquity,* July, 1945. V. 11, pp. 49-56.

Willey, Gordon Randolph (1945)
"Middle Period Cemetery in the Virú Valley, Northern Peru." *Washington Academy of Science Journal,* Feb., 1947. V. 37, pp. 41-47.

Willey, Gordon Randolph (1951)
"American Archaeology". *Science,* Sept. 14, 1951. 114; Sup. 3.

Willey, Gordon Randolph (1953)
Prehistoric settlement patterns in the Virú Valley, Perú. Washington, U.S. Government Printing Office, 1953. xxii, 453 p.

Willey, Gordon R. and Corbett, John (1954)
Early Ancón and early Supe culture. (Columbia Studies in Archaeology and Ethnology.) New York Columbia University Press, 1954. xix, 173 p.

Willson, Robert W. (1924)
Astronomical notes on the Maya Codices, vii, 46 p. (In Papers of the Peabody Museum of American archaeology and ethnology, Harvard University, Vol. VI, No. 3, 1924).

Xerez, Francisco de [ms. 1533] (1929)
. . . *Conquista del Perú, y Viaje de Hernando Pizarro desde Caxamarca hasta Jauja (Sevilla 1534 escrito por Francisco de Xerez y Miguel de Este, edición preparda por Antonio R. Rodríguez Moñino . . . con facimiles.* Badajoz, Arqueros, 1929, 202 p.

Xerez, Francisco de [ms., 1533] (1917)
. . . *Las relaciones de la conquista del Perú por Francisco de Jerez y Pedro Sancho, secretarios officiales de Don Francisco Pizarro (1532-1533).* Nota biográficas y concordancias con las cronicas de Indias, por Horacio H. Urteaga . . . Biografias de Jerez y Sancho, por Carlos A. Romero . . . Lima, Sanmarti y ca., 1917. 224 p.

Yasser, Joseph (1932)
A theory of evolving tonality. New York, American Library of Musicology, 1932. 381 p.

Zevallos Quiñones, Jorge (1944)
Toponimia Preincaica en el Norte del Peru. Estudios Yungas I. Lima, 1944.

Zevallos Quiñones, Jorge (1947)
"Un Diccionaria Castellano-Yunga". Estudios Yungas II. Sobretira de la *Revista del Museo Nacional.* Toma, XV, pp. 163-188. 1947.

Zevallos Quiñones, Jorge (1948)
"Los Gramaticos de la Langua Yunga". Estudio Yungas III. *Cuadernos de Estudio,* Instituto de Investigaciones Historicas, Pontifica Universidad Catolica del Peru, V. 3, No. 6, pp. 40-67. 1948.

Index

The index has been prepared so that it will be of use to both the scholar and the general reader. References to photographs have been included only where it was felt that they were essential, or where the subject matter was not mentioned in the text of the book.

Addenda

p. 38

Kosok last saw Peru more than a decade ago, and although many changes have taken place, the general observations made in this and subsequent chapters are still valid. The 1960 census has recently been tabulated, although all the data have yet to be analyzed. It will provide a good basis for comparing the population figures the author lists in his charts to see how much real change has taken place in the past twenty years.

p. 180

Subsequent to the termination of the writing of this manuscript, Dr. James Ford undertook extensive investigations in the Lambayeque-Leche area for the American Museum of Natural History, the results of which are soon to be published.

p. 216

After the completion of the manuscript, Tello's studies in the Casma valley were published and Donald Collier undertook further detailed investigations in the valley, the results of which are due to appear shortly.

p. 244

Piura-Chira. Many of Dr. Petersen's studies have been published subsequently, largely in Peruvian journals.

Balsa or Guayaquil River Boat.

(with Fig. 23, Chapter 24)

A. Prow

B. Aft

C. Cabin

D. Poles that serve as masts

E. Sails

F. Cross beams

G. Board that serves as wooden protector and steering rudder

H. Kitchen

I. Flasks for water

J. Main ropes (rigging)

K. Main ropes (rigging)

L. Floor or deck

THE PERUVIAN COASTAL RIVERS AND VALLEYS
(from the Rio Grande to Ecuador) and their relationships to the Chimú Empire.

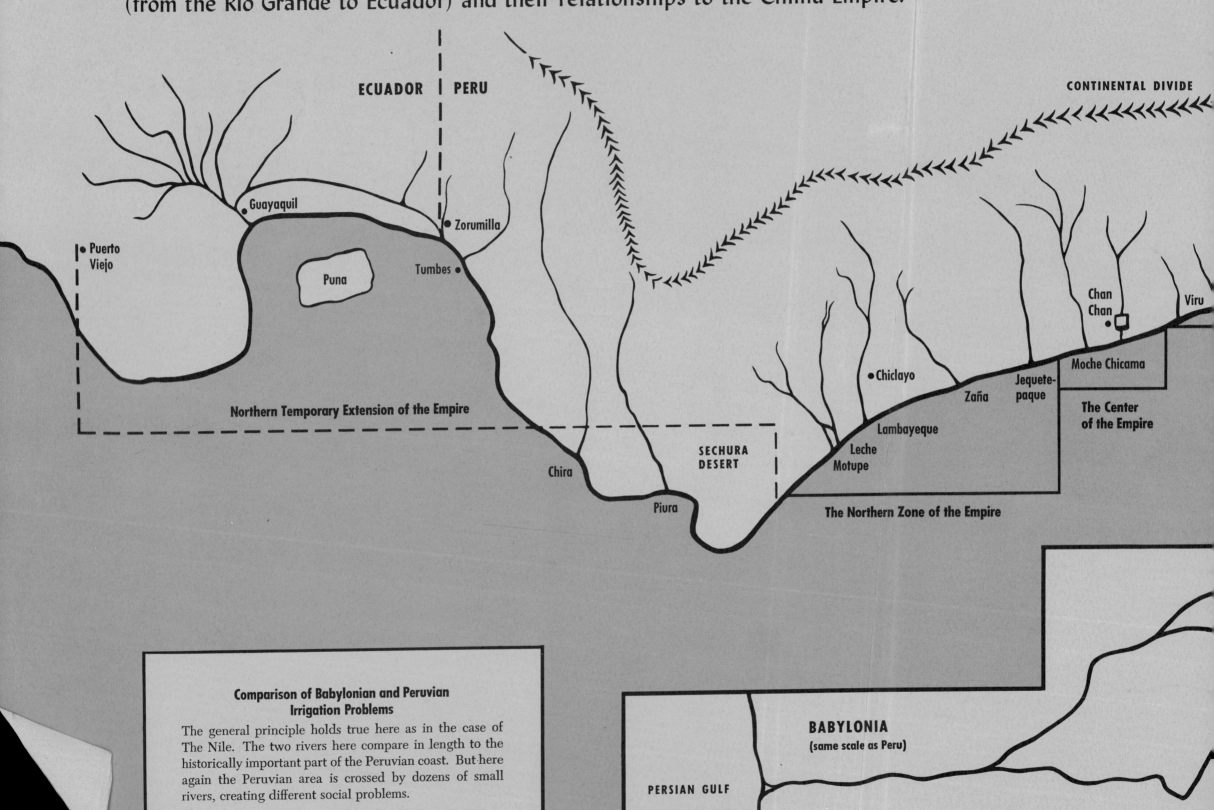

ECUADOR | PERU

CONTINENTAL DIVIDE

Guayaquil

Zorumilla

Puerto Viejo

Puna

Tumbes

Chan Chan

Viru

Moche Chicama

Chiclayo

Zaña

Jequete-paque

The Center of the Empire

Northern Temporary Extension of the Empire

Lambayeque

Leche
Motupe

Chira

SECHURA DESERT

The Northern Zone of the Empire

Piura

Comparison of Babylonian and Peruvian Irrigation Problems

The general principle holds true here as in the case of The Nile. The two rivers here compare in length to the historically important part of the Peruvian coast. But here again the Peruvian area is crossed by dozens of small rivers, creating different social problems.

BABYLONIA
(same scale as Peru)

PERSIAN GULF